THE GLOBAL ANTI-MONEY LAUNDERING REGULATORY LANDSCAPE IN LESS DEVELOPED COUNTRIES

The Global Anti-Money Laundering Regulatory Landscape in Less Developed Countries

NORMAN MUGARURA
Researcher with Global Action Research and Development Initiative (Garadi) Limited, UK

Routledge
Taylor & Francis Group
LONDON AND NEW YORK

First published 2012 by Ashgate Publishing

Published 2016 by Routledge
2 Park Square, Milton Park, Abingdon, Oxon OX14 4RN
711 Third Avenue, New York, NY 10017, USA

First issued in paperback 2017

Routledge is an imprint of the Taylor & Francis Group, an informa business

British Library Cataloguing in Publication Data
Mugarura, Norman.
The global anti-money laundering regulatory landscape in less developed countries.
1. Money laundering. 2. Money laundering – Developing countries – Prevention. 3. Money – Law and legislation.
I. Title
364.1'68–dc23

Library of Congress Cataloging-in-Publication Data
Mugarura, Norman.
The global anti-money laundering regulatory landscape in less developed countries / by Norman Mugarura.
p. cm.
Includes bibliographical references and index.
ISBN 978-1-4094-4346-9 (hardback : alk. paper) 1. Money laundering--Developing countries—Prevention. 2. Money laundering—Prevention—International cooperation.
I. Title.
K1089.M836 2011
345'.0268—dc23

2011045507

ISBN 13: 978-1-138-11005-2 (pbk)
ISBN 13: 978-1-4094-4346-9 (hbk)

Contents

List of Abbreviations

AIDS	acquired immunodeficiency syndrome
AML/CFT	anti-money laundering/combating the financing of terrorism
ARS	alternative remittance systems
BCCI	Bank of Credit and Commerce International
BIS	Bank for International Settlements
CDD	customer due diligence
CJA	Criminal Justice Act
CTAG	Counter-Terrorism Action Group
CTC	Counter-Terrorism Committee
EAC	East African Community
ECOSOC	United Nations Economic and Social Council
ECOWAS	Economic Community of West African States
EDU	European Drug Unit
EEC	European Economic Community
EFTs	Electronic funds transfers
EU	European Union
EUROPOL	European Police Office
FATF	Financial Action Task Force
FDI	foreign direct investment
FIU	Financial Intelligence Unit
FSAP	Financial Sector Assessment Programme
FSF	Financial Stability Forum
FTR	Financial Transaction Reporting
GDP	gross domestic product
HIV	human immunodeficiency virus
ICT	information and communications technology
IFIs	international financial institutions
IGG	Inspector General of Government
ILO	International Labour Organization
IMF	International Monetary Fund
INTERPOL	International Criminal Police Organization
IOSCO	International Organization of Securities Commissions
KYC	know your customer
NCCT	Non-Cooperative Countries or Territories
NCIS	National Criminal Intelligence Service
NGOs	non-governmental organizations
NRM	National Resistance Movement
OAS	Organization of American States

OECD	Organisation for Economic Co-operation and Development
OFCs	offshore financial centres
OGBS	Offshore Group of Banking Supervisors
POCA	Proceeds of Crime Act 2002
SADC	Southern African Development Community
SAPs	Structural Adjustment Programmes
SIS	Schengen Information System
SOCA	Serious Organised Crime Agency
TI	Transparency International
UCB	Uganda Commercial Bank
UN	United Nations
UNCAC	United Nations Convention against Corruption
UNDCP	United Nations Drug Control Programme
UNDP	United Nations Development Programme
URA	Uganda Revenue Authority
WTO	World Trade Organization

Foreword

The book has been precisely written to strike a balanced approach to the study of money laundering in the asymmetric global marketplace. It underscores the importance and challenges of harnessing a global anti-money laundering framework, taking into account the dynamics of development in less developed economies. In conceptualizing the need for a global anti-money laundering framework, the book highlights a dichotomy of challenges. First, there are challenges in relation to the dynamics of the market economy such as deregulation, liberalization and conflict of laws. Secondly, there are challenges inherent in the domestic economy such as corruption, general systemic failure and lack of infrastructural capacity. In deconstructing the aforementioned challenges, the book delineates a need to consolidate the existing global anti-money laundering/combating the financing of terrorism (AML/CFT) framework so that it is capable of delivering the envisaged AML/CFT standards globally. For the global anti-money laundering framework to work globally, it should be designed with an ethos which reflects the prevailing global climate in which it operates.

While the book proffers insights into money laundering and its predicate offences, it also discusses the infrastructure that facilitates money laundering and a wide range of predicate offences. The thrust of the book is that the global anti-money laundering framework cannot translate locally into practice unless it creates something of a level playing field for the member countries subject to it. Apparently, the playing field is not leveled, which potentially plays in favour of some countries while undermining the ability of others to harness the prescribed global anti-money laundering regimes. The precarious environment in some countries is manifested in the absence of local capacity building, the prevalence of corruption and the absence of tailored reforms to pertinent and novel challenges in particular countries. Thus, the book proffers an alternative approach for further studies and policy development on money laundering, fronted on well-sequenced reforms domestically and, where necessary, at a global level. This approach is an essential requirement, if not a prerequisite, in order for states to domesticate desired global anti-money laundering regimes. The proliferating global anti-money laundering regimes, desirable as they may be, are implemented locally and are inherently prone to the prevailing local environment. For instance, developing countries are deficient in economic and social infrastructure, and are constrained by limited resources and requisite education, not to mention the prevalence of corruption. The above challenges are compounded by a lack of institutional and structural capacity to harness global anti-money laundering standards locally. Similarly, the institutional and structural weaknesses in some countries have translated into an environment conducive to criminal exploitation, while diminishing the same state's capacity to counteract new challenges, such as money laundering. In the majority of less developed economies, efforts towards harnessing global AML/CFT regimes are derailed by many factors, which it is perhaps needless to reiterate. In part, this predicament translates into an environment for criminal exploitation and renders societies vulnerable in confronting their common challenges. In view of the varying dynamics of development, this book wonders whether countries still need to be clustered together and treated as one or whether regions should forge different arrangements and simply coexist as different entities.

Thus, this book is an essential read for policy and intellectual reasons. In relation to policy, it underscores externalities of the global system on individual local societies. It articulates that in view of overlapping global exigencies such as money laundering and its predicate threats, countries have very little choice but to come together by way of harmonization of internal policies and adopting other common initiatives. For instance, there is a need for a common legal grid to enable countries to deal with conflict of laws and different jurisdictions, and also with regard to sharing resources such as intelligence information. Some states have been sidelined as a result of their participation in the globalization of markets and, in my view, this has been due to the fact that these states have failed to position themselves properly in the face of global changes.

At an intellectual level, the book proffers a scholarly alternative to the study of money laundering in a global regulatory landscape. It highlights the ethos of global AML/CFT regimes, articulating the challenges that this global framework has to confront. While the manuscript would have benefited from the author's earlier scholarly work, this was distinctly done to underscore the broader objectives for writing this book.

Preface

The book articulates that the global anti-money laundering/combating the financing of terrorism (AML/CFT) framework replicates global asymmetries of power in both approach and reality and cannot afford a level playing field to the majority of less developed countries. Globalization generally and the global anti-money laundering regimes specifically are information-driven, and the ability of societies at rudimentary stages of development to harness the potential synergies of the global system is significantly curtailed by the inefficiency of 'local societies' to harness meaningful information. In many developing countries, there are weak or no centralized data registry centres to process and supply data to AML/CFT agencies such as the Financial Intelligence Units (FIUs) and the police. Information is deemed to be meaningful if it is society-oriented and informed by the challenges facing the society in question. Information is the prerequisite for the effective enforcement of laws and regulations. Information is essential for the construction of the money trail, given that the money laundering process would have been executed in stages; however, requisite information is also essential for law enforcement agencies in order to secure a successful prosecution of the alleged money laundering/terrorist culprits. Without the requisite information, these agencies will not be able to function properly in enforcing the implementation of laws and in ensuring that when violations occur, they do not go unsanctioned.[1] I have deconstructed the global AML/CFT framework within the context of some domestic jurisdictions to demonstrate its limitations as a global framework.

The book illuminates the challenges to an effective global AML/CFT environment in some jurisdictions. The aforementioned environment potentially dictates the ease of harnessing normative global AML/CFT standards in a country. The AML/CFT control paradigms, which have evolved at the level of the Financial Action Task Force (FATF) or at a regional level (for example, the EU) and have been adopted by states as a regulatory framework, are difficult to apply, let alone enforce, given that the majority of these regimes function on the strength of generating good information on present and future bank clients. Similarly, in many developing economies, either there is no data generated to help quantify and evaluate the magnitude of money laundering/terrorism threats or the little data generated is too patchy to properly inform any policy choices. Underdevelopment and its attendant shortcomings have generated significant, if not insurmountable,

1 Ian Carrington and Heba Shams, 'The Elements of Effective AML/CFT Framework: Legal, Regulatory, and Best Institutional Practices to Prevent Threats to Financial Stability and Integrity', Seminar on 'Current Development in Monetary and Financial Law', Washington DC, 23–27 October 2006.

challenges for financial and law enforcement agencies in some countries with regard to developing requisite measures against both local and global-oriented crimes.

The last part of the book underscores the need for countries to first address their novel development challenges before they countenance the adoption of global regimes on money laundering and its predicate crimes. Individual countries will have to address the question of infrastructure deficiencies at home as a prerequisite for assimilating the desired anti-money laundering standards into their domestic law. As such, there is a need to co-opt some developing countries onto the committees charged with the responsibility of producing the global anti-money laundering standards to ensure that the proliferating regimes have an ethos not only of representivity but also of legitimacy in different societies.

Acknowledgements

In part, this book is a culmination of hard work, inspiration and the influence of people like John Strawson, Professor Mads Andenas, Professor George Walker, Dr Richard Alexander, Professor Kofi Oteng Kufuor, Dr Frank Byamugisha of World Bank Washington and Professor Mondo Kagonyera. I am thankful to each one of them for their contribution towards my academic and professional development.

I wish to pay tribute to my parents, who in those formative years impressed on me the importance of education to someone's life. The fact that I understood and internalized the education cause in my early years has instilled in me a sense of academic insatiability. I vividly remember being told that education is a platform where 'the son of a minister and the son of a peasant vie for the same office'. As a matter of fact, writing this book goes a long way towards fostering my early childhood dream.

As ever, I remain indebted to my family, friends and colleagues for their support and encouragement; and, most importantly, I thank God who is my anchor in all my aspirations. To cap it all, this book is a product of hard work, discipline and above all the innate desire to succeed. Perhaps finally I should say that I alone remain responsible for any errors and infelicities it might contain.

Chapter 1
The Conceptualization of Money Laundering Offences and Typologies

Introduction

This chapter explores the genesis of money laundering and its underlying offences (hereinafter the money laundering predicate offences). Money laundering is an elusive concept that involves the illicit movement of funds generated from drug trafficking, human trafficking, terrorism, motor vehicle trafficking, etc. In view of this, this chapter addresses multiple issues such as the scope, nature and money laundering typologies.[1] Specifically, it outlines money laundering offences and why it is a preferred method of avoiding law enforcement, its strategies and techniques, and its relationship to other forms of crimes. Money laundering can be described as an opportunistic crime because not only does it 'lubricate the wheels' of other organized crimes, it is also exploited as a strategy to transmit the proceeds of crime to their destination and purpose. Thus, unless robust money laundering countermeasures are devised, it has the potential to fuel the commission of transnational organized crime such as terrorism, drug trafficking and human trafficking. Since money laundering is a transnational crime, its typologies are likely to differ from society to society.[2] Criminals in some countries might choose to launder their profits, while in others they might simply decide to spend them. In this regard, the explosion of corruption and counterfeit currency crimes in some countries constitute money laundering predicate crimes. Thus, the last part of this chapter addresses the nexus of corruption and money laundering within the broad context of money laundering predicate offences.

The Early History of Money Laundering

The term 'money laundering' is relatively new, having come into parlance in the mid-1970s. According to the *Oxford English Dictionary*, the term first came into use

---

1 Directive 2001/97/EC [2001] OJ L 344/76.

2 For example, tax evasion is a crime in the USA, yet not only is it perfectly legal in Switzerland, it is often encouraged in the quest to maximize shareholders' wealth and investors' returns.

in connection with the Watergate Scandal in 1973–1974.[3] It is derived from the early practice of American criminal organizations operating laundromats as cash-intensive businesses to hide their criminal wealth. It has become the accepted term ever since in relevant legislation and legal texts. It can be found, for example, in titles such as the US Money Laundering Control Act (1986) and the 1990 European Convention on Money Laundering, Search, Seizure and Confiscation of Crime Proceeds.[4] Money laundering was not criminalized in the USA until the passage of Money Laundering Control Act. The earliest legal development against money laundering took place in the USA with the passage of Bank Secrecy Act 1970.[5] This Act fully recognized the link between money laundering, including security fraud and the global dimension of the problem.[6] It required banks to report cash transactions of $10,000 or more and this provision was also enacted in the Money Laundering Act 1986, which for the first time defined money laundering as a federal crime.[7]

In the UK, money laundering was not a distinct offence but would be prosecuted under various statutes in the 1980s. Section 22 of the Theft Act 1968 provided the framework for the prosecution of launderers who dishonestly handled stolen assets. The most famous case to be prosecuted under this provision was the Brink's-Mat bullion robbery case. Michael Relton, a former solicitor, was successfully prosecuted under this provision of the Theft Act 1968. The concept of money laundering in the UK can also be traced back to the House Lords' decision in *R v. Cuthbertson* (1980).[8] This decision revealed the failure of forfeiture laws to deprive the offender of the proceeds of crime. The defendants were engaged in long-term criminal activity involving the supply of controlled substances. They are said to have generated over £750,000, some of which was placed in bank accounts in Switzerland and France. Pleading guilty, the defendants were convicted and the court ordered that their assets be forfeited. The defendant appealed to the House of Lords against the sentence and the forfeiture orders of their assets. The question of law presented before their Lordships was the interpretation of the Misuse of Drugs Act 1971 and the section on which the court was empowered to order the forfeiture of the aforementioned assets.[9] It was concluded that the powers of the court to order the forfeiture of assets did exist, but only as long as the asset in question was a tangible property and not choses in action such as cheques or other

3 Jeffrey Robinson, *The Laundrymen* (London: Pocket Books, 1998), quoted in Heba Shams' paper 'Using Money Laundering Control to Fight Corruption: An Extraterritorial Instrument', 7 *Law and Business Review of the Americas* (2001): 85–133.

4 Shams, 'Using Money Laundering Control to Fight Corruption'.

5 Ibid.

6 Ibid.

7 See the United Nations Drug Control Programme website: www.unodc.org (date accessed 22 November 2011).

8 [1980] 2 All ER 401.

9 Ibid.

intangibles.[10] In 1986 the Drug Control Act was passed, which was to consolidate confiscation orders of criminal assets by stripping criminals of the proceeds of their criminal activities. Section 24 of the Act creates an offence of assisting another to retain the proceeds of drug trafficking. However, to secure a successful prosecution, the defendant must demonstrate that he/she knew or suspected that the owner of the property has been engaged in drug trafficking or has benefited from drug trafficking.[11] Yet, s. 24 was only applicable in relation to the confiscation of the proceeds of drug trafficking, an issue that for some time confined money laundering to drug trafficking. This was later to be addressed by states following the adoption of United Nations (UN) instruments such as the United Nations Convention against Transnational Organized Crime in 2000 signed at Palermo (hereinafter the Palermo Convention).

The Definition of Money Laundering

Money laundering is defined as a process of manipulating legally or illegally acquired wealth in a way that obscures its existence, origin or ownership for the purpose of avoiding law enforcement.[12] Money laundering describes a deliberate, complicated and sophisticated process by which the proceeds of crime are camouflaged, disguised or made to appear as if they were earned by legitimate means. It is a three-stage process, which is as follows: (i) the dirty money must be severed from the predicate crime generating it; (ii) it must be characterized by a series of transactions designed to obscure or destroy the money trail in order to avoid detection; and (iii) the criminal proceeds must be reinvested in furtherance of the objectives of the business (launderer). In Article 3(1) of the United Nations Convention Against Illicit Traffic in Narcotic Drugs and other Psychotropic Substances (1988), states are required to enact legislation necessary to establish a modern code of criminal offences relating to illicit trafficking in all its different dimensions.[13] The scope of criminalization should cover a comprehensive list connected to drug trafficking – from production, cultivation and possession to the organization, management and financing of trafficking operations.[14] This article

---

10 Shams, 'Using Money Laundering Control to Fight Corruption'.

11 Ibid.

12 Ibid.

13 W.C. Gilmore, *Dirty Money: The Evolution of Money Laundering Counter-Measures* (Strasbourg: Council of Europe Publishing, 1999), p. 161.

14 D.P. Stewart, 'Internalising the War on Drugs: The UN Convention Against Illicit Traffic in Narcotic Drugs and Psychotropic Substances', 18 *Denver J. International Law and Policy* (1990): p. 387.

requires each party to the Convention to establish money laundering as a criminal offence in its domestic law when it is committed internationally.[15]

In Article 3(1)(b), each state party is required to establish as a criminal offence:

> the conversion or transfer of property knowing that such a property is derived from any offence or offences established in accordance with subparagraph (a) of this paragraph or from an act of participation in such offence or offences, for purposes of concealing or disguising the illicit origin of the property or of assisting any person who is involved in the commission of such offence or offences to evade the legal consequences of his action. The concealment or disguise of the true nature, source, location, disposition, movement, rights with respect to, or ownership of property, knowing that such property is derived from an offence or offences established in accordance with subparagraph (a) of this paragraph or from an act of participation in such an offence or offences.

Article 3(1)(c) provides that each party render as criminal: 'The acquisition, possession or use of property, knowing at the time of the receipt, that such property was derived from an offence or offences established in accordance with subparagraph (a) of this paragraph or from an act of participation in such offence or offences.'[16] Article 3 creates a framework for criminalization and treating money laundering as a serious offence, and would ease state cooperation in relation to confiscation, mutual legal assistance and extradition of alleged money laundering criminals. The Convention is particularly important because all parties are obliged to establish Article 3(1) offences as criminal offences in their domestic law.

Thus, money laundering involves the following when committed intentionally:

- The conversion and transfer of property, knowing that such property is derived from criminal activity, for the purpose of concealing or disguising the illicit origin of the property or of assisting any person who is involved in the commission of such activity to evade the legal consequences of his/her action.[17]
- The concealment or disguise of the true nature, source, location, disposition, movement, rights with respect to or ownership of property, knowing that such property is derived from criminal activity or from an act of participation in such activity.
- The acquisition, possession or use of property, knowing at the time of receipt that such property was derived from criminal activity or an act of

15 For this, see Article 3(3), which says that 'knowledge, intent or purpose' required as an element of the offence may be inferred from an objective factual circumstances.

16 Gilmore, *Dirty Money*.

17 This definition derives from Article 3, s. 1(b) of the United Nations Convention Against Illicit Traffic in Narcotic Drugs and Psychotropic Substances 1988, signed in Vienna (hereinafter the Vienna Convention).

participation in such activity.
- Participation in, association to commit, attempts to commit and aiding, abetting, facilitating and counselling the commission of any of the actions mentioned in the foregoing indents.
- Knowledge, intent or purpose required for the commission of the above-mentioned money laundering activities should have been carried out in the territory of another state or in that of a third country.[18]

'Property' means assets of every kind, whether corporeal or incorporeal, movable or immovable, tangible or intangible, and legal documents or instruments evidencing title or interests in such assets.[19]

The element of conversion is central to the study of money laundering offences because it marks the point at which illicit cash is turned into a less suspicious form, so that the true source or ownership is concealed and a legitimate source is created. A shortcoming of the Vienna Convention is that it was specifically limited to the laundering of the proceeds of drug trafficking. Following the Vienna Convention, a number of countries based their anti-money laundering laws on this framework, limiting the definition of this offence to the laundering of drug profits. Subsequently, there has been a move to extend the definition of money laundering to include the proceeds of other serious criminal activities, such as smuggling, fraud, serious financial crimes and the sale of stolen goods.[20] The 1996–1997 survey by the Financial Action Task Force (FATF) on money laundering measures noted that, along with drug trafficking, financial crimes (bank fraud, credit card fraud, investment fraud, advance fee fraud, bankruptcy fraud embezzlement, etc.) were the most mentioned sources of the proceeds of crime.[21] Many countries have now taken action to extend the scope of their money laundering offences to include a wider range of all predicate offences.

18 This is the United Nations Drug Control Programme (UNDCP) definition of money laundering adopted from its anti-money laundering unit programme paper, 'An Overview of the UN Conventions and International Standards Concerning Anti-Money Laundering Legislation', February 2004.

19 Article 3, s. 1(b) of the Vienna Convention.

20 Rick McDonnell, 'Money Laundering Methodologies: International and Regional Counter-Measures', National Crime Authority, NSW, paper presented at the Australian Institute of Research in Sydney, May 1998.

21 'An Overview of the Global Money Laundering Problem: International Anti-Money Laundering Standards and the Work of the Financial Action Task Force', in Rick McDonnell, above, note 20.

The Extent of the Global Money Laundering Problem

Estimating the amount of money laundered has been recognized as problematic (if not impossible) because of the covert nature of the crime. However, some estimates have been developed which give the rough magnitude of the problem. In 1987, the UN estimated the value of drug trafficking worldwide at US$300 billion, much of which would be laundered. Other estimates[22] have been made which put the amount at between US$300 and US$500 billion of dirty money that is introduced into the global financial system each year, or roughly two per cent of global GDP.

The Outcome of Money Laundering

The definition of money laundering envisages several outcomes:

- The launderer intends to hide the existence of the wealth or its amount, as in the case of a tax evader who wants to shelter his/her wealth.
- He/she could also be intending to hide or disguise the owner of the generated wealth, as in the case of a drug lord who wants to obscure the money trail that might lead to his/her detection by severing the link between him/her and the funds through a shell company or a trust.
- He/she could be intending to hide the way it is put to use, where the money is intended for investment in a criminal or terrorist organization.
- He/she could be intending to disguise the origin of funds by fabricating another legitimate source of wealth.

The outcome of the laundering process depends on the purpose of the launderer himself/herself, as well as on the law and law enforcement in the jurisdiction where the activity is taking place.[23] The money launderer's chief objective is to reinvest the illegal wealth in another illegal enterprise by obscuring the ownership of the money or its trail to the illegal destination. Disguising the source and legitimizing it will be irrelevant when the launderer invests his/her wealth in jurisdictions which operate a lax approach to the illegality of funds.

Avoiding Law Enforcement

Any money laundering operation ultimately aims at circumventing law enforcement and evading the reach of the law. The purpose of the launderer is to

---

22 Rick McDonell, 'Regulatory Challenges for the 21st Century', paper presented at the Australian Institute of Criminology in Sydney, 7–8 May 1998.

23 B.A.K. Rider, 'Taking the Profits Out of Crime', *Journal of Money Laundering Control* (2001): pp. 2–3.

secure or avoid the confiscation of his/her ill-gotten wealth or to avoid or evade the tax authorities. For those who extend money laundering to civil wrongs, the launderer's purpose could be to avoid the enforcement of a court ruling against his/her assets in a divorce case.[24]

Strategy

Drug trafficking, like any other form of criminal activity, is highly cash-intensive. Indeed, in the case of hard drugs (heroin and cocaine), the physical volume of notes received from street dealing is much larger than the volume of the drugs themselves.[25] Reliance on cash as a central medium of exchange in turn gives rise to at least three common factors:

- drug dealers need to conceal the true ownership and origin of the money;
- they need to control the money; and
- they need to change the form of the money.

Money laundering can be summarized as the conversion of illicit cash to another asset, the concealment of the true source or ownership of the illegally acquired proceeds and the creation of the perception of legitimacy of the source and ownership.[26]

In their efforts to achieve the above goals, money launderers have resorted to the use of a variety of techniques. The most common ones include: currency smuggling; the conversion of cash into negotiable instruments; the creation or use of facilities offered by financial and tax havens; the establishment and use of front or shell companies; the use of currency and brokerage houses; the creation of false or inflated invoices; the use of casinos and other gambling enterprises; the use of credit cards obtained from tax haven banks; the use of facilities provided by underground or parallel banking systems; and resorting to cash purchases.[27] As will be noted, the techniques of money laundering are innumerable, diverse, complex, subtle and secret. What is not in dispute is the ability of the launderer to manipulate the legitimate process in his/her transactions. Analysis of the Canadian money laundering police files[28] revealed that over 80 per cent had an international dimension, suggesting that the perpetrators of this trade exploit the transnational movement of goods, capital and people, in the same way as the legitimate

24 Shams, 'Using Money Laundering Control to Fight Corruption'.

25 P. O'Brien, 'Trafficking Narco-Dollars: The Evolution of a Potent Weapon in the Drug War', 21 *Inter-American Law Review* (1990): p. 643.

26 Ibid.

27 Ibid.

28 M.E. Bearer et al., *Tracing Illicit Funds: Money Laundering in Canada* (Ottowa: Ministry of Solicitors General of Canada, 1990): p. 304.

business community does in this global era. As the EU Commission has noted, the internationalization of economies and financial services are opportunities which are seized upon by money launderers to carry out their criminal activities, since the origin of funds can be better disguised when put beyond the reach of the national authorities where the crime was initially committed.[29] This warrants a need for international cooperation in evolving an international framework in relation to money laundering challenges, such as with regard to bank secrecy laws and making sure that money laundering is criminalized internationally.

Typologies of Money Laundering

Money laundering patterns are said to fall into three distinct categories. The first is internal money laundering, characterized by the laundering of the proceeds of crime committed within a given country or assets to be used in committing more crimes there – an example would be the prominent case of the 'daga' trade in South Africa. The second is incoming/inflowing money laundering, which entails the laundering of assets derived from crimes committed outside the country and reintroduced as investment – the most notorious of this type being foreign currency importation. The third category is outgoing money laundering, which very closely mimics the classical cases. In this typology, the proceeds of crime committed within the country are exported to one or more countries, as highlighted by the case of counterfeit currency in Uganda. The overriding objective[30] of the launderer is to get the money to the international money markets at some stage, whereby total flexibility can be achieved. The origin having been totally concealed, the beneficiary can pose as a rich person who invests anywhere in the world legitimately using the banking system at will.

The Process of Money Laundering

The acts or transactions that constitute money laundering are limited only by the purpose for which they are structured and the skill of the launderer. There are an almost unlimited number of ways in which the launderer can achieve his/her purpose. This process encompasses the three money laundering stages, which are covered separately below.

29 This was the overriding objective of the first European Anti-Money Laundering Directive of 1991.

30 This section draws on a panel discussion paper on money laundering presented by Mr Kessy Herman to the Interim Executive of Eastern and Southern Africa Anti-Money Laundering Group (ESAAMLG) in South Africa.

Money Laundering Techniques

Money can be laundered using one of the following techniques:

- Investing the dirty money in legitimate businesses, either through shell companies or through genuine companies using pseudonyms.
- Where the launderer acquires assets from the proceeds of crimes.
- Depositing of money in banks in non-cooperative countries and remittances through banking channels to the host country.
- Use of non-banking channels to transfer money (such as hawala and hundi), which is now a common method of remitting money to many parts of the world. For example, this method is popular among Ugandan and other East African citizens in sending money to their countries;
- Over-invoicing of goods in seemingly normal business transactions.
- Routing money through tax haven countries – the Cayman Islands and other Caribbean territories have been very prominent in this respect.

These techniques are further broken down in each of the stages (placement, layering and integration) through which the money laundering is processed.

The first stage is the placement stage, where the illegitimately acquired or destined assets are placed into the financial system. This initial stage can also involve the greatest risks for the culprit, since the placement stage often requires substantial sums of money across the counters of a bank or other financial institution. According to Rider,[31] 'money in flight will first be noticeable when it literally first splashes into the pool'. Thus, money laundering operations are more noticeable, and thus easier to stop, when money is first introduced into the system (the placement stage), since deposits without an apparently bona fide commercial reason will tend to arouse suspicion at the point of face-to-face contact with the bank. However, detection at this stage can often be avoided by the process known as 'smurfing', which involves the use of what is a small army of individuals who deposit cash sums[32] which fall below the reporting threshold. These 'smurfs' are often known to the banks and banking institutions which deal predominantly or exclusively in cash.[33] It may be said that individual bankers are in the best position

---

31 Ibid.

32 C. Howard, 'The *Mens Rea* Tests for Money Laundering Offences', 4 *New Law Journal* (1998): pp. 118–19. This article distinguishes between the following categories of the mental state that constitute knowledge: (i) actual knowledge; (ii) wilfully shutting one's eyes to the obvious; (iii) wilfully and reckless failing to make such inquiries as an honest and reasonable person would make; (iv) knowledge of circumstances which would indicate the facts to an honest and reasonable person; and (v) knowledge of circumstances which would compel an honest and reasonable person on inquire further.

33 Cash from unknown persons in mixed denominations is often a cause of suspicion. For this reason, many drug traffickers and professional launderers have sought to operate

to monitor and report suspicious financial transactions. However, attempts to stop money laundering at the placement stage has put considerable pressure on banks and indeed on the tradition of the legal systems of countries. Several issues arise here: not only is there the bank's requirement to report to the authorities knowledge or suspicion of illicit activities, but there is also the duty the bank owes to the customer based on the principle of customer confidentiality.[34]

During the placement stage, one or all of the following are likely to occur:

- Physical disposal of bulk cash proceeds. Because large volumes of cash may draw attention to their illegal source and carry the continuous risk of theft or seizure, criminals are motivated to exchange small denomination bills for larger bills, to deposit cash and buy financial instruments or otherwise dispose of bulk cash promptly.
- Structuring/smurfing of cash transactions (deposits, monetary instrument purchases, etc.) in order to evade the common regulatory requirement that transactions which exceed a certain amount of money must be recorded and sometimes reported.
- Bank complicity, where money laundering is facilitated when bank personnel are corrupted, intimidated or controlled.
- Misuse of exemptions. The unsupervised unilateral ability of a financial institution to exempt itself or its customers from a reporting or recording regime can offer money launderers a way in which to avoid an audit of their cash transactions.
- Committing of licit and illicit funds. The committing of funds and establishing front companies is a way to take advantage of these circumstances by obscuring illicit proceeds in a forest of licit transactions (co-mingling) or masking them with the appearance of legitimate receipts of a largely cash business activity (a front company).
- Assets purchased with cash. Large-scale purchases can support a luxurious lifestyle, change the form of the proceeds from conspicuous to inconspicuous, or can be used to obtain major assets which will be employed to further the criminal enterprise.
- Currency smuggling. The cross-border smuggling of currency and monetary instruments by various methods accomplishes the desired physical transfer without leaving an audit trail.[35]

What generally happens at this stage can be illustrated by the following two metaphors:

---

from behind the cover of cash-intensive businesses, such as casinos, bars or restaurants.

34 *Tournier v National Provincial Union Bank of England* [1924] 1 KB 46.

35 Robinson, *The Laundrymen*, p. 35.

- Money laundering is analogous to throwing an object[36] (for example, a stone) into water. As soon as the object is thrown into water, one can see the ripples where it first hit, but as it sinks and goes deeper, the ripples disappear with it, to a point where they can no longer be seen. At some point, it is hard to tell that the object was even thrown into the water. Drawing on this metaphor, it has been said that unless money laundering is prevented at the placement stage, it becomes very difficult to control at the layering or integration stage when it has 'sunk deeper' within the financial system.
- Money laundering typologies[37] have also been explained in the following 'laundry' analogy. The 'hand wash' is when a criminal organization uses the money (generally small amounts) to buy goods and services for the organization. The 'family washing machine' is when the criminal organization or family launders its money according to family goals and in collusion with banks or financial institutions. Washing programmes can also consist of a short cycle, such as opening a deposit account in a bank in the name of a given person and depositing the money there, or a long cycle, which involves terms such as 'pre-wash', 'wash', 'rinse' and 'drying' to describe the different stages from cleaning the money to its investment in legitimate activities. Then there is the 'condominium washing machine', when several families belonging to the same criminal syndicate (such as the Mafia) organize a laundering enterprise with the complicity of someone in a bank or financial institution. Last, but not least, is what is called the launderette, where a criminal organization offers criminals and criminal syndicates a money laundering service with different cycles: a short cycle for cleaning the money only or a long cycle which includes all the activities from laundering to investment.

The second stage is the layering or agitation stage, where numerous transactions arise that are designed to act as a smokescreen to disguise the true origin of the money:

- One of the many methods used at the layering stage is over-invoicing regarding the value of imported goods.
- The use of gold is also much favoured by money launderers, in view of its highly mutable qualities. Whether in the form of ingots, rings, bracelets, pendants or ornaments, the value remains constant, so therefore a single piece of gold can be changed many times in order to disguise its original form without any significant change in its worth. This approach (to a great extent) mirrors parallel calls to transplant interpretations of knowledge on the basis of the case law on constructive trusts into the sphere of criminal

36 Ibid.

37 D. Savona, 'Mafia Money Laundering versus Italian Legislation', 3 *European Journals of Criminal Policy and Research* (1993): p. 35.

law in order to include a broadly defined concept of wilful blindness.

- The creation of a false paper trail involves the intentional production of false documentary evidence to disguise the true source, ownership, location, purpose of or control over the funds.
- Cash converted into money instruments – once illicit proceeds have been placed into a bank or other financial institution, they can then be converted into monetary instruments such as traveller's cheques, letters of credit, money orders, cashiers' cheques, bonds or stocks. Conversion into monetary instruments allows the proceeds to be more readily transported out of the country without detection, to be deposited into other domestic financial institution accounts, pledged for loans, etc.
- Tangible assets purchased with cash and converted in order to offset transaction costs. The identity of the parties may be obscured by untraceable transactions, so the assets become difficult to locate and seize.
- Electronic funds or wire transfers. This is possibly the most effective layering method available to money launderers. It offers criminals much-needed speed, distance, a minimal audit trail and virtual anonymity amid the enormous daily volume of electronic funds transfers (EFTs), all at a minimal cost.

The third stage in the money laundering process is the integration or reintegration stage. This stage occurs when the dirty money has been safely placed and then layered to the extent that it is safe to return to the launderer via a legitimate financial system. In effect, the illicitly gained proceeds of the original criminal activity have been cleaned by the time they reach the integration stage. This stage encompasses the following activities:[38]

- Real estate transactions, where property can be bought by shell corporations using illicit proceeds. The property can then be sold and the proceeds appear as legitimate sales proceeds. A reduced price can be declared and partial payment made in cash to the seller, guaranteeing a paper profit when the property is resold at the market value. Inflated prices can be established by a series of trades, enabling the last seller to show a legitimate source of substantial (although fictitious) profit or providing justification for inflated loan transactions.
- Front companies and sham loans, whereby the owner can pay his/her foreign laundering subsidiary interest on the loan and deduct it as a business expense, thereby reducing his/her tax liability.
- Foreign bank complicity. This form of money laundering is committed using accomplice foreign banks and represents a higher order of criminal sophistication, presenting a very difficult problem both at the technical and

38 The three stages in the laundering of dirty money are intended to give a simplistic overview of what in reality is a complex and sophisticated process.

political levels. Such a bank can conceal many incriminating details relating to persons and transactions, not to mention providing sham loans secured by criminal proceeds, while guaranteeing immunity from law enforcement scrutiny due to the protective banking laws and regulations.
- False import/export invoicing, involving fictitious transactions, over-valuation of entry documents and/or over-valuation of exports serving to justify fund transfers involving criminal proceeds.[39]

It has to be said that the above stages are not cumulative constituent elements of money laundering in the sense that they should all exist before an offence is committed. The commission of any one of them could be sufficient for guilt to arise. However, it is improbable that layering or integration could occur with placement having preceded it. As is apparent in the three stages of money laundering, there are instances when it is committed without the placement stage. While there are instances where all three stages are clearly discernible, the variability and complexity of the money laundering process can result in cases where only a number of these stages occur, where they occur simultaneously or where they overlap.[40] This has led to a number of alternative models to the three stages:

- The two-phase model distinguishes between money laundering in the first degree (concerning the laundering of money stemming directly from illegal acts) and money laundering in the second degree, indicating mid- or long-term operations through which the laundered money appears as a legal income and is restructured in the legitimate financial system (recycling).
- The circulation model, which is based on the cycle of water and is divided into seven stages.[41]
- The four-sector model, in which the sector contains a refinement process.
- The destination/teleological model, based on diverse money laundering targets (e.g. integration, investment, tax evasion and the financing of organized crime).

39 E.U. Savona and M.A. De Foe, 'International Money Laundering Trends and Prevention/Control Policies', in E.U. Savona (ed.), *Responding to Money Laundering: International Perspectives* (New York: Harwood Academic Publishers, 1997), pp. 27–8.

40 Ibid.

41 Schematically the cycle goes as follows: rain (insertion of cash) – insertion of water into the soil (first wash) – creation of undercurrent waters (creation of reserves) – creation of underground seas through drainage (preparation and transportation abroad) – recollection in the underground seas (preparation for legitimation) – water pumping station (entrance to the legitimate financial system) – biological cleansing installations (second wash) – consumption/use (transportation and investment) – evaporation (legal reintroduction into the country of origin) – new rain (new insertion of cash from criminal activities). This model is cited in Valsamis Mitsilegas, *Money Laundering Counter-measures in the European Union: A New Paradigm of Security Governance versus Fundamental Legal Principles* (Dordrecht: Kluwer Law International, 2003), p. 29.

As far as the criminal underground community is concerned, money laundering is embedded primarily in its potential to avoid detection of the underlying criminal activity that generates the profit.[42] In addition, money laundering can sustain the enjoyment of profit from crime or its reinvestment in future criminal activities. Moreover, money laundering facilitates the development of transnational networks and links with criminal environments of disparate origins. Law enforcement authorities in many parts of the world have come to the conclusion that by combating money laundering activities, they can disrupt the cycle used by criminal groups to derive benefits from illegal profits, and thereby weaken or even destroy their viability. If the primary motivation behind syndicated crime is economic, and the economic gain is removed, the crime will cease.

Sophisticated attempts to conceal the sources of money can involve hundreds (sometimes thousands) of bank accounts in numerous jurisdictions in an attempt to create as complex a web as possible. This makes it difficult or impossible to trace transactions, presenting law enforcement authorities with huge administrative barriers against obtaining financial details.[43]

It must be said that in any type or stage of the money laundering process, the goal remains the concealment of the true ownership and origin of criminal proceeds and changing its form by constantly maintaining control.[44] This element of concealment or disguise is integral to the conceptualization of the money laundering phenomenon and is essential to distinguish it from the simple hiding of illicit proceeds.[45] This is not always taken into account by certain theories on the process of money laundering, especially in models such as the 'hand wash', which involves the use of a small amount of money to buy goods. This does not involve an intention to conceal the origin of the criminal proceeds and may not involve the use of credit or financial institutions.

The *Actus Reus* of Money Laundering Offences

In the context of an EU Directive,[46] the conduct that describes money laundering consists of: the conversion or transfer of property; the concealment or disguise of its origin; its acquisition or possession or use; and the participation or association to commit, attempt to commit and aiding, abetting, facilitating and counselling the commission of any of the acts. It also involves conduct which in effect is similar

42 Savona and De Foe, 'International Money Laundering Trends'.

43 Jarrod Wiener, 'Money Laundering: Transnational Criminals, Globalization and the Forces of Redomestication', 1 *Journal of Money Laundering Control* (1997): pp. 54–66.

44 Ibid.

45 United Nations Office on Drugs and Crime, www.unodc.org (date accessed 22 November 2011).

46 Council Directive of 10 June 1991 on prevention of the use of financial systems for the purposes of money laundering (91/308/EEC), OJ L 166, 28 June 1991, at 77.

to the offences of handling of the proceeds of crime. This is a well-established offence in many EU Member States,[47] except that as money laundering it would incur a higher penalty.[48] In the UK, s. 329 of the Proceeds of Crime Act (POCA) 2002[49] criminalizes the mere possession of criminal property. It can rightly be noted that the conduct that constitutes money laundering extends beyond the mere handling of stolen goods (as in the UK Theft Act 1968) because there is a need for action beyond mere possession (for example, assisting in the retention or removal of property for the benefit of another person).[50] The POCA 2002 assimilates the money laundering offences introduced by the Criminal Justice Act 1988 as amended by the Criminal Justice Act 1993. Section 93A(1)(a) of the Criminal Justice Act 1988 focused on assistance when the retention or control by or on behalf of another (A) of A's proceeds of criminal conduct is facilitated, whether by concealment, removal from the jurisdiction or transfer of nominees or otherwise. However, in order for the prosecution to secure a conviction against a money launderer, it must prove that he/she had a requisite *mens rea* of the offence.

The *Mens Rea* of Money Laundering Offences

In criminal justice, most notably with regard to the presumption of innocence, the prosecution must prove that the launderer knew that the money was derived from unlawful activity. The prosecution must also prove that by manipulating the funds, the accused intended to hide its origin, nature, location, ownership or any other aspect thereof as described in the definition of the offence.[51] This burden of proof can be very onerous, especially in view of the complexity of money laundering operations and the extensive use of shell companies and bearer securities.[52] To render this burden manageable, there is a growing consensus to allow for the reliance on inferential evidence. This is also set out in the Vienna Convention framework (1988), which provides that 'knowledge, intent or purpose' required as an element of the offence set forth in para. 1 of this article may be inferred from objective factual circumstances.[53] As noted in *R v Harmer*, the defendant's

47 Article 1(3).

48 Mitsilegas, *Money Laundering Counter-measures in the European Union*, p. 107.

49 This legislation is truly universal in nature, for not only does it encompass universal mandatory reporting, it also has the unique effect of drawing all the relevant offences of money laundering under a single, unified statute. The previous incremental system has been replaced, almost in its entirety, by a complete legislative framework aimed at reducing the ability of criminals to engage with the financial system to launder their illicit gains.

50 P. Alldridge, *Money Laundering Law* (Oxford: Hart Publishing, 2003), p. 92.

51 Article 3(1) of the Vienna Convention.

52 Ibid.

53 Article 3(3), which reads that 'knowledge, intent or purpose required as an element of the offence set forth in paragraph 1 of this article may be inferred from objective factual circumstances'.

knowledge may be inferred from factual circumstances where that inference is absolutely compelling.[54]

It will always be necessary for the prosecution to prove that the property was in fact the proceeds of crime or drug trafficking. Under s. 93C(1) of the Criminal Justice Act 1988[55] and s. 49 (1) of the Drug Trafficking Act 1994, there is an express reference to dealing with the proceeds of crime and, as a result, it is essential for the prosecution to prove the source of money so as to make clear that the alleged property is a proceed of crime.[56] It will also be incumbent on the prosecution to prove that the defendant knew of the foundation facts on which he/she ought to have formed the suspicion.[57] The requirement for the 'reasonable grounds to suspect' is a subjective test that seems to oblige the prosecution to establish that the defendant himself/herself had formed the suspicion and that it was based on reasonable grounds.[58]

Money laundering is thus established in cases where the defendant either knew or reasonably ought to have known that the money in question was the proceeds of crime.[59] The efforts to adopt a broad framework have led to the additional element of suspicion in the *mens rea* of a number of offences constituting or relating to money laundering. This is the case with regard to assisting another to retain the benefits of criminal conduct and tipping off.[60] Valsamis Mitsilegas contends that the *mens rea* requirement is more stringent in the offences of concealing or transferring proceeds of drug trafficking of a third person and of assisting another to retain the proceeds of terrorist-related activities. In both cases the knowledge element will have to be accompanied by the defendant having the reasonable grounds to suspect the origin of the property from drug trafficking in the first case and an engagement in terrorist activities in the second.[61] Section 330(2) of the UK

---

54 *Kwan Ping Bang* [1979] AC 609, 615.

55 Fundamentally, the Criminal Justice Act 1993 introduced the concept of mandatory reporting – where in the course of his/her trade, profession, business or employment, a person knows or suspects that another person is engaged in drug money laundering, he/she is under a legal duty to report his/her knowledge or suspicion to the authorities. See s. 26B of of the Drug Trafficking Offences Act 1986, as inserted by s. 18 of the Criminal Justice Act 1993.

56 For a discussion on the requisite mental element of the offence, see the case of *R v Montila (Steven William)* [2004] UKHL 50; [2004] WLR 3141 (HL).

57 Mitsilegas, *Money Laundering Counter-measures in the European Union.*

58 *R v Harmer (Roy Peter)* [2005] EWCA Crim 1; [2005] 2 Cr App R 2 (CA, Crim Div).

59 R.E. Bell, 'Prosecuting the Money Launderer: Who Acts for the Organised Crime', 3(2) *Journal of Money Laundering Control* (1999): p. 107.

60 See ss. 93A and 93D of the Criminal Justice Act 1988 as amended by the Criminal Justice Act 1993.

61 Section 14(2) of the Criminal Justice Act 1993 and s. 53(1)(b) of the Northern Ireland (Emergency Provisions) Act 1991.

Proceeds of Crime Act (POCA) 2002[62] further extends the *mens rea* requirement of the offence of failure to disclose, having reasonable grounds for knowing or suspecting that the property was the proceeds of crime.[63] This is particularly important for professionals dealing with the regulated sector. The failure to report suspicion or knowledge of money laundering is, in accordance with s. 334(2)(b), punishable on indictment by a maximum of five years' imprisonment or an unlimited fine. It is important to note that the offence of failing to disclose knowledge or suspicion of money laundering is strictly limited to knowledge or suspicion of money laundering and does not extend to cover 'all-crime' money laundering.[64] The facts or circumstances of the substantive offence that must be proved are that the proceeds are criminal as defined in s. 340 (3)(a), where the alleged offender must know or suspect that the property is criminal. Perhaps also worthy of mention is that knowledge can also be inferred from objective factual circumstances. The scope of money laundering offences as set out in Articles 5 and 6 of the Palermo Convention encompasses a wide range of activities that generate illicit proceeds of crime.

Money Laundering Predicate Offences

The Council of Europe Anti-Money Laundering Convention of 1990 defines predicate offences broadly to include 'any criminal offence as a result of which proceeds were generated that may become the subject of laundering'.[65] While the FATF approach leaves the choice of whether to include or exclude corruption as a predicate offence for money laundering to national legislatures, the approach of the Council of Europe does not seem to offer such a choice.[66] According to the UK approach on money laundering, predicate offences are defined by s. 93A of the Criminal Justice Act 1993, which extends the predicate offence of money laundering to include 'any criminal conduct which constitutes an offence triable on indictment in the Crown Court'.[67] Countries are given the discretion to exclude

62 The POCA 2002 simplifies the law, dispensing with the need for the prosecutor to prove that the defendant was aware of the type (drugs or other criminality) of illicit provenance of the property.

63 In a situation where a person intended to make a necessary disclosure but failed to do so, he/she will not be guilty of the offence under the provisions provided that he/she has a reasonable excuse for his/she failure to disclose.

64 R. Stokes and A. Arora, 'The Duty to Report under the Money Laundering Legislation within the United Kingdom', 5 *Journal of Banking Law* (2004): pp. 332–56.

65 Article 1(e) of the Convention on Laundering, Search, Seizure and Confiscation of the Proceeds from Crime (11 November 1990), available at www.conventions.coe.int/treaty/en/treaties/html/141.htm (date accessed 22 November 2011).

66 Stokes and Arora, 'The Duty to Report under the Money Laundering Legislation within the United Kingdom'.

67 Ibid.

crimes committed abroad or to eliminate those crimes that they do not deem truly relevant from the definition of domesticate predicate crimes.[68]

Substantive Money Laundering Offences in the UK

There are six distinct money laundering offences which apply in England and Wales:

1. concealing, disguising, converting, transferring or removing from the UK;
2. entering into or becoming concerned with an arrangement which facilitates the acquisition, retention, use or control of criminal property;
3. acquiring, using or having possession of criminal property;
4. failing to disclose knowledge or suspicion of money laundering, which came to his/her attention by virtue of his/her position as the nominated officer in the regulated sector;
5. failing to disclose knowledge or suspicion of money laundering where the offender is another nominated officer; and
6. the disclosure of information prejudicial to an investigation, i.e. 'tipping off'.

The Acquisition, Use and Possession of the Proceeds of Crime

It is a separate offence under s. 22 of the Theft Act 1968 for a person to handle stolen goods or their proceeds, knowing or believing them to be stolen goods, or to dishonestly assist in the retention, removal, disposal or realization of such goods by or for the benefit of another person or if he/she arranges to do so.[69] Section 329 of the POCA 2002 which replaces s. 51 of the Drug Trafficking Act 1994 and s. 93B of the Criminal Justice Act 1988, creates a unified position on those who deal with or those who come into possession of the proceeds of crime. This section catches all those who help directly or indirectly in the removal, disposition or retention of criminal property with requisite subjective knowledge or suspicion as provenance. It is therefore a defence for those who take possession of the proceeds of crime in the course of their official duties, such as the police and law enforcement agencies. It will therefore be upon the defendant to prove innocence on this position, as illustrated by their lordships in the case of *R v Gibson* (2000).[70]

---

68 Marco Arnone, 'International Anti-Money Laundering Programmes: Empirical Assessment and Issues in Criminal Regulation', 13(3) *Journal of Money Laundering Control* (2010): p. 226.

69 C.M.V. Clarkson and H.M. Keating, *Criminal Law: Text and Materials* (London: Sweet & Maxwell, 1998), p. 836.

70 [2000] Crim LR 479.

The Offence of Concealing, Disguising, Converting, Transferring or Removing Criminal Property from the UK

This offence is underscored by s. 327 of the POCA 2002 and will be committed by any person who either conceals,[71] disguises, converts, transfers or removes criminal property from the UK.[72] What is noteworthy with regard to this offence is the vastly broad scope of the offence covered by the section and indeed the expansive definition of the offence.[73] The section will catch those engaged in money laundering activities, that is, as per the definition, but will also extend to standard banking practices, such as transfers, conversions and sending funds abroad through wire transfers. In effect, this section combines two offences from the earlier legislation – those of concealing or disguising criminal proceeds and converting or removing from the jurisdiction criminal proceeds for the purposes of avoiding a prosecution for a money laundering offence or in order to avoid an enforcement order, and either concealing or disguising, converting or transferring criminal proceeds with the knowledge or reasonable grounds to suspect that the funds were criminally derived.[74]

The POCA 2002 abolishes the distinction between laundering the proceeds of drug trafficking activities and laundering the proceeds of other criminal activities, which was the chief characteristic of the previous regimes under the Criminal Justice Act 1988 and Drug Trafficking Act 1994.[75] It also abolishes any requirement that the conduct in question amounts to an indictable offence in the UK, as was previously the case under the Criminal Justice Act 1988. Thus, the laundering of any criminally derived property,[76] whether or not the conduct in question would amount to an indictable offence, is now a criminal offence.

In relation to the offence in earlier legislation, namely that of confiscation orders, and the second offence, namely that of containing the objective *mens rea* before the person may be convicted of concealment, these have been amalgamated.[77]

71 Section 327(1)(a) of the POCA 2002.

72 The other elements of the offences are covered by ss. 327(1) (b), (1)(c), (1)(d) and 327(2)(e) respectively.

73 See, for example, what constitutes concealing or disguising in the definition under s. 327 (3) of the above regime.

74 Section 31 of the Criminal Justice Act 1988.

75 See Part 7 of the POCA 2002 in relation to double criminality set out under s. 340 of the same regime.

76 'Property' is criminal property if: (i) it constitutes a personal benefit from criminal conduct or it represents such a benefit (in whole or in part and whether directly or indirectly); and (b) the alleged offender knows or suspects that it constitutes or represents such a benefit. Criminal conduct is conduct which constitutes an offence in any part of the UK or would constitute an offence in any part of the UK if it occurred there. It is immaterial who carried out the criminal conduct, who benefited from it and whether it occurred before or after passing of the Act. See s. 340(3) of the POCA 2002.

77 Section 340 of the POCA 2002.

The offence of concealing criminal property is now committed solely through concealing, disguising, converting, transferring or removing criminal property from the UK provided that the person cannot avail himself/herself of one of the statutory defences. However, to bring a successful prosecution, the necessary element of prosecution must be established in order for the property to be criminal by virtue of s. 340(3), but the alleged offender must also know or suspect that the property is criminal. The above section provides the definition of criminal property, which includes two components: that the property constitutes a benefit from criminal conduct (s. 340(3)(a)); and that the alleged offender knows or suspects that it constitutes such a benefit (s. 34(3)(b)). Interestingly, it is the suspicion element in the absence of specific criminality in relation to allegedly laundered criminal proceeds that has been the cause of much concern for practitioners in the interpretation of money laundering offences.[78] The drafters of the POCA 2002 intended to relax the onerous requirement for the prosecution to have to prove underlying criminality – an issue that had in the past caused problems for courts in successfully prosecuting money laundering offences. In *R v Whitham* (2008),[79] the decision of the court demonstrates that suspicion alone could suffice in bringing a prosecution for money laundering against the defendant. For example, having a substantial and unexplained substantial sum of money or a sudden increase in one's assets could be seen as evidence of money laundering. The draconian confiscation of suspected assets could then follow. The defendant would then then be given the opportunity before the court to prove otherwise. It is an offence under s. 327 of the POCA 2002 for the defendant to conceal, disguise, convert, transfer or even remove criminal property from its jurisdiction.

Failure to Disclose in the Regulated Sector

Under s. 330 of the POCA 2002, a person commits an offence where through the course of his/her business in the regulated sector, he/she knows or suspects that another person is engaged in money laundering and fails to make the required disclosure as soon as practically possible.[80] Suffice it to say that this offence creates a

78 D. Bentley and R. Fisher, 'Criminal Property under POCA 2002 – Time to Clean Up the Law?, 2 *Archbold News* (March 2009).

79 [2008] EWHC Crim 239; see also *Wilkinson v DPP* [2006] EWHC 3012 and *Hogan v DPP* [2007] EWHC 978.

80 There will be no offence where the person is a professional legal adviser and the information or other matter which causes him/her either to know or suspect money laundering came to him/her in privileged circumstances. This defence is elaborated on in s. 330(10), which provides that: 'information or other matter comes to a professional legal adviser in privileged circumstances if it is communicated or given to him/her: (a) by (or representative of) a client of his in connection with the giving by the adviser of legal advice to the client, (b) by (or representative of) a person seeking legal advice from the adviser, or (c) by a person in connection with legal proceedings or contemplated legal

universal duty to disclose knowledge or suspicion of money laundering, something which previously had been limited to the laundering of drug trafficking or terrorist funds.[81] This offence is structured on a tripartite basis and all requirements must be proved beyond reasonable doubt in order to secure a successful prosecution under this section. First, the person must know or suspect or have reasonable grounds for knowing or suspecting that another person is engaged in money laundering. Secondly, the information upon which his/her knowledge is based, or which gives him/her reasonable grounds for such knowledge or suspicion, must have come to him/her through the course of business in the regulated sector. What constitutes the regulated sector is defined in broad terms. It is defined in negative terms, with Sched. 9, para. 3 providing:

> A business is not in the regulated sector to the extent that it engages in any of the following activities –
>
> (a) The issue of withdrawal share capital within the limit set by section 6 of the Industrial and Provident Societies 1996 Act;
>
> (b) The acceptance of deposits from the public within the limit set by section 7(3) of that Act by a society registered under that Act;
>
> (c) The acceptance of deposit from the public within the limit set by section 7(3) of that Act by such a society;
>
> (d) Activities carried out by the Bank of England;
>
> (e) Any activity in respect of which an exemption order under section 38 of the Financial Services and Markets Act 2000 has effect if it is carried on by a person who is for the time being specified in the order or falls within a class of person.

The scope of the regulated sector encompasses a range of professional businesses including, for example, bankers, accountants and members of the legal profession. These professionals are under a duty to disclose and failure to comply with this requirement will result in criminal and heavy penal consequences.[82]

Thirdly, and perhaps lastly, the person must not fail to make the necessary disclosure[83] as soon as reasonably practicable after the information relating to

---

proceedings'. However, this defence is restricted in s. 330(11), which provides that where the information or other matter is communicated or given with the intention of furthering a criminal purpose, the legal privilege defence is unavailable.

81 Section 340(3), (4) of the POCA 2002.

82 Ibid.

83 Under s. 334 of the POCA 2002, failure to report is punishable by, where tried summarily, imprisonment for a term not exceeding six months. Where the offence is tried

possible money laundering offences has come to his/her attention.[84] The meaning of 'required disclosure' is clarified in s. 330(5), which defines this in terms which essentially refer to 'reporting up the line', that is, the person must make a disclosure to a nominated officer (defined in s. 330(9) as referring to the person appointed to receive and handle money laundering disclosures in the disclosures company or alternatively to any person authorized to receive such disclosures by the Director General of the Serious Organised Crime Agency (SOCA)).[85]

The jeopardy of the bank is clearly demonstrated in the case of *Squirrel Ltd v National Westminster Bank Plc and HM Customs and Excise* (2005).[86] Squirrel Ltd held a bank account with NatWest that was £200,000 in credit. Without warning or explanation of its supposedly unusual actions to its customer, the bank froze the account. Squirrel applied to the court for an order that NatWest unfreeze the account and disclose the reason for its conduct. Apparently, it transpired that Squirrel Ltd was under investigation by HM Customs and Excise for VAT-related offences, and accordingly the bank suspected that the funds in Squirrel Ltd's account represented criminal property.[87] Two issues were raised by this scenario: (i) unfreezing would amount to a breach of s. 328 of the POCA 2002 (entering into an arrangement to facilitate the use of criminal property); and (ii) disclosing to Squirrel the reason for its decision to freeze the account would cause the bank to breach s. 333 (tipping off). The court ruled that the course of action adopted by the bank was unimpeachable, even though there were no material facts before the court to justify that the funds in the respective bank account represented criminal property. The court expressed that even if Squirrel Ltd were entirely innocent, there was no question of the bank being required to compensate Squirrel Ltd for damages suffered. However, the court found itself powerless to impeach the position of the bank, even though there was nothing material before the court to justify the conclusion that the funds in the ban (as alleged) was criminal property. Squirrel Ltd's predicament was compounded by the fact that it could not afford legal representation without access to its funds. In essence the inference drawn from this case is that courts will require financial institutions to comply with anti-money laundering legislation regardless of the detrimental effect it might have on the relationship between the financial institution and its customers. The reporting regimes in the above section are so onerous on the bank that has reasonable ground to suspect, as demonstrated in Squirrel Ltd, that it should freeze the account instantly. This is so that even if the bank processes a cheque to transfer the money

on indictment, the offence is punishable by a maximum of five years' imprisonment and an unlimited fine.

84 E. Radmore, 'Money Laundering Prevention: Effect of the New Law on Solicitors', 16(5) *Comp. Law* (1995): p. 155.

85 J. Wadsley, 'Professionals as Policemen', 275 *Conv.* (1994): p. 281.

86 [2005] EWHC 664.

87 The bank did not want to be seen as if it was entering into an arrangement to facilitate the use of criminal property, contrary to s. 328 of the POCA 2002.

into the account of another person without making due inquiry where it should have, it could be liable for facilitating the use or control of criminal property and hence be committing an offence under s. 328 of the POCA 2002.[88] For professionals advising a client on the matter that might involve the legal advisor or the client being involved in money laundering, steps should be taken to make an authorized disclosure, as clearly demonstrated by their Lordships' decision in *P v P* (2003).[89] This case is of particular importance in relation to legal advisors not falling foul of s. 328 of the POCA 2002 in relation to having inadvertently participated in an arrangement which facilitates the acquisition, retention, use or control of criminal property. The case of *Bowman v Fels* (2005)[90] sheds more light on the interpretation of s. 328 of the POCA 2002 and its relevance to the legal professions. The underlying facts were that the relationship between the claimant and the defendant ended, and the claimant asserted a right to a beneficial interest in the property that they had occupied together, but which was registered in the defendant's sole name. In preparing for trial, the claimant's solicitors suspected that the defendant had included in his business accounts the cost of non-business-related work carried out at the property, and notified the National Criminal Intelligence Service (NCIS) by virtue of their perceived obligation under s. 328. The important issue to be determined was whether s. 328 means that, as soon as a lawyer acting for a client in legal proceedings discovers or suspects anything in the proceedings that may facilitate the acquisition, retention, use or control (usually by his/her own client or his/her client's opponent) of 'criminal property', he/she must immediately notify the NCIS of his/her belief if he/she is to avoid being guilty of the criminal offence of being concerned in an arrangement which he/she knows or suspects facilitates money laundering.

The court concluded that the proper interpretation of s. 328 was that it was not intended to cover or affect the ordinary conduct of litigation by legal professionals. This included any step taken by them in litigation, from the issue of proceedings and the securing of injunctive relief or a freezing order up to its final disposal by judgment. The court did not consider that either the European or the UK legislation could have envisaged that any of these ordinary activities would fall within the concept of 'becoming concerned in an arrangement which facilitates the acquisition, retention, use or control of criminal property'.

The overriding importance of the banks' duty to report suspicious transactions has also been reiterated in the recent case of *Shah v HSBC Private Bank* (2009).[91] In this case the High Court underscored the importance of HSBC's statutory obligation to report suspicious transactions. The facts of this case related to the delayed payment of US$4 million from the accounts of Mr and Mrs Shah following a suspicious activity report to a designated person in Zimbabwe. An

88 *K v National Westminster Bank and others* [2006] EWCA Civ 1039.

89 [2003] EWHC Fam 260.

90 [2005] EWCA Civ 226.

91 [2009] EWHC 78.

intended recipient of the money reported the matter to the authorities, who then froze the account of Mr and Mrs Shah, which included funds of US$300 million. The claimants challenged HSBC, alleging that it had breached its implied term in the contract to take reasonable care and to comply with the instructions, and had breached confidentiality. The traditional position has always been that in the event of conflict between common law and statutory law, statutory law would always take precedence. The court held that the common law duty of confidentiality alleged by the claimants (Mr and Mrs Shah) had been overridden by the provisions of the POCA 2002 and hence the bank had acted lawfully within the provisions of s. 328 of the POCA 2002. It also needs to be noted that for the bank to secure a successful prosecution, it needs to file a suspicious activity report (SAR) as soon as practically possible. If the bank delays in filing a SAR, it could jeopardize the trail on the grounds of Article 6 of the European Convention on Human Rights (ECHR). Such a scenario has been underscored by the case of *RCPO v C* (2010),[92] where a solicitor had fraudulently laundered money through the firm's accounts. Due to delays in bringing the prosecution, the defendant was cleared of all six counts of money laundering after the judge ruled that a fair trial was impossible. Had the court proceeded with the trial, it would have been in breach of Article 6 of the ECHR.

Therefore, the suspicion-based reporting regime in the above case and in *Squirrel Ltd v NatWest Bank Plc and HM Customs and Excise* (2005), which is still operative in the UK, is vulnerable to attack through recourse to human rights principles and jurisprudence.[93] Confidentiality in financial dealings and status is an important facet of one's private life and, as such, ought to be protected as far as reasonably possible by law. Confidentiality is also a feature of the bank–customer relationship, and indeed any professional relationship, based on trust, loyalty and fair dealing, not to mention contract law.[94] A person who fails to disclose may argue that he/she was justified in doing so under Article 8(1) of the ECHR.[95] The only exceptions to public bodies are set out in Article 8(2), where the following can be established. The five legitimate justifications are: where national security is at stake, there is the need to protect national safety or the economic well-being of the country, prevention of disorder or crime, protection of health or morals, and the protection of freedom of others.[96] The traditional principle of banking confidentiality created by the contract between the customer and the bank (as a

92 [2009] EWCA Crim 97.

93 The application of Article 8(1) of the ECHR has a negative effect on the disclosure requirements under s. 330, since it prohibits a public body (for example, courts) from interfering with an individual's right to privacy.

94 Robert Stokes, 'The Banker's Duty of Confidentiality, Money Laundering and the Human Rights Act', 3 *Journal of Banking Law* (2007): pp. 502–20.

95 Ibid.

96 James Otty, 'Money Laundering and Human Rights', *New York Law Journal* (2001): p. 634.

confidant) and data protection could be undermined under the provisions of Article 8(2). Any common law disclosure of confidential information held by a banker in respect of a customer must also be proportionate[97] to the legitimate aim pursued. The case of *Sunderland v Barclays Bank Ltd* (1938)[98] underscores problems with regard to the critical nature of the principle of proportionality. 'Proportionality' was defined as 'a deliberately flexible concept whereby each specific interference with conventional rights had to be analysed on its individual merits'. The doctrine of proportionality may require the review of a court decision to assess the balance which the court has struck, not merely whether it is within the range of rational or reasonable decisions. The proportionality test may go further than the traditional grounds of review, inasmuch as it may require attention to be directed to the relative weight accorded to the interests and considerations: *R v Ministry of Defence, ex parte Smith* (1996).[99]

Tipping Off

The remaining offence under the POCA 2002 is that of tipping off – where a professional or those working in the regulated sector make a disclosure that is likely to prejudice a money laundering investigation being undertaken by the law enforcement agencies.[100] It is in fact worthy of mention that where the person does not know or suspect that the disclosure was likely to be prejudicial, he/she does not commit an offence.[101] The offence of tipping off is highlighted by the case of *Governor and Company of the Bank of Scotland v A Ltd* (2001).[102] In this case, the bank made enquiries in respect of a number of accounts opened by A Ltd into which substantial sums of money were transferred. The police advised the bank that money laundering investigations were being carried out into the activities of the company and asked it not to reveal the information to A Ltd. The bank was fearful that it would risk being sued by the company if it failed to pay money held in the accounts or by third parties as constructive trustees if it did. As such, it was in an invidious position of 'damned if you don't, damned if you do'. The Court of Appeal indicated that it was important in such a situation for the bank to file an interim declaration under r. 25.1(1)(b) of the Civil Procedure Rules (CPR), naming the Serious Fraud

97 Proportionality seeks to establish the balance between democratic principles of tolerance, pluralism, broadmindness and 'necessity'. Interference with the provisions of Article 8(1) will only be necessary in a democratic society when it is proportionate to the legitimate aim being pursued.

98 (1938) 5 LDAB 163.

99 [1996] QB 517.

100 Section 333 of the POCA 2002, which replaces ss. 53 and 58 of the Drug Trafficking 1994 and s. 93D of the Criminal Justice Act 1988.

101 Section 333(2) of the POCA 2002.

102 [2001] 1 WLR 751.

Office as the defendant. In these circumstances, the bank would clearly be protected against the criminal liability of 'tipping off'. In another case, *C v S* (1991),[103] a bank made a disclosure in action or documents, which might have revealed the existence of ongoing enquiries by the NCIS as it then was.[104] The purpose of the application was an attempt by the company (C) to trace the sums of money that it alleged had been misappropriated by others. The bank had earlier made a disclosure to the NCIS of suspicious transactions and was fearful that disclosure of the documents might breach the tipping off provisions of s. 93D of the Drug Trafficking Act 1994. It was also in an invidious situation where, on the one hand, it would be criminally liable if it complied with the first instance order for disclosure, while on the other hand, it would be liable to contempt of court if it failed to do so. An *ex parte* application was made to the High Court *in camera* in an attempt to resolve the dilemma and the original disclosure order was revoked, allowing the bank not to disclose information to the NCIS (now replaced by SOCA).[105]

It is a defence in the UK that a person who should disclose neither knew nor suspected that another person was engaged in money laundering and had not been provided with the required training by his/her employer.[106] This defence is available where the person is charged with the s. 330(2)(b) offence, namely where the professional has reasonable grounds for knowing or suspecting that a person is engaged in money laundering-related activities but, by virtue of the omission of the training to detect possible money laundering vehicles, fails to disclose as required.[107] This serves as a reminder to those institutions within the regulated sector that the legislative framework under which they operate is geared to revolve around the disclosure of information concerning money laundering, and this is something, in turn, that is dependent on the training that such institutions provide to their employees to detect suspect transactions and clients.[108]

The Bank's Liability in Money Laundering Offences

The bank's duty of disclosure could potentially conflict with the duty of confidentiality owed to the customer by virtue of the contractual obligations

103 [1991] 1 WLR 1551.

104 This has now been replaced by SOCA.

105 Edward Rees and Andrew Hall, *Proceeds of Crime Act* (Oxford; Oxford University Press, 2002), pp. 108–11.

106 Section 330(7) of the POCA 2002.

107 Indeed, this was the case for a junior employee facing criminal sanctions for negligently failing to disclose suspicion or knowledge that money laundering was about to be committed.

108 D.P. Stewart, 'Internalising the War on Drugs: The UN Convention Against Illicit Trafficking in Narcotic Drugs and Psychotropic Substances', 18 *Denv. Journal of International Law and Policy* (1990): p. 387.

created between the bank and the customer. However, if the bank knowingly assists in the receipt of deposits generated from money laundering, it could be liable as an accessory to the alleged money laundering offences.

The Bank's Duty of Confidentiality

If money has been laundered into a suspected bank account and the claimant needs to follow his/her money in the respective bank account, what would be the position of the bank, given the contractual relationship between the bank and the customer? The bank–customer relationship is governed by the common law principle of confidentiality to its customers, but again this duty is not 'set in stone', as we have already illustrated in the case of *Shah v HSBC Private Bank* (2009). It is an established principle in English common law that the relationship between a bank and a customer is a contractual one, and that the bank has a legal duty arising out of this contract to protect the information relating to a customer which it has received as a confidant.[109] An implicit term of the contract is that the bank should not disclose to third parties either the state of the customer's account, any of his/her transactions with the bank or any information relating to the customer acquired through the maintenance and administration of the account.[110] In *Tournier v National Provincial Union Bank of England* (1923),[111] Bank LJ clearly argued that this duty extends at least to 'all the transactions that go through the account … even beyond the period when the account is closed … [and] extends to the information obtained from other sources than the customer's actual account'.[112]

While the duty not to disclose is a legal one arising out of the law of contract, it is not an absolute one, but is qualified. The first qualification is where there is a duty to the public to disclose; the second is where disclosure is under a compulsion by law; the third is where the interest of the bank requires disclosure; and the last is where disclosure is made with the express or implied consent of the customer.[113] Implied consent is manifested in a situation where, for instance, the customer has filled in a consent form and has authorized the bank to pass information on to a third party.

---

109 The nature of this relationship is clearly articulated in *Foley v Hill* [1848] 2 HL Cas. 28 and *Joachison v Swiss Bank Corporation* [1921] 3 KB 110; see also Lord Chorley and P.E. Smart, *Leading Cases in the Law of Banking*, 4th edn (London: Sweet & Maxwell, 1998), p. 88.

110 Atkin LJ's *dictum* in *Tournier v National Provincial and Union Bank of England* [1923] All ER 550–558.

111 [1923] All ER 550.

112 E. Ellinger, E. Lomnicka and R.J.A. Hooley, *Modern Banking Law*, 3rd edn (Oxford: Oxford University Press, 2005), p. 152.

113 Ibid.

There are circumstances in which the courts have allowed money to be followed at common law into the hands of a subsequent transferee,[114] and the position of the law seems to assert the common law right to follow an asset and to recover it in personal action, just as much as in the case of a debt.[115] The instructive example in this situation is the Court of Appeal's decision in *Banque Belge Pour L'Etranger v Hambrouck* (1921),[116] in which the facts of the case were as follows. The first defendant, Hambrouck, having fraudulently obtained a number of crossed cheques drawn or purporting to be drawn in his favour by his employer, paid these into a bank account opened in his name for that purpose and, after the proceeds had been collected by his bank from the claimant banker and credited to his account, drew cheques on that account in favour of his mistress, the second defendant, who paid them into her own bank account with the third defendant. The claimant's bank thereupon brought an action against all three defendants for the declaration that the money paid by the second defendant into her account with the third defendant was the property of the claimant, and an order for payment to them. The third defendant paid the sum in question into the court and was dismissed from the action.

The claimant succeeded against the remaining defendant, and the second defendant appealed. The Court of Appeal rejected the appeal, contending that the right to follow the money had and received was lost by the appellant's payments of money into the banking account, upholding the decision of the trial judge. Both Banks LJ and Atkin LJ were of the opinion that the money, having been paid to the third defendant and by them into the court, was clearly identifiable as money to which the claimant was entitled and which it could thus recover at common law in an action for money had and received.[117] As third parties, banks could find themselves as accessories to money laundering offences.

The Bank's Liability as an Accessory

If a bank knowingly accepts deposits realized from the sale of criminal property, it could be liable as an accessory to the crime of aiding and abetting money laundering. The law on accessories is set out in the Accessories and Abettor Act 1861: 'Whosoever shall aid, abet, counsel or procure the commission of any indictable offence … shall be liable to be tried, indicted and punished as a principal offender.'[118] Where two or more people agree to an act in prohibited

114 *Banque Belge Pour L'Etranger v Hambouck* [1921] 1 KB 321.

115 *Re Diplock* [1947] 1 Ch. 716, at p. 746.

116 [1921] 1 KB 321.

117 Alastair Hudson, *Principles of Equity and Trusts* (London: Cavendish Publishing, 2004), pp. 433–65.

118 The liability of secondary offenders is governed by s. 8 of the Accessories and Abettors Act 1861.

circumstances, the law has long adopted a view that they should be liable for the direct and agreed consequences of that joint enterprise. The only problem would be when one of the parties exceeds what was agreed.[119] For the defendant to be liable in a joint-enterprise offence, the defendant (the bank in this case) must have had the necessary *mens rea* in relation to its own conduct, notably an intention to encourage the commission of money laundering. This could take the form of *mens rea* in respect of the principal offence and its consequences, or it could involve *mens rea* in relation to the mental state of the principal offender.[120] Similarly, the foregoing situation could also elicit issues of conspiracy to commit money laundering under the Conspiracy Act 1977. Section 1(2) of this Act requires that in order for the defendant (the bank) to be liable for an offence of conspiracy, the defendant must intend or know that the prohibited circumstances will exist when the offence is committed. Since conspiracy is a crime of specific intent, the prosecution will have to prove that the bank has committed the conduct and the outcome of the substantive money laundering offences.[121] In the case of *Gray v Johnson* (1968),[122] it was clearly established that this applied if the bank had misapplied the funds, amounting to a breach of trust, or where the bankers were privy to the intent to make the misapplication of the trust funds.[123] Equally, banks are not under any fiduciary obligation as trustees to their customers or third parties, but in circumstances where there has been *mal fides* (for example, in situations where they are sufficiently aware of money laundering), they may be liable to the victim of this conduct as 'a constructive trustee'.[124] Banks will not be made a constructive trustee simply because it acts as the agent of the trustee in transactions within their legal powers, unless they have assisted with the knowledge and fraudulent design on the part of the trustees.[125] As such, for a prosecution to succeed, it will have to clearly articulate a causal relationship between the defendant's intention (in this case the bank) and the commission of the substantive offences, which is the basis of conspiracy.[126]

If the bank converts negotiable instruments, a frequently used method in the layering stage of the money laundering process, it could be liable for the tort of conversion. Equally, where the bank has knowingly received funds which have been misappropriated in breach of trust or fiduciary duty, it will be liable

119 *R v Powell and another; R v English* [1977] 4 All ER 545 (HL).

120 Clarkson and Keating, *Criminal Law, Text and Materials*, pp. 546–7.

121 In the Canadian case of *Claiborne Industries Ltd v National Bank of Canada* (1989) 59 DLR (4th) 533, the release of lender's security to the plaintiff, which was subsequently taken by the defendant through his private company, was found to constitute conspiracy to defraud the bank.

122 [1968] LR 3 HL 1.

123 *Tassell v Cooper* (1850) 9 CB 509.

124 Ross Cranston, *Banks' Liability and Risks* (London: Lloyd's of London Press Ltd, 1995), pp. 64–5.

125 Ibid.

126 Ibid.

for 'knowing receipt'. Knowing receipt is a form of secondary liability where the wrongdoer is primarily liable for the act or omission committed.[127] This is a form of personal liability rather than proprietary liability that is manifested in a situation where the bank receives the funds properly and then applies them for its own benefit.[128] One of the prerequisites for knowing receipt is where the money has been disposed of in breach of trust and where the bank has applied the money for its own benefit.[129] The prosecution will have to prove that the bank had knowledge that it was misapplying the money in breach of trust. The liability of the bank will be by way of its officers and agents, who have requisite knowledge of the money or its proceeds.[130] Knowledge is delineated as 'actual knowledge' or 'constructive knowledge'. The bank is deemed to have knowledge where it wilfully shuts its eyes to the obvious, wilfully or recklessly fails to make inquiries that an honest and reasonable bank would make, has knowledge of circumstances which would indicate the facts to an honest and reasonable bank, or has knowledge of circumstances which would compel an honest and reasonable bank to inquire further.[131] Constructive knowledge is to be inferred from objective factual circumstances if the defendant is not able to explain or to provide evidence exonerating him/her of the alleged money laundering offence.[132]

It is possible that the bank could also be liable for knowing assistance if it acts to facilitate fraud on the trustees either by the receipt of information in breach of confidence or where it induces a breach of trust or a fiduciary.[133] In *Barnes v Addy* (1874),[134] for the bank to be liable for this form of liability, there has to be 'a dishonest and fraudulent design' on the part of the trustees. In addition, there has to be an element of fault, although knowledge has been said to suffice.[135] The dishonest test adopted in relation to the above is the Cunningham subjective test rather than an objective bystander test, otherwise known as the Caldwell test for recklessness.[136] This would involve questions like: would an honest and reasonable bank have acted differently at the time? This question will assist the prosecution on determining the liability of the defendant in alleged money laundering offences.

---

127 Ross Cranston (ed.), *Principles of Banking Law* (Oxford: Oxford University Press, 2003), p. 192.

128 Ibid.

129 *Agip (Africa) Ltd v Jackson* [1990] Ch 265.

130 M. Bryan, 'When Does a Bank Receive Money?', 3 *Journal of Business Law* (1995): p. 165.

131 *Baden Devaux and Lecuit v Societe Generale pour Favoriser le Developpement du Commerce et de l'Industrrie en France SA* [1992] All ER 161, 235.

132 Section 3(1)(b) in the definition of money laundering offences according to the Vienna Convention.

133 P. Finn, 'The Liability of Third Parties in Knowing Receipt or Assistance', in D. Waters (ed.), *Equity, Fiduciaries and Trusts* (Ontario: Caswell), p. 197.

134 (1874) LR 9 Ch. App. 244.

135 *Agip (Africa) Ltd v Jackson* [1990] Ch 265.

136 *R v Ghosh* [1982] QB 1053.

There are many typologies of money laundering and these will vary from country to country. In some countries, money laundering crimes are inextricably linked to corruption.

Corruption as a Typology of Money Laundering

There is a correlation between corruption[137] and the offshoot growth of financial crimes such as money laundering. In many cases where money launderers cannot achieve their aims through the use or threat of the use of violence, corruption will be the alternative. Corruption takes many forms, including bureaucratic corruption, where officials take bribes, or political corruption, which includes politicians taking bribes to award contracts, influence elections or provide patronage. Grand corruption involves the misuse of power by heads of state, ministers and top officials for private pecuniary profit, and even noble cause corruption, where the instruments of government such as the intelligence services are used to provide financial and other support for criminal activity, including assisting terrorism, providing secret arms supplies beyond the scrutiny of political processes and laundering secret funds.[138] The United Nations Convention against Corruption (UNCAC) criminalizes the laundering of the proceeds of crime, setting out measures to prevent money laundering in Article 14. It also criminalizes activities such as the bribery of national and foreign national officials of public international organizations (Articles 15 and 16), the embezzlement, misappropriation or other diversion of property by a public official (Article 17), the abuse of positions by a public official in order to obtain an undue advantage (Article 19), trading in influence (Article 18), illicit enrichment (Article 20) and bribery and embezzlement of property in the private sector (Articles 21 and 22).[139] Article 23 underscores what constitutes criminal activity within the context of money laundering. It covers situations where a person converts or transfers property in illicitly obtained goods for the purposes of concealing its provenance. Corruption has also been fuelled by globalization and its attendant liberalization paradigm, which has created opportunities for corruption in the in the same way as it has for legitimate businesses.[140] Then are there asymmetries in the global economy and its dynamics in some regions.

---

137 Susan Rose-Ackerman, *Corruption and Government: Causes, Consequences and Reform* (Cambridge: Cambridge University Press, 1999), p. 13.

138 Barry Rider, *Corruption: The Enemy Within* (Dordrecht: Kluwer Law International, 1997), pp. 8–34.

139 Indira Carr and Miriam Goldby, 'Recovering the Proceeds of Corruption: UNCAC and Anti-money Laundering Standards', 2 *Journal of Business Law* (2011): pp. 171–7.

140 Indira Carr, 'Strategic Improvement in the Fight Against Corruption in International Business Transactions', 2 *Journal of Business Law* (2006): p. 375.

The financial services markets (for example, the stock exchange) in many parts of Africa are not yet developed because investing in shares is still misconceived to be the preserve of the privileged class.[141] This is presumably explained by two reasons: the nature of the laidback society in which financial markets operate and the poor dissemination of information that generally abounds in societies at a rudimentary stage of development. Political instability and its attendant negative effect has not only created an unfriendly market environment but has also been exploited for criminal purposes, including financial abuse. The stock market is still in its infancy in many parts of Africa, which has a negative effect on its financial markets. For instance, the Ugandan stock exchange was established in 1999, and in Kenya, a country that until recently had managed to enjoy a relative period of calm since independence, the stock market has been riddled by corruption.[142] In a society with a developed stock market, there is the likelihood of some financial discipline because regulators are aware that any laxity and poor oversight of financial institutions, especially in a globalized market environment, will trigger systemic failures.

In some parts of the world, corruption and political instability have created opportunities for criminal groups of all shapes and sizes to thrive. These two factors are prevalent in the majority of African countries, which have faced enormous challenges in regulating their financial markets. Criminal groups are always on the lookout for any opportunities to exploit. Organized criminal groups have resorted to money laundering in different countries not only to cleanse the proceeds of crime but also as a means to move criminal proceeds around. They achieve this by using money laundering techniques such as smurfing, the establishment of front companies, the acquisition of commercial and non-commercial properties, remittances through non-official banking channels and foreign remittances. In vulnerable societies with poor salary schemes, public officials can easily be bribed to turn a blind eye to the obvious, providing an avenue for criminal exploitation – including money laundering.

In Uganda, for instance, corruption is so widespread that it cannot simply be confined to being committed in a handful of public sector areas.[143] Corruption practices span both the formal and informal sectors of the economy, such as the judiciary with regard to proper dispensation of justice[144] and the army,

141 This problem was decried by the Chief Executive Officer of the Ugandan Stock Exchange while addressing students at the Makerere University Business School, Kampala, Uganda. See the *New Vision* (Ugandan daily newspaper), 26 March 2008.

142 This refers to the post-election inter-tribal violence sparked by the alleged vote-rigging by the government of Mwai Kibaki, which has marred the situation in much of Kenya since January 2004.

143 According to the World Bank Institute report (2004), the cost of corruption in both rich and poor countries was estimated at $1,000 billion ($1 trillion) per year: seen the World Bank website at www.worldbank.org (date accessed 22 November 2011).

144 *New Vision,* 26 April 2008.

where officers have been found inflating the payroll size in the form of 'ghost employees'.[145] Actually, corruption is so ingrained in Ugandan society that it has more or less become an acceptable norm, notwithstanding the anti-corruption legislation[146] by the government. There is also employment-related corruption manifested in the form of political meddling, patronage and giving token jobs largely to the politically well connected.[147] In Uganda and Kenya, for instance, job allocation is sublimated to political whims, sidelining the market mechanisms in job allocation. This has generated a negative effect on markets and it has also inhibited the process of domesticating global anti-money laundering/combating the financing of terrorism (AML/CFT) regimes and other development initiatives. Corruption and its attendant environment have created market distortions, relegating the well educated to the sidelines of the market, while ironically elevating cronies and relatives of politicians to prestigious offices. Fair enough! However, my only quarrel with this is that corruption undermines the fabric of society and it has an adverse effect on markets and regulations. Money laundering and its predicate offences cannot be fought without fully harnessing the work of auditors, accountants, supervisors, engineers, lawyers, secretaries, administrators, etc.

Conclusion

It can rightly be said that the current AML/CFT framework is a patchwork of complimentary regimes that have evolved at various inter-state levels, but significantly the normative AML/CFT standards are embodied in the revised 40+9 recommendations of the FATF.[148] While this chapter has delineated the substantive and secondary money laundering offences in the UK, it is possible that what constitutes money laundering offences in the UK might not do so in other parts of the world. Many countries would have transposed supranational AML/CFT regimes encapsulating local particularities of money laundering-related threats. However, given the overlapping nature of money laundering offences, coupled with different jurisdictions and legal systems in different parts of the world, it soon became apparent that countries would need to adopt a uniform AML/CFT

145 *New Vision*, 27 March 2008.

146 The Leadership Code (2002): this law aims to combat corruption of public officials, whereby they have to declare their assets every year. If there is a mismatch in an official's declared wealth, he/she may be asked to account for it. The creation of the Leadership Code in Uganda has empowered the Inspector General of the Government to freeze accounts pending investigation and to prosecute offenders allegedly in breach of this statute.

147 In well-established cases, jobs are awarded for electioneering purposes, apparently being traded in return for supporting particular candidates.

148 For more information on the FATF, see its website at: www.fatf-gafi.org (date accessed 22 November 2011).

framework. As such, many countries have adopted the FATF recommendations and the Basel guidelines, as well as signing up to international conventions (for instance, the Vienna Convention (1988) and the Palermo Convention (2000) on money laundering). The adoption of these regimes was deemed essential to creating a uniform global framework against the threat of money laundering. Thus, this chapter has offered insights into the dynamics of money laundering – its definition, scope and attendant threats or offences. However, money laundering committed through the infamy of corruption by many dictators also requires political and sociological analysis. The money that is laundered at a global level amounts to millions, if not billions of dollars annually,[149] often stolen from countries with deep-seated poverty and characterized by a widespread lack of basic necessities such as food, clean drinking water, health, education and housing. Similarly, where the proceeds of money laundering are recovered, a constructive trust should always be declared in the interest of the beneficiaries who have suffered as a result of the money laundering.

Perhaps unsurprisingly, many dictators are sucked into exposing those they rule to a life of misery and deprivation by raiding national treasuries, stealing national wealth and demanding bribes and commissions from the poor. We can also infer that money laundering is caused by a lack of good leadership in places where it is committed. A leader should always be the alchemy of a great vision with the interests of the society he/she leads at heart. Thus, exposing people to misery manifested in the negative effect of money laundering does the exact opposite. This predicament is demonstrated by the legacy of many world leaders and other dictators, who have been tainted by corruption and money laundering. President Mobutu of Zaire is believed to have stolen $4 billion, not to mention the money stolen by Sani Abacha of Nigeria, Daniel Arap Moi of Kenya, Slobodan Milosevic of Serbia, Ferdinand Marcos of the Philippines, 'Papa Doc' Duvalier of Haiti and former President Suharto of Indonesia, to name but a few.

Thus, the challenge of legal asymmetries, even within the same legal traditions (in relation to the definition and characterization of money laundering offences), could be overcome when states subscribe to the globalization of money laundering laws. The creation of an AML/CFT framework has created a level playing field in various areas of money laundering and its predicate threats, and it has eased technical deficiencies in some countries, fostering a stable global financial community. A stable global system has the potential to generate economic and social synergies to all countries, developed or developing; conversely, unstable societies will impede economic development because they encourage the commissioning of money laundering offences.

149 The IMF estimates laundered money to account for between $2 billion and $5 billion of the world's GDP.

Chapter 2
The Dynamics of Globalization and Money Laundering

Introduction

This chapter underscores the dynamic nature of global anti-money laundering/combating the financing of terrorism (AML/CFT) framework. It demonstrates that the global AML/CFT framework is not only desirable but is also an imperative to ensure a coordinated and robust implementation of internationally agreed AML/CFT standards on a forward-looking basis.[1] It is internationally accepted that this framework is necessary in order to prevent criminal organizations from abusing the financial system as well as to overcome weaknesses in the anti-money laundering laws of individual countries.[2] For example, foreign banks which operate in Uganda have managed to circumvent the absence of AML/CFT laws by exploiting the parent-grown banking policies, which have to be applied in formulating local policies in all international branches. It has to be said that if domestic and foreign laws are not aligned together by the passing of enabling legislation nationally, it can engender an environment for exploiting the reputation of some banks and causing regulatory arbitrage to the disadvantage of foreign banks.[3]

In view of the fact that the globalization of markets is fraught with economic asymmetries, the system has naturally tended to favour developed countries over less developed countries. Thus, the majority of developing countries are naturally at a disadvantage and cannot access the benefits of the global system. As demonstrated by some sections of this book, asymmetries of power in the global system have the potential to resonate into AML/CFT regimes in relation to the way in which they have evolved or are harnessed at an inter-state level. Similarly disparities in the global economy have generated an environment where the benefits of the global system, regardless of what the issue might be, cannot be evenly distributed among stakeholder countries.[4] Furthermore, it has become

---

1 F. Bilali, 'The Role of the World Bank', *Fordham Law School Occasional Papers* 1 (2004): p. 111; see also J. Gieger, 'The Case for Harmonisation of Securities', 241 *Columbia Business Law Review* (1997): pp. 299–307.

2 This was precisely the reason for the adoption of the Vienna Convention in 1988.

3 If foreign banks are tightly regulated when their local rivals are not, they will not be able to compete with their local rivals.

4 This explains the demise of the first East African Community in 1977 before it was resurrected in 1999. The government of Uganda under Idi Amin was unhappy with

increasingly evident that criminal organizations have ruthlessly exploited the market economy for their ends. For example, through legitimate international trade and the use of commercial products, such as letters of credit or electronic money transfers, criminals have been able to launder the proceeds of crime from one place to another with ease.[5] These challenges have also been exacerbated by the advent of cyber-markets, offshore financial centres and increased investment vehicles which are ruthlessly exploited to evade AML/CFT regulations and other risk-management models.[6] This situation justifies the need for a robust global AML/CFT framework.

A Brief Overview of the Global AML/CFT Framework

The global AML/CFT framework is underscored by the 40+9 FATF recommendations and the UN treaties, such as the the Vienna Convention (1988) and the Palermo Convention (2000). Then there are the EU Directives on money laundering, the Bank for International Settlement (hereinafter the Basel Committee Supervisory Standards) and other regimes on money laundering offences. These bodies have pioneered guidelines on money laundering which governments struggling with both the design and implementation of AML/CFT measures can draw upon. In the examination of global regimes on AML/CFT, I have utilized the work of the Basel Committee Standards, the FATF, the European Anti-Money Laundering Directive and the anti-money laundering treaties of the UN as constituting a global anti-money laundering framework.[7] The adoption of normative AML/CFT standards is assessed against the FATF compliance framework in an individual member country.[8] The FATF compliance framework on money laundering and the combating of terrorism was designed in 2004 (and

the disproportionate distribution of the accrued benefits between the three East African countries of Kenya, Tanzania and Uganda.

5 Louise Shelley, 'Transnational Organised Crimes: A New Authoritarianism', in H. Richard Friman and Peter Andreas (eds), *The Illicit Global Economy & State Power* (Lanham, MD: Rowman & Littlefield, 1998), pp. 25–40.

6 D. Caruso, J. Elvin, A. James and S. Negreira, 'Trade Related Money Laundering Schemes Pose Increased Threats to Financial Institutions', EY Anti-Money Laundering Team, *Payment Efficiency and Risk Reduction Bulletin* (Summer 2000): p. 2.

7 While the above regimes are the most prominent ones, they are supplemented by a myriad of other global AML/CFT regimes such as FATF specialist AML/CFT regional bodies, the Commonwealth Secretariat regimes and many more. For a concise overview of these regimes, see Doug Hopton, *Money Laundering: A Concise Guide for all Businesses* (Aldershot: Ashgate, 2005), pp. 5–9.

8 FATF (2004) anti-money laundering framework, available at www.fatf-gafi.org (date accessed 22 November 2011); see also Norman Mugarura, 'The Effect of Corruption Factor in Harnessing Global Anti-Money Laundering Regimes', 13(3) *Journal of Money Laundering Control* (2010): p. 272.

updated in February 2009).[9] The thrust of the FATF methodology is to encourage a country's compliance with international AML/CFT standards. These standards are contained in the FATF recommendations 2003 and the nine FATF special recommendations on terrorist financing (2001, updated in February 2008).[10] The methodology is designed to assist assessors in compiling a comprehensive AML/CFT report/mutual evaluation report. The FATF also provides a framework for identifying legal, regulatory and financial mechanisms adopted by a country to implement a robust AML/CFT system. The FATF methodology is currently used by the FATF-style regional bodies, the World Bank and the International Monetary Fund (IMF). The assessment of a country's compliance with the AML/CFT framework should be based on relevant underlying information, such as the quantity and type of predicate offences for money laundering, the vulnerability of a country to money laundering or terrorist financing, the method, techniques and trends used to launder money or fund terrorist, the structure of a country's financial system and the nature of the sectors dealing with designated non-financial business and professions, the nature of the underlying criminal justice system and the changes that have been introduced to introduce the AML/CFT system nationally.[11]

The effective AML/CFT system in a country should focus on assisting a legal and institutional framework[12] based on the following elements:

1. Laws that create money laundering and terrorist financing offences and make it possible to freeze, seize and confiscate the proceeds of a crime and terrorist funding.[13]
2. Laws, regulations or in certain circumstances other enforcement measures that impose the required obligations on financial institutions and designated non-financial businesses and professions.[14]
3. An appropriate institutional or administrative framework, laws and other measures that provide the competent authorities with the necessary duties, powers and sanctions to enforce AML/CFT legislation.

---

9 FATF (2004) anti-money laundering framework, available at www.fatf-gafi.org (date accessed 22 November 2011).

10 Ibid.

11 These measures have been identified by the FATF (2004, updated in July 2009) as constituting the necessary AML/CFT framework for countries in transposing their international anti-money laundering obligations. These requirements are also replicated in all other global institutions whose mandate includes AML/CFT. As a matter of fact, these measures provide a comprehensive overview of the global anti-money laundering framework.

12 FATF Methodology/Compliance guidelines with its 40 recommendations and its 9 special recommendations (27 February 2004, updated as of February 2009).

13 Recommendation 3 of the FATF.

14 Ibid., Recommendation 4.

4. Laws and other measures that give a country the ability to offer the widest range of international cooperation. This is regarded as essential in ensuring that the whole system is effectively implemented.

The above framework is designed to provide evaluators/assessors on the country's compliance with the AML/CFT framework or its tools to do so. In view of this framework, the assessors are able to compile a detailed report on the country's ability to implement the FATF AML/CFT framework. The constituent elements of the FATF framework are as follows:

1. The respect of principles such as transparency and good governance.
2. A proper culture of AML/CFT compliance that is shared and reinforced by government, financial institutions, designated non-financial businesses and professions, industry trade groups and self-regulatory organizations (SROs).
3. Appropriate measures to prevent and combat corruption, including, where information is available, laws and relevant measures, jurisdictions, participation in regional or international anti-corruption initiatives (such as the UN Convention against Corruption). The impact of adopting these measures should be to enable a country to apply the required standards locally.
4. There should be a reasonably efficient court system which ensures that judicial decisions are properly enforced.
5. The need for high ethical and professional requirements for police officers, prosecutors, judges, accountants, etc. and measures and mechanisms to ensure that these are observed.

The absence of an effective AML/CFT infrastructure in a country could highlight inherent weaknesses in its ability to transpose a normative AML/CFT framework. Where the state in question has not implemented the necessary AML/CFT regimes, there will be loopholes in the global system due to interconnectedness of states. States cannot effectively coexist in fighting the war against money laundering/financing of terrorism in the absence of the harmonization of laws, norms, procedures and systems. There is no functional central authority to enforce compliance with normative anti-money laws or standards when states stubbornly refuse to implement emerging anti-money laundering norms. The global system therefore remains complex for some countries, but generally the global regimes have proved problematic to harness due to inequalities in the global economy. The issue of the regional integration of markets has generated opportunities within member countries such as the easy movement of labour, capital and services across national borders. However, there is abundant evidence to suggest that such opportunities can also be exploited for criminal purposes. For instance, the growth of motor vehicle trafficking crimes (a microcosmic aspect of cross-border threats) in the East African region[15] is attributable to the relaxation of border controls between the East African member countries. The removal of border controls between these countries was part and parcel of the East African Community initiative. Many governments have had to come together on overlapping global challenges, aligning their laws and policies so as to achieve their common interests.

With regard to money laundering, it is essential to establish the range of activities that constitute money laundering predicate offences. Article 2(h) of the Palermo Convention (2000) defines predicate offences as 'any offence/s as a result of which proceeds have been generated that may become the subject as an offence as defined in Article 6 of the Convention'. Predicate offences are offences which generate illicit proceeds that are subsequently converted into less suspicious assets. The process of converting illicit assets into less suspicious forms is essential, as it marks the stage where the true source or ownership of the new illicit assets is concealed and a legitimate source is created. In this book we have adopted a methodology that captures the predicate crime area where illicit proceeds are generated and assimilated into the financial system (laundered). The limitation of Vienna Convention anti-money laundering framework[16] was that it was specifically limited to the laundering of the proceeds of drug trafficking. After the adoption of the Vienna Convention in 1988, states were limited to creating their anti-money laundering laws to the proceeds from drugs. Thus, the definition of money laundering has been extended to include the proceeds of other serious criminal activities (smuggling, fraud, serious financial crimes and the sale of stolen goods).[17] The 1996–1997 survey by the FATF[18] on money laundering measures

15 Ibid.

16 Money laundering is defined in Article 3(1)(b) as follows: 'The conversion or transfer of property, knowing that such property is derived from any offence or offences established in accordance with sub-paragraph (a) of this paragraph, or from an act of participation in such offence or offences, for the purpose of concealing or disguising the illicit origin of the property or of assisting any person who is involved in the commission of such an offence or offences to evade the legal consequences of his action; the concealment or disguise of the true nature, source, location, disposition, movement, rights with respect to, or ownership of the property, knowing that such property is derived from an offence or offences established in accordance with subparagraph (a) of this paragraph or from an act of participation in such an offence.' Subparagraph (a) refers to illicit drugs trafficking.

17 Rick McDonnell, 'Money Laundering Methodologies: International and Regional Counter-Measures', National Crime Authority, NSW, paper presented at the Australian Institute of Research, Sydney, May 1998.

18 The FATF is working closely with the IMF and the World Bank to develop a common methodology for assessing the measures taken by jurisdictions to combat money laundering. This common methodology was agreed in October 2001 and it was decided that it should be used for one year on a mutual evaluation basis conducted by the FATF. The common methodology means that the IMF, the World Bank and others – including the FATF-style regional bodies – will have a uniform basis with which to assess the level of implementation of AML/CFT measures. These measures include more stringent customer

noted that along with drug trafficking, financial crimes (bank fraud,[19] credit card fraud, investment fraud, advance fee fraud, bankruptcy, embezzlement, etc.) were the most frequently mentioned sources of the proceeds of crime.[20] The EU Council of Ministers approved the revisions to the EU's Anti-Money Laundering Directive.[21] This Directive broadens the definition of targeted criminal activity from drug offences (as per the original Directive) to include proceeds from other crimes.[22]

Many states have revised their anti-money laundering legislation in line with the revised definition of predicate offences.[23] The shortcoming of the Vienna Convention on money laundering was its failure to capture all activities generating the illicit proceeds of crime.[24] Thus, money laundering can be established directly through the examination of reported money laundering cases, but it can also be inferred from clandestine criminal activity. In a direct approach methodology, money laundering is quantified from prosecuted and recorded money laundering cases in national courts. These cases can potentially provide insights into the scale and typology of money laundering offences in respective countries. Conversely,

---

identification, enhanced reporting of transactions and enhanced scrutiny when considering whether the approve the establishment of bank branches, subsidiaries or representative offices. The FATF is working with several international bodies to ensure a global level of coordination. For example, evaluation conducted using the common methodology will provide a basis for the World Bank, the UN and other providers of technical assistance to better assess needs and provide the necessary assistance to jurisdictions with deficiencies in their systems. See Claes Norgren, 'The Control of Risks Associated with Crime, Terror and Subversion', 7(3) *Journal of Money Laundering Control* (2004): pp. 201–6.

19 A large-scale laundering operation involving one or more of a country's financial institutions and how this could put the global financial institutions at risk was underscored by the Bank of Credit and Commerce International (BCCI). Banks can lose their credibility and soundness and subsequently lose investor confidence.

20 'An Overview of the Global Money Laundering Problem, International Anti-Money Laundering Standards and the Work of the Financial Action Task Force', quoted in McDonnell, 'Money Laundering Methodologies: International and Regional Counter-Measures'.

21 Council Directive 91/308/EEC of June 1991.

22 The Directive also imposes anti-money laundering obligations on 'gatekeepers', requiring a broad range of professional (including independent legal professionals, accountants, auditors and notaries) to abide by anti-money laundering regulations with 18 months of the date of adoption. See the International Narcotics Drug Control Strategy Report issued by the US Department of State, March 2001.

23 For example, the POCA 2002 in the UK, adopted to align the UK anti-money laundering framework with the EU second Anti-Money Laundering Directive of December 2001.

24 National authorities must adopt a normative AML/CFT based on the FATF 40+9 recommendations. Of course, this is supplemented by other anti-money laundering regimes, such as those recommended by the Basel Committee on the Regulation and Supervision of Banks.

an indirect approach to the study of money laundering has used the prevalence of predicate offences in a country to delineate the scale of money laundering activities. In 1997, the FATF ad hoc group, for example, estimated the magnitude of money laundering by focusing its efforts on gathering data in relation to drug consumption, production and pricing.[25] Using an indirect approach in 1987, the UN estimated drug trafficking worldwide to amount to US$300 billion, much of which would be laundered. Other estimates have been made of US$300–500 billion of 'dirty money' that is poured into the financial system each year, or roughly two per cent of global GDP.[26] However, money laundering by its very nature occurs outside the normal range of official statistics and cannot be properly estimated. The IMF estimates that the amount of money laundering occurring on an annual basis could be between two and five per cent of global GDP. This translates to somewhere between US$600 billion and US$1.5 trillion.[27]

Following the Vienna Convention and with the adoption of the Palermo Convention, money laundering is no longer treated as a derivative offence. Money laundering offences are committed whenever a person commits any activity involving the proceeds of crimes (otherwise known as predicate offences).[28] Therefore, crime activities such as motor vehicle trafficking, credit card theft, corruption and terrorism fall within the extended definition of money laundering. As a matter of fact, money laundering is sustained and fuelled by globalization and its processes, as will be discussed below.

What is Globalization?

The term 'globalization' is not amenable to a specific definition and is thus conceptually confusing. It is used differently to denote different meanings for different people – politicians, journalists, policy makers, academics or even laypeople.[29] In general, the term 'globalization' refers to developments in the political, economic and cultural spheres. While definitions of the current global system abound, there is one common denominator: the growing interconnectedness

25 W.C. Gilmore, *International Efforts to Combat Money Laundering* (Cambridge: Grotius Publications Ltd, 1992), pp. 5–10.

26 L.P. Raine and F.J. Cilluffo (eds), 'Global Organized Crime: The Empire of Evil', *Center for Strategic and International Studies Washington* (1994): p. 39.

27 Available on the IMF website at www.imf.org (date accessed 22 November 2011).

28 Activities that constitute money laundering offences are underscored by Articles 5 and 6 of the Palermo Convention in 2000. Articles 5 criminalizes participation in an organized criminal activity and Article 6 deals with the criminalization of money laundering proceeds.

29 For an illustrative explanation of the confusion surrounding the term 'globalization', see Heba Shams, *Legal Globalization: Money Laundering Law and Other Cases*, vol. 5 of the Sir Joseph Gold Memorial Series, International Financial & Economic Law (London: British Institute of International and Comparative Law, 2004), Chapter 3.

of economies due to innovations in technology and enhanced transport systems. States are no longer single-handedly able to control the parameters within which they can chart their economic, social and political fortunes.[30] At a European level, efforts at globalization are manifested in the establishment of a single European market,[31] which brings citizens and corporations from different countries increasingly into contact. The abolition of border controls between Schengen states[32] and the integration of Western and Eastern European countries has created benefits, but it has also created opportunities for illicit transactions across borders.[33] The creation of the single European market – the underpinning objective of the EU – has been replicated in other regions such as the Southern African Development Community (SADC) in Eastern and Southern African countries. It is now certain that due to the emerging trade agreements between member states, borders have become more porous than ever.[34] This means that criminals can easily slip through relaxed border controls by exploiting the free movement of workers, capital and services created by such integration.

Specifically, economic globalization is concerned with the removal of barriers to trade and investment, and the movement of capital across national boundaries.[35] Globalization is a ubiquitous word that shows how events and activities in one part of the world come to have significant consequences for distant people and communities. It is a sociological, cultural, political or economic concept of a series of time-space compressions. Globalization implies the allegedly irreversible process geared towards the formation of a single world economy, with societies and cultures driven by technology and the transnationalization of investment and money capital.[36] In its ideological usage, globalization signifies the deregulation of national economies through trade liberalization, with the removal of trade barriers

30 J. Wiener, 'International Crime in the New Geopolitics: A Core Threat to Democracy', in W.F. McDonald (ed.), *Crime and Law Enforcement in the Global Village* (Highland Heights, KY and Cincinnati, OH: Academy of Criminal Justice Science and Anderson Publishing Co. Ltd, 2000), p. 112.

31 The Single European Act (SEA) was created by the European Communities Act in 1986 to provide a framework for cooperation in various areas under the competence of the Community, for example, a power to veto decisions.

32 This Agreement provided for the abolition of border controls between the EU and participative Member States. The Schengen Agreement was initially agreed by Belgium, France, Germany, Luxembourg and the Netherlands. It was incorporated into Community law via a protocol appended to the Treaty of Amsterdam (1997). The purpose of the Schengen Agreement was to lift customs and immigration controls in participating member countries. Denmark, Ireland and the UK derogated from the Schengen Agreement for reasons of their special geographical boundaries.

33 Wiener, 'International Crime in the New Geopolitics', p. 27.

34 McDonald (ed.), *Crime and Law Enforcement in the Global Village*.

35 Ibid.

36 Frank Fukuyama, *The End of History and the Last Man* (Harmondsworth: Penguin, 1992), p. 19.

as an attendant benefit of economic integration. As borders literally 'implode' and the movement of people increases across national borders in response to increased communication and transport systems, states have found it increasingly difficult to counter the movement of criminals across national borders. In light of the above contentions, globalization could mean a process of social change of both geographical and political dimensions. In the geographical sense, it represents the change in time and space within which social relations are conducted, as well as the growing consciousness of this spatial change. In the political sphere, globalization represents the balance of power and the pre-eminent role of non-state actors.[37]

In a legal context, the term 'globalization' remains troublesome because, by nature, the proliferating AML/CFT regimes cannot be independent and often are not accountable to their own governments,[38] not to mention that some of the global AML/CFT regimes emerge through ad hoc arrangements as an imperative of market exigencies.[39] Constitutionally, governments govern by the principle of the separation of powers, which creates a framework for the distribution of legitimate powers and decision making between the judiciary, the executive and the legislature. In this context, the legal usage of the word 'globalization' in international law remains problematic in the absence of a global constitution articulating a framework for states to inter-relate with each other. This would explain in part the existing disparities in relation to the way in which emerging global regimes are applied and enforced. Forging together, either by states or regions, on a regulated issue area requires a clear framework, spelling out modalities for the shared engagement of purpose. At an EU operational level, for instance, treaties are transposed into domestic law subject to the principle of subsidiarity,[40] which implies that the treaty provisions can only be effective if they have been ratified by all Member States. It is my contention that the EU offers significant insights as a microcosm of globalization and the way in which global initiatives, in their various manifestations, should be properly harnessed.

In relation to money laundering, globalization has created instrumentalities for criminal exploitation (such as the Internet) and the enhanced means of

37 Heba Shams, *Legal Globalization: Money Laundering Law and Other Cases*, vol. 5 of the Sir Joseph Gold Memorial Series, International Financial & Economic Law (London: British Institute of International and Comparative Law, 2004), p. 27.

38 Kern Alexander, Rahul Dhumale and John Eatwell, *Global Governance of Financial Systems: The International Regulation of Systemic Risk* (Oxford: Oxford University Press, 2000), p. 37.

39 This is highlighted by the Basel Committee Banking and Supervisory Standards.

40 Subsidiarity is a fundamental concept designed to achieve an appropriate balance between the institutions of Europe and the interests of Member States. Where the Community has exclusive competence in a legislative area, the principle of subsidiarity has no application, and where the Community gives concurrent powers to Member States to act in certain areas, it will act so long as the Community has not exercised that power anywhere. It has to be said that where there is conflict, EC law has primacy over national law.

transferring money from one place to another. This facilitates the ease with which laundered money can be moved about. Contemporary criminal groups are capable of manipulating an array of tools to disguise their criminal activities, without regard to international borders. In the words of a US Treasury official, 'once the funds go abroad either through our financial systems or having been physically smuggled, there is virtually a smorgasbord of business structures, supported by laws of dozens of countries, which serve to obscure ownership, and frustrate the government's ability to unravel schemes'.[41] Funds can be moved among corporate entities and financial institutions in many countries in a split second through wire fund transfers, making more and more difficult to untangle the path of the funds at every stage.[42] There are three stages of money laundering: placement, layering and integration. The placement stage is where the illegitimately acquired assets are placed into the financial system. The the layering stage is where numerous transactions arise, which are designed to work as a smokescreen to disguise the true origin of the money.[43] The integration stage is where illicit assets, after they have been cleansed, find their way back into the mainstream financial system.

Globalization has come to be associated with a variety of specific trends: an increasing reliance upon the market, a significant growth in influence of international markets and institutions in determining the viability of national priorities, a reduction in the role of the state and the size of its budget, the privatization of various functions that were previously considered to be the exclusive domain of the state, the deregulation of a range of activities and the increased role of civil society organizations.[44] It is my contention that the contemporary crime trends have become too complex and ubiquitous to be explained by open border theory alone. This would be to under-estimate the complexity of the global system.

Open Borders and the Crime Floodgates Theory

There are two theories underpinning the notion of the open borders and crime nexus: in the first theory, opening borders is seen as a *sine qua non* of opening crime floodgates. The second theory, advanced by advocates of globalization,

41 FinCeN Trends, Financial Crimes Enforcement Network, US Treasury Department, 'International Cooperation Against Money Laundering Gains Momentum', Guidance Notes for Mainstream Banking, Lending and Deposit Taking Activities, London, 1996, p. 5.

42 Ibid., p. 6.

43 For these stages, see Mugarura, 'The Effect of Corruption Factor in Harnessing Global Anti-Money Laundering Regimes', pp.77–8.

44 This has been adopted from the statement of the Committee on Economic, Social and Cultural Rights on Globalisation and Economic Social and Cultural Rights of 11 May 1998, available at www.unhchr.ch/htm.menu2/6/cesnote.htm (date accessed 20 August 2008).

dismisses the connection of relaxed border controls and a proportionate increase in crimes. This section discusses these theories and articulates the likely impact of each theory with regard to generating money laundering and its predicate offences. The above theories aside, what is not in dispute is the fact that decisions, formerly the domain of sovereign states, are taken at the peripheral level but are implemented within the state. Therefore, it can be said that the traditional state, which is of course circumscribed by borders, is emasculated by the growth of supranational initiatives.[45] The enhanced global media system and technologies of rapid communication and travel have rendered national borders porous and permeable by people travelling for all sorts of reasons. As such, the issue of removing border controls – a facet of most regional trade agreements – generates benefits but also brings with it certain negative externalities that have already been outlined. Therefore, the issue of borders has been a difficult one to explain by way of theories based on what might be happening in one region alone.[46] The above situation is illustrated by studies carried out on this subject in Canada and the UK.[47]

In some political discourses, opening internal borders is analogous to opening crime floodgates.[48] However, the dichotomy of open borders and crime floodgates has not been supported by empirical evidence and is dismissed as baseless.[49] The above mythology of crimes and opening borders has been exploited for the sake of political expediency.[50] There are two reasons advanced to explain this contention: first, the notion of terrorism as a transnational crime has long predated the advent of regional integration.[51] Opening borders and crime floodgate theory is over-emphasized to create 'a ring of steel' around some regions, for example, Europe, in order to repel the threatened flood of immigrants from less developed regions of the world. Sceptics try to articulate a clear link between illegal immigrants and serious crimes. In case of terrorism, for instance, the removal of internal borders is likely to have very little impact on the overall levels on the spread and planning of terrorist crimes as the control of frontiers has never prevented terrorism in the past.[52] The same view applies to drug trafficking because strict border controls as

45 Some of these initiatives, such as the EU, are predicated on the philosophy of the free movement of workers and capital, hence curtailing any state controls in relation to the above fields.

46 Ian Taylor, 'International Drug Trade and Money Laundering: Border Controls and Other Issues', 8(2) *European Sociological Review* (1992): pp. 181–93.

47 Ibid.

48 Ibid.

49 A. Palmer, 'Global Crusade Can Never Be Won', *Sunday Telegraph*, 31 August 1997.

50 There is evidence that some political parties have sought to exploit the anti-immigration sentiments to gain an advantage in elections.

51 The Convention for the Prevention of Terrorism in 1937 adopted by the League of Nations as a framework for the prevention and punishment of terrorism.

52 John Benyon, 'An Audit of Crime, Policing and Criminal Justice Issues', *Law and Order Review* (1994): p. 87.

a mechanism for controlling crimes spilling over to the other side of the border constrains supply, but, conversely, it increases demand and high prices. This works as a 'pull factor' for drug traffickers and intrinsically money laundering because of the increased market prices for drugs.[53]

It has to be said that the nature of contemporary crimes cannot be controlled through national borders alone. For instance, it is a challenge for law enforcement agencies to control telecommunication-related crimes, such as the theft of intellectual property rights, the electronic dissemination of offensive materials, electronic money laundering and electronic vandalism through physical land borders.[54] The prospect of cyber crimes has threatened to pose fresh problems for policing since they cut across geographical, social and political and gendered boundaries, calling into question conventional notions of space, place and time in the narrow confines of modern states.[55]

Far from the hype attributed to relaxed border controls (often exploited for political reasons), this book cannot flatly dismiss the nexus of open borders and crimes theory. It is my contention that border controls should not only be relaxed due to market imperatives but for other considerations as well.[56] However, relaxed border controls could send the wrong message to drug traffickers, criminals involved in small arms trafficking, illegal immigration and other threats. Owing to this, the question of linking border controls and crime floodgates should be approached with a sense of caution. Traditionally borders represent operational limits for law enforcement agencies from the other side of the border. Different borders connote different languages and the possibility of language barriers, different legal systems, different laws and procedures.[57] As such, money laundering is a complex issue spanning the individiual state's remit and hence the need for concerted global measures.

The Overlapping Nature of Money Laundering Offences

Money laundering is not only intrinsic to the activities of organized crimes, but if left unchecked by the absence of the adoption of appropriate measures at a global level, it can be exploited to engender a new authoritarianism capable of displacing

53 Palmer, 'Global Crusade Can Never Be Won'.

54 Benyon, 'An Audit of Crime, Policing and Criminal Justice Issues'.

55 Ibid.

56 Studies carried out in the UK in the run-up to the Schengen Agreement (1985) revealed that abrupt searches by the police, immigration and customs officials on cars and trucks crossing the borders into the UK revealed that opening borders could undermine British security. See Taylor, 'International Drug Trade and Money Laundering: Border Controls and Other Issues'.

57 Europol Publication available at http://parliament.uk/parliamentary committees/ lords eu select committee.cfm (date accessed 28 October 2009).

legitimate governments.[58] Besides the fact that money laundering metaphorically provides the fuel to lubricate the wheels of the underground shadow economy, it is also embedded in the international banking system. The shadow economy connotes the informal economy which exists alongside the formal economy. Money laundering has become a complex issue for governments, anit-money laundering policy makers and enforcement agencies in a changing globalized crime landscape. The complexity of money laundering is illustrated by the fact that money laundering offences could be committed in the UK by an American citizen who channels the money to Uganda in South African currency. The differences and fragmentation of national AML/CFT legislation have facilitated the growth of illicit criminal activity around the world.[59] This is compounded by the fact that criminals have gained access to new markets by exploiting discrepancies between legal systems of countries in different parts of the world.[60] The emergence of new market-oriented economies has meant that criminals have developed the capacity to operate on a worldwide scale.[61] The growth of supranational institutions, such as the EU, the global media system, technologies of rapid telecommunications and travel, and the boundaries between states have become more porous and permeated than ever before.[62] The official line between domestic and non-domestic crimes has become blurred and this has become apparent in the area of crime and the criminal justice system.[63] Unless the global and local systems are harmonized such that there is some measure of parity, the envisaged global AML/CFT framework will remain beyond the reach of some societies. It would be wrong to propose or even suppose that the global AML/CFT framework can successfully apply globally in total disregard of what happens nationally.

Equally, the large volume of legitimate capital moving into the global financial system at any one particular point, coupled with the reduced regulatory controls on the movement of capital, has made it possible for large amounts of money to enter the global financial markets unnoticed.[64] The widespread use of international money transfers has facilitated criminal activity in the same as it has facilitated

58 For example, telecommunications, the Internet and travel have been ruthlessly exploited to perpetuate money laundering-related crimes.

59 D. Murphy, 'Contemporary Practice of the United States', 94(4) *American Journal of International Law* (2000) pp. 695–700.

60 Shams, *Legal Globalization*, p. 65.

61 This is highlighted by the global financial crisis (2007–2010) which started in the US sub-prime market (involving mortgages) before spreading swiftly to other jurisdictions because of globalization and its processes.

62 Shelley, 'Transnational Organised Crimes: A New Authoritarianism'.

63 M.F. McDonald, 'The Globalization of Criminology: The New Frontier in the Frontier', *Journal of Transnational Crime* (1995): pp. 6–7.

64 FATF Asia Secretariat, 'Disposal of Proceeds of Crime Money Laundering Methods', Workshop Report of the Expert Group in Hong Kong, 14 November 1996.

legitimate businesses to move funds internationally in a disguised way.[65] This can potentially disrupt audit trails as law enforcement is stymied by jurisdictional and legal boundaries. Indeed, this is not to mention the growing diversification of international financial instruments and differences in controls and regulations between countries. In such an environment, it is easy for those contemplating money laundering to have ample opportunity to do so.[66] The lightly regulated financial centres are targeted by criminals in order to cleanse their illegally acquired assets and then reintroduce these into developed financial centres after they have been cleansed.[67] The transition towards a market economy can make it easier for criminals to invest their illicit proceeds in the newly privatized enterprises, following the adage that 'crime follows opportunity'. In the first place, the market economy has created opportunities for criminals to invest their dirty money where opportunities abound.[68] Secondly, the proliferation of financial markets has induced a dramatic increase in the number of jurisdictions offering financial services without appropriate controls or regulation while banking secrecy laws is still an uphill challenge in many jurisdictions. In South Africa, money generated from daga trafficking is said to be invested in the South African stock exchange, real estate and currency trading on the open market.[69] The growing complexity of money laundering schemes explains why the threats posed by money laundering cannot be defeated through national law enforcement agencies alone.[70] The issue of criminal law remains exclusively within the domain of individual states and therefore sometimes states that are less than willing to cooperate in order to protect their sovereignty. As such, states must come together to circumvent challenges that are either inherent within the individual states or within the global system itself.[71]

There are so many challenges to states in their quest to harness global regimes, not least economic asymmetries and their varied impact on envisaged normative measures. As a matter of fact, poorly regulated jurisdictions have undermined the efficacy of global regimes by being predisposed to worsening standards of risk

---

65 See the case of the BCCI, which closed down in 1991, following the discovery of massive fraud and money laundering by US regulators. The BCCI had grown to become the world seventh-largest private bank with assets of US$23 billion and with operations in 72 countries. The chief victim of the bank malpractices were depositors and governments in developing economies. See George A. Walker, *International Banking Regulation: Law, Policy and Practice* (Dordrecht: Kluwer Law International, 2000), pp. 10–59.

66 Ibid.

67 Ibid.

68 Shelley, 'Transnational Organised Crimes: A New Authoritarianism'.

69 Charles Goredema, 'Observations on Typologies of Money Laundering', Institute of Security Studies Paper, March 2003.

70 Anthony P. Maingot, 'Money Laundering Schemes', 37(4) *Journal of Anti-American Studies and World Affairs* (1995): p. 1–24.

71 Alex Van Sickle, 'Should There Be a European Criminal Code?', 73 *London Progressive Journal* (2009): p. 2.

management of their financial institutions.[72] Criminals who perpetuate money laundering are likely to thrive in an environment where there is a weak and poor regulatory system in place.[73] Weak regulatory financial systems, lax enforcement and corruption practices are key factors that render certain jurisdictions vulnerable to money laundering offences.[74] Equally, such an environment has made it easier for international drug traffickers and other criminal organizations such as terrorist groups to move money to pariah states with ease.[75] Through the ubiquitous global system, risks generated from one part of the system are able to navigate to other jurisdictions with ease. Regulatory shortcomings in some countries have generated significant challenges for policy makers in other jurisdictions.[76] For example, the issue of counterfeit currency in Uganda in early 2000 was undoubtedly spurred on by the reduced supervisory oversight by the Bank of Uganda. There was no comprehensive framework on money laundering with regard to identification, seizure and forfeiture of the instrumentalities of money laundering crimes.[77] Thus, it can be inferred that the explosion of financial crimes or money laundering in some regions is attributable to a weak domestic economy rather than globalization and its exigencies. On a positive note, globalization can offer solutions to embedded challenges in some countries. As has already been noted, foreign banks operating in Uganda have managed to circumvent the tenuous legal system in the country by exploiting the parent-grown banking policies, which have to be applied to all international branches. However, if the domestic and foreign laws are not properly aligned through the harmonization of inter-state laws, there is a likelihood of regulatory arbitrage at the expense of foreign banks.[78] I am thus inclined to argue that adopting a robust global AML/CFT framework is essential in order to overcome imperfections in the market such as free riding and regulatory arbitrage. These are common features of states that apply different regulatory regimes.

Furthermore, given that the global system is technologically embedded, the system naturally tends to favour developed economies which have made advances

72 Some countries such as Bermuda, the Cayman Islands, Cyprus, Malta, Mauritius and San Marino are very attractive to money launderers. See D. Murphy, 'Contemporary Practice of the United States', p. 667.

73 Beth A. Simmons, 'The International Politics of Harmonization: The Case of Capital Markets', 55(3) *International Organization* (2001): p. 601.

74 D. Murphy, 'Multilateral Listing of States as Money Laundering Havens', 94(4) *American Journal of International Law* (2000): pp. 695–6.

75 Ibid.

76 Julian Harris, 'Risk Territories', *Company Lawyer* (2008): pp. 1–3.

77 This has caused problems to major multilateral banks, which have had to rely on internal systems developed by their main offices and used by all their branches globally. Barclays Bank has developed specific anti-money laundering policies, for example, its 2001 Africa policy for the prevention of money laundering.

78 In an environment where laws are arbitrarily applied, foreign banks can easily be out-competed by their local rivals.

in technological development as opposed to their less developed counterparts.[79] Since globalization presupposes states working together to overcome their overlapping challenges, inequalities or asymmetries are disadvantageous in the sense that they inhibit the transposition of normative AML/CFT laws internally.[80] For countries to keep pace with the requirements of the global AML/CFT regimes, they have no choice but to enhance their level of information and communications technology (ICT) development.

Organized Criminal Groups

There are numerous organized criminal groups operating globally. Therefore, this section does not seek to discuss the entire organized criminal enterprise system but to tease out the connection between organized crime and money laundering. Organized criminal groups, as the phrase suggests, represents an established network of criminal organizations that are coordinated in order to perpetuate the underground criminal industry. Organized criminal organizations forge transnational criminal alliances in other countries and enter into informal agreements organized around common interests.[81] These agreements are illegal and are enforced illegally either through murders, abductions or gun crime, occasionally turning major cities into quasi-battlefields. Globalization has spawned an illegal market in smuggling, human trafficking, piracy, the trading in illegal goods and services and illegal immigration.[82] It should be noted that any money derived from criminal activity and subsequently integrated into the mainstream financial system under circumstances of concealment of the provenance of funds will constitute money laundering under international money laundering counter-measures.[83] Money laundering offences can be committed by both legitimate and illegitimate businesses. These organizations are often well structured and some have the capacity to compete for recognition with established governments.[84]

---

79 Our own estimation of high-tech consumption in countries like Uganda is that less than 10 per cent of the population has access to television sets, let alone telephones and the Internet – things which in Western countries are more or less taken for granted. There is no way a person living in Uganda, Tanzania or Kenya can enjoy the same benefits as a person in a Western country in terms of technology-related benefits. These benefits are essential imperatives in developing a robust global AML/CFT infrastructure.

80 Philip Jenkins, 'Failure to Launch: Why Do some Social Issues Fail to Detonate Moral Panics?', 35 *British Journal of Criminology* (2009): p. 5.

81 J. Wiener, *Globalisation and the Harmonisation of Law* (London and New York: Pinter, 1999), p. 3.

82 Margaret E. Beare (ed.), *Critical Reflections on Transnational Organised Crime, Money Laundering and Corruption* (Toronto: University of Toronto Press, 2005), p. 5.

83 Ibid.

84 The Japanese Yakuza are said to be major shareholders in the biggest Japanese banks, while the Russian Mafia are said to own 80 per cent of privatized industries in

Criminal organizations have tapped into the benefits generated by the globalization of markets in the same effective way that legitimate businesses do. The work of transnational criminal groups is underscored by clandestine criminal activities in the UK. It is the medium by which drugs, cheap alcohol and cigarettes which have evaded legal duties are made available to local communities, not to mention illegal immigration and the investment of illegal proceeds of money into the mainstream economy.[85]

This chapter demonstrates that to understand the threat posed by money laundering on the global economy, it is necessary to explore the *modus operandi* of criminal syndicates and their extensive money laundering-fuelled operations. The most prominent criminal syndicates involved in money laundering are: the Chinese triads, the Russian Mafia, the Colombian cartel, the Japanese Boryokudan (also known as the Japanese Yakuza), the Italian Mafia, Nigerian criminal groups and Turkish criminal groups.[86] The Chinese triads and the Japanese Yakuza are among the most prominent groups involved in Asian transnational crimes. The triads are mostly based in Hong Kong, Macao and Taiwan, but have their affiliate groups in other regions, while the Italian Mafia is based in Sicily.[87] Much as these criminal groups may operate individually, they also forge some links with other criminal groups.[88] The triads are involved in a variety of illegal activities ranging from drug trafficking, money laundering, corruption, credit-card forgery and fraud, counterfeit identification and migrant smuggling.[89] The world's largest triad group is based in Hong Kong with an estimated membership of between 47,000 and 60,000 individuals carrying out criminal activities worldwide. Unlike the triads, the Yakuza syndicates are relatively open societies, some of whose members have been known to have their own business cards complete with the Yakuza emblem. Some of their organizations even publish magazines and newsletters. The Yakuza has an estimated membership of 80,000 people. Their worldwide criminal enterprises include the drugs and arms trade, money laundering, the penetration of legal business enterprises and the inflation of land prices. As the largest criminal group in Japan, the Yakuza is said to have an estimated total revenue of between US$25 billion and $38 billion.[90]

Russia. See Shelley, 'Transnational Organised Crimes: A New Authoritarianism'.

85 Roger Gaspar, Director of Intelligence of NCIS (now replaced by SOCA), commentary on transnational crimes in the UK (*BBC News Online*, 2001).

86 Jeffrey Robinson, *How Criminal Groups are Taking up Canada* (Toronto: McClelland Stewart Inc, 1999), p. 7.

87 James Dubro, 'Trends in Organised Crimes', *Transnational Consortium Periodical* (2002): p. 114.

88 Ibid.

89 Ibid.

90 James Dubro, *Dragon of Crime* (Ontario: Octopus Publishing Group, 1992), pp. 240–241.

Organized criminal groups have resorted to money laundering in different countries as a mechanism of cleansing the tainted proceeds of crime and integrating the cleansed proceeds into the mainstream financial system. They achieve this by the use of many techniques, not least those used by legitimate businesses. There are different money laundering techniques, but popular among them with regard to the transfer of money is *hundi* or *hawala*, an alternative banking channel (commonly used among the Asian community based abroad).[91] In this method, the money is deposited with a local agent, who sends instructions to his/her counterpart in the native country to pay a specified amount of money to a named person in the native country. Given that concealment is an important component of money laundering, potential money launderers prefer this method since there is no audit or accounting trail, as the system works on trust.[92]

There are multiple methods used by transnational criminal groups to launder criminal proceeds, not least the use of ghost beneficiaries, front houses and fractious companies. In India, for example, money laundering is indulged in by corporate houses to evade taxes, as well as by organized criminal groups to launder dirty money.[93] Money laundering techniques include 'smurfing', the establishment of front companies, the acquisition of commercial and non-commercial properties, remittance through *hawala*, legitimate business and foreign remittances. Likewise, the transfer of money by Nigerian criminal gangs correlates with attempts to legitimize the proceeds of crime by concealing their true origin and ownership. The organized criminal groups involved in drug trafficking repatriate money from abroad by the direct purchase and sale of luxury items like cars and jewellery. Other methods include the over-invoicing of goods and trading in stocks and shares.[94] In Pakistan, money laundering has links with drug trafficking, smuggling, tax evasion and corruption. The popular methods of disguising the proceeds of crimes by Pakistan's criminal gangs include *hawala*, investment in real estate, over-invoicing of exports and under-invoicing of imports. This has been exploited to enhance the process of transferring money from one place to another and cutting queues, but *hawala* has also been exploited for criminal expediency, particularly for money laundering and the financing of terrorism.[95] The growth in organized crime activities in many parts of the world and the sophistication of money laundering schemes are so pervasive that the state is literally said to be in disarray.

91 *Hawala* money transmission services have proliferated in many parts of London and in other European countries.

92 Dubro, *Dragon of Crime*.

93 Barry Rider (ed.), *Corruption: The Enemy Within* (Dordrecht: Kluwer Law International, 1997), pp. 8–34.

94 James Dubro, *Dragon of Crime*.

95 Ibid.

The Limits of the Contemporary State

The notion of a state traces its origin back to the Peace of Westphalia in Germany (1648).[96] This divided Europe into independent units, crystallizing the present form of a state.[97] The concept of statehood is defined, as formulated in Article 1 of the Montevideo Convention on the Rights and Duties of States (1933), as 'the political community that possesses a defined territory and a permanent population, and is subject to an organised form of government, capable of engaging in international relations'.[98] In the contemporary global era, markets and states are embedded within each other and shaped by their mutual interaction. Globalization has made it necessary to break with a state-centred paradigm to international law.[99] In the first place, some threats to peace and security are non-state based and not amenable within the traditional state paradigm. The state paradigm to international law defines national security within the realm of the state, regardless of the challenges that modern states face. As such, the concept of the state is said to be anachronistic because it limits international law to states, excluding not only regional actors but also representations of transnational market forces in global society. The definition of the state has remained unchanged and is still confined[100] within the traditional Montevideo Convention.[101] Formal definitions have remained unchanged, as has the concept of statehood as rigid and unable to respond to contemporary global changes. Since modern societies are dynamic, the legal framework within which societies are governed should equally be dynamic to assimilate the changes ushered in by the system.[102]

Transnational criminal activities have the potential to undermine both weak and strong states with impunity. However, in less developed countries which have weak structures and tenuous legitimacy, the power wielded by transnational criminal groups can even rival the power of sovereign states.[103] As such, governments have found it imperative to adopt a number of common initiatives through which such

96 It is this treaty that ended the destructive Thirty Years War in Europe. It was convened in German in 1644 and after three years of tough negotiations, all major European states agreed to abide by the territorial integrity of each other. For a detailed on this treaty, see Ian Brownie, *Principles of Public International Law* (Oxford: Clarendon Press, 1998), p. 114.

97 Ibid.

98 Shams, *Legal Globalization*, p. 102.

99 Sean O. Rain, 'States and Markets in the Era of Globalisation', 26 *Annual Review of Sociology* (2000): p. 187.

100 The state as an entity of international law should possess a permanent population, a defined territory, a government and the capacity to engage in relations with other states.

101 Rosalyn Higgins, *Problems and Process: International Law and How We Use it* (Cambridge: Cambridge University Press, 1994): Chapter 3.

102 Ibid., pp. 1–2.

103 Maria Los, 'Beyond the Law: The Virtual Reality of Post-Communist Privatization', 4 *Journal of Government and Crime Control* (2004): pp. 239, 244–5.

novel challenges can be managed. Intergovernmental and sectoral bodies have emerged in response to money laundering and the financing of terrorism and their underlying offences, assisting national governments in improving their AML/CFT infrastructure. The contemporary securitarization encompasses threats that are broad enough to undermine societies in the dispensation of their responsibilities. The transnational element of security has undermined the fabric of society in three dimensions: against the individual, the state and the international system of states.[104] Some of the aforementioned threats are insidious and pervasive to national sovereignty due to the permeability of national borders. In the current global environment, societies have been sidelined by the activities of organized criminals, such as corruption, fear of violence or intimidation, threats to national security and state control, creating a rival authority structure, or a state without a state-based system, a black market economy and infiltration of the state and financial institutions by criminals.[105]

As has already been noted, the state has been emasculated by the dynamics of globalization. States have either reconstituted at a regional or a wider global level, understandably for good reasons, but on the other hand they are constrained by either regional or global initiatives and cannot exercise their full sovereignty.[106] The question of sovereignty is illustrated by the case of the accession of the UK to the European Economic Community (EEC) in 1972, now the EU.[107] While there are benefits to Member States accruing from the EU, the emerging EU institutions have seemingly undermined the British Parliament by derogating legislative powers away to Brussels. The EU will legislate in all areas of national importance except where a Member State has derogated or entered into a reservation on some or all aspects of a particular treaty.[108] Section 3 of the Treaty of Accession in 1972 articulates that in the event of a potential conflict between national and EU laws in the UK, the latter has to take precedence. Lord Denning, decrying the erosion of British sovereignty as a result of the pervasive character of EU treaties, likened it to 'an impending estuary'. In the case of *Bulmer v Bollinger* (1974),[109] he had this to say: 'Parliament has decreed that the treaty henceforward to be part of our law. It is in force to any Statute.' In effect this means that the state has been undermined by the perverse nature of global initiatives in areas where it fundamentally needs to have a strong presence, as illustrated above. The erosion of state sovereignty, as already noted, explains the dismissive attitude of some states. To protect the widespread interests of the state and to exercise the authority of the state, it has

---

104 P. Williams, 'Transnational Criminal Organisations and International Security', 36(1) *Survival* (1994): p. 94.

105 Ibid., pp. 32–40.

106 Owing to this, Phil Cerny predicts the end of the state.

107 Amended by the Treaty of Amsterdam (1997).

108 Any EU Member State may exercise its right to stay out of any treaty arrangements in the name of national self-interest under the principle of subsidiarity.

109 [1974] 3 WLR 202, pp. 215–16.

been deemed more essential to remain statist than to uphold treaty obligations or other constraining obligations.[110] However, market integration is essential in order to create development opportunities and ease dualities in the global economy.

Dualities in the Global Economy

Globalization presupposes unity of purpose on overlapping global challenges and is sidelined by the fact that the implementation of the envisaged standards is locally oriented and prone to the dynamics of development at local level. The global community has not managed to develop a functional global jurisdiction or government within which the envisaged policy standards can be implemented and sidelined by the dictates of national development. The contemporary global AML/CFT as it stands cannot be successfully implemented unless its ethos reflects the prevailing global market conditions. National governments will have to create robust institutions through which to fight money laundering and its predicate offences. National institutions are essential to ensure that the envisaged AML/CFT regimes are properly implemented.

The strength of any regulatory regime depends on the ability of states to generate and harness the requisite information for their development purposes. States at rudimentary stages of development are deficient in terms of requisite information and therefore they are unable to devise appropriate strategies to deal with their apparent global threats. Since globalization or the global AML/CFT framework is information-driven, it has to be said that the current global framework must be fed and sustained by its ability to generate requisite information. Some of the AML/CFT-specific regimes (for example, the Know Your Customer (KYC) campaign) functions on the basis of generating good information on prospective bank clients. The above AML/CFT standard will not easily translate into practice, especially in countries that are deficient in terms of their infrastructure capacity. Arguably, in the above environment, these states are vulnerable to money laundering-related challenges. In many African states, either there are no data registry centres to help collect, collate, quantify and evaluate data on money laundering-related crimes or the little data generated is too patchy to properly inform any policy choices. The absence of data registry centres to feed information to agencies charged with the responsibility of crime control has severely hampered national anti-money laundering initiatives. Similarly, the absence of an adequate information portfolio on money laundering typologies has also undermined the creation of effective policy measures and strategies to put states one step ahead of criminals.

The process of translating AML/CFT norms cannot succeed unless they are transposed through robust national institutions. In some countries, there is a myriad of challenges, not least the absence of functional institutions and other

---

110 Michael Likosky, *Transnational Legal Processes Globalization and Power Disparities* (London: Butterworths, 2002), p. 19.

manifestations. Record keeping is not only slow in coping with the upsurge of the modern global system, but is also unable to handle the imperatives of development. There is also the issue of corruption, where judges and other court officials may simply overlook the facts and evidence, having received a 'kickback' from the money launderer. The influence of academics in developing countries is limited (if not non-existent) with regard to the evolution of development policies. There is also the absence of robust research institutions, which presents enormous challenges in fighting local and global crimes. There is the need to establish robust research centres in local universities to feed information to respective policy bodies when developing appropriate AML/CFT policies. Similarly, there is a need to create local foresight agencies to ensure the internalization of laws and strategies against the threat of money laundering and terrorism.

The strength of AML/CFT regulatory regimes and the ease with which they can be transposed domestically are dictated by the ability of the individual states to generate and harness requisite information. In this regard, states at rudimentary stages of development are sidelined with regard to generating meaningful information against their apparent and contemporary global threats. Since globalization generally or the global AML/CFT framework specifically are information-driven, it can be inferred that for countries to harness the current global framework on money laundering, they will have to develop the capacity to process, collate and evaluate the requisite information on money laundering. Some AML/CFT-specific regimes (for example, KYC) function on the basis of generating good information on prospective bank clients. In this book, it is argued that the envisaged AML/CFT standards cannot translate into practice, especially in countries with tenuous infrastructures and systems. In such an environment, the system will be vulnerable to sophisticated money laundering schemes. The dismal absence of data registry centres to provide data to agencies which are charged with the responsibility of crime control has severely hampered the work of local anti-money laundering agencies. As such, it has been posited that technological development and wider infrastructural development are needed to protect societies from the perverse effects of the global system.

The issue of economic asymmetries either between states or within regions undermines the efficacy of global AML/CFT regimes in terms of the way in which these regimes are evolved and harnessed in different states.[111] The global AML/CFT laws ahave been developed and greatly influenced by developed countries, which understandably is necessary given that someone has got not only to provide leadership but also the resources needed to create the normative AML/CFT regimes.[112] However, the challenge arising from a lack of representation of

111 Most global AML/CFT regimes developed courtesy of the US influence, e.g. Vienna Convention (1988) and the regimes created by the FATF in 1989 but subsequently adopted by other countries.

112 This point is illustrated by Basel II as a capital harmonization framework in banks, but, in addition, as I will demonstrate later, the global AML framework is oriented

many countries for which such a system is created is that some aspects of the AML/CFT regimes are manifestly insensitive to the interests of less developed economies. The Basel Capital Accord,[113] in its assessment of different risk profiles, has been criticized as unwise for prescribing a standard eight per cent threshold of bank assets in a volatile market environment. The capital adequacy framework demonstrates the challenges of adopting a global framework in societies that are subject to varying levels of development.[114] The political dimension is that states either adopt or refuse to adopt global AML/CFT laws whenever it suits them. Some countries may resent and literally refuse to transpose global AML/CFT laws for their own economic self-interest. Empirical studies on money laundering indicates that countries which operate bank secrecy laws do so to take advantage of the positive externalities generated to the economy as a result of such laws. For example, Swiss officials have recognized that bank secrecy has contributed enormously to Switzerland's high standard of living.[115] The issue of bank secrecy laws, coupled with weak supervisory oversight of financial institutions, may attract the flow of funds from tax evaders and money launderers to poor countries and territories. Equally, if adopting stringent AML/CFT laws drives potential business and jobs away, countries will always want to err on the side of caution before adopting the supposedly pervasive regimes. The stringent adoption of AML/CFT regimes in some developed countries, for example in the USA, is known to drive money launderers and drug traffickers deep underground, from where it becomes difficult to dislodge them.[116] These contentions help to shed light on why some countries have preferred to hover on the sidelines, literally with 'one leg in and the other leg out' in the transposition of global AML/CFT regimes locally. In other words, countries cannot afford to ignore the question of national self-interest. This would also seem to imply that the process of transposing global AML/CFT laws

---

towards the G10 financial markets. While it is important to adopt a uniform anti-money laundering framework, its adaptaion is dictated by some factors at a local societal level.

113 Under the capital adequacy framework, all internationally active banks must hold capital to the value of eight per cent of risk-weighted assets plus off-balance sheet commitments. This agreement was necessary in the sense that it would enhance the capital position of the banks so as to enable them to absorb losses due to the debts and other exposures resulting from less developed countries. But there was also a need to forestall a possible competition in regulatory laxity by setting a harmonized capital framework where supervisors would apply the same standard and would prevent free riding off of the reputation of less regulated international banks.

114 The eight per cent capital reserve will favour highly capitalized Western banks, giving them a competitive advantage.

115 Lisa Troshinsky, 'Ex-Nat West Lawyer Fears "Know Your Customer" Fall Out', *International Banking Regulator*, 5 August 1996. For information about the Swiss private banking industry, see Ian Rodger, 'Survey of the Swiss Banking Industry', *Financial Times*, 26 October 1995, p. 3. However, in the author's view, this is ironic, since Switzerland hosts the Bank for International Settlements and it should provide exemplary leadership.

116 Simmons, 'The International Politics of Harmonisation', p. 607.

cannot be wholeheartedly embraced in countries sidelined by the global market economy.

The global system generally and the global AML/CFT regimes specifically are information-driven, which presupposes that countries should first generate some capacity in ICT. This also implies that countries at rudimentary stages of development are constrained by their dynamics of development from harnessing the global system because of their inherent weaknesses. For instance, the ability of data registry centres to collect process and supply data to AML/CFT agencies such as the police or Financial Intelligence Units (FIUs) is extremely limited, if not non-existent, in some societies. Information is deemed to be meaningful if it is oriented and informed by the challenges of society. Information is a prerequisite for the effective enforcement of laws and regulations. Information is essential for the construction of the money trail, given that the money laundering process would have been executed in stages, but, in addition, requisite information is essential if law enforcement agencies are to secure a successful prosecution of those allegedly involved in money laundering and terrorist activities. Without requisite data on a regulated issue area, law enforcement agencies cannot function properly in enforcing laws and also in ensuring that violations do not go unsanctioned.[117]

Conclusion

The prevailing global climate (in its various manifestations) should be taken into account in the evolutions of normative AML/CFT framework. The global AML/CFT climate has in this chapter been underscored by the following developments: ICT, porous land borders, inequalities and underdevelopment in the world and, in some countries, the absence of the necessary AML/CFT institutions. Such an environment has the potential to influence national and international anti-money laundering institutions such as courts, specialist AML/CFT institutions (for example, the Inspector General of Governments in Uganda) and regional AML/CFT initiatives (for instance, the EU) in different ways. In some developed economies, information generated on money laundering is overwhelming, while, by contrast, there is a dismal absence of requisite information (to properly inform policy on money laundering) in developing countries. The absence of requisite information on crime typologies undermines the efficacy of law enforcement authorities in terms of constructing money trails to apprehend perpetrators of money laundering crimes. Therefore, these asymmetries highlight the challenges

117 Ian Carrington and Heba Shams, 'The Elements of Effective AML/CFT Framework: Legal, Regulatory, and Best Institutional Practices to Prevent Threats to Financial Stability and Integrity', Seminar on Current Development in Monetary and Financial Law, Washington DC, 23–27 October 2006, available at www.worldbank.org (date accessed 22 November 2011).

to the conceptualization of money laundering and its related predicate crimes globally.

The transposition of global anti-money laundering standards such as KYC should be implemented pragmatically, taking into account the varying dynamics of development in individual countries. It is evident that many countries are not able to implement such AML/CFT regimes. As a paradigm of money laundering control at AMF/CFT policy levels, such as the FAFT and the Basel Committee, financial institutions must know their customers. Apparently, KYC, adopted by states, is difficult to apply, let alone enforce, given that it functions on the strength of generating good information on present and future bank clients.[118] In the majority of developing countries, either there is no data to help quantify and evaluate the magnitude of money laundering/terrorism threats or the little data generated is too patchy to properly inform any policy choices. This situation has generated significant challenges for financial and law enforcement agencies in developing strategies against both local and global-oriented crimes. As a prerequisite for harnessing the AML/CFT regimes, it is essential for countries to first take a step back and address their embedded development challenges. For instance, it is essential for countries to first address the question of infrastructure deficiencies at home as a prerequisite of harnessing normative AML/CFT laws. The need for a AML/CFT policy framework should reflect the prevailing global market conditions, which cannot be exclusive of local conditions. In this regard, we propose that various AML/CFT oversight committees should have a broad representation to take into account the challenges of applying evolved norms globally. Thus, it would seem that widening the composition of AML/CFT committees is essential in order to ensure that proliferating regimes have an ethos not only of representativeness but also of legitimacy in different countries.

---

118 The ability of a state to harness the global AML/CFT framework is dictated by the availability of resources and a requisite infrastructure. Therefore, countries which are deficient in resources and such infrastructure development are likely to lag behind others in transposing normative AML/CFT regimes into their own system.

Chapter 3
The Global Anti-Money Laundering/ Countering the Financing of Terrorism Framework

Introduction

This chapter underscores the dynamics of the putative AML/CFT framework. This framework is made up of diverse AML/CFT regimes that have evolved at various institutional levels. Some of these regimes have evolved under the auspices of the UN treaties, some are regional-based initiatives, while others are ad hoc arrangements between certain market domains and hence are rightly market-oriented.[1] Thus, this chapter proffers insights into the envisaged AML/ CFT normative standards which individual member states are required to transpose nationally. The global anti-money laundering framework includes but is not limited to the following regimes: the Vienna Convention of 1988; the FATF; the Council of Europe; and the Basel Committee under the auspices of the Bank for International Settlement.[2] In 2001, the UN Security Council adopted nine Special Resolutions on Countering the Financing of Terrorism, calling on member countries to implement them in combating money laundering and the financing of terrorism. Ideally, this meant that money laundering and the financing of terrorism would henceforth be enforced within the framework of Chapter 7, in particular Articles 40 and 41 of UN Charter of 1945.[3] The last part of the chapter explores other bodies that have a significant influence on money laundering and its predicate crimes such as the Intelligence Financial Units (Egmont Group), the Financial Stability Forum (FSF) and the World Bank/IMF.

1 Other initiatives include the International Convention for the Suppression of the Financing of Terrorism (1999), the International Organization of Securities Commissions (IOSCO), the African initiatives such as the Convention on the Prevention and Combating of Terrorism in Africa (Algiers Convention) and the New Partnership for Africa's Development (NEPAD) (1999), and many more in Asia and worldwide.

2 Ilias Bantekas and Susan Nash, *International Criminal Law* (London: Cavendish Publishing, 2003).

3 Chapter 7 spells out a range of sanctions that may be taken against a member state deemed to be in violation of international peace and security standards under Article 39 of the UN Charter.

The global efforts towards combating financial systemic abuse, financial crime and specifically money laundering intensified in the late 1980s due to the growing concerns about drug trafficking. However, it also needs to be noted that the evolved global anti-money laundering laws were precipitated by the overlapping challenge of illicit drug tracking, particularly in the USA, which was seen as an affront to the fabric of human society. There is an adage that 'crimes follow opportunity', and thus the USA was at the receiving end of illicit drug trafficking presumably because of its economic clout. The prevalence of illicit drug trafficking would later be sensationalized as a war, code-named a 'war on drugs' and made a central national policy, particularly under President Richard Nixon in the early 1970s.

The 'War on Drugs' in the USA

The prevalence of drugs in the USA in relation to production, distribution and consumption, sensationalized by the 'war on drugs' campaign, was seen as a threat to humanity and the fabric of human society. The widespread use of narcotic drugs was not only perceived to have adverse social effects, but also was seen as an assault on social justice and civil liberties and a factor encouraging tax evasion, disrespect of the law, erosion of the work ethic, and violence and corruption in relation to the lucrative black market.[4] The need to control illicit drugs also had other objectives, such as the need to guard against the adverse effect associated with drug use, which could potentially create a drug culture, dependence on drugs and its consequent social effects. The widespread use of narcotic drugs such as cocaine and morphine was attributed to a lack of legal proscriptions and medical ignorance of the dangers posed by drug use. In 1937 President Franklin D. Roosevelt appointed Harry Anslinger as the first Commissioner of Narcotics. Subsequently in the same year, the marijuana tax was passed to outlaw the possession or sale of the drug for any purpose.[5] Congress would later pass the Narcotic Control Act 1956, imposing a mandatory sentence of offenders from 10 to 20 years for those caught re-offending.[6] In 1968, President Nixon politicized the drug problem during his presidential campaign and would later make drug control the government's central national policy. The President partly exploited the nation's discomfort with the civil rights-led urban riots and rising street crime rates for his political expediency, and he would

4 S. Wisotsky, *Breaking the Impasse in the War on Drugs* (Westport, CT: Greenwood Publishing Group, 1986), p. 303; see also Margaret E. Beare (ed.), *Critical Reflections on Transnational Organised Crime, Money Laundering and Corruption* (Toronto: University of Toronto Press, 2005), p. 145.

5 MaryBeth Lipp, 'A New Perspective on the War on Drugs: Comparing the Consequences of Sentencing Policies in the United Sates and England', available at http://digitalcommons.lmu.edu/cgi/viewcontent.cgi?article=2422&context=llr (date accessed 1 December 2011).

6 Ibid.

also use the war on drugs campaign as a front to suppress the black militants in the civil rights movement.[7] He would also influence the adoption of the Comprehensive Drug Abuse Prevention and Control Act of 1970, which merged various federal anti-drug statutes and established a schedule of controlled substances.[8] It can certainly be argued that President Nixon's failure to criminalize money laundering and to focus his war on drugs campaign on vulnerable street users than the 'drug kingpins' demonstrated that he probably had other ulterior motives.[9]

While drug trafficking was proscribed in various pieces of US legislation, money laundering was not, until the passage of Money Laundering Control Act in 1986.[10] The Bank Secrecy Act (BSA) 1970 (otherwise known as 'Currency and Foreign Transaction Reporting') did not directly address money laundering *per se*.[11] The BSA 1970 fully recognized the link between money laundering – including security fraud – and the global dimension of the problem and asked financial institutions to cooperate with the government in forestalling the looming threat of money laundering.[12] The Act required banks to report cash transactions of $10,000 and this provision was also enacted in the Money Laundering Act 1986, which for the first time defined money laundering as a federal crime.[13] The BSA 1970 also required banks to keep records of cash purchases of negotiable instruments, file reports of cash transactions exceeding $10,000 (daily aggregate) and report suspicious activity that might signify money laundering, tax evasion and other criminal activities.

---

7 Ibid.

8 In addition to the legislation, the President created the Office of Drug Abuse Law Enforcement when the division of the Justice Department resisted his edict to target street-level dealers instead of 'drug kingpins'. See Eva Bertram et al., *Drug War Politics: The Price of Denial* (Berkeley, CA: University of California Press, 1996).

9 In the southern USA, whites identified blacks who were addicted to cocaine. There were long-held racial prejudices and levels of intolerance that were exploited to create lopsided laws. There were also stereotypes manifested in the existence of the fear that cocaine engendered Herculean qualities in blacks, making them invincible. The American public similarly stigmatized Chinese immigrants, who were linked to the widespread use of opium. The unchecked use of opium smoking would undermine American society with crimes such as rape, murder and other forms of violence. The war on drugs had a political undertone reflecting American society at that time – for example, it had some racial connotations. See Lipp, 'A New Perspective on the War on Drugs'.

10 In this Act, Congress also removed the lopsided federal judiciary approach to customizing sentences based on the individual circumstances of each case. The removal of discretion also fell in line with the aims of the Sentencing Act 1984, which was designed to avoid unwarranted sentencing disparities among defendants found guilty of similar crimes.

11 Shams, *Legal Globalization.*

12 Ibid.

13 United Nations Office on Drugs and Crime website: www.unodc.org (date accessed 1 December 2011).

In addition, it was also recognized that the increasing globalization of trade in financial services, spurred on by advancements in communication technology, might facilitate money laundering and hence there was an urgent need for a framework to deal with money laundering-related issues.[14] Money laundering would henceforth be given priority in many multilateral organizations. Leading the inter-agency group is the FATF and the affiliated regional organizations such as the Eastern and Southern Africa Anti-Money Laundering Group (ESAAMLG). These anti-money laundering regimes can be analysed on two levels: those regimes formed under the auspices of the UN with a specialized focus on money laundering and its underlying predicate offences, and those regimes adopted in response to the exigencies of the global financial market economy. It soon became evident that despite the efforts of individual national governments against drug trafficking, they remained vulnerable to the threat of illicit drug trafficking unless they acted together through the UN.

The United Nations Convention Against Illicit Traffic in Narcotic Drugs and other Psychotropic Substances 1988 (Vienna Convention)

The adoption of the Vienna Convention in 1988 was preceded by a series of General Assembly Resolutions[15] where the concern over drug abuse was expressed by delegates from many national governments. In these Resolutions, drug abuse and trafficking was viewed as being of increasing concern in the international arena, which led to the General Assembly Resolution 39/141 of December 1984 entitled 'Draft Convention against Trafficking in Narcotic Drugs and Psychotropic Substances.'[16] The securitization of drug abuse and trafficking through their conceptualization as a threat and the priotization of the adoption of counter-measures resulted in the call for a specialized conference[17] to deal with the fight against drug trafficking. In adopting a similar securitization discourse, the then Secretary-General of the UN[18] stated that existing resources were inadequate to deal with the drug plague, which was contaminating, corrupting and weakening the very fabric of society. In its preamble, Resolution 40/121 characterizes the activities of transnational criminal organizations engaged in drug trafficking as a 'threat to the well being of people; the stability of democratic institutions; and

14 Bantekas and Nash, *International Criminal Law*.

15 The First was the General Assembly Resolution 35/195 of December 1980. See, for instance, the third preamble of Resolution 35/195.

16 'The UN Economic and Social Council, 'Implementation and Development of International Instruments on the Control of Narcotic Drug, and Psychotropic Substances', a Report of the Secretary-General, DOC.E/CN, 7/1987/2 of 17 June 1986, p. 2.

17 M. Anderson, *Policing the World: Interpol and the Politics of International Police Co-operation* (Oxford: Oxford University Press, 1989), pp. 41–2.

18 The then UN Secretary-General was Javier Pérez de Cuéller.

the sovereignty of states' and calls in its second paragraph for maximum priority to be given to the fight against drug production, demand and traffic and related international activities.[19] Resolution 40/122, on the other hand, expressed the same concerns through the decision to convene the conference in 1987 at the ministerial level: 'as an expression of political will of national, regional and international levels and to adopt a comprehensive multi-disciplinary outline of future activities which focuses on concrete and substantive issues directly relevant to the problems of drug abuse and illicit trafficking'.[20] There were challenges faced by law enforcement officials with regard to investigating the flow of money across national borders, but there was also a need for an international framework within which states could respond to the overlapping character of money laundering offences. The treaty offers a meticulous definition to the specific elements that encompass trafficking in drugs and other related drug substances. Thus, these concerns led to the adoption of the Vienna Convention in 1988.

The Parameters of the Convention

The Convention creates an anti-money laundering framework on a wide range of issues, such as: the definition and characterization of the offence; the requisite inter-state cooperation, including mutual legal assistance and extradition arrangements; and enforcement mechanisms, including stripping criminals of the profits realized from money laundering and other predicate crimes. In Article 3(1), state parties are required to enact legislation necessary to establish a modern code of criminal offences relating to illicit trafficking in all its different dimensions.[21] The scope of criminalization should cover a comprehensive list connected to drug trafficking, from production, cultivation and possession to the organization, management and financing of trafficking operations.[22] The article requires each party to the Convention to establish money laundering as a criminal offence in its domestic law when committed internationally.[23]

In Article 3(1)(b), each state party is required to establish as a criminal offence:

> The conversion or transfer of property knowing that such a property is derived from any offence or offences established in accordance with subparagraph (a) of this paragraph or from an act of participation in such offence or offences, for purposes of concealing or disguising the illicit origin of the property or of assisting any person who is involved in the commission of such offence or

19 Anderson, *Policing the World.*

20 The Vienna Convention.

21 Gilmore, *Dirty Money*, p. 161.

22 Stewart, 'Internalising the War on Drugs', p. 387.

23 For this, see Article 3(3), which says that 'knowledge, intent or purpose required as an element of the offence may be inferred from objective factual circumstances'.

> offences to evade the legal consequences of his actions. The concealment or disguise of the true nature, source, location, disposition, movement, rights with respect to, or ownership of property, knowing that such property is derived from an offence or offences established in accordance with subparagraph (a) of this paragraph or from an act of participation in such an offence or offences.'

For a uniform application of money laundering framework among states, Article 3(1)(c) provides that each state party render the following as criminal: 'The acquisition, possession or use of property, knowing at the time of the receipt that such property was derived from an offence or offences established in accordance with subparagraph (a) of this paragraph or from an act of participation in such offence or offences.'[24] Article 3 is very significant because by establishing the parameters for criminalization and treating money laundering as a serious offence, the drafters ensured that cooperation in respect of confiscation, mutual legal assistance and extradition would be forthcoming. The Convention has been hailed,[25] particularly in relation to extradition, a subject which is addressed by Article 6. Because all parties are obliged to establish Article 3(1) offences as criminal offences in their domestic law, any requirements of dual criminality, that is, the offence is criminal in both jurisdictions, in a party's extradition should be met. At a practical level, an Article 3(1) provision signifies that states which have accepted to transpose the above international instrument must similarly accept to fully comply with its treaty obligations and their attendant effects.[26] Governments are obliged to comply with obligations created by the treaty because of the international law principle of *pacta sunt servanda*.[27] Governments would comply with international treaties largely because of the need to promote the ideals embodied in the treaty. However, the reality might sometimes differ from country to country because of the varied dynamics of development. Also worthy of mention is the fact that even if every country were to sign the Convention, its implementation would still remain the responsibility of individual countries, which is a complicated issue for the international community to police.

It has to be said that although there has been a universal recognition of the fact that illicit drug trafficking offences are extraditable offences, narcotics-related money laundering is a new criminal offence for many states and has not been traditionally recognized as an extraditable offence. The universal recognition of narcotics-related money laundering as an extraditable offence is one of the most important provisions established by the Vienna Convention.[28] The enforcement

24 Gilmore, *Dirty Money*.

25 The US delegates for example hailed it as being very robust.

26 D.W. Sproule and P. St-Denis, 'The UN Drug Trafficking Convention: An Ambitious Step', *Canadian Yearbook of International Law*, (1989): pp. 263–70.

27 See Article 36 of the Vienna Convention on the Law of Treaties, 23 May 1969 (which entered into force on 27 January 1980).

28 Sproule and St-Denis, The UN Drug Trafficking Convention'.

mechanisms under the Convention, which are designed to impact on the financial aspect of drug trafficking, is the provision for confiscation of the profits derived from criminal activity. In view of this provision, a number of states have enacted legislation towards that end.[29] Stripping criminals of profits generated from criminal activities is increasingly being seen as an effective way to combat drug-related crimes and also as a means of carrying out justice by restoring the criminal to the position he/she would have been in prior to the commission of these crimes. There was a need for enhanced international cooperation to facilitate states in their efforts against the threat of drug trafficking and money laundering. Accordingly, individual states are urged to enact domestic forfeiture legislation enabling the state in question 'to identify, trace, seize, freeze or forfeit property or proceeds located in the requested states, where property was allegedly derived from or used in drug trafficking and drug money laundering in violation of laws of the requesting state'. In so doing, the Convention creates a framework for undermining the efforts of those who are moving money internationally within the financial system, particularly to jurisdictions where there is customer confidentiality or bank secrecy legislation in place as a deterrent. The existing bank secrecy laws are used in many instances to obstruct cooperation and the provision of information needed for the investigation of allegations of drug-related offences.[30] The Convention acknowledges the indispensability of domestic courts in the fight against money laundering and its predicate crimes. Thus, Article 5(3) empowers each state party's courts or relevant authorities to order that a bank, financial or commercial records be made available before the local judge for examination. Similarly, no party shall decline to act under the provisions of this paragraph on the grounds of bank secrecy. The exclusion of bank secrecy as a justification for declining to act may prove to be one of the most important measures in combating narcotics-related money laundering operations.[31]

Parties to the Convention are encouraged to enter into detailed bilateral and multilateral confiscation agreements in order 'to enhance the effectiveness of international co-operation pursuant to the above article'.[32] However, in the absence of bilateral agreements or treaties, Article 5(4)(f) stipulates that that the Convention would suffice in those circumstances. Article 5(6) addresses the need to ensure that proceeds derived from and instrumentalities used in illegal trafficking cannot escape forfeiture simply because their form has been changed or they have been commingled with other property.[33] At the same time it was felt necessary to provide that Article 5 shall not be construed as prejudicing the rights

---

29 D. McClean, 'Seizing the Proceeds of Crime: The State of the Art', 38 *International Criminal Law Quarterly* (1998): p. 334.

30 This is identified as one of the biggest problems in fighting crimes by the UN conference on drug abuse in 1987.

31 McClean, 'Seizing the Proceeds of Crime'.

32 W.C. Gilmore, 'International Action Against Drug Trafficking: Trends in United Kingdom Law and Practice', 24 *International Lawyer* (1990): pp. 388–90.

33 Ibid.

of bona fide third parties.[34] The extradition procedures shall be expedited as much as possible by simplifying the rules of evidentiality relating to the offence and other requisite extradition procedures.[35]

The Vienna Convention provides modalities for extradition of alleged money laundering offenders to jurisdictions which have made a formal request and to have offenders produced before the respective jurisdiction's courts of law. Extradition shall be subject to the laws of the requested party as laid down in Article 6(5). The extradition procedure, the standard of proof and the defences to extradition are to be defined exclusively by the domestic law of the requested party. Article 6(5) must be read together with Article 3(1) and Article 10, which amend bilateral extradition treaties to preclude the denial of extradition on the grounds of Article 3(1) offences: 'fiscal, political or politically motivated offences'.[36] If the party makes extradition conditional on the existence of a treaty and it receives a request for extradition from another party with which it has no extradition treaty, it may consider this Convention as the legal basis for extradition in respect of any offences to which this article applies. On the other hand, parties which do not make extradition conditional on the existence of a treaty shall recognize offences to which this article applies as extraditable offences between themselves.[37] The requested state may refuse to comply if to do so substantially leads its judicial or other competent authorities to believe that compliance would facilitate the prosecution or punishment of any person on account of his/her race, religion, nationality or political opinion, or would cause prejudice for any of those reasons to any person affected by the request.[38]

The Vienna Convention also creates provisions for mutual legal assistance in relation to serious drug trafficking offences. For instances, Article 7(1) provides that 'the parties shall afford one another, pursuant to this article, the widest measure of mutual legal assistance in investigations, prosecution and judicial proceedings in relation to criminal offences established in accordance with article 3(1). This provision is an invitation to states to examine the possibility of doing so'.[39] The assistance, which may be requested in this mini-mutual legal assistance treaty, includes: the taking of evidence or statements; effecting the service of judicial documents; executing searches and seizures; examining objects and sites; providing information and evidentiary items; providing relevant documents and records including bank, corporate or business records; and identifying or tracing proceeds and instrumentalities of evidentiary purposes, providing information

34 Articles 5(8) and 7(2) of the 1988 Vienna Convention.

35 Ibid., Article 6(7).

36 Gilmore, 'International Action Against Drug Trafficking'.

37 Articles 6(4) and 6(5) in respect of the conditions that accompany the extradition of fugitive offenders under Article 3(1) offences of the same framework above.

38 Article 6(6) of the Vienna Convention 1988.

39 Ibid., Article 7(2).

and evidentiary items.[40] Similarly, in order to enhance the fight against money laundering, Article 7(5) imposes the following duties on states: 'it is an obligation for state parties to enact an implementing legislation, if necessary, to modify domestic bank secrecy laws to permit execution of the request for bank records under the convention'. In addition, with respect to individual requests for bank records under the Convention, this provision obliges the requested party to grant the request if the only reason to refuse the request would be bank secrecy laws.[41] The state parties may afford one another any other form of mutual legal assistance allowed by the domestic law of the requested party. According to Article 7(4), parties shall facilitate and encourage, to the extent consistent with their domestic law and practice, the presence or availability of a person in custody who consents to assist in the investigations or participate in the proceedings.

Money laundering is an integral part of transnational organized criminal enterprises and is used as a strategy to achieve two fundamental objectives: to evade detection and capture of those who plan and execute money laundering schemes; and to enhance enjoyment of the ill-gotten proceeds of crime. As such, the role of the authorities in pursuing the money trail is becoming increasingly cumbersome. The sophistry in which members of organized crime groups perpetuate their nefarious activities has certainly become a great source of concern to governments and law enforcement agencies all over the world. The concerted efforts of various countries in relation to transnational organized crime is indicative of the fact that transnational crime groups cannot be managed unilaterally by one country. It is therefore imperative that criminalizing participation in organized criminal groups and developing an anti-money laundering framework takes into account the worldwide context within which criminals operate. While the Vienna Convention was the very first anti-money laundering framework adopted, it has now been superseded by the Palermo Convention 2000.

The United Nations Convention against Transnational Organized Crime 2000 (Palermo Convention)

In order to stem the spread of international organized crimes, the UN General Assembly adopted the Convention against Transnational Organized Crime

40 Ibid.

41 'United Nations Convention Against Illicit Traffic in Narcotic Drugs and Psychotropic Substances', 101st Session, Senate, Executive Report 101–5 (2006), p. 185.

(otherwise known as the Palermo Convention)[42] in December 2000.[43] This Convention contains a range of provisions specifically designed to reinforce the fight against transnational organised crimes; and committing countries that ratify it to implement its provisions into domestic national law.

In relation to fighting money laundering, the Palermo Convention obliges each state subject to a treaty to implement and criminalize money laundering, including all serious predicate crimes of money laundering, whether committed within or outside of the country, and permit the required criminal knowledge or intent to be inferred from objective facts;[44] In Article 2(1), an offence is transnational in nature if 'it is committed in more than one State; it is committed in one state but a substantial part of its preparation, planning, direction or control takes place in another State; it is committed in one State but involves an organised criminal group that engages in criminal activities in more than one state; and lastly, it is committed in one State but causes substantial effects in another State'.

States are obliged to establish regulatory regimes to detect and deter all forms of money laundering, including customer identification, record keeping and the reporting of suspicious transactions;[45] States are also required to authorize the cooperation and exchange of information among administrative, regulatory, law enforcement and other authorities, both domestically and internationally, and consider the establishment of financial intelligence unit to collect, analyse and disseminate information.[46] In addition, the Palermo Convention also creates provisions to enhance international cooperation.[47] It creates modalities on matters such as extradition, mutual legal assistance on civil and criminal matters, transfer of proceedings and conducting joint investigations. State parties are required to provide the necessary technical assistance to developing countries so that they

42 This Convention came into force on 29 September 2003, having been signed by 147 countries and ratified by 82 countries. For details on the adoption of the Palermo Convention, see www.undoc.org.undocc/crime_cicp_signatures_convention.html (date accessed 12 September 2007). This Convention was adopted pursuant to an intergovernmental ad hoc committee whose mandate was to discuss the elaboration, as appropriate as possible an international instrument addressing trafficking in women and children, combating the illicit manufacturing and trafficking of firearms, their parts and components and ammunition, and the illegal trafficking in and transporting of migrants including by sea. The UN General Assembly resolution mandated the ad hoc intergovernmental committee to continue its work on the elaboration of the above Convention in accordance with Resolutions 53/111 and 53/114 of December 1998. Under Resolution 54/129 of December 1999, the UN General Assembly invited the intergovernmental ad hoc committee to host a high-level political conference in Palermo for the purpose of signing the Palermo Convention and its three protocols.

43 www.undcp.org/adhoc/palermo/convmain.html (date accessed 12 September 2007).

44 See, in particular Articles 5, 6 and 7 of the Palermo Convention.

45 Ibid., Article 7.

46 Ibid., Article 7(1)(b).

47 Ibid., Article 7(3) and (4).

are able to take measures to deal with transnational organized crimes.[48] It has to be noted that the Palermo Convention subsumes and extends the anti-money laundering framework under its predecessor. State parties are obliged to undertake measures to transpose their international obligations into domestic law. Following the adoption of international conventions such as the Palermo Convention, the EU has responded by issuing Directives to transpose its international obligations. The AML/CFT framework in the EU is underscored by the Directives issued by its institutions.

The European Anti-Money Laundering Directives: Overview and Application

Europe has long been at the forefront of fighting money laundering, as demonstrated by its early initiative by the Council of Europe (1990).[49] The Council of Europe Convention in 1990 was to adopt a framework for harmonization of practice and policy on money laundering, tracing, seizure and confiscation of the proceeds of crimes within EU Member States. The EU subsequently issued three Anti-Money Laundering Directives (1991, 2001 and 2005) to bring a certain degree of harmonization of the money laundering laws within its Member States. As always, harmonization initiatives tend to generate tensions among EU Member States and there are several discerning trends in the EU anti-money laundering drive: (i) the link with FATF standards and discussions is both strong and, in many ways, binding; (ii) G7 members such as the UK and France are at the forefront of proposals and are more eager to push for comprehensive regional standards; (iii) countries with long-established offshore status, most notably Luxembourg, are experiencing intense pressure to address the potential weaknesses in their AML/CFT regulatory framework.[50] It is important to mention that the European Anti-Money Laundering Directives are also adopted to bring EU law into line with its international obligations, such as the FATF recommendations on AML/CFT. The EU has been very robust about the implementation of its anti-money laundering obligations. The relationship between the EU Directives and the FATF recommendations is underscored by the fact that every time the FATF adopts new recommendations, the EU responds by adopting measures to transpose those obligations within its Member States. For example, when the FATF issued its first 40 recommendations, the European Council adopted its First Anti-Money Laundering Directive in June 1991.[51] When the FATF revised its recommendations in 1996 to extend their scope to 'designated non-financial businesses and professions', the

48 Ibid., Articles 16–30.

49 Eleni Tsingou 'Global Governance and Transnational Crimes: Opportunities and Tensions in Global Anti-Money Laundering Regimes', CSGR Working Paper No. 161/05, May 2005.

50 Ibid.

51 OJ L 166 of 28 June 1991.

EU Council issued the Second Anti-Money Laundering Directive in December 2001. For the first time, lawyers were brought within the scope of the European Directive in order to oblige them to report suspicious transactions to their national anti-money laundering authorities.

The Second European Directive took the form of amendments to the First Directive, inserting a new provision requiring Member States to ensure that obligations laid down in the Directive were imposed on, among others, notaries and other independent legal professionals when they assist in the planning or execution of any activities which effectively constitute money laundering.[52]

The Directive was created in response to fears among leaders of EU Member States that an integrated financial system could permit drug trafficking and money laundering to flourish, thereby undermining the integrity of the financial system and disrupting the market.[53] They were also troubled by the prospect of ad hoc efforts to curb money laundering by individual nations, which they perceived would have a negative effect on a unified system. Thus, the Directive prescribes a series of measures to be adopted by all Member States in their approach to money laundering.

The Directive prohibits the knowing acceptance and disposition by financial institutions and non-bank finance companies of the proceeds of non-drug-related crimes, as well as the proceeds of narcotics trafficking.[54] It thus requires Member States to criminalize the laundering of the proceeds of drug offences as set out in the Vienna Convention and 'any other criminal activity designated as such for the purpose of this Directive by each Member State'.[55] The Directive primarily focuses on the prevention and detection of money laundering by way of enacting prevention and detection provisions within financial institutions.[56] It applies to all financial institutions because of their potential vulnerability to money laundering schemes. Financial institutions are defined in the Directive as 'undertakings whose business is to receive deposits or other repayable funds from the public and to grant credit for their own account'.[57]

The Directive defines financial institutions as 'an undertaking other than credit institutions whose main activity is to carry out one or more of the functions listed

52 In relation to the list of what constitute predicate crimes, see Recommendation 12(h) of the FATF.

53 The Second Anti-Money Laundering Directive (91/308/EEC).

54 The EU leaders voiced their fear that 'when credit and financial institutions are used to launder proceeds from criminal activities, the soundness and stability of the institutions concerned and confidence in the financial system would be jeopardized'.

55 Kern Alexander, 'Multinational Efforts to Combat Financial Crimes and the Financial Action Task Force', 2(5) *Journal of International Financial Markets* (2000): pp. 178–90.

56 Ibid.

57 The EU Directive adopts the definition of credit institution from the First Banking Directive 77/780/EEC as amended by Directive 89/646/EEC (hereinafter the Second Banking Directive).

in the Second Banking Directive.[58] These functions include lending (consumer and mortgage credit), financial leasing, money transmission services, guarantees and commitments, trading for its own account or for a customer's account, money broking, portfolio management and advice'.[59] Financial institutions also include insurance companies authorized in accordance with the insurance directives such as Directive 79/267/EEC as amended.[60] Credit and financial institutions include branches located in European states whose home offices are based outside Europe.[61] Article 12 of the Directive provides that Member States must extend either all or part of the Directive to professional categories and other credit and financial institutions referred to in Article 1, which engage in activities that are likely to be used for money laundering purposes. This would include casinos and the proliferating money changing or lending businesses that have become prevalent largely in response to the current dynamics of the global market.[62]

The Third Anti-Money Laundering Directive had a very broad mandate, not least extending its remit regarding lawyers to include money used for the financing of terrorism. The Second Anti-Money Laundering Directive defined the basic principles on the prevention of money laundering in Europe.[63] The Third Anti-Money Laundering Directive also introduced a risk-based approach to customer due diligence, creating a dual reporting regime for low-risk clients (Article 9) and enhanced due diligence in situations regarded as being likely to be used for money laundering.[64] The latter covers situations where there is no face-to-face interaction with the client, for example, where the transaction is made online, over the telephone, etc., as well as relating to cross-border banking relationships and a new category of politically exposed persons residing abroad (Article 10). The broad mandate of the above European Directives aside, these Directives are transposed as a framework on AML/CFT within individual EU Member States. Failure to comply with the EU Directive will justify the need for sanctions.

58 See, in particular, Article 1 of the Second Anti-Money Laundering Directive.

59 Directive 89/646/EEC, in particular numbers 2–12 and 14 of the list attached to the Directive.

60 Kern Alexander, Rahul Dhumale and John Eatwell, *Global Governance of Financial Systems: International Regulation of Systemic Risk* (Oxford: Oxford University Press, 2006), p. 276.

61 Ibid.

62 Directive 91/308/EEC.

63 Council Directive 91/308, 1991, OJ L 166 77. Pursuant to this, the European Council of Ministers passed Directives, which in turn were to be implemented by the EU Member States through the creation of enabling legislation at home.

64 OJ L 309, 25 November 2005, p. 15.

The Sanctions Mechanism under the Directive

There are two types of sanctions regimes operative in Europe and in all other UN member countries. These are specific sanctions designated to implement UN resolutions, in particular under Articles 40 and 41 of the UN Charter 1945. There are also EU autonomous sanction regimes including arms embargo, trade sanctions, flight bans and restriction of admission for countries aspiring to join the EU. The EU Directive prescribes a range of duties on credit and financial institutions to take appropriate measures to ensure the full application of its provisions, and in particular the penalties to be imposed for infringement of the measures adopted.[65] The European Commission brought its first action to enforce the Anti-Money Laundering Directive in May 2000, when it instituted proceedings against Austria for failing to enact the necessary laws to implement the Directive. In pursuit of Article 226 of the EC Treaty, the Commission alleged that Austrian legislation did not comply with the European Anti-Money Laundering Directive. In particular, it contended that Article 40 of the Austrian Banking Act wrongly provided for exemption to the obligation to identify customers when opening passbook accounts. This had the effect of allowing people to open as many passbook accounts as they desired without declaring their identity.[66] Such a provision was clearly inconsistent with the Directive, which requires Member States to enact laws prohibiting financial institutions from keeping anonymous accounts and requiring them to take appropriate measures to identify customers.[67] Austria responded to this action and to pressure from other international bodies (for example, the FATF) by amending Article 40 to prohibit the issuing of anonymous passbook accounts after 1 November 2000, as well as imposing an obligation to identify all depositors after this date (with the exception of transfer securities deposits).[68]

The Directive demonstrates that the EU has adopted the strictest anti-money laundering standards across the globe. The Directive perpetuates 'Know Your Customer' (KYC), the concept first introduced by the Basel Committee on Banking Supervision and later broadened in the FATF recommendations. It adds teeth to the suspicious transaction reporting standards advanced by the FATF by making such reporting mandatory.

To broaden the extraterritorial effect of the Directive, the EU anti-money laundering legislation is not only confined to candidate countries or offshore jurisdictions, but continuously seeks to incorporate agreements to bind non-Member States.[69] According to the European Commission, the standard clause refers to efforts and cooperation to avoid money laundering and the establishment

65 Article 14.

66 Directive 91/308/EEC.

67 Alexander, Dhumale, and Eatwell, *Global Governance of Financial Systems*.

68 See the FATF, 'Money Laundering', press release, OECD, 15 June 2000.

69 EU Commission Report, 1998, p. 7.

of suitable standards against money laundering equivalent to those adopted in the EU and in other international bodies such as the FATF.[70]

The Extension of Predicate Offences

The international initiatives adopted to combat the threat of money laundering, for example, the Vienna Convention and the Council of Europe Convention, were limited in scope because they only focused on the criminalization of the proceeds from narcotics trafficking only. However, the Strasbourg Convention and the FATF provide for the optional extension of criminalization to additional categories of predicate offences. The scope of money laundering predicate offences is clearly elaborated in the glossary to FATF 40 recommendations to encompass the following: participation in organized criminal groups and racketeering; terrorism, including the financing of terrorism; trafficking human beings and illegal migrant smuggling; sexual exploitation, including that of children; illicit trafficking in narcotic drugs and psychotropic substances; illicit arms trafficking; illicit trafficking in stolen and other goods; corruption and bribery; fraud; counterfeiting currency (such as 'bicupuli' from Uganda); counterfeiting and piracy of products; environmental crimes; murder or grievous bodily harm, kidnapping and hostage taking; robbery or theft; smuggling; extortion; forgery; piracy; and insider trading and market manipulation.

The above definitional framework had been adopted by the 1991 Second Anti-Money Laundering Directive, which sought to extend the scope of money laundering in line with the foregoing criminal activities. This was largely a reflection of the policy agenda from the 'war on drugs', which had served the justification for the initial money laundering counter-measures against the multi-faceted threat of organized crime.[71] It also reflects the views of experts who advised that the limitation of money laundering only to drug trafficking would render the Directive ineffective. This was tendered in the UN report as follows: 'The time may have come to end the artificial division of criminal money into categories depending on the nature of the crime.'

As far as the EU anti-money laundering framework is concerned, the issue of money laundering predicate offences has been partly addressed in the

70 The recent EU common strategy on Russia and the European Council common strategy on Ukraine. See also the Common Action Plan on Drugs between the EU and Central Asian States (Kazakhstan, Kyrgyzistan, Tajikistan and Uzbekistan), Council doc.12353/02. Brussels, 25 September 2002.

71 Alexander, Dhumale, and Eatwell, *Global Governance of Financial Systems*.

specific context of third pillar measures on fraud[72] and confiscation.[73] In its first Commission Implementation Report, the European Parliament adopted a motion whose resolution point 5 calls on all Member States, insofar as they have already not done so, to extend their legislation on combating money laundering not only to money derived from drug trafficking but also to money generated from professional and organized crime.[74]

The connection between drug trafficking and money laundering is clearly highlighted by the adopted text under the Third Anti-Money Laundering Directive that:

> Member states shall ensure that the obligation laid down in this Directive are imposed on the following institutions: credit institutions (as defined previously); Financial institutions (as defined previously); and on the following legal or natural persons acting in exercise of their professional activities: auditors, external accountants and tax advisors, real estate agents, notaries and other independent legal professionals, when they participate, whether: by assisting in the planning or execution of transactions for their clients concerning, (i) buying and selling of real property or business entities; (ii) Managing of clients' money, securities or other assets; (iii) opening of management of bank, savings or securities accountants; (iv) organisation of contribution necessary for the creation, operation or management of companies; (v) creation, operation or management of trusts, companies or similar structures; (b) or by acting on behalf of and for their client in any financial or real estate transaction, dealers in high value goods, such as precious stones or metals, or works of art, auctioneers, whenever payment is made in cash and in amount of EUR 15,000 or more.

The need for the extension of money laundering predicate offences was also reiterated in the Tampere European Council conclusions, which called for a 'uniform and sufficiently broad scope' of predicates (para. 55). This position was

---

72 The second protocol of the Convention on the Protection of the European Communities' Financial Interests (OJ L 221 19 July 1997, p. 11) criminalizes the laundering of proceeds of fraud, at least in serious cases, and active and passive corruption (Articles 1(e) and 2).

73 The Joint Action on money laundering, the identification, tracing, freezing and confiscation of the instrumentalities and the proceeds from crime (OJ L 333, 9 December 1998, p. 1) calls on Member States to ensure that no reservations are made to Article 6 of the Council of Europe money laundering inofar as serious offences are concerned. See in particular Article 1(b).

74 W.C Gilmore, 'European Parliament Committee on Legal Affairs and Citizens' Rights: Report on the First Commission's Report Submitted to the European Parliament and to the Council on the Implementation of the Directive on the Prevention of the Use of the Financial System for the Purpose of Money Laundering' (91/308/EEC) (CM (95) 0054-C4-0137/95).

also reflected in the EU's view on the proposed Palermo Convention.[75] Article 1(5) of this Convention states that 'in the money-laundering field, the convention should extend a broad range of offences, and in particular should be consistent with the 40 Recommendations of the Financial Action Task Force'. This particular provision was incorporated as an acknowledgement that the international trends of money laundering justified the need to facilitate suspicious transaction reporting and international cooperation in this area.[76] Rather than following the all-crime prohibition, the Commission opted for an extension to cover, along with the drug offences of the 1991 text, the following conduct: participation in the activities linked to organized crime; and fraud, corruption or any other illegal activity that is damaging or likely to damage the EU's financial interests.[77] Another prevalent trend following the adoption of the Second Anti-Money Laundering Directive was the increasing use of the wider financial and non-financial institutions for money laundering purposes. This was considered to be the result of money laundering counter-measures and the increased level of compliance by credit and financial institutions, prompting launderers to shift towards non-regulated professions for their activities.[78] This trend was also associated with the growing sophistication of money laundering activities, which involve a wide range of intermediary professions of varied expertise.[79]

The growing role of professionals such as accountants, solicitors and company-formation agents was heavily emphasized, since they were frequently mentioned in money laundering cases.[80] In establishing sophisticated businesses that conceal money laundering, it is the professionals that provide advice and an extra layer of respectability to money laundering operations.[81] The FATF addressed these concerns by revising the 40 recommendations in 1996. Recommendation 8 (formerly 9) was revised to ensure that Member States equally apply anti-money laundering standards to non-financial institutions which are not subject to formal prudential supervisory regimes in all countries such as *bureaux de change*.[82] Recommendation 9 (formerly 10), on the other hand, requires national authorities to consider the extension of the duties of the recommendations to 'the conduct of financial activities as a commercial undertaking by businesses or the professions, which are not financial institutions, where such conduct is not allowed or not

75 Joint Position of 29 March 1999 defined by the Council on the basis of Article k.3 of the Treaty of the European Union, on the proposed United Nations Convention against Organized Crime, OJ L 87, 31 March 1999, p. 1.

76 Recitals 12 and 13.

77 United Nations Convention against Organized Crime, OJ L 87, 31 March 1999.

78 FATF, *Annual Report 1996–1997*, para. 16.

79 Mitsilegas, *Money Laundering Counter-Measures in the European Union.*

80 The Second Banking Directive brought lawyers within the scope of the money laundering reporting regime, now subsumed into the Third Anti-Money Laundering Directive.

81 FATF 1998/1999 annual report, para. 47.

82 Ibid.

prohibited'. In the same context, the Parliament proposed the extension of the *ratione personae* scope of the Directive[83] to cover a wide range of professions at risk of being involved in money laundering or abused by money launderers.[84] The indicative list includes both financial and non-financial professions, such as estate agents, art dealers, auctioneers, casinos, *bureaux de change*, transporters of funds, notaries, accountants, advocates, tax advisors and auditors.[85]

The EU anti-money laundering counter-measures have been emboldened by the Third Anti-Money-Laundering Directive, which consolidates the earlier Directives on the same issue.[86] This Directive reflects the changed regulatory market environment and typologies of money laundering as per the revised 40 recommendations of the FATF. In particular, the revision was designed to extend the scope of predicate offences, providing guidance on customer identification requirements, which now take place on the basis of a risk-based approach,[87] taking into account categories of individuals such as politically exposed persons (PEPs) and the misuse of corporate vehicles.[88] As a strategy to undercut terrorist funding, which is largely fuelled by money laundering, the Third Anti-Money Laundering Directive signalled a concerted effort on the part of the EU to use money laundering counter-measures in fighting the threat of terrorism.[89] The provision of customer identification has been expanded to introduce various levels of due diligence, which may range from simplified due diligence, in particular in the course of correspondent cross-border banking with third countries, and include transactions with politically exposed persons or where the use of shell banks is involved.[90] With regard to enhanced reporting requirements, Member States are asked to establish financial intelligence units (FIUs) with the specific mandate of accessing national

---

83 Gilmore, 'European Parliament Committee on Legal Affairs and Citizens' Rights'.

84 Ibid.

85 Underscored by Resolution point 1(a) of FATF, *Annual Report 1996–1997*.

86 The Second Banking Directive expanded the scope of predicate offences and introduced more compliance obligations on professionals such as lawyers, accountants, notaries and estate agents.

87 It enshrines the risk-based approach currently used by the regulated sector in the UK and equally it sets out professional guidance issued by, among others, the British Bankers' Association's Joint Money Laundering Steering Group (JMLSG).

88 Mitsilegas, *Money Laundering Counter-Measures in the European Union*, pp. 118–19.

89 After 9/11, the FATF extended its mandate to cover not only money laundering but also the financing of terrorism. Some of the new measures include the monitoring of wire transfers, the regulation of alternative remittance systems and enhanced measures in reporting standards.

90 Article 14 allows Member States to permit institutions and persons covered by the Directive to rely on third parties to meet the requirements of customer due diligence under certain conditions.

databases, notwithstanding that data protection provisions under national law may prohibit access to the individual person's file.[91]

What we can say in relation to money laundering predicate offences is that the extended definition of predicate offences is seemingly vague and is likely to cause more challenges than it actually overcomes. It is very broad and seems to subsume traditional crimes, such as theft and robbery, that fall within the realm of domestic states. This is likely to cause some confusion and tension between domestic and global institutions which might want to rely on this framework in prosecution of overlapping money laundering offences. This is particularly so in the absence of a global court specifically set up to dealing with overlapping money laundering crimes.

The FATF

The most prominent intergovernmental agency on money laundering and the financing of terrorism is the FATF.[92] The FATF is a free-standing specialist body concerned with the multilateral enhancement of AML/CFT capacity of countries globally.[93] It is made up of 36 member states or territories and four affiliate regional organizations and maintains a small secretariat based at the offices of the Organisation for Economic Co-operation and Development (OECD) in Paris.[94] The preventive role of the financial system against the threat of money laundering has been substantially enhanced through the initiatives of the FATF.[95] It is given the task of examining measures needed to combat money laundering, largely in recognition of the enormous extent of the drug problem, organized crime and money laundering. Although located at the OECD, where it maintains a small secretariat, the FATF is an independent body. It is the principal anti-money laundering multilateral organization. In addition, it is a voluntary task force and not

91 Under Article 21, para. 3, Member States must ensure that FIUs have full access, directly or indirectly and on a timely basis, to the financial, administrative and law enforcement information that they may require to properly execute their duties.

92 J.W.E Sheptycki, *Issues in Transnational Policing* (London: Routledge, 2000), pp. 136–50.

93 It was established by the G7 nations in July 1989 and its membership extends to 31 member countries, representing the advanced capitalist countries.

94 The detailed information about the FATF can be found on its website, available at www.oecd.org/fatf/40recs_en.htm (date accessed 7 April 2011). The FATF has supported the development of FATF-like bodies outside the European region, such as the Caribbean Financial Action Task Force, the Asia/Pacific Group on Money Laundering and the EAASAMLG.

95 It was basically designed to ensure that the financial system and institutions are not utilized for the purposes of money laundering and to consider additional preventive measures in this field.

a treaty organization; its 40 recommendations do not constitute a binding national convention but provide a guideline framework for combating money laundering.

Before 1989, few countries had explicit anti-money laundering laws. The creation of the FATF was influenced by the USA and France at the Paris Economic G7 Summit in 1989.[96] As far as the USA was concerned, the FATF would create another front to on which to fight the war on drugs. For other countries, it would provide a multilateral front on money laundering and indeed the FATF has established itself as a global anti-money laundering framework with the mandate to create global AML/CFT standards. Specifically, it provides a framework for analysing and keeping abreast of money laundering trends, but also streamlines the Basel Committee anti-money laundering regimes by issuing a list of 40 recommendations. These recommendations are updated regularly and it has a transnational reach on all matters of money laundering and combating the financing of terrorism.[97] Each of the 36 member nations furnishes information annually on the status of its domestic implementation of the 40+9 recommendations and submits to an onsite assessment by the FATF. Does this small membership of 36 countries mean that non-members are exempted from the FATF recommendations? The answer is no, because these recommendations have been co-opted by the World Bank and and IMF as conditions for borrowing from these agencies. Today, many countries are required by the World Bank and the IMF to apply the FATF revised 40+9 recommendations to demonstrate their preparedness to fight money laundering and its related predicate threats. Similarly, the FATF recommendations are essential as a global framework on money laundering.[98] In 1997, the FATF ad hoc group estimated the magnitude of money laundering by focusing its efforts on gathering data in relation to drug consumption, production and pricing.[99] Using an indirect approach in 1987, the UN had estimated drug trafficking worldwide to be US$300 billion, much of which would be laundered. Other estimates have been made at US$300–500 billion of 'dirty money' that is poured into the financial system each year, or roughly two per cent of global GDP.[100] Money laundering is influenced by the dynamics of globalization, such as porous land borders, the infrastructure of the Internet and a liberalized market economy.

Although the FATF recommendations were initially non-binding, some of them have become mandatory. For example, all member countries must

96 Michael Levi and Peter Reuter, *Money Laundering* (Chicago: Chicago University Press, 2006), p. 289. The G7 countries are Canada, France, Germany, Italy, Japan, the UK and the USA. See the FATF website at www.fatf-gafi.org (date accessed 1 December 2011).

97 Gilmore, *Dirty Money*, pp. 93–5.

98 The FATF has undergone successive revisions in 1990, 1999, 2003 and 2004, with each revision addressing a new threat in the fight against money laundering and the financing of terrorism.

99 Gilmore, *International Efforts to Combat Money Laundering*, pp. 5–10.

100 L.P. Raine and F.J. Cilluffo (eds), *Global Organized Crime: The Empire of Evil* (Washington DC: Center for Strategic and International Studies, 1994), p. 12.

criminalize money laundering and require financial institutions to implement vigilant KYC procedures and other necessary transparency procedures. However, FATF member countries take a political commitment to combat money laundering by implementing the recommendations. Besides the exercise of self-assessment and mutual evaluation, the FATF, in close collaboration with its members and other organizations, conducts regular typology exercises to uncover new money laundering techniques and to develop strategies for countering them.[101]

The FATF's anti-money laundering efforts encapsulated within its 40+9 recommendations relate to the enforcement of criminal laws and complementary measures in the financial sector, as well as international cooperation.[102] The recommendations that apply to law enforcement can be grouped into the following categories: (a) the criminalization of money laundering; (b) the seizure and confiscation of the proceeds of money laundering; (c) suspicious transaction reporting; and (d) international cooperation in the investigation, prosecution and extradition of suspects in money laundering-related crimes. Recommendations dealing with financial sector regulations relate primarily to customer identification and record-keeping requirements, which are commonly referred to as KYC standards.[103]

This chapter has examined the mandate of the FATF in three parts. First, the recommendations set out the general framework, justifying their adoption on the ground of the need for rapid tough action and practical measures.[104] In this context, the recommendations refer to the growing dimensions and the increasing awareness of the problem of money laundering which would justify a reinforcement of the Vienna Convention provisions in the field, as well as to avoid the risk of

---

101 Gilmore, *International Efforts to Combat Money Laundering*, p. 19.

102 The FATF has since assumed an active role in the implementation of the recommendations. W.C. Gilmore observes that this takes place in the following ways: the extension of money laundering predicate offences from drug offences to serious offences determined as such by each country (Recommendation 4); the application of appropriate measures in terms of the conducting of financial activities by non-bank financial business or professions (Recommendation 9); the application of appropriate measures to non-bank financial institutions, even those which are not subject to a formal prudential supervisory regime in all countries (Recommendation 8); the mandatory reporting of suspicious transactions (Recommendation 15); the consideration of further measures in respect of shell corporations, acknowledging their potential for abuse (Recommendation 25); the expansion of the recommendations dealing with customer identification (in particular Recommendations 10 and 13); in the same context, the proactive consideration of new technologies that might favour anonymity (Recommendation 13); the strengthening of measures in respect of *bureaux de change* (Recommendation 8); the introduction of measures relating to the cross-border movement of currency (Recommendation 22); and the utilization of controlled delivery operations in a money laundering context (Recommendation 36).

103 Recommendation 36.

104 Recommendation 3.

discrepancy between national measures, and a call to build upon and enhance the Basel Statement of Principles and to proceed towards harmonization of practical aspects not covered.[105] Secondly, the recommendations are devoted to the general improvement of the national legal system to combat money laundering.[106] Article 5 attempts to extend the definition of money laundering by calling for an extension of the scope of the offence to 'any other crimes for which there is a link to narcotics, or, alternatively, to criminalise money laundering based on all serious offences, and/or on all serious offences that generate proceeds of or on certain serious offences. The third part constitutes the cornerstone of the FATF initiative, aims at the enhancement of the role of the financial system',[107] their scope extending to bank and non-bank financial institutions.[108] The institutions concerned are called upon to comply with a series of duties, which are covered below.

The Customer Identification Requirement

Financial institutions[109] are required to satisfy themselves as to the identity of 'their customers', whether they are dealing with occasional or usual customers. Identification must be established by official or any other satisfactory documents.[110] This requirement aims to ensure that the financial system is not used as a channel for criminal funds. As such, the institutions have to make reasonable efforts to determine the true identity of all customers requesting their services. According to this requirement, banks are no longer allowed to hold anonymous accounts. In this case, the bank needs to satisfy itself as to the independence and reliability of information relating to third persons. Particular care is taken in identifying the ownership of all accounts and those using safe custody facilities.

Where the institution suspects that the customer is just a nominee account holder, for example, holding an account on behalf of another, or where the account holder is a company, it must satisfy itself as to the identity of the principals on

105 Mitsilegas, *Money Laundering Counter-Measures in the European Union.*

106 Recommendations 4–8.

107 Recommendations 9–29.

108 Recommendation 9.

109 These are persons or entities whose activities include: lending; financial leasing; transfer of money or value; trading in foreign exchange, derivatives, securities, commodities, futures and the like; life insurance and other investment-related insurance.

110 Before opening accounts, the financial institutions should undertake customer due diligence to ensure that no anonymous or fictitious accounts are opened. Documents like passports, photo-card driving licences and at least two recent utility bills should be obtained for the purposes of ascertaining the identity of natural persons. In the case of artificial persons, proof of incorporation or similar proof to establish legal status, the identity of directors, trustees or partners and proof of authority from which they derive power to bind such persons are required.

whose behalf the accounts are conducted.[111] Likewise, ongoing due diligence should be conducted relating to the transactions undertaken at the behest of the customer to ensure that information submitted by the customer is consistent. It is imperative that the source of the funds is legitimate and checks should be made and evidence procured to make certain that this is the case.[112] Enhanced due diligence and monitoring is necessary for politically exposed persons as there are prominent public figures who may abuse their positions. While dealing with cross-border correspondent banks or other cross-border firms, additional due diligence measures should be undertaken, which include: (i) understanding the business of the correspondent institution; (ii) determining that it has rigorous money laundering checks and regulatory supervision in place; and (iii) ascertaining if any money laundering investigation was carried out against it.[113] Records on the customer and the transaction should be maintained for the minimum of five years. This is necessary to provide a paper trail to the authorities in case they need to take legal action against the customer for any criminal activity.[114] The transaction should be examined in detail, especially those which are complex for no apparent reason. Customer due diligence and record keeping are also applicable to designated non-financial business and professionals in the following situations: casinos, when the transactions are equal to or above the applicable designated threshold; real estate agents in transactions involving the buying and selling of real estate; dealers in precious metals and precious stones regarding cash transactions equal to or above the designated threshold; lawyers, notaries or other independent legal professionals and accountants with respect to transactions involving the buying and selling of real estate; the management of client money securities or other assets; the management of bank, savings or securities accounts; and the organization of contributions for the creation, operation or management of companies. It also involves the creation, operation or management of legal persons or arrangements and the buying and selling of business entities. To counter all this, institutions are advised to build internal controls in their systems and to ensure adequate compliance management and employee training policies which do not restrict employee disclosure of suspicious activities.[115]

---

111 This is done in line with Recommendation 15 of the FATF Recommendations 1989.

112 Rashmi Sharma, *Due Diligence and Money Laundering* (Leeds: EMIS Professional Publishing Ltd, 2005), pp. 4–6.

113 Ibid.

114 Ibid.

115 Anu Arora, 'Money Laundering Regulation', Finance and Credit Law, C *Informa Professional (2005)*.

Compliance with the Law

Those in charge of banks should ensure that business is conducted in conformity with high ethical standards, ensuring that laws and regulations pertaining to financial transactions are adhered to. As regards transactions executed on behalf of customers, it is accepted that banks may have no means of knowing whether the transaction stems from or forms part of criminal activity. In an international context, it may be difficult to ensure that cross-border transactions are in compliance with the regulations of another country. Nevertheless, banks should not set out to offer a service or provide active assistance in transactions that they have good reason to suspect are associated with money laundering activities. They should cooperate fully with national law enforcement authorities to the extent permitted by specific local regulations relating to customer confidentiality. Care should be taken at the initial transaction stage to avoid providing support or assistance to customers seeking to deceive law enforcement agencies through the provision of altered, incomplete or misleading information.

Financial Transaction Reporting (FTR)

Most jurisdictions which have money-laundering regulations in place require financial institutions, designated non-financial institutions and professionals to have a fully-fledged anti-money laundering officer.[116] Employees are required to report suspicious activities to the money laundering officer, who will then take it up with the FIU. Employees are required to receive appropriate training on anti-money laundering procedures on suspicious transactions and reporting lines.[117] The recommendation states that: 'Financial Institutions should pay special attention to all complex, unusual or large transactions, and unusual patterns of transactions, which have no apparent economic or visible lawful purpose.' Banks should examine the background and the intentions behind such transactions to the fullest extent possible, and they should record their findings in writing in order to assist the relevant authorities.[118] If financial institutions suspect that funds are connected to criminal activity, 'they should be permitted or required to report promptly their

116 Section 340 of the POCA 2002, one of the UK's anti-money laundering regimes, requires financials institutions to make disclosure to designated anti-money laundering persons in a regulated sector.

117 It is a defence for an employee who fails to report any suspicious transaction due to not knowing that the transaction was actually suspicious. Conversely, employers who fail to train their employees on money laundering may be prosecuted.

118 Directorate For Financial, Fiscal and Enterprise Affairs, OECD (FATF Money Laundering Report 11 (B), 1990).

suspicions to the competent authorities'.[119] To promote this reporting duty, the recommendation suggests that financial institutions should be immune from civil and criminal liability when they make such reports in good faith.[120] For example, recommendation 14 states that: 'Financial Institutions should maintain, for at least five years, all necessary records on transactions, both domestic and international, to enable them to comply swiftly with information requests from the competent authorities. Such records must be sufficient to permit reconstruction of individual transactions (including the amount and type of currency involved, if any) so as to provide, if necessary, evidence for prosecution of criminal behaviour.'[121]

Sanction Mechanisms for Non-Compliant Member States

In 1996, the FATF adopted a formalized policy of issuing sanctions to members that failed to translate its 40 recommendations into practice.[122] The FATF sanction policy consists of a series of graduated steps designed to pressure member countries into enacting the reforms necessary to achieve compliance. The initial steps include the issuing of a letter from the FATF President to the non-complying governments and the dispatch of a special delegation led by the FATF President to the country concerned. More serious measures include urging financial institutions worldwide to scrutinize all business relations and transactions with persons, companies and financial institutions domiciled in the relevant country under the provisions of recommendation 21[123] and ultimately to suspend the respective country from the FATF.[124] The FATF has invoked the most severe sanction underpinned by its rules, in particular recommendation 21, on two occasions. The first case involved the government of Turkey in 1996, after exhausting all other means to encourage the government of Turkey to enact legislation criminalizing money laundering and to take other measures necessary to adhere to the 40 recommendations. The FATF issued a press release cautioning financial institutions in respect of transactions with persons or businesses domiciled in Turkey.[125] The public shame that was created by the statement and the Turkish government's aspirations to become a

119 Ingo Walter, *The Secret Money Market: Inside the Dark World of Tax Evasion, Financial Fraud, Insider Trading, Money Laundering, and Capital Flight* (London: HarperCollins, 1990), p. 157.

120 Ibid.

121 Mitsilegas, *Money Laundering Counter-Measures in the European Union*, pp 23–30.

122 Directorate for Financial, Fiscal and Enterprise Affairs, 'OECD, Financial Action Task Force on Money Laundering', 1996–7 (FATF Report VII above).

123 Recommendation 21 in Appendix 1 and perhaps also the Explanatory Notes for the same recommendation thereto.

124 FATF Report VII, pp. 109–93.

125 'FATF on Money Laundering Issues a Statement about Lack of Anti-Money Laundering Law in Turkey', OECD press release of 19 September 1996.

member of the EU led Turkey to enact a law making money laundering a criminal offence and to implement other mandatory FATF recommendations.[126] The second time that the FATF invoked its sanctions was in June 2002 against Austria. Austria was already under investigation by the European Commission when in 1999 FATF began to investigate Austrian bank secrecy laws. The FATF investigations exposed Austria to negative publicity in a period when it was under international scrutiny because of the investigation of the right-wing Freedom Party in its governing coalition. On 3 February 2000, the FATF threatened the ultimate sanctions against a member country – including the threat of suspension from the FATF – unless Austria fulfilled two conditions. It asked Austria to make a clear statement that all necessary steps to eliminate the system of anonymous passbook accounts in accordance with the 40 recommendations would be taken by June 2002. It also required Austria to introduce the bill prohibiting the opening of anonymous passbook accounts and to eliminate existing anonymous accounts. The Austrian government responded in June 2000 by stating that it would conform completely to the FATF's demands.[127] On 7 June 2000, the First Chamber of the Australian Parliament adopted an amendment to the Banking Act which would lead to the elimination of anonymous passbook savings accounts. The measure adopted by the Austrian government addressed the concerns of the FATF and significantly enhanced the Austrian anti-money laundering programme.[128]

Although the FATF does not have the formal authority to issue sanctions against governments of non-member countries, it may nevertheless apply Recommendation 21 to financial institutions operating in non-member jurisdictions that have not complied with the FATF recommendations. For example, it may require its members to impose restrictions on financial institutions that operate in non-complying offshore jurisdictions. The FATF threatened this course of action in the case of the government of the Seychelles, which had enacted a law designed to facilitate money laundering.[129] The FATF admonition drew a great deal of international media attention, prompting some governments to issue statements of their own condemning the same law.[130] The ensuing international pressure forced the government of the Seychelles to enact another piece of legislation effectively rescinding the EDA.

The FATF has taken the work of the Basel Committee much further by stressing the importance of requiring its member to implement its standards. In

126 'FATF on Money Laundering Welcomes New Anti-Money Laundering Laws in Turkey', OECD press release, 1 February 1996.

127 'FATF on Money Laundering Welcomes Proposed Austrian Legislation to Eliminate Anonymous Passbook', OECD press release, 15 June 2000.

128 Mitsilegas, *Money Laundering Counter-Measures in the European Union.*

129 'FATF on Money Laundering Condemns New Investment Law in the Seychelles', OECD press release, 12 December 1996.

130 G. Graham, 'Seychelles Condemned over Money Launderers Charter', *Financial Times*, 2 February 1996.

1991, it issued a statement indicating that its members had agreed to a process of mutual assessment to ensure that the 40 recommendations were being put into practice.[131] The members also agreed to expand the membership of the FATF and to influence non-member jurisdictions to follow the 40 recommendations.[132] Thus, the significant work of the FATF is devoted to promoting compliance with the 40 recommendations and to cultivating an anti-money laundering infrastructure.[133] Therefore, as part of its mandate, the FATF conducts onsite peer evaluation of its members' adherence to the 40 recommendations.[134] An evaluation team comprising legal, regulatory and law enforcement experts from member states visits the relevant country and conducts a thorough review of the anti-money laundering infrastructure. The findings are published in a report, which is reviewed internally by the FATF membership.[135] The FATF also provides guidelines for identification of those jurisdictions that did not cooperate in taking measures against money laundering so as to encourage them to implement international anti-money laundering standards adopted by the FATF.[136] This process involves the use of 25 criteria against which to identify detrimental rules and practices that impede international cooperation in the fight against money laundering. These include loopholes in financial regulations that allow no or inadequate supervision of financial institutions, weak licensing or customer identification requirements, excessive financial secrecy provisions or a lack of suspicious transaction reporting systems. There is also the issue of weak commercial regulations in relation to the identification of beneficial ownership and registration of business entities, obstacles to international cooperation, both in administrative and judicial items, and inadequate resources for preventing, detecting and repressing money laundering.[137]

As part of the review process,[138] the FATF established four regional groups to begin the process of considering the position in a number of jurisdictions, both within and outside the FATF's membership.[139] In June 2000, the FATF

---

131 FATF Report VII above, *note, 129.*

132 At the 1990 summit in Houston, all member countries were invited to participate in the fight against money laundering and to implement the recommendations of FATF. See FATF Report (1990), *note* 130.

133 Ibid.

134 Ibid.

135 Gilmore, *Dirty Money*.

136 FATF Report, Feb., 2000, above, *note, 130.*

137 FATF Report on Non Co-operative Countries and Territories, 14 February 2000, pp. 4–7.

138 The FATF agenda has proved a powerful instrument of reform because within 10 years of its inception, its membership has grown to 26 countries, three observer countries and two international organizations.

139 There is one in Africa, the Caribbean, the Middle East and Asia. These regional FATF groups are meant to coordinate efforts on money laundering within the context of their respective regions.

established the names of all non-cooperative countries. These include Andorra, Anguilla, Aruba, the Bahamas, Barbados, the British Virgin Islands, the Maldives, the Marshall Islands, Monaco, Montserrat, Nauru, Samoa, St Lucia, St Kitts and Nevis, St Vincent, the Turks and Caicos Islands and Vanuatu.[140] The FATF works closely with other international agencies (for example, the World Bank, IMF and the UN General Assembly) to ensure its recommendations are easily coordinated and implemented.

The Interplay between the FATF and the UN General Assembly

It should be noted that the sanction mechanisms established by the FATF are further strengthened by the nine UN General Assembly Resolutions adopted in 2001. In an extraordinary plenary in Washington DC (October 2001), the FATF adopted a resolution extending its mandate to countering the financing of terrorism.[141] This was in response to a series of terrorist attacks, including in Kenya and Tanzania (1998) and later in the USA on 11 September 2001. It would now work closely with other agencies including the UN Security Council to bring the enforcement of countering the financing of terrorism under Chapter VII of the UN Charter. Similarly, states would no longer have to treat the FATF recommendations as non-binding soft law regimes – they would also be required to pass domestic legislation translating the nine special recommendations on the financing of terrorism at home. The UN Security Council would treat the financing of terrorism as a security threat within the purview of Article 39 of the UN Charter1945.[142] The respective state's failure to cooperate with its obligations under the UN Charter could justify the invocation of both economic and military sanctions under Articles 40 and 41 of the UN Charter.[143] It is therefore essential to explore the remit of the UN General Assembly resolutions on countering the financing of terrorism.

The UN General Assembly Resolutions

After the simultaneous bombing of the US embassies in Kenya and Tanzania by terrorists in 1998, the UN Security Council adopted two special resolutions,

140 Mitsilegas, *Money Laundering Counter-Measures in the European Union.*

141 www.oecd.org/fatf/terFinance_enhtm_documents (date accessed 15 November 2011).

142 The UN Security Council shall determine the existence of any threat to the peace, breach of the peace or act of aggression and shall make recommendations, or decide what measures shall be taken in accordance with Articles 41 and 42 to maintain or restore international peace and security.

143 Sanctions are an important tool to enable the Security Council to exert pressure on a country which has failed to comply with its obligations under the UN Charter (1945).

1267 and 1373 (1999), as provisional measures taken under Article 40 of the UN Charter.[144] These resolutions were specifically adopted to undermine the efforts of terrorists through the financial sector. The International Convention for the Suppression of the Financing of Terrorism (December 1999) defines the primary objective of terrorism as 'to intimidate a population, to compel a government or an international organization to do or to abstain from doing an Act'.[145] While this definition does not have money laundering as it is primary target, the underlying logic is that the cutting of terrorist funding has the potential to undermine terrorist operations wherever they are planned, interrupting the flow of arms and materials to terrorist groups, their ability to train and travel, as well as cutting off other logistics.

States should now ensure that financial institutions implement the sanction regimes adopted by the UN General Assembly. Resolution 1267 imposes a wide range of sanctions against the Taliban regime in Afghanistan for activities relating to providing sanctuary and training to international terrorists.[146] Specifically, Resolution 1267 required UN member countries to freeze funds and other financial resources (including property owned or controlled by the Taliban) as designated by a committee established under Resolution 1267.[147] UN Resolution 1333 (2000) relates to the asset freezing of members of the Taliban regime, Osama bin Laden and any persons associated with him, including Al-Qaeda, as designated by the 1267 Committee of the UN General Assembly. The term 'associated' is used to refer to acts or activities indicating that an individual, undertaking or entity is associated with Osama Bin Laden, Al-Qaeda and the Taliban. This includes, although is not limited to, the following:

> Participating in the financing, planning, facilitating, preparing or perpetuating acts or activities by, in conjunction with, under the name of, on behalf of, or in support of; Supplying, selling or transferring arms or related materials to;
>
> Recruiting for or
>
> Otherwise supporting the acts or activities of Osama Bin Laden, the Al-Qaida organisation and the Taliban or any cells, affiliate sprinter group or derivative thereof.[148]

144 The countering the financing of terrorism framework is underscored by the UN Convention for the Suppression of the Financing of Terrorism (1999).

145 Doug Hopton, *Money Laundering: A Concise Guide for all Businesses* (Aldershot: Ashgate, 2005), p. 6.

146 William Blair and Richard Brent, *Banks and Financial Crimes: The International Law of Tainted Money* (Oxford: Oxford University Press, 2008), pp. 63–70.

147 S/RES/1999, para. 4(b).

148 Ibid.

In order to make the above resolutions easily to implement within member countries, the UN Security Council adopted Resolution 1363, which was adopted on 30 July 2001. This resolution creates mechanisms for implementing Resolutions 1267 and 1333, including establishing a monitoring group of five experts, reporting to the 1267 Committee, and the sanctions enforcement support team of 15 experts under the monitoring group. In order for the above resolutions to function properly, Resolution 1363 required member countries to enforce and strengthen Resolutions 1267 and 1333 of the UN General Assembly. UN Security Council Resolution 1390, adopted on 16 January 2002, required member countries to *inter alia* freeze without delay any funds and financial assets of Osama bin Laden, members of the Al-Qaida organization and the Taliban regime, and other persons and entities associated with them, as designated in the list by Resolution 1267 committee pursuant to the earlier UN General Assembly Resolutions 1267 and 1333.

However, the delegates recognized that the wholesale application of anti-terrorist measures would have a counter-productive effect and exemptions were necessary. The UN General Assembly Resolution 1452, adopted on 20 December 2002, creates provisions for member countries to exempt certain funds and other financial assets or economic resources, notably those necessary for basic expenses (such as payment for food, mortgages, medicines, medical treatment, etc.). UN General Assembly Resolution 1455, adopted on 17 January 2003, calls upon member countries to *inter alia* take urgent measures, both legislative and administrative, against nations, other individuals or entities operating in their territory to prevent and punish violations of the asset freezing provisions under Resolutions 1267, 1333 and 1390. These would have far-reaching consequences for banks that failed to honour their obligations under Resolution 1267 in particular. Furthermore, under UN Resolution 1526, adopted on 30 January 2004, member countries were required to cut the flow of funds and other financial assets or economic resources to persons and entities associated with Osama bin Laden, the Al-Qaida organization and the Taliban, taking into account appropriate international codes and standards for combating the financing of terrorism. This would include those designed to prevent the abuse of non-profit or charitable organizations and alternative remittance systems. Member countries were urged to implement comprehensive international anti-money laundering standards embodied in the FATF 40+9 recommendations. This requirement is provided by UN Resolution 1617, adopted on 29 July 2005. This resolution to a large extent reiterates the obligations of member countries relating to persons and entities associated with Osama Bin Laden, the Al-Qaida organization and the Taliban regime in Afghanistan.

There was also a need to adopt another resolution, UN Resolution 1730, which was adopted on 19 December 2006, that would further streamline the sanction mechanisms against designated persons. This resolution was passed after a request from the UN Secretary-General and requires member countries to establish Security Council subsidiary organs as focal points to coordinate the operations of different committees. These focal points would receive delisting requests from persons and entities listed by various sanction committees of the UN Security Council, including the Resolution 1267 Committee, and for these to be incorporated by the sanction committee into their own procedures. Finally, Resolution 1735, adopted on 22 December 2006, provided clarification on the following points:

- information to be provided on the proposed persons and entities for inclusion in the consolidated list, including identifying those parts of the information that can be publicly published;
- setting out requirements in relation to delisting from the consolidated list, specifically as to whether there was a mistake in the original inclusion of the person or entities or whether the person or entity continues to meet the criteria for inclusion as set out in Resolution 1617;
- providing mechanisms for delisting those people or entities that had severed links with Osama bin Laden, the Al-Qaida organization and the Taliban regime. These moves would help the international community in fighting money laundering and financing of terrorism.

Furthermore, the FATF also works closely with the Wolfsberg Group in offering guidelines and principles of best banking practice in relation to money laundering and countering the financing of terrorism. The Wolfsberg Group first issued its principles in October 2000 and these have subsequently been revised to reflect desired changes.

The Wolfsberg Group

The Wolfsberg Group is an association of 11 international banks whose mandate includes developing financial services industry standards and related products for KYC and AML/CFT policies.[149] The Group was established in 2000, at the Château Wolfsberg in north-eastern Switzerland, in the company of representatives from Transparency International whilst working on drafting anti-money laundering guidelines for private banking.[150] The Group published a series of papers on the financing of terrorism as well as on anti-money laundering principles for correspondent banking and the Wolfsberg Statement on Monitoring Screening and

149 This Group consists of the following leading international financial institutions: Banco Santander, Bank of Tokyo-Mitsubishi-UFJ Ltd, Barclays, City Group, Credit Suisse, Deutsche Bank, Goldman Sachs, HSBC, JP Morgan Chase, Société Générale and UBS. Detailed information about the Wolfsberg Group can be found on its website: www.wolfsberg-principles.com (date accessed 1 December 2011).

150 The Wolfsberg Anti-Money Laundering Principles for Private Banking were subsequently published in October 2000 (and revised in May 2002). The Group has just recently issued a paper offering guidelines on international trade finance (2011).

Searching. In 2004, the Group focused on the development of a due diligence model for financial institutions in cooperation with Bankers Almanac, thereby fulfilling one of the recommendations made in the correspondent banking principles.[151]

The Wolfsberg Group has issued guidelines on anti-money laundering, all of which aim to provide guidance on a number of areas of banking activity where standards had yet to be fully articulated by lawmakers or regulators. The published papers are always intended to provide guidelines and assistance to industry participants and regulatory bodies in relation to shaping their own policy measures on combating money laundering/the financing of terrorism.[152]

In 2007, the Wolfsberg Group, working in tandem with Transparency International and the Basle Institute on Governance, issued a guideline paper on corruption. Transparency International describes the role of the Wolfsberg Group and financial institutions as crucial in supporting international efforts towards combating corruption. The statement against corruption articulates measures that financial institutions may consider in order to prevent corruption in their own operations and to protect themselves against the misuse of financial institutions. The Wolfsberg Group has also issued a statement endorsing measures to enhance the transparency of international wire transfers in order to promote the effectiveness of global anti-money laundering and anti-terrorist financing programmes. In short, the statements or papers published by the Wolfsberg Group offer guidelines to banks, particularly on various challenges relating to money laundering and the financing of terrorism.[153]

It is also essential here to explore the influence of other international institutions which actively help to foster a robust global AML/CFT framework. These institutions include but are not limited to the FIUs (the Egmont Group), the FSF, the World Bank and the IMF. In view of this, this chapter also explores the mandate of the FIUs in spearheading the fight against money laundering/the financing of terrorism.

---

151 It also issued a statement, 'The Wolfsberg Statement on AML Screening and Searching' (2009).

152 It issued a paper in June 2006 consisting two sets of guidance: 'Guidance on a Risk-Based Approach for Managing Money Laundering Risks and AML Guidance for Mutual Funds and Other Pooled Investment Vehicles'. It also published guidelines on 'AML Issues in the Context of Investment and Commercial Banking and Correspondent Banking, which Complement the other Sets of Guidelines on Beneficial Ownership, Politically Exposed Persons'.

153 See the Wolfsberg Group website: www.wolfsberg-principles.com (date accessed 1 December 2011).

FIUs: The Egmont Group

The Egmont Group was set up in 1995 under the sponsorship of the FATF, with the membership consisting of FIUs from 80 jurisdictions. It derives its name from the venue in Brussels where the first meeting of the FIUs was held in June 1995. The FIUs are responsible for receiving, analysing and disseminating the disclosure of financial information concerning the suspected proceeds of crime in order to counter money laundering.[154] The Group fosters communication among FIUs, has a secure website for sharing information and has produced a model information agreement. This information is then passed on to the appropriate government authorities for further action. The Group recently complied a list of 100 cases handled by FIUs around the world. The most common indicator of money laundering offences as identified by the Group are as follows: large-scale cash transactions; unusual underlying business transactions (cross-border travel in order to undertake simple transactions); unrealistic business turnover; large and/or rapid transfer of funds; unrealistic wealth compared to the client's profile; unusually high rates of return for low-risk business activities; unrealistic explanations given by customers for account activity; unwarranted high-security risk-personal transfer of valuable assets; new customers attempting large transactions with no supporting rationale; unusually complex methods of purchasing financial products involving deposits at a variety of branches and times for no logical reason (possible evidence of smurfing); the re-emergence of known financial criminals in the financial services sector; attempts to avoid the identification of the final beneficiaries of accounts; complex fund structures; possible client involvement in previous crimes; the identification of false documents; suspicious activity of client associates; the deliberate concealment of fund ownership; change of account behaviour without explanation; multiple amounts paid into personal accounts without explanation; transfer of assets at well below (or above) the market rate; over-complex fund movements; multiple transactions below the reporting threshold (€15,000 or £10,000); illogical business activity, for example, sending multiple cheques for cashing at a higher charge; the multiple use of money transmission services; and unconnected parties channelling funds to a single account.[155] The Group also provides technical assistance in setting up and running the FIUs. It does this work in collaboration with other agencies such as the FSF.

---

154 Rashmi Sharma, Financial Stability Forum (FSF), available on the internet at: www.fsforum.org/home/home.html (date accessed 15 December 2007).

155 Ibid.

The Finanical Stability Forum (FSF)

The FSF was convened in 1999 to promote international stability through information exchange and international cooperation.[156] In March and April 2000, the FSF Working Group on offshore financial centres (OFCs) issued a report on the role of OFCs with respect to global financial stability.[157] It is comprised of national authorities (central bank, prudential regulators and government representatives), international organizations (for example, the IMF) and international regulatory organizations, such as the Basel Committee.[158] It is important to reiterate that the underpinning objectives of the Basel Committee were to promote and coordinate international financial stability, improving the functioning of markets as well as reducing systemic risks.[159] Among the integrity standards, four are relevant to money laundering, including access to sharing financial information and generating transparency of ownership structures. The FSF also published a classification of OFCs in terms of the perceived quality of supervision and the degree of cooperation, in part to establish the priority jurisdiction for assessment. The FSF has called on the IMF to take responsibility for developing, organizing and carrying out a process for assessment of the adherence of OFCs and other standards.[160] There are many more organizations in this regard,[161] but for our purposes the FIUs, OFCs, the World Bank and the IMF are the most notable ones.

The World Bank and the IMF

The World Bank and the IMF undertake wide programmes that encapsulate promoting stronger financial, economic and legal systems internationally.[162] Both of these institutions encourage financial institutions to adopt robust supervisory standards and legal and institutional frameworks to prevent financial sector abuse. The IMF surveillance function under Article IV of the Articles of Agreement involves intensive exchange with each member country on its economic and

156 Ibid.

157 Ibid.

158 Rhys Bollen, 'The International Financial System and Future Global Regulation', *Journal of International Banking Law* (2000): p. 462.

159 Rashmi Sharma, Financial Stability Forum (FSF), available on the internet at: www.fsforum.org/home/home.html (date accessed 15 December 2007).

160 OFC concerns were discussed by the Executive Board on 10 July 2000, available at www.financialstabilityboard.org/ (date accessed 1 December 2011).

161 There is the Inter-American Drug Abuse Control Commission (CICAD); the Offshore Group of Banking Supervisors (OGBS); the United Nations Drug Control Programmes (UNDCP); and the International Money Laundering Information Network (IMoLN).

162 Bollen, 'The International Financial System and Future Global Regulation'.

financial systems.[163] The IMF staff will examine the economic and legal system of the member country to identify potential vulnerabilities and advise it to take corrective measures and polices. The IMF has adopted several discrete initiatives designed to strengthen the financial stability and to prevent global crises.[164] In 1999, the IMF, together with the World Bank, adopted Financial Sector Assessment Programmes (FSAPs) as a centrepiece for inquiring into the health and stability of member countries. The mandate of both the World Bank and the IMF will cover the country's banks, securities, money markets, foreign exchange and payment systems as well as assessing regulatory, supervisory and legal frameworks of financial institutions.[165] It is this work of the World Bank and the IMF which has relevance to fighting money laundering and its related predicate offences. By undertaking a regulatory assessment programme to establish any vulnerability in the system, states are subsequently advised to take desired corrective measures.

It should be noted that the World Bank and the IMF play a fundamental normative role of promoting an anti-money laundering environment by encouraging financial sector reforms within individual countries.[166] The IMF helps national authorities to strengthen their supervisory and regulatory systems, which in turn helps to promote the safety and soundness of the financial sector and to create an environment that prevents financial system abuse.[167] In order for states to attract foreign direct investment (FDI), they are required to adopt a robust legal system that guarantees the interests of investors. Thus, the World Bank and the IMF impose conditions on many countries so that they demonstrate a realistic effort to internationalize and align their economies to normative international standards. Countries are asked to implement the Basel Capital Accord in order to qualify for financial assistance and as part of World Bank and IMF FSAPs.[168] As part of the financial sector reforms, international financial institutions (IFIs) monitor the observance of international standards, codes and best practice in the areas of financial supervision, prudential regulation, transparency of fiscal and monetary policies, and data provision and dissemination in order to foster financial and market integrity.[169] Therefore,

163 William E. Holder, 'The International Monetary Fund's Involvement in Combating Money Laundering and Financing of Terrorism', 6(4) *Journal of Money Laundering Control* (2003): p. 383.

164 Ibid.

165 Ibid.

166 Under the existing IMF policies, anti-money laundering issues other than those relating to financial sector regulation and supervision are covered under surveillance and conditionality, as with other governance matters. See the 1997 Guidance Note on Funds Experience in Governance Issues (Executive Board Meeting 01/14 February 2001), available at www.imf.org (date accessed 1 December 2011). The monitoring and surveillance function of the Bank is supported by Article IV of the Articles of Agreement.

167 See the IMF policy paper, 'Enhancing Contributions to Combating Money Laundering', available at www.imf.org (date accessed 1 December 2011).

168 Ibid.

169 Ibid.

international financial institutions have engineered the adjustment of laws and systems to the level of prescribed international standards on money laundering.[170]

Technically, the World Bank and the IMF have assisted countries in identifying and addressing structural and institutional bottlenecks that contribute to a lack of market integrity and the potential for financial abuse.[171] It participates in targeted international efforts to combat money laundering based on its mandate and expertise.[172] These institutions have helped countries to put in place strong economic, financial and legal foundations as their principal contribution towards the fight against financial abuse. The World Bank's technical assistance is geared towards reorganizing customs and institutions, developing transparent and effective treasury departments, spearheading procurement and auditing reforms within governments.[173] Public education efforts and training programmes in investigative journalism, accounting and auditing can be offered support by the international community support fund operated by the World Bank.[174]

In light of these challenges, the World Bank has initiated tailored programmes in areas of anti-corruption, good governance and public financial management.[175] It has supported more than 600 lending and non-lending activities in approximately 90 countries aimed at stimulating institutional reforms needed to reduce corruption and strengthen governance.[176] These include, for example, adaptable programme loans and technical assistance operations designed to enhance capacity and reform incentives in the civil service (including employees of financial regulatory services), reforms in public sector management systems and, in tax and customs administration, strengthened legal, judicial and regulatory reforms, as well

170 For the detailed reading on the role of the World Bank and the IMF in promoting the desired anti-money laundering framework, see N. Mugarura, 'The Mechanisms for Harmonisation of Global Anti-Money Laundering Laws: An Institutional Framework', *ExpressO* (2010): pp. 1–33.

171 See the 'Strategy for the Financial Sector: Draft Report (R2000-169) August 19, 2000', in a paper by the World Bank Board of Executive Directors on 19 October 2000, available at www.worldbank.org (date accessed 1 December 2011).

172 The World Bank and the IMF work in collaboration with the FATF, OECD and IOSCO in bolstering the financial supervisory regimes.

173 Beare (ed.), *Critical Reflections on Transnational Organised Crime, Money Laundering and Corruption*, p. 99.

174 Susan Rose-Ackerman, 'Economics of Corruption in Developed Countries, a Review of Issues', Working Paper, Berkeley: Centre for International and Development Economics Research, February 1996.

175 For more detailed information on the Bank's governance, anti-corruption and public sector reform programs, see 'Helping Countries Combat Corruption: Progress in the Bank since 1997', September 2000, and 'Reforming Public Institutions and Strengthening Governance: A World Bank Strategy Paper', November 2000, available at www.worldbank.org (date accessed 1 December 2011).

176 Ibid.

as encouraging reforms to establish mechanisms for combating public sector corruption.[177]

The World Bank has stepped up its efforts in several areas which underpin a robust market environment such as strengthening legal, judicial and institutional reforms, corporate governance, accounting and auditing as well as market transparency.[178] It particularly focuses its efforts on small states, which are susceptible to potential financial abuse, including money laundering, and assists them by putting in place the policy and institutional foundations specifically designed to reduce the risk of market abuse.[179] In relation to money laundering, the Bank supports legislation that outlaws anonymous banking accounts, improves of the KYC mandate, modifies secrecy legislation to verify the implementation of the KYC requirement and implements anti-money laundering regimes.[180] It has also encouraged and supported the introduction of banking laws and regulations, tax laws and regulations, the development of financial management through proper accounting and auditing systems, legal and judicial reforms for policy-based lending as well as reforms relating to economic and development issues.[181] In order to support the desired structural reforms, the Bank introduced the 'Institutional Development Fund' to provide grants for projects such as 'the preparation of new legislation, public procurement and associated training, or the carrying of studies to diagnose the problems inhibiting the proper functioning of the civil service and the judiciary'.[182] In my view, less developed countries should be given grants but not loans to support the development of an effective infrastructure to harness global initiatives. At the moment, a one-size-fits-all approach favours developed countries, which are naturally endowed with an environment where the envisaged AML/CFT standards can be easily implemented.

Conclusion

The terms 'global' and 'international' in relation to AML/CFT regimes can be used interchangeably – the difference simply being a matter of nomenclature. However, it would seem that global regimes are market-oriented as a result of the exigencies

177 Ibid.

178 The First Annual Small States Forum: Background Information Document, 25 September 2000, available at: www.worldbank.org/smallstates (date accessed 1 December 2011).

179 'Strategy Paper for the Financial Sector: Draft Final Report (R2000-169)', August 2000.

180 See www.worldbank.org (date accessed 1 December 2011).

181 Nancy Zucker Boswell, 'Combating Corruption: Focus on Latin America', 3 *SW. J. L. & TRADE AM.* (1996): pp. 179–89.

182 'The World Bank and Legal Technical Assistance', World Bank Policy Research Working Paper No. 1414, 1995, available at: www.worldbank.org (date accessed 1 December 2011).

of the global market system, while international regimes have evolved based on treaties or other sources of international law. International treaties adopted in relation to money laundering include but not are limited to the Vienna Convention, the Palermo Convention and the three EU Anti-Money Laundering Directives. As have already been demonstrated, the three Anti-Money Laundering Directives were adopted by the EU to transpose the UN anti-money laundering framework into its own system. However, the EU as a jurisdiction is uniquely singled out as part of the global anti-money laundering network because some aspects of it, such as the sanction mechanisms, have an extraterritorial reach. As a jurisdiction, the EU has its own specific sanctions regimes that are independent of the UN sanctions under Chapter VII of the UN Charter and hence qualifies it as part of the global AML/CFT framework. As regards the FATF and Basel Committee regimes on supervisory standards, these are market-oriented and would have evolved in response to the exigencies of the globalization of financial markets, especially in the G10 countries. These regimes are said to be ad hoc and adopted by developed G10 countries to protect their internal financial markets. However, the FATF and Basel regimes have been co-opted by the World Bank and the IMF as requirements for borrowing (lending conditionalities). As a matter of fact, market-oriented regimes have been criticized as undemocratic, given the way in which they evolve and are subsequently enforced globally.

Traditionally, AML/CFT regimes based on treaty provisions must be transposed by signatory states for them to generate a binding legal effect. Treaties are binding subject to ratification and are only effective once they have been transposed into substantive national law. The transposition of a treaty into substantive national law is a process where a member country's parliament adopts measures to transpose the treaty by way of passing enabling legislation. The transposition of a treaty will henceforth provide a framework for domestic courts to interpret and apply the envisaged treaty provisions. It is also important to note that in dualist countries, international treaties cannot generate direct effect at home until they have been transposed nationally. As regards monist countries like France, once treaties have been ratified, they become part of national law without recourse to further measures in parliament. It should be noted that the transposition of anti-money laundering model laws is dictated by many factors at a state level, not least national politics. Some states might refuse to transpose treaties on the grounds of national sovereignty and national self-interest. Some states might transpose treaties in a manner that either constricts the scope of their international obligations, while others might simply employ delaying tactics in the implementation of normative AML/CFT laws.

Soft law regimes, such as those developed by the Basel Committee Principles on Banking and the Supervision of Banks, and the recommendations of the FATF, are traditionally not meant to be legally binding. Soft laws are created more or less like guidelines, notwithstanding that some could have an element of enforceability, such as the FATF recommendations and the World Bank financial sector reforms. As guidelines, soft law norms are deemed essential in filling gaps in the law, providing guidelines on normative standards that could eventually create a basis for crystallization into hard law.[183] The FATF and the Basel Committee supervisory standards are now co-opted into the World Bank and IMF conditionalities for borrowing from the these agencies. The experience of some countries in domesticating global anti-money laundering standards clearly shows that prescribing regimes is one thing, but transposing and enforcing the same regimes locally is indeed another, which is dictated by many factors. This would seem to explain why there is a significant gap in the law of money laundering within and between regions, even though there is a global framework in place. It is possible that global regimes on any envisaged policy issues can be created by states or market domains if they so wish, but the enforcement and application of engendered regimes should always be pragmatic, taking into account the dynamics of development at a local level. Individual member countries must adopt adjustments based on the local dynamics of development so that global anti-money laundering regimes can work effectively locally. This is presumably the reason why some countries have not fully transposed measures against money laundering and its predicate offences such as terrorism.

While the focus of this chapter was to explore the global AML/CFT framework, there are also numerous bilateral treaties exclusively binding respective states. These treaties create regimes based on mutual legal assistance and the investigation and prosecution of crimes[184] and create individual frameworks for bilateral cooperation on matters such as extradition. These regimes are used to obtain and preserve evidence, but also to provide assistance and facilitate the confiscation of criminal proceeds and instrumentalities.[185] Mutual legal assistance treaties (MLATs) based on multilateral regimes have been criticized as being weak in specificity (for example, the Vienna Convention), the language used being little more than hortatory and key features such as forfeiture and freezing orders often being omitted. Besides, states have shown a tendency to transpose MLATs in a constricted way that further undermines their application. In view of these weaknesses, bilateral treaties are seen as more effective than MLATs. Lastly and obviously not least is that where there is a conflict between states with regard to the application of norms of international law and national law, the former would take precedence. This implies that much as states can enter into bilateral arrangements, they are still bound by their international obligations on parallel treaties or otherwise. Globalization and its dynamics have made the need for states to work together on overlapping global challenges such as money laundering more of an imperative. As a matter of fact, as regards money laundering and terrorism,

---

183 By this, we simply mean state practice.

184 Jimmy Gurule, 'The United Nations Convention Against Illicit Traffic in Narcotic Drugs and Psychotropic Substances – A Ten Year Perspective: Is International Cooperation Merely Illusory?', 22(74) *Fordham International Law Journal* (1998): pp 88–9.

185 For instance, the USA has entered into such treaties with countries like the Cayman Islands, Colombia, Mexico, Panama, Switzerland, Thailand and others.

states have appreciated a need for the global anti-money laundering paradigm reflecting the contemporary challenges to the international community.

Chapter 4
The Evolution of a Global Anti-Money Laundering Paradigm

Introduction

The primary purpose of this chapter is to demonstrate that the global anti-money laundering framework is not only necessary but is essential for states in relation to the threats posed by money laundering and the financing of terrorism. The global AML/CFT framework is vital, given the overlapping nature of money laundering and its related predicate crimes. In addition, the contemporary crime typologies are shaped and influenced by the dynamics of globalization. The interplay of globalization and money laundering is underscored by the dynamics of the global market economy such as porous land borders, ICT and its offshoot effects and the challenges posed by the liberalization of markets, especially on tenuous economies. Finally, this chapter examines the role played by domestic courts in fostering an environment for the transposition of a normative AML/CFT anti-money laundering framework.

The term 'money laundering' as already elucidated in the preceding chapter, indicates the practice of concealing assets to avoid any discovery of unlawful activities involved in their generation.[1] It connotes a process of manipulating legally or illegally acquired wealth in a way that obscures its existence, origin or ownership for the purpose of avoiding law enforcement.[2] Money laundering describes a deliberate, complicated and sophisticated process by which the proceeds of crime are camouflaged, disguised or made to appear as if they were earned by legitimate means.[3] It is a three-stage process initiated when the potential launderer severs the dirty money from the predicate crime generating it, followed by a series of transactions designed to obscure or destroy the money trail in order to foil pursuit and reinvesting the proceeds of crime in furtherance of the objectives of the launderer.[4] Money laundering[5] is described as 'the conversion or transfer of property; the concealment or disguise of its origin; its acquisition or possession

1 Nicholas Ryder, 'The Financial Services Authority and Money Laundering: A Game of Cat and Mouse', 67(3) *Cambridge Law Journal* (2008): p. 635.

2 Shams, *Legal Globalization*, p. 130.

3 Ibid.

4 Gilmore, 'International Action Against Drug Trafficking'.

5 See the Council Directive of 10 June 1991 on the prevention of the use of financial systems for the purposes of money laundering (91/308/EEC), OJ L 166, 28 June 1991, at 77.

or use; and the participation or association to commit, attempts to commit and aiding, abetting, facilitating and counselling the commission of any of the acts'.[6] It also involves conduct which in effect is similar to the offence of handling the proceeds of crime. The phrase 'money laundering' is said to have been first used in the 1930s.[7] However, it became a state-of-the-art term in the 1970s and gained prominence during the Watergate investigation in the USA in 1973–1974.[8] An extensive body of anti-money laundering laws starting proliferating from the 1970s onwards.

Given the transnational ethos of money laundering crimes and its consequent adverse effect on global markets, it has become an imperative for governments to create multilateral regimes against money laundering and its predicate crimes.[9] For example, the US BSA 1970 was passed as a response to drug trafficking in the USA and bank secrecy laws operated by offshore financial centres.[10] Technically, however, the BSA did not go far enough in forestalling the threat of drug trafficking globally because of its jurisdictional limits. Specifically, it was adopted to prevent criminals from using financial institutions in transmitting the illicit proceeds of crime. Hence, financial institutions would be required to keep records in relation to financial transactions such as cash purchases, to negotiable instruments and to file reports on transactions exceeding US$10,000 (daily aggregate). The US government would push for the adoption of the UN treaty to create an international framework on money laundering, which led to the creation of the Vienna Convention in 1988.[11]

The antecedents of the Vienna Convention were a series of General Assembly resolutions[12] where the concern over drug trafficking was expressly discussed by delegates from many national governments. Drug abuse and trafficking were viewed as of increasing concern in the international arena, which led to the General Assembly Resolution 39/141 of December 1984 entitled the 'Draft Convention against Trafficking in Narcotic Drugs and Psychotropic Substances'.[13] The securitization of drug abuse and trafficking through their conceptualization as a threat and prioritization of the adoption of counter-measures resulted in the call for

6 Gilmore, 'International Action against Drug Trafficking'.

7 J. Robinson, *The Laundrymen* (London: Verso, 1995), p. 12.

8 Shams, *Legal Globalization.*

9 Initially Money Laundering regimes were limited to proceeds of drug trafficking but in the post Vienna (1988) era this changed to encompass a range of offences.

10 Shams, *Legal Globalization.*

11 Gilmore, 'International Action against Drug Trafficking'.

12 This is set out in the third preamble of General Assembly Resolution 35/195, where the issue of drug abuse was expressed as an issue of major concern by delegates of many national governments.

13 See 'The UN Economic and Social Council, Implementation and Development of International Instruments on the Control of Narcotic Drugs and Psychotropic Substances', a report of the Secretary-General, DOC.E/CN. 7/1987/2 of 17 June 1986, at 2.

a specialized conference[14] to deal with the issue. Adopting a similar securitization discourse, the then UN Secretary-General[15] stated that existing resources were inadequate to deal with the drug plague, which was contaminating, corrupting and weakening the very fabric of society.[16]

In December 2000, the Palermo Convention and its attendant three protocols were adopted. The Palermo Convention not only supersedes the Vienna Convention in its definitional limits of money laundering, but it also creates four additional specific crimes: participation in organized criminal groups, money laundering, corruption and obstruction of justice. In addition, it establishes modalities for the extradition of wanted criminals: through mutual legal assistance, law enforcement and cooperation in the area of information exchange.[17] The 1996–1997 survey by the FATF[18] on money laundering measures noted that along with drug trafficking, financial crimes (bank fraud,[19] credit card fraud, investment fraud, advance fee fraud, bankruptcy, fraud, embezzlement, etc.) were the most frequently mentioned sources of the proceeds of crime.[20] The EU Council of Ministers approved the revisions of the EU's Anti-Money Laundering Directives, aligning it to necessary changes in Europe.[21] The Second Anti-Money Laundering Directive broadens the definition of targeted criminal activity from drug offences (as per the original Directive) to include proceeds from other crimes.[22] Many countries have now

14 Anderson, *Policing the World*, pp. 41–2.

15 The then United Nations Secretary-General was Javier Pérez de Cuéller.

16 This consolidates and supersedes the antecedent laws that were enacted by the UN on drug trafficking, for example, the Single Convention on Narcotic Drugs (1961) and the Protocol amending the 1961 Single Convention of Narcotic Drugs in 1972.

17 Article 1 of the Palermo Convention of 15 December 2000.

18 The FATF has worked closely with the World Bank and the IMF to develop a common methodology for assessing the measures taken by jurisdictions to combat money laundering. This common methodology was agreed in October 2001 and it was established that it should be used over one year for a mutual evaluation conducted by the FATF. The common methodology means that the World Bank, the IMF and others (including the FATF-style regional bodies) will have a uniform basis on which to assess the level of implementation of AML/CFT measures. See Claes Norgren, 'The Control of Risks Associated with Crime, Terror and Subversion', 7 *Journal of Money Laundering Control* (2004): pp. 201–6.

19 A large-scale laundering operation involving one or more of a country's financial institutions and how that could put the global financial institutions at risk was underscored by the case of the BCCI.

20 'An Overview of International Anti-Money Laundering Standards and the Work of the Financial Action Task Force', (2005), available on the FATF website at www.fatf-gafi.org (date accessed 1 December 2011).

21 Council Directive 91/308/EEC of 10 June 1991.

22 The Directive also imposes anti-money laundering obligations on 'gatekeepers', requiring a broad range of professionals (including independent legal professionals, accountants, auditors and notaries) to abide by anti-money laundering regulations within 18 months of the date of adoption.

taken action to extend the scope of their money laundering offences to include a wider range of all predicate offences because they recognize the limitations of the Vienna Convention in capturing all the activities that generate the illicit proceeds of crime.[23]

Porous Land Borders: Implications and Threats

Economic globalization, which connotes the removal of barriers to trade and investment, and the movement of labour and capital across national boundaries, has diminished the importance of land borders. With the array of modern telecommunications, banking, travel and financial systems which now span the globe, criminal elements in various parts of the world now find it easy to move people, money or goods across national borders than they did in the past.[24] The above challenge, coupled with the persisting differences and fragmentation of AML/CFT legislation at an individual state level, has contributed to an increase in transnational criminal activities.[25] In fact, just as legitimate businesses are increasing internationally due to the globalization of markets, criminal enterprises are equally seeking to develop both their structure and illicit activities at an international level.[26] Criminals gain access to new markets by taking advantage of discrepancies between the legal systems of countries in different parts of the world. Today's international criminal organizations are 'adaptable, sophisticated, extremely opportunistic and immersed in a full range of illegal and legal activity'.[27] The frequent use of money generated from illegal activity has enabled criminals to launder 'dirty money', enabling them to create even more profit. Criminals are also known to apply criminal tactics (such as manipulation, murder and intimidation) to get ahead in their legal business organizations.[28]

There is anecdotal evidence suggesting that transnational criminal groups are able to work globally in countries where legal or bureaucratic loopholes allow

---

23 Article 3.

24 This is underpinned by Article 39(3) and (4) (formerly Article 48(3) and (4)) of the Treaty of Rome (1957) on the free movement of workers. Although Member States are required to protect themselves from having to admit those who can cause real disruption and insecurity of the state, these provisions can be exploited by criminals seeking to further their criminal projects.

25 See the point discussing the way in which ECOWAS was exploited by Nigerian criminal gangs in the following paragraph.

26 Mitsilegas, *Money Laundering Counter-Measures in the European Union*, Chapter 1.

27 Ibid.

28 Mexican drug gangs are known for violence, sometimes making major cities the settings for gun battles and killing their victims with impunity, but the same thing is also true in some parts of South Africa.

them to take advantage of the system.[29] Organized criminal gangs are said to take advantage of the prevailing climate of liberalization and regional trade agreements, which are attended by certain benefits such as the free movement of labour, services and capital.[30] Used cars are smuggled into these countries from the Western world. In Nigeria, stolen cars find their way into the country through the international borders of neighbouring West African states.[31] In East Africa, there has been a steady trend in the growth of money laundering crimes due to the relaxation of border controls. For instance, motor vehicles stolen from Tanzania and other countries of the Great Lakes and Southern African regions have been recovered in Uganda. On the other hand, vehicles stolen from Uganda have been recovered in other nearby countries. In all these cases, criminals have taken advantage of the relaxed border controls in many regions.[32] In 1999, a total of 32 vehicles stolen from neighbouring countries were recovered from Uganda and 18 Ugandan-registered cars were recovered from neighbouring countries.[33] As opposed to the above situation, there is no incidence of motor vehicle trafficking across the Indo-Pakistani border because of the strict border controls there.[34] Arguably, opening borders should be sequenced to ensure that liberalizing economies are not exposed to the harsh dictates of the global system at an unprecedented scale.[35]

As a money laundering predicate area, the trafficking of people[36] has become as pernicious and lucrative as the trafficking of drugs and firearms. Globalization is characterized by asymmetries on different fronts. In some societies it has created opportunities for criminal exploitation due to increased investment in some societies, while in others it has induced wars, poverty, misery and blatant

---

29 This draws on a paper, 'Transnational Criminal Activity: A Global Context' published by the Canadian Security Intelligence Service, 17 August 2000, available at: www.csis-scis-scrs.gc.ca/eng/miscdocs/200007_e.html (date accessed 10 May 2009).

30 In the West African sub-region, there is a protocol for the free movement of persons and goods under the auspices of ECOWAS, a policy which criminals take advantage of in order to indulge in the trafficking of stolen goods.

31 Charles Goredema, 'Money Laundering in the Southern Africa: Incidence, Magnitude and the Prospects for its Control', a paper delivered at the Institute of Security Studies in South Africa, 12 October 2004.

32 Ibid.

33 These figures were tendered by the daily Ugandan newspaper the *New Vision* on 20 April 2000.

34 Ibid.

35 Trafficking in persons shall mean 'the recruitment, transportation, transfer, harbouring or receipt of persons by means of threat or use of deception, of the abuse of power or of the position of vulnerability or of the giving or receiving of payments or benefits to achieve the consent of the person having control over another person, for the purpose of exploitation'. See Article 3 of the Protocol to Prevent, Suppress and Punish Trafficking in Persons Especially Women and Children 2000.

36 Reliable estimates by *The Economist* (26 August 2000) indicate that at that point there were between 200 million and 300 million people being trafficked every year.

violations of basic human rights because of arms trafficking in societies that occupy a peripheral position in the global economy. Because of this, immigration is seen as a rational human response to what has been characterized as the 'pull and push' factors.[37] It is an established fact that people trafficking has flourished from war-ravaged countries (such as Somalia, Congo, Ethiopia and Iraq), where people smugglers prey on the plight of the victims.[38] In addition, the global technological revolution has created an environment where shopping for women, children and body parts can be conducted on the Internet.[39] People who are being trafficked already know where they want to go and what to do there through the abundant information being churned out by the global media and hence the increased consciousness created by this. Similarly, the perpetrators of the above crime are able to coordinate their business by taking advantage of the advanced technological developments in many parts of the world. Criminals are able to evade capture by manipulating information, encoding information in encrypted languages in order to cover their trail. Traffickers profit from the non-existent sanctions in many parts of the world, exploiting the existing trade agreements such as in relation to the free movement of workers, capital and services in the case of the EU. The organized crime industry is intrinsically linked to money laundering because it provides the means to move the proceeds of crime about.[40]

The Role of ICT

The advent of ICT has created an infrastructure (in terms of transportation, banking and finance) that provides an improved business environment in which to deliver goods and services.[41] However, criminals and terrorists have recognized the potential of the Internet and have ruthlessly exploited it. The Internet has been used as a tool for perpetuating crimes not only within countries but also across national borders. Hackers have broken into bank computers, transferred funds to their own accounts and extorted banks, but criminals also use computers and computer networks to sell their products on the Internet, while at the same time

37 Peter Stalker, *The No-Nonsense Guide to International Migration* (London: Verso, 2001), p. 10.

38 Ibid.

39 Natasha Jarvie, 'Control of Cyber Crimes – Is an End to Our Time on the Internet a Price Worth Paying?', 9(3) *Computer and Telecommunications Law Review* (2003): pp. 76–81.

40 Stalker, *The No-Nonsense Guide to International Migration*.

41 The Internet ignores borders and criminals are able to use it as a tool to harm victims across national borders. In the absence of an appropriate legal framework to punish those who use the Internet to harm others, it will continue to be exploited for criminal purposes.

using encrypted language to evade government surveillance.[42] Due to advances in Internet-related technology, money is said to have become a digital blip through telecommunication channels. Large volumes of money are transferred within the international electronic network with little more documentation than an ordinary sales receipt, which greatly frustrates the construction of money trails.[43] Once money has been translated into electronic impulses that contain information about the money, it becomes exceptionally difficult to trace as it navigates its way through electronic systems in and out of the jurisdictions of several states.[44] Criminals take advantage of the speed and complexity of electronic funds transfers (EFTs)[45] to conceal the provenance of such funds. In this electronic age, the speed with which transactions take place has rendered it difficult to effectively monitor the status of funds that are received by financial institutions.[46] Once dirty money has entered the financial system, it becomes very difficult to separate illicit transactions from bona fide transactions. In one of the methodologies used to committee money laundering offences, criminals will violate the confidentiality of information stored on the computer system.[47] Credit cards or bank account details can be accessed and used for money laundering purposes. Criminals can, for example, hack into a computer in order to obtain information which they then use to commit other crimes, such as the fraudulent purchase of goods and services or the fraudulent transfer of funds.[48] Conversely, communication data generated by criminals on the

---

42 R.W. Downing, 'Shoring up the Weakest Link: What Law Makers Around the World Need to Consider in Developing Comprehensive Laws to Combat Cyber Crime', available at www.cybercrime.gov/juvenilepld.htm (accessed 30 July 2007).

43 Bruce Zagaris and Scott MacDonald, 'Money Laundering, Financial Fraud and Technology: The Perils of an Instantaneous Economy', 4 *George Washington Journal of International Law and Economics* (1992): p. 63.

44 Ibid., p. 66.

45 EFTs may involve numerous intermediary banks and many payment orders. Intermediaries sometimes use different protocols to complete the transfer, which can leave bits of information out along the way, and sometimes the intermediaries will not even know the name of the originator or the payee, only the name of the two banks on either side of the chain. This makes the construction of paper trails difficult and hence this is a preferred medium for money laundering.

46 George Kaufman, 'Bank Contagion: A Review of the Theory and Evidence', 8 *Journal of Financial Services Research* (1994): pp. 123–45.

47 The Convention on Cybercrime addresses computer-related forgery and fraud, although these provisions do not necessarily require authorized access. Accordingly, Article 7 states that: 'Each party shall adopt such legislative and other measures as may be necessary to establish as criminal offence under domestic law, when committed intentionally and without any right to the input, alteration, deletion or suppression of computer data, resulting in unauthentic data with the intent that it be acted upon for legal purposes, as if it was authentic, regardless of whether or not data is directly readable and intelligible.'

48 Unauthorized Computer Access (Provisional Translation) Law No. 128 of 1999, Article 3 (Japan), available at: www.cybercrimelaw.net/countries/japan.html9 (date accessed 17 May 2008).

Internet can be a vital tool in establishing money laundering/financing of terrorism trails with regard to the provenance and eventual movement of criminal assets.[49] This is possible by ensuring that the criminal's contacts and movements are traced from location to location. For instance, the police in the UK have successfully used records of phone and text messages as evidence to secure the conviction of suspected criminals.[50] As such, the police and other law enforcement agencies can access phone and email records of suspected money launderers/financers of terrorism in order to bring them to book.[51]

The Liberalization of the Financial Economy and Money Laundering

Financial liberalization refers to measures directed at diluting or dismantling regulatory controls over institutions, structures, instruments and activities of agents in different segments of the financial sector.[52] However, a string of recent global financial crises has demonstrated the vulnerability of local economies to the dictates of a liberalized financial economy. Criminals are also known to exploit the benefits of a liberalized market economy to their full advantage.[53] Examples are the issuing of counterfeit currency in Uganda in the early 2000s and the recent global financial crisis. These two events strengthen the viewpoint that the liberalization of markets is good and bad at the same time.[54] First, it is appreciated how through inter-bank markets a crisis generated in one part of the globe can trigger a chain reaction throughout the system. Secondly, in several economies, the liberalization of financial institutions such as banks rendered supervisory oversight difficult. It induced the retreat of states from effective regulatory supervision, information gathering and the enforcement of prudential norms for fear of not wanting to be seen going back towards state control.[55] The process of capital account liberalization in Uganda, which had been undertaken since 1987,

---

49 *Evening Standard*, 19 November 2009, p. 6.

50 Ibid.

51 Phone and email traffic records have played an important role in securing the conviction of three men jailed for life for conspiring to blow up planes flying between Heathrow and the USA in August 2006.

52 Jayah Ghosh, 'The Economic and Social Effects of Financial Liberalization: A Primer for Developing Countries', UN Economic and Social Affairs, available at www.un.org/esa/desa/papers (date accessed 1 December 2011).

53 Michael McKee, 'Financial Markets Turmoil and the Biggest Banks: Lessons to be Learned', 23(8) *Journal of Banking and Regulation* (2008): p. 404.

54 It creates benefits by easing the free movement of capital but it can also play into the hands of criminals.

55 Schneider Benu, 'Capital Account Liberalization: A Developing Country's Perspective', paper delivered at the Overseas Development Institute, 21 June 2000.

saw the rapid expansion of the banking and non-banking[56] sector after 1994.[57] Some of the proliferated banks were poorly supervised[58] and, when compounded by the relaxed foreign exchange controls by the Bank of Uganda (the regulator of financial institutions), opened potential loopholes that were quickly exploited for criminal expediency.[59] The liberalized financial market economy was exploited by criminals to launder money in the form of Ugandan counterfeit currency and other foreign currencies.[60] This was potentially devastating for the economy, since the negative publicity generated by the awareness of some Ugandans abroad with currency counterfeits in various denominations undermined the government's efforts to attract investors into the country.[61] Besides undermining the health and stability of financial institutions, in a globalized business environment, the threat of money laundering can potentially cause contagious effects.[62]

Poorly regulated financial centres are characterized by a lack of risk control mechanisms such as the absence of teller machines, hand-counted money or even the absence of the necessary infrastructure.[63] Capital account liberalization and the too hasty dismantling of capital controls have left countries exposed to the harsh dictates of rapid capital movement and its offshoot vulnerabilities (such as the Ugandan-type counterfeit currency). With regard to counterfeit currency from Uganda, the money would be co-mingled with clean money and introduced into the financial system through shopping, by exploiting a liberalized business

56 Some Forex Bureaux, for example, 'Give and Take', were found to have been aiding and abetting money laundering. Similarly, in 1996, an employee of the Oriental Forex Bureau was intercepted at Entebbe International Airport trying to siphon one billion Ugandan shillings in foreign denominations out of the country. When interviewed by the police, he confessed that he had on a number of occasions taken money out of the country to places like London, Pakistan and India under concealment.

57 L.A. Kasekende, 'Capital Account Liberalisation in Uganda: The Ugandan Experience', paper presented at the Overseas Development Institute, London 21 June 2000.

58 There were few currency controls, no disclosure or reporting requirements and few regulations or investigations, as these were deemed to be a step backwards towards a regulated economy.

59 A lack of expertise in managing risks, appropriately combined with the rapid growth of lending, makes screening and monitoring increasingly difficult to enforce in developing countries.

60 The case of currency counterfeiting in Uganda was underscored by the case of a prominent Ugandan businessman, Alhaj Nassar Ssebagala, in Boston, USA. His case was investigated by the US Secret Service (which was created as a law enforcement agency with the competence to investigate the counterfeiting of US currency) and he was sentenced to six months in prison.

61 Money laundering may also frustrate government attempts to implement fiscal policies, since large-scale movements of funds may be counter-intuitive to the anticipated behaviour of rational investors.

62 Razeen Sappideen, 'The Regulation of Credit, Market and Operational Risk Management under the Basel Accords', *Journal of Business Law* (2004): p. 60.

63 The Ugandan daily newspaper *The Monitor*, 30 May 2005.

environment.[64] Criminals have been known to exploit every weakness in the system and to survive in a poorly regulated environment.[65] Conversely, it would seem that liberalization works better in an environment where there is a developed infrastructure with internal controls to protect the economy from unscrupulous behaviour. In the absence of appropriate regulatory and supervisory infrastructure, market access in financial services will only have a notional value.[66]

The World Bank has conceded that unless liberalization is carefully managed, it can potentially open up avenues for corruption. In countries like Russia, which were expected to make a rapid transition into the market economy, capital accounts turned out to be an opportunity to strip assets and ship wealth abroad.[67] Liberalization has undermined the political credibility and regulatory capacities of many states, contributing to a more generalized process of political decay. This reduces incentives for probity on the part of officials and politicians, and creates widespread social alienation from the political process.[68] Liberalization has also created opportunities for money laundering as regulatory mechanisms have become weakened, there is no longer any need for economic justification for money transfers and it has become easier to exchange and transfer currencies and capital.[69] In some countries (for example, six of the 13 SADC member countries), there is no legislation on money laundering and there are no well-trained personnel to handle the complexities of the modern global system.[70] Obviously, in developing countries, law enforcement agencies are deficient, due not only to a lack of capacity but also to the lack of know-how in detecting and countering money laundering. One example demonstrating the challenges faced by some jurisdictions is that of the Meridian Biao Bank in Tanzania, which was found to have been cleverly established to take advantage of Tanzania's lack of experience and requisite expertise in international banking and financial regulation.[71] The bank offered friendly customer service and as such attracted rich customers and huge deposits. Eventually the bank lost over US$30 million of depositors' money

64 Ibid.

65 Shelley, 'Transnational Organised Crimes: A New Authoritarianism', p. 25.

66 Mahmood Bagheri and Chizu Nakajima, 'Optimal Level of Financial Regulation under the GATS: Regulatory Competition and Cooperation Framework for Capital Adequacy and Disclosure of Information', 5(2) *International Journal of Economic Law* (2004): p. 157.

67 Joseph Stiglitz, *Globalization and its Discontents* (London: W.W. Norton & Co, 1999), p. 53.

68 B. Harris-White and G. White, 'Corruption, Liberalisation and Democracy', 17 (2) *IDS Bulletin* (1996): p. 2.

69 Ibid., p. 3.

70 Uganda, Malawi and Tanzania are some examples.

71 Prince M. Bagenda, 'Combating Money Laundering in the SADC Sub-region: The Case of Tanzania', in Charles Goredema (ed.), *Monograph No. 90* (2003), p. 19, available at www.iss.co.za/pubs/Monographs/No90/Contents.html (date accessed 1 December 2011).

through poor supervisory oversight. It was found to have been over-exposed on foreign exchange markets.

Money launderers would have cleverly identified weaknesses in the financial system, wherever they are, before they struck.[72] In the first place, international investors (very much a facet of modern globalization) have a tendency to engage in momentum trading and herding, which can be destabilizing for developing economies.[73] Secondly, international investors, together with domestic residents, tend to engage in speculative attacks on developing countries' currencies, thereby causing instability that is not warranted based on the economic and policy fundamentals of those countries.[74] Conversely, financial integration can help to transmit crises generated from one part of the globe to another. The extent of damage afflicted to economies usually depends on the level of interconnectedness. In the long run, there is the contagious risk as healthy countries are literally infected when bad news from unhealthy regions starts filtering through. Potentially, such a situation would disrupt markets as investors panic and start to withdraw their money abruptly for reasons unrelated to the domestic economy. Finally, financial globalization creates a palatable climate for governments (even though they are democratically elected) to incur debts which might aggravate over-borrowing.

The transition towards a market economy has created an environment for criminals to invest their illicit proceeds in newly privatized enterprises, epitomized by the adage that 'crime follows opportunity'.[75] In the first place, the market economy has created opportunities for criminals to invest their dirty money where there are opportunities in the same way that legitimate business does.[76] Secondly, the increasing integration of financial markets has induced a dramatic increase in the number of jurisdictions offering financial services without appropriate controls or regulation, while banking secrecy laws are still an uphill challenge in many jurisdictions. Equally, poorly regulated jurisdictions also contribute to worsening standards of risk management of financial institutions.[77] Criminals who perpetuate money laundering are always on the lookout for opportunities to exploit any glaring loopholes in the regulatory and supervisory system. In the case of counterfeit currency in Uganda, which exploded in response to the idiosyncrasies of a liberalized market economy, there was no comprehensive framework on

72 Tanzania, *Business Times*, July 2006.

73 Eswar Prasad, Kenneth Rogoff, Shang-Jin Wei and M. Ayhan Kose, 'Effects of Financial Globalization on Developing Countries: Some Empirical Evidence', IMF, 17 March 2003, p. 10, available at www.imf.org/external/np/res/docs/2003/031703.pdf (date accessed 1 December 2011).

74 Underscored by the East Asian financial crisis of 1997/8 and its wider effects on global markets.

75 It is alleged that 80 per cent of privatized industries in Russia are under the control of the Russian Mafia.

76 Shelley, 'Transnational Organised Crimes: A New Authoritarianism'.

77 Alexander, 'Multinational Efforts to Combat Financial Crimes and the Financial Action Task Force'.

money laundering with regard to the identification, seizure and forfeiture of the instrumentalities of money laundering crimes.[78] Therefore, the spread of financial crimes is partly attributable to a weakened domestic economy rather than the exigencies of the global system.

The most recent global financial crisis underscored the susceptibility of financial markets to perverse global forces.[79] It should be noted that the recent global financial crisis, as well as by the East Asian financial crisis in 1997/1998 and other global crises all have one thing in common: they have helped to demonstrate the dangers posed by a liberalized market economy internally, but also how opening markets can potentially undermine the entire world financial community due to the interconnectedness of economies. The recent global financial crisis underscores the potential dangers inherent in the globalization of financial markets.[80] The inter-bank links have the potential to act as a conduit in transmitting crises from one part of the world to another.

It has become more or less predictable that whenever the financial crisis unfolds, banks respond by tightening the regulatory regimes. This has been manifested by the nationalization of banks such as Northern Rock in the UK and other rescue measures replicated in other countries. The challenge with this reactive approach is its weakness in providing a stable working framework capable of cautioning financial institutions against the vagaries of the global system. In terms of fighting money laundering, for example, unless there is a robust framework in place, it is possible that criminals who perpetrate money laundering will relocate to lax financial centres and particularly to cash-based economies. Many countries in developing countries are cash-based economies and as such are prone to organized criminal activity. Poorly regulated financial centres can be exploited to perpetuate a wide range of financial crimes, as the Ugandan counterfeit currency has already demonstrated. In my view, liberalization should not be undertaken prematurely in countries with a tenuous regulatory infrastructure, even though it is important for the purpose of enhancing capital flows such as attracting FDI. It is therefore essential for countries, regardless of their level of development, to embrace and translate the global AML/CFT framework into domestic law. Posturing based on national self-interest will only play in favour of the potential launderer or terrorist.

78 This has caused problems for major multinational banks, which have had to rely on internal systems developed by their main offices to be used by all their branches globally. Barclays Bank has developed specific anti-money laundering policies, for example, 'Africa Policy for the Prevention of Money Laundering' (2001).

79 This crisis started in the USA sub-prime markets, but spread widely to other economies due to inter-bank links.

80 William K. Tabb, *The Amoral Elephant: Globalization and the Struggle for Social Justice in the Twenty-First Century* (Berkeley, CA: Monthly Review Press, 2001), pp. 99–126.

Quark Investors: The BCCI

There are many banking scandals involving money laundering such as the failure of Barings Bank, the involvement of Mexican banks in laundering the illicit proceeds of drug trafficking, the Bank of New York's alleged involvement in laundering for the Russian Mafia, and obviously the frequently cited case of the BCCI.[81] This BCCI saga demonstrated how criminals masquerading as investors can exploit a liberal business climate to consolidate their criminal underground enterprises. The global structure of the BCCI was manipulated to ensure that the illegal operations of the bank remained beyond the scope of supervisors and regulators. The above case is also important to demonstrate how poorly supervised bank establishments can be infiltrated and exploited for criminal purposes.

The BCCI was established in 1972[82] by a group of bankers from Pakistan, with financial and technical support from America and major investment from the ruler of Abu Dhabi and the wealth of Saudi Arabian citizens.[83] It was said that, by 1990, it had stated assets of US$20 billion spread across over 70 countries and was the largest private bank in the world. By this time, the bank had split into two companies, with BCC SA based in Luxembourg and BCCI Overseas based in the Cayman Islands under the Luxembourg holding company BCCI Holdings.[84] The object of this structure was to avoid the scrutiny of supervisors by fragmenting itself into obscure financial centres, yet maintaining a close link with customers who could put large deposits at the bank's disposal.[85]

First, with regard to supervision, the BCCI did not fit within the model on which the Basel Committee had focused – that is, the parent bank subject to supervision in one country, with branches and subsidiaries subject to supervision in the host country.[86] Secondly, the BCCI scandal demonstrated how criminally minded international bankers could outwit regulators and accountants with national remits. The BCCI, with its Luxembourg registration, London headquarters, Middle-Eastern shareholders and worldwide operations, was regulated by everyone and yet no-one.[87] It therefore became apparent that the law enforcement authorities needed to reconstruct the financial trail in order to prosecute the supposed launderers.

81 Ryder, 'The Financial Services Authority and Money Laundering', p. 638.

82 It grew to be the largest private bank in the world, expanding from 146 branches in 32 countries to over 400 branches in 73 countries by 1977.

83 Rowan Bosworth-Davies, 'Deviant Legitimacy – A Theory of Financial Crime', 4(1) *Journal of Financial Crimes* (1997): pp. 7–16.

84 Ibid.

85 George A. Walker, 'International Financial Supervisory Crisis – The Collapse of the BCCI and the 1992 Basel Minimum Standards', CCLS Research Paper, May 2005.

86 Walker, *International Banking Regulation: Law, Policy and Practice*, p. 12.

87 The USA took unilateral action, amending its International Banking Act 1978 to bolster the Federal Reserves' authority over foreign bank operations.

The structure of the bank[88] and the fact that financial institutions do not always maintain the requisite records of verified customer identification data relating to the parties involved in executing wire transfers made it difficult to prosecute culprits involved in the BCCI financial abuse conundrum.

Following the US authorities' operation code-named 'Operation C-Chase', the accounts of the BCCI in Florida and Panama were implicated in the transfer of funds from drug trafficking, while certain BCCI officials had also offered to launder money through other BCCI international offices. Bank officers received cash undercover, which they wired to various branches around the world, notably in Europe – London, Paris or Luxembourg.[89] These branches would then issue certificates of deposit in branches nearer home in the Bahamas or Barbados.[90] The traffickers could then take out loans at these branches with the certificate of deposit as collateral and the loans would be repaid from the original deposits by the bank.[91] The law enforcement authorities were faced with the problems emanating from differences in the legal systems and with the procedural difficulties that foreign jurisdictions applied to protect their sovereignty. The legal and regulatory differences also meant that information gathered by businesses and professions in relation to financial transactions that were carried out from country to country could not confidently be utilized to construct the money trail after it had been routed through foreign jurisdictions.[92] The conviction of the bank for money laundering charges was a clear blow to stemming the tide of rumours about the bank's reputation. It added plausibility about the BCCI as a dirty bank and created a negative public image for it. As such, it was forced to close its Florida office.[93]

In relation to the bank's role in money laundering, the relaxed supervision of the BCCI was vehemently exploited for drug trafficking and using the bank as a conduit to move illicit proceeds about. But, in addition, the BCCI as a global bank appeared to solicit close relations with those involved in organized crime.[94] Moreover, there was a glaring failure on the part of the regulators of the bank to provide adequate supervisory oversight for branches that operated in their

88 The segmented structure ensured that corporate records were spread worldwide and the regulation and audit of the BCCI was fragmented across different jurisdictions without any single jurisdiction having consolidated access to all bank records.

89 Walker, *International Banking Regulation.*

90 Ibid.

91 Ibid.

92 Sarah Jane Hughes, 'Policing Money Laundering through Funds Transfers: A Critique of Regulation under the Bank Secrecy Act', 67 *Indiana Law Journal* (1992): p. 283.

93 Nikos Passas, 'The Genesis of the BCCI Scandal: The Corruption of Politics and Politics of Corruption', 23(1) *Journal of Law and Society* (1996): pp. 57–72.

94 In 1988, seven officials of the bank were arrested in Tampa on charges of drug trafficking and money laundering.

jurisdiction but were incorporated in other jurisdictions.[95] The complex global structure of the BCCI was exploited to perpetrate fraud, corruption, insider dealing and money laundering.[96] The Bank of England argued that it had failed to act earlier than it did under UK law because it was not the home-country supervisor, as the BCCI was wholly owned by a Luxembourg holding company. This seemingly justified the Bank of England's inaction since it had no responsibility for overseeing the BCCI's global activities, which were administered mainly from its London offices.[97]

The BCCI's global structure also sheds light on the supervisory challenges posed by the transnational operations of financial conglomerates.[98] The segmented corporate structure of the bank ensured that corporate records were spread worldwide and that the regulation and audit trail was fragmented across different jurisdictions without any single jurisdiction having consolidated access to all the bank's records. To compound the problem, the BCCI ensured that all important documents were kept in jurisdictions that adhered to strict bank secrecy and were thus protected by it.[99] The structure of the bank was designed to ensure that bank operations remained beyond the reach of any prosecuting authority or jurisdiction, as lamented by the New York District Attorney: 'here you have financial statements, profit and loss filed in Washington, filed in Virginia, filed in Tennessee, filed in New York and audited by auditors who are beyond the reach of law enforcement'.[100] International financial conglomerates today are providing an array of products and services, including not only the traditional offerings of loans and deposits but also, *inter alia*, insurance, investment services and tax and estate planning.[101] Modern financial institutions conduct diversified operations across borders to diversify their earnings and enhance profits. The liberalization of restrictions on capital flows across national borders has also increased international

---

95 This occurred in the context of the Bank of England's efforts to supervise the London branch operation of the BCCI. It had operated for many years with its principal place of business in London, where it administered a global web of affiliates and holding companies registered in Luxembourg and the Cayman Islands.

96 Alexander, Dhumale and Eatwell, *Global Governance of Financial Systems*, p. 48.

97 *Three Rivers District Council v Governor and Company of the Bank of England (No. 3)* [2000] 2 WLR 1220.

98 This term is used to describe multifunctional financial firms that often serve as holding companies for subsidiaries and affiliates which provide a wide range of financial service activities.

99 IMF, 'Current Developments in Monetary and Financial Law', seminar paper, Washington DC, 23–27 October 2006, p. 8.

100 'The BCCI Affair: A Report to the Committee on Foreign Relations', US Senate (December 1992, 102d Congress 2d Session Senate Print 102–4), Chapter 9.

101 Keith Pooley, 'Legal Regulatory Requirements Regarding Capital Adequacy and Other Supervisory Issues', Groupe de Contact seminar paper, Christ's College, University of Cambridge, 9 September 2003.

lending and deposit taking.[102] It would seem that adopting a global AML/CFT framework would provide countries with an opportunity to prosecute alleged money laundering offences.

The Role of Domestic Courts

The role of courts in the domestication of normative anti-money laundering standards cannot be over-emphasized. First, the courts provide a common law function of adjudicating decisions as guidelines for the prosecution of future cases.[103] Secondly, the court as an institution engenders norms that ensure the assimilation of recommended anti-money laundering norms into local societies on a forward looking basis. Traditionally, the court's influence in the translation of laws is paramount,[104] but also, as already noted, courts interpret laws to create judicial decisions or guidelines to enhance the translation of anticipated changes into society. In view of this, the courts must be prepared to provide the intellectual interface for internalizing international AML/CFT norms nationally without displacing national laws.[105] As this presupposes, the courts must transcend the notion of law in the narrow confines of individual state jurisdiction, but should also look at the broader picture of achieving common objectives.

The case for a specialist court on money laundering crimes is advocated on the grounds that its absence works against the fostering of a robust AML/CFT culture globally. The function of courts, among other things, is to adjudicate decisions based on the facts in accordance with the values, traditions and principles of society. However, questions of national polity and administrative feasibility are determined by parliament and the legislature. The proposed court would bring its mandate to bear on global relations between different stakeholders in default of a global government and constitutional powers to govern. The court should play a complimentary role with domestic courts to ensure the smooth transposition of desired AML/CFT norms into the local context.[106] It should be noted that in performing their judicial functions, the courts are guided by the values and traditions of the society – a cherished common law tradition or the underlying constitutional

102 Ibid.

103 This tradition is based on the legislative supremacy of parliament – a tenet of the tripartite separation of powers.

104 Where the law has become obsolete with regard to the imperatives of development, as illustrated in the case of *Fisher v Bell* [1961] 1 QB 394, courts will refer the respective statute back to parliament to bring it into line with the necessary changes in society.

105 Sidney W. Richards, 'Legitimacy of the Supreme Court in the Context of Globalisation', 4(3) *Utrecht Law Review* (2008): p. 104.

106 Hilaire Barnett, *Constitutional & Administrative Law* (Abingdon: Routledge-Cavendish, 2006), p. 12.

principles.[107] I am inclined to argue that the court is a required interface for the success of every society, to the extent that no government can afford to dispense with it. As far as I am concerned, the absence of a global government creates a vacuum insofar as the legitimacy of global institutions is concerned. The creation of a global anti-money laundering court would go a long way towards enhancing the assimilation of global AML/CFT regimes, but also foreclosing any weaknesses that are inherent in global regimes.

It would seem that the role of courts is subordinate, since they rely heavily on the work of the legislature in the creation and translation of norms. This function is constitutional whereby the courts, just like any other state institutions, must work in tandem to uphold the will of parliament rather than to override it. As this would suggest, the independence of the courts is curtailed as they must concede in the event of conflict with parliament as a matter of constitutional law. There are occasions when courts have had to use their discretional powers, providing leadership in certain areas of law without recourse to parliament – judicial activism.[108] A global court should be constituted with a mandate to bind all participating states in matters of money laundering and to ensure that money laundering offences are not tried in mainstream courts. Prescribing laws at the FATF and other anti-money laundering institutional level is essential, but is not enough in itself, as already elucidated in the earlier sections of this study.

In international law, an overlapping crime would be prosecuted in the state where it was committed. This is based on the *lotus principle*, which lays out that a state has jurisdiction to try another state's national provided that the alleged offences were committed within its territory.[109] However, from the UK's point of view, the courts will have jurisdiction over alleged money laundering offences committed outside the UK where the defendant is a UK resident. Where the asset subject to money laundering is received by someone innocently, it will be caught by the legal principle of money had and received.[110] The claimant is allowed to assert his/her ownership over the property by demonstrating the following: (i) the legal title to the money; (ii) that the defendant received it; and (iii) that the receipt was unjust due to a vitiating factor.[111] Owing to the above factors, the claimant is allowed to claim for restitution for unjust enrichment. The defence allows the

107 *R v Secretary of State for the Home Department, ex parte Adam* [2000] 2 AC 477.

108 These are extreme where the government feels constrained for some reason not to antagonize the rights of citizens or to divide society.

109 This was underscored in the Canadian case *United States v Burns* (2001) SCC 7, file No. 26129. In this case, the Supreme Court of Canada said that a person who chooses to leave Canada leaves behind Canadian law and procedures and must generally accept the local law, procedures and punishments which the foreign state applies to its citizens.

110 Zachary Douglas, in William Blair and Richard Brent (ed.), *Banks and Financial Crimes: International Law of Tainted Money* (Oxford: Oxford University Press, 2008), pp. 343–7.

111 *Lipkin Gorman v Karpnale* [1991] AC 548.

defendant to set against his/her enrichment the amount of disenrichment that he/she has sustained but would not otherwise have sustained had it not been for the enrichment.[112] Where the defendant is domiciled in the UK, the legal position is that he/she will be tried by the UK courts according to English law.[113] However, where the defendant is domiciled in another country, the UK courts do not have jurisdiction to try the defendant in that country, save where it was expressly chosen as the preferred choice of forum.[114] Equally, where another country has already initiated proceedings on the matter, even though the UK courts have jurisdiction, they will have to stay proceedings. But if the defendant was domiciled in a country like Uganda which has not passed a law specifically on AML/CFT, matters would be complicated. Most likely the courts would not have the mandate to prosecute the defendant, unless perhaps under customary law. The absence of a specific law proscribing certain crimes could jeopardize the global efforts on money laundering, let alone the fact that the vacuum created can potentially be exploited so that the defendant can stay put.

Since different jurisdictions have different ways of interpreting AML/CFT – narrowly or broadly depending on the national AML/CFT policy framework – the global court could be put forward as a neutral judicial organ. The reason for this is that some societies are too weak and corrupt to properly oversee the prosecution of money laundering offences nationally.[115] As if this is not enough, judicial officers caught in the process of money laundering will undermine the dispensation of justice against alleged offenders, who after all may be accomplices. Through the process of elaboration of the emerging AML/CFT norms, the courts would ease and enhance the crystallization of soft law norms into hard law, easing the enforceability of engendered norms. There is an intricate issue that money could have been aided and abetted by international banks through correspondent banking or accepting deposits in disregard of customer due diligence requirements.

Similarly, some global initiatives are often perceived as pervasive to national economies as regards asserting their national development programmes as independent sovereign states. Therefore, the legitimacy of AML/CFT regimes would be greatly enhanced by the creation of a global court. The court would help to make the engendered AML/CFT initiatives legitimate in the eyes of participating countries. If the mandate of the global court has been constituted in agreement with participating nations, it would create a sense of global legitimacy necessary to foster the same initiatives globally. It would seem prudent that countries subject

112 Ibid.

113 Ibid.

114 Article 2 of the Judgement Regulations instituted on or after 1 March 2002. The Judgement Regulations would apply because the subject matter is a civil and commercial matter (Article 1(1)).

115 This is likely to raise the issue of national sovereignty, but unless governments are able to compromise a measure of their national sovereignty for the good of a functional global system, global regimes will not function properly.

to global regimes should be closely involved in designing AML/CFT measures. Failure to co-opt states in initiatives where its sovereignty is required will elicit a sense of resentment, which is presumably why some states may perceive global AML/CFT laws to be extraneous.[116] Some countries have ratified international conventions on money laundering, such as the Palermo Convention of December 2000, but have fallen short in passing enabling legislation domestically. For example, in Uganda, money laundering is not a specific offence and is treated as a derivative crime. While crimes that generate money laundering are proscribed and sanctionable under national law, money laundering is not a distinct offence. As such, at present the courts are not able to prosecute the alleged money laundering offenders because of the absence of law and policy covering this area. In addition, countries which have been sidelined by the global economy tend to resent global regimes, alleging that anything global is a front for exploitation. This situation is clearly illustrated by the case of the Seychelles. In 2001, the government of the Seychelles passed a law, the Economic Development Act, offering protection and immunity from prosecution to any person who invested more than US$100,000 in the country, regardless of whether the money was the proceeds of money laundering. The proposed law sparked international condemnation of the Seychelles and although the law was withdrawn under international pressure, the fact that the Seychelles had dared to pass such an Act was indicative of the fact that national self-interest is likely to supersede global interests. It would seem that transposing global AML/CFT standards is more or less off the development agenda of the majority of developing counties for reasons not of their own making, such as resource constraints as well as political and economic imperatives.

The AML/CFT system can work as long as there are certain prerequisites, not least the availability of a physical and economic infrastructure to foster a positive AML/CFT environment. There is evidence to corroborate the fact that the transposition of AML/CFT initiatives in developing countries is derailed due to the following factors. Courts in some jurisdictions are sidelined by staffing shortages, often having to contend with no judges or prosecutors to preside over the proper dispensation of cases submitted before them for hearing. As such, suspected offenders – money launderers or other criminals alike – have languished in prisons longer than necessary.[117] The absence of a robust judicial system and well-trained judges in many societies has inhibited the development of a transnational legal order which would ease the transposition of global AML/CFT laws locally. The lack of the requisite level of education in some jurisdictions has rendered judges less dexterous in handling the complexities of the modern international legal order. This presumably underpins the reason why the current global AML/CFT framework has not been internalized into many developing countries.

116 Norman Mugarura, 'The Subdued Giant: The Predicament of the Law in Harnessing Global Markets', 17(2) *African Journal of International and Comparative Law* (2009): p. 330.

117 With regard to rights articulated by Articles 6(1) and 8(1) of the ECHR.

Suffice to say that in many countries, corruption has undermined national efforts towards supporting local institutions. Corruption undermines the efficacy of already-established local institutions (including courts) as well as the fabric of society as a whole. In many societies, pursuing and securing justice against alleged offences is very expensive, given the money paid in bribes or the exorbitant costs incurred in initiating legal proceedings in courts of law. In such a situation, those who cannot afford the high cost of initiating legal proceedings will have their rights literally trampled upon by the very institutions created to secure and promote citizenry rights.

Conclusion

Money laundering and its underlying predicate crimes have failed to go away despite the proliferation of global anti-money laundering laws. It would seem that money laundering is intrinsically linked to the complexity of the international banking system, but it is also embedded in the complex global economy system itself. The current global threats have undermined the functioning of societies at three levels: the individual, the state and the international community. The permeability of national borders has made some states to lose much of their significance and the fabric of society has been undermined by organized crime, corruption and money laundering. Thus, money laundering and its dynamics can best be understood if viewed within the fluidity of the modern global market environment

While states have evolved global regimes, the implementation of engendered regimes is still inhibited and undermined by inward individualistic state posturing. Furthermore, it can be said that economic disparities between economies has also not helped to foster the adoption of normative AML/CFT regimes internationally. On the contrary, it has generated an offshoot challenge of free-riding, regulatory arbitrage and regulatory failure caused by an uncoordinated regulatory system. We are in total agreement that global regulatory measures against money laundering and the financing of terrorism are essential and need to be formulated on a global basis.[118] However, we are also cognisant of the dangers of making false assumptions that the global AML/CFT can effectively apply across the board irrespective of the underlying local challenges to transposing global regimes. The implementation of global AML/CFT regimes should be pragmatic, taking into account the dynamics of development in individual countries. These dynamics include challenges in technology, the regulatory environment and other aspects of infrastructural development. There is a need for normative reforms to support the envisaged AML/CFT laws. The desired reforms should adopt a forward-looking

118 Mahmood Bagheri and Chizu Nakajima, 'Optimal level of Financial Regulation under GATS: Regulatory Competition and Cooperation Framework for Capital Adequacy and Disclosure of Information', 5(2) *International Journal of Economic Law* (2004): p. 157.

AML/CFT paradigm that combines the needs of the local and the global. However, it should be noted that there is no country that can afford to stay statist, however seemingly powerful that state is. Traditionally, states have always coexisted, but they should not create regimes which they are not going to implement. Desired reforms should be realistic and society-oriented in order to properly caution the society against the exigencies of money laundering and the financing of terrorism.

It is an absolute imperative for global AML/CFT regimes to be enforced pragmatically, bearing in mind inequalities of development and the attendant constraining effect in some states which are subject to the above regimes. The wide asymmetries in the global economy have resonated in terms of implementing an AML/CFT regulatory framework and have undermined unity between states. Global regulatory regimes, including those on money laundering, should be drafted with exemptions, perhaps based on the model of mutual recognition in Europe. Mutual recognition – a model of regulating financial markets in Europe – should be adopted globally because it provides a measure of harmonization for foreign and host regulatory authorities to coexist without conflict. In adopting the above regulatory model, it was recognized that EU Member States are characterized by different internal legal systems (in terms of contract law and employment law) and different regulatory environments coexisting within EU law. Therefore, without mutual recognition, whereby states accept to surrender part of their sovereignty in order to coexist with other legal systems in different Member States, an integrated single European market would never be possible. Mutual recognition also implies and requires mutual trust fostered through the adoption of common rules. Mutual recognition and minimum harmonization are accompanied by other pillars such as home country control and the single banking licence.[119] With regard to the principle of 'home country control', the home country undertakes to control and supervise its financial institutions as a substitute for host country supervision.[120] In order for mutual recognition to function properly, countries will have to accept the legal systems of other countries domestically. However, mutual recognition is difficult to apply where some countries have not defined money laundering as a distinct offence at all.

States must demonstrate the desire to go beyond the mere prescription of international regimes and transpose their AML/CFT obligations to avoid an uncoordinated system and its offshoot regulatory arbitrage between stakeholder countries. As we have already noted, states have no choice but to transpose AML/CFT to attract FDI. Besides, the World Bank and the IMF have co-opted global AML/CFT regimes and now require borrowing countries to demonstrate their preparedness to transpose the Basel Committee and FATF regulatory standards.[121] Similarly, investors would want to be assured that there is an effective system of

---

119 Ibid.

120 Ibid.

121 This duty exists as a contract between the customer and the bank, but also by virtue of the Data Protection Act 1998. See Ross Cranston, *Principles of Banking Law*

laws and that when violations occur, offenders are punished. It should be noted that states have little choice but to transpose their AML/CFT obligations into domestic law since there is no state that can afford to stay on the sidelines of globalization and its exigencies. If a state decides not to adopt normative AML/CFT regimes, it will render itself vulnerable to money laundering and its predicate offences, such as terrorism and corruption. As the recent global financial crisis has probably highlighted, the inaction of one state towards its international obligations can also engender consequent problems in another state.

(Oxford: Oxford University Press, 2003), p. 168; and also the frequently cited case of *Tournier v National Provincial and Union Bank of England* [1924] 1 KB 461.

Chapter 5
Corruption and the Domestication of Global Anti-Money Laundering Schemes

Introduction

This chapter examines the effect of corruption on the transposition of global anti-money laundering regimes such as customer due diligence (CDD) into the narrow context of some jurisdictions. It demonstrates how corruption (in its various manifestations) can undermine the ability of states to transpose its CDD measures, as well as institutions through which AML/CFT regimes function. CDD is a core anti-money standard which requires banks to know their customers at the inception of the relationship and to continuously monitor their customers as the relationship progresses. Since corruption undermines the efficacy of local institutions, it has to be inferred that corruption undermines society's capacity to forestall challenges such as money laundering. Therefore, in an inherently corrupt system, the prescribed AML/CFT regimes cannot function properly in achieving their intended purposes.[1] This chapter posits that corruption and money laundering are literally kith and kin and should be given the same level of attention at the international level. It argues that the dangers posed by corruption to the global economy are far greater than the dangers posed by money laundering in some countries. It explores the issue of corruption both as a cause and predicate offence of money laundering. Therefore, the design of an effective global AML/CFT framework should encompass measures against corruption since the envisaged AML/CFT regimes cannot translate into practice at a local level in an environment of corruption. Corruption and money laundering are embedded within each other and this chapter demonstrates that anti-corruption measures need to be enacted and implemented first in order for anti-money laundering laws to work.

The Nexus of Corruption and Money Laundering

Corruption is an economic crime that generates illicit proceeds, which in money laundering terms qualifies it as a predicate offence. The term 'predicate offence' circumscribes all the activities which generate the laundered proceeds of a crime. Corruption is defined as 'the abuse of public office, either to commit some act in breach of a duty or to demand some kind of favour in return for doing something

1 The FATF revised 40+9 recommendations adopted in 1989 and 2003 respectively.

which one is bound to do anyway, that is, for a private gain'.[2] Corruption often involves improper or unlawful behaviour on the part of officials in the public sector, whether politicians or civil servants, in which they enrich themselves or those who are associated with them.[3] The World Bank defines corruption as 'the abuse of public office for a private gain'.[4] This definition is fairly straightforward and is designed to cover a whole range of criminal activities that fall within its delineated framework. Thus, corruption can be construed as a specific type of violation against moral norms and values of society for selfish personal reasons. Corruption is a domestic offence when it is committed within the boundaries of a single country, for example, an official of the government offering a bribe to secure a business contract in a company registered in a country. Transnational corruption on the other hand transcends national boundaries and occurs within many jurisdictions. An obvious example of this is when hypothetically an American company offers bribes to a government official in Uganda, for example, in order to secure its interests in a government contract. But the bribe can also be given by an official of the government to gain a contract in a foreign country. In both cases it is corruption. In relation to the World Bank definition, its potential limitations are that it fails to capture corruption committed in the private sector, such as bribery in private businesses. Another manifestation of private sector corruption can be in the form of corporate fraud where, for example, a director of a company defrauds it of millions of dollars.[5] Private sector corruption would seem to be more prevalent in the economies of developed countries, while public sector corruption is rampant in developing countries.[6]

In many developing countries, money laundering schemes are inextricably linked to corruption. Corruption is both as a cause and predicate offence of money laundering. Either the laundered assets are the proceeds of corruption or the process of laundering is facilitated by corrupting law enforcement agencies or officials in the financial institutions in order to place illicit proceeds into the system.[7] The centrality of corruption in facilitating money laundering-related

2 Richard Alexander, 'Corruption as a Financial Crime', 30(4) *Company Lawyer* (2009): pp. 98–104.

3 Cyrille Fijnaut and Leo Hubert, *Corruption, Integrity and Law Enforcement* (*The Hague*: Kluwer Law International, , 2002), p. 3.

4 Vito Tanzi, 'Corruption Around the World: Causes, Consequences, Scope and Cures', IMF Working Paper, WP/98/63. 1998. See also Shams, 'Using Money Laundering Control to Fight Corruption'. I had the opportunity to access this paper as an international economic law student in 2005.

5 Here so many cases abound, not least Bernie Madoff, who allegedly defrauded the company of $65 billion.

6 It is true that developed economies dominate the global business landscape and as such companies tend to employ corruption to give them an advantage over their rivals. See Tanzi, 'Corruption Around the World: Causes, Consequences, Scope and Cures'.

7 Charles Goredema, 'Money Laundering in Southern Africa: Incidence, Magnitude and Prospects for its Control', Institute of Security Studies, Paper 92, October 2004, p .4.

threats, such as drug trafficking, prostitution, small arms trafficking and illegal currency trafficking, has destroyed the myth that corruption is a domestic political issue for which individual states cannot be held liable.[8] Therefore, the design of anti-corruption policy measures should encompass the effective implementation strategy of CDD such as KYC and the proper enforcement of anti-corruption laws.[9]

It also needs to be noted that money accrued from corruption constitutes criminal property under the global AML/CFT framework.[10] Criminal property is defined as 'property of any kind that one knows or suspects to be derived from criminal conduct'.[11] In the UK, for example, criminal conduct includes not only offences committed in the UK, but also any act which, although it was committed abroad, would have constituted an offence had it been committed in the UK.[12] Therefore, the remit of this definition covers British residents who embezzle government money in their own countries before coming to the UK. For example, somebody who occupies a position in which he/she is expected to work in the interests of the state and then embezzles government funds or who abuses his/her position in any other way such as taking a bribe will have committed a criminal offence.[13] Another example could be a situation where a government official accepts a gift from a representative of or the agent of a company in return for agreeing to influence a bid for a contract.[14] The causes of corruption are many and vary from society to society where corruption is committed. In developing countries, there is a complicit culture of corruption caused by greed and ostentatious lifestyles that cannot be sustained by people's meagre incomes. This has translated into a form of moral hazard that is corroding the core of many societies. In my view, corruption as culture varies from society to society and is thus culturally relative. The action that may be viewed as constituting corruption in one society may be viewed differently in another.[15] Whatever perception of corruption one has, corruption is in my view inextricably linked to money laundering and other forms of financial abuse.[16]

8 The centrality of corruption in facilitating cross-border threats is expressed in the preamble of the United Nations Convention against Corruption (UNCAC), 9 December 2003.

9 This proposition is in line with Article 52(5) and (6) of the UNCAC, which came into force in 2005.

10 In the UK, this is defined by s. 340(2) of the POCA 2002.

11 See Recommendation 1 of the FATF.

12 Section 340(2)(b) of the POCA 2002.

13 Alexander, 'Corruption as a Financial Crime'.

14 Such behaviour amounts to criminal conduct as defined under s. 340(1) of the POCA 2002.

15 The perception of corruption among the majority of Ugandans is that corruption is a sign of being thrifty and progressive or developmental to put it another way. This mentality is so entrenched that in my view, fighting corruption will be for sometime to come remain a big challenge for the government.

16 Alexander, 'Corruption as a Financial Crime'.

The nexus between corruption and money laundering has manifested itself in the form of tax evasion, the looming threat of counterfeit currency and swindling government funds, often at the expense of government development programmes.[17] Corruption is not unlike other problems of wrongdoing, such as fraud, money laundering, terrorism and other forms of lawlessness. In many societies, the aforementioned threats have become difficult to eliminate because of corruption – which has more or less become a normative practice. This is so despite some countries having campaigned vigorously and adopted laws against corruption.[18] Kickbacks, commissions or representation fees are sought in return for rigging bids; that is, manipulating the laws adopted to govern the privatization process. There is also the issue of corruption where judges and other court officials may simply overlook the facts and evidence, having received a kickback from a money launderer. This, apart from weakening support for deregulation and the promotion of market reforms, creates laxity in creating laws to govern market reforms.[19] Lax financial regulation has attracted money launderers because to a large extent in such an environment, the authorities do not fully cooperate with international efforts aimed at suppressing the threat of money laundering.[20]

There is a close connection between corruption[21] and the concomitant growth of financial crimes such as money laundering. In many cases where money launderers cannot achieve their aims through the use or threat of the use of violence, corruption will be the alternative. Corruption takes many forms, including bureaucratic corruption, where officials take bribes, or political corruption, which includes politicians[22] taking bribes to award contracts, influence elections or provide patronage. Grand corruption involves the misuse of power by heads of

17 Apparently corruption has become endemic and a multi-faceted issue. Funds given in aid by Western governments are often siphoned out back to Western banks by corrupt leaders. The ongoing corruption case involving three former Ugandan Ministers of Health over the diversion of GAVI Funds extended to facilitate the treatment of malaria, tuberculosis and HIV/AIDS underscores this point. This situation has been replicated elsewhere in Africa – for example, it is alleged that money extended to the government of Lesotho for the same purposes has been diverted by corrupt officials to buy posh houses in South Africa. For more information on this case, see Alexander, 'Corruption as a Financial Crime', p. 2.

18 The Leadership Code 2002, under which leaders in public offices are supposed to account for their wealth prior to taking office. The Code was enacted pursuant to Article 3 of UNCAC, where member states were mandated to take necessary measures to fight corruption, including imposing punitive measures against those who perpetuate corruption in government.

19 Rose-Ackerman, *Corruption and Governments*, p. 27.

20 Ibid.

21 Ibid., p. 7.

22 Classic cases cited on corruption include Mobutu Sese Seko in Zaire, Hastings Kamuzu Banda in Malawi, Sani Abacha in Nigeria, Ferdinand Marcos in the Philippines and Daniel Arap Moi in Kenya. For the detailed account of corruption in Africa, see the

state, ministers and top officials for private pecuniary profit, and even noble cause corruption, where the instruments of government such as the intelligence services are used to provide finance and other support for criminal activities, such as assisting terrorism, providing secret arms supplies beyond the scrutiny of political process and laundering secret funds.[23]

Prominent Cases of Grand Corruption and Money Laundering

The world is awash with cases and scandals of corruption on a grand scale, demonstrated by examples such as the following: Suharto, the former President of Indonesia, and his family are said to have stolen and amassed a personal wealth of US$45 billion during his 32 years in power;[24] Ferdinand Marcos, while in power for 20 years in the Philippines, is believed to have stolen an estimated US$10 billion; Mobutu Sese Seko in his 30 years as President of Zaire, is believed to have stolen a whopping US$30 billion, much of which was either money that had been given to Zaire in development aid or accrued from illegal mineral deals with international businesses.[25] Much of this money is said to have been siphoned out to friendly countries both in Africa and elsewhere. Sese Seko was known by the World Bank and the IMF to be appropriating 30–50 per cent of the national budget for capital investment every year.[26] However, the World Bank did not stop lending to his regime until 1993 and nor did it intervene in any other way.[27] Corruption is deemed to be a political matter which the World Bank and the IMF have no mandate over, as it is deemed to be an internal political matter of an individual country.[28] Investigations by the Swiss Federal Banking Commission (SFBC) found US$660 million belonging to the former President Sani Abacha of Nigeria in Swiss banks.[29] In 1999, the Swiss government called upon five private banks in Switzerland to freeze accounts held in the name of Abacha's son, Mohammed, believed to contain millions of dollars plundered from the Nigerian Central Bank

---

Transparency International Report (September 2009), available at www.transparency.org/news_room/in_focus/2009/gcr2009 (date accessed 3 December 2011).

23 Barry Rider, *Corruption: The Enemy Within* (The Hague: Kluwer Law International, 1997), pp. 8–34.

24 Jackie Johnson, 'In Pursuit of Dirty Money: Identifying Weaknesses in the Global Financial System', 5(2) *Journal of Money Laundering Control* (2001): p. 128.

25 Ibid.

26 Susan Hawley, 'Exporting Corruption: Privatisation, Multinationals and Bribery', 2000, available at www.psrast.org/corrupt.htm (date accessed 3 December 2011).

Ibid.

27 Ibid.

28 Article IV mandates the World Bank and the IMF to intervene only for economic reasons and not politics.

29 Johnson, 'In Pursuit of Dirty Money'.

and oil revenues.[30] In January 2000, the Swiss bank froze £390 million in accounts belonging to Abacha and his associates.[31] A further US$540 million was located in Luxembourg and Liechtenstein. An unspecified amount of money was allegedly deposited with Barclays Bank and efforts to recover it by the Nigerian government have seemingly faltered due to technicalities.[32] It is estimated (as nobody can put an exact figure on the amount) that Abacha in his ten years as the President of Nigeria is believed to have stolen a total of US$5 billion.[33] Similarly, money extended to some countries in aid and to assist with the treatment of diseases such as malaria, tuberculosis and HIV/AIDS has simply vanished, courtesy of officials and politicians in corrupt governments.[34] It can therefore be inferred that in an inherently corrupt system, laws, systems and procedures adopted to fight money laundering and its underlying offences cannot function effectively. In English law, money received as bribes is recoverable as it is deemed to be money held on a constructive trust in the interest of the principal. The issue here is illustrated by the decision in the case of *AG of Hong Kong Kong v Reid*.[35] The defendant (Mr Reid) had already successfully been prosecuted and was serving a jail term, but this notwithstanding, the government of Hong Kong decided to bring a civil law claim to recover the properties which Mr Reid had bought in New Zealand. In this case, judgement was awarded in favour of the government of Hong Kong as the aforementioned properties were bought from the proceeds of crime and therefore were deemed to have been held on trust for the principal, in this case the government of Hong Kong. According to Lord Templeman: 'When a bribe is accepted by the fiduciary in breach of his duty, then he holds that bribe on trust for the person to whom the duty was owed.'[36]

Similarly, if the property in question has since appreciated in value, the defendant cannot be entitled to the surplus in excess of the original value of the property as he/she would have benefited from his/her illegal conduct, that is, the breach of duty. If this were to be allowed, the defendant would be benefiting from his/her illegality, which goes against the ethos of English law.[37] It would seem on the basis of the evolved precedent in the above case that money stolen as a result of corruption is money held on trust in the interest of countries where it would have originated. It is therefore vital as part of the wider anti-corruption measures that

30 Hawley, 'Exporting Corruption'.

31 Ibid.

32 Johnson, 'In Pursuit of Dirty Money'.

33 Ibid.

34 The embezzlement of GAVI Funds in Uganda – money that was meant for the above purpose, which disappeared as the result of the actions of three government Ministers of Health – clearly supports the above point.

35 [1994] 1 AC 324.

36 Alexander, 'Corruption as a Financial Crime'.

37 This is regarded as the 'golden rule' on which I have had the pleasure to teach students in contract law at an undergraduate degree level.

states cooperate in ensuring that assets accrued from stolen wealth are recovered by societies from where the money originally emanated. However, the assets in question will have to be identified in order to be recovered under what in English law is known as common law tracing. Where the asset has been used to purchase other assets, then it might be advisable to identify the beneficial interests of the claimant in those new assets. In relation to corruption, the money originally stolen from the government might have been used to purchase a house in England and it is this house that becomes subject to common law tracing. Where the original asset has dissipated, equity allows the claimant to identify what remains of the original asset in the hands of the defendant. If the trust asset has been mixed, given the fact that money accrued from corruption is money deemed to be held on constructive trust in the interests of its rightful beneficiaries, the defendant is deemed to have used his/her own money first and whatever remains is deemed to be the trust fund.[38] Assuming that the defendant uses money which was initially accrued in corruption to buy a house, he/she then sells the house and uses the proceeds to buy a car and deposits the balance into his/her account, the money in the account would be held on trust (constructive trust) in the interest of rightful beneficiaries. Alternatively, where in a mixed fund the defendant spends all the money previously in the account and then buys shares to the value of the trust fund, the second withdrawal is deemed to be the trust money and the shares will be trust assets.[39] This discussion lays down what ought to be the approach in relation to stolen assets held in various jurisdictions courtesy of corrupt government individuals. In relation to the money stolen by different corrupt leaders, the beneficiaries should file court proceedings where those assets are held in order to restore them to the countries from which the assets originated. Thus, asset recovery is a vital part of the global strategy against the threat of corruption. As such, every country should establish an assets recovery agency through which to recover and restore stolen assets to countries from which they were stolen. For instance, the creation of the Assets Recovery Agency in the UK, a role now subsumed into SOCA since 2008, is a step in the right direction. The concept of returning stolen assets back to the bona fide owners not only deprives criminals of the opportunity to enjoy the proceeds accrued from looted assets but it is also the right thing to do in relation to getting the property back to its rightful owners. Asset recovery was deemed to be an important strategy in undermining money laundering enterprises. The premise for asset recovery is an admission that the alleged money launderer apprehended at Heathrow might just be a tip of the iceberg after all. In any case, he/she might even be an innocent victim of circumstances. For example, he/she could just be an errand runner on an official mission to deliver a briefcase (unaware of the contents) on behalf of a powerful politician from a dictatorial government somewhere. However, if

38 This position is delineated by the English case of *Re Hallett's Estate* (1879) 13 Ch D 696.

39 A. Pugh-Thomas, 'The Bank – An Attractive Deep Pocket Defendant (Part 2)', *Journal of International Banking Law* (1999): p. 52.

the criminal property is targeted, then it has the potential to undermine further business operations of criminal syndicates. The concept of confiscation of criminal property is an *in rem* proceeding (which can be civil or criminal) and unlike *in personam* procedures can dispense with the requirement of criminally convicting a suspect.[40] An *in rem* proceeding does not necessarily create offences against the person (alleged money launderers or corrupt officials), nor is it designed to impose fines, penalties or even imprisonment on an individual, but instead to ensure that wrongful gains are disgorged. Another obvious advantage of forfeiture proceedings is that the trial can proceed without the defendant necessarily having to appear before the court. However, given the insidious nature of money laundering and corruption crimes, it might not be easy to identify where the criminal property is in order to institute recovery proceedings. Since the effectiveness of assets recovery agencies depends on the robustness of local institutions, the agencies cannot work properly in less developed economies where institutions are more or less dysfunctional. This is precisely why states should ratify UNCAC to ease inter-state relations on matters of corruption. The central plank of UNCAC is the return of stolen assets back to their countries of origin. Article 51 creates a provision in relation to the return of assets plundered by political leaders to their countries of origin. Article 43 calls on member states to extend the widest possible mutual legal assistance in relation to the investigation and prosecution of offences as defined in the Convention. For the expeditious recovery of stolen assets, victim countries, especially developing countries, are asked to foot the bill incurred in repatriating these assets, or at least having it deducted from the value of the assets. The detailed guidelines for expeditious asset recovery to countries of origin are set out in Article 57 of UNCAC.

It does seem that corruption is more rampant in developing countries than it is in developed countries (a view corroborated by Transparency International Reports), presumably because of their weak democratic institutions and the reduced accountability of state officials. Powers are concentrated around the state and certain individuals, allowing them the latitude to commit corrupt acts in various manifestations and remain at large. Corrupt leaders in many developing countries have an enormous degree of discretion that will enable them to do literally whatever they want. They can use this discretion to influence the creation of laws in parliament as well as to exercise their enormous discretion over the proliferation and interpretation of laws that have been created to run the country.[41]

---

40 *In rem* proceedings can be prosecuted by administrative agencies such as SOCA and the Assets Recovery Agency in the UK. On the other hand, *in personam* proceedings are prosecuted through the court system, requiring the defendant to appear before the magistrate. See Keith Fisher, 'In Rem Alternatives to Extradition for Money Laundering', 25 *International and Comparative Law Review* (2003): p. 408.

41 In many countries, presidents appoint judges and other judicial officers such as the attorney general. In a way this is done to ensure that the appointed judges do the president's bidding or else, in the next reshuffle, their jobs cannot be guaranteed.

In many developing countries, corrupt politicians are elected to high political offices democratically. They would have accumulated wealth in advance to be used to further this cause or would have been funded by their parties to ensure that they are elected to particular positions. The *raison d'être* for this is that corrupt governments are sustained by making sure that they have majority representation in parliament in order to push through desired programmes, but also to use their positions to amass wealth and to protect their economic empire from crumbling.[42] On the contrary, honest, intelligent people of high integrity are sidelined by corrupt regimes as they are perceived literally as what one would call 'a thorn in the side'. In so doing, development is undermined as the most talented people are excluded or relegated to minor positions. In order to combat this, corruption can easily be checked through transparent and democratic institutions in developed countries. These democratic institutions would have engendered democratic values and practices to set the standards that every appointed leader is expected to adhere to. Therefore, although corruption is committed in developed countries as well as in developing countries, the difference is that corruption in developed countries is rarely perpetuated through state institutions.[43] In developing countries, corrupt leaders are believed to steal almost 50 per cent of the money meant to fund national budgets, whereas 70 per cent of the population lives on less than US$1 a day.[44] These are the countries that should have been the ultimate beneficiaries of the laundered money and are rightfully entitled to it.

Suffice it to say that laws and systems established to govern societies will be manipulated to foster the interest of corrupt regimes. Corruption is so lethal that it impoverishes economies, threatens democratic institutions and undermines the rule of law, obviously not to mention the fact that it promotes money laundering and the growth of the whole range of criminal activities. It should be noted that money generated as a result of corruption constitutes the proceeds of crime under the extended definition of money laundering.[45] But corruption is also used to facilitate the process of placing tainted money into the mainstream financial system and to get it wired out of the country in a legitimate form.[46] The international community must unite in formulating a framework to facilitate the repatriation of plundered wealth and subsequently to reverse some of the damage inflicted on societies

42 This would seem to explain why corrupt governments are never exposed until they have relinquished power and attendant state protection. Mobutu Sese Seko of Zaire and Sani Abacha of Nigeria are two cases that demonstrate this point, but the list of such cases is endless.

43 This can only be the case of a few bad apples within government departments. In developed countries there are strong institutions to ensure checks and balances, which is not the case in developing countries.

44 Transparency International Report (December 2007), available at www.ti.org (date accessed 6 October 2009).

45 Article 1(1) of the Palermo Convention of December 2000.

46 This is one of the many techniques through which tainted money finds its way out of the country where it has been looted to a safe haven somewhere else.

by corrupt politicians or officials. To a large extent, money stolen as a result of corruption would have been diverted from reaching those who needed it most. This chapter postulates that as more and more countries embrace the AML/CFT framework of regulatory laws, it will undercut money laundering by rendering it a potentially more risky business.[47]

Corruption has created an environment where criminal groups in all their various manifestations are able to establish a stronghold in many countries.[48] Organized criminal groups have resorted to money laundering in different countries to cleanse the proceeds of crime.[49] Money laundering techniques include smurfing, the establishment of front companies, the acquisition of commercial and non-commercial properties, remittance through non-official banking channels and foreign remittance. In vulnerable societies with low salaries, public officials can easily be bribed to turn a blind eye to the obvious, providing an avenue for criminal exploitation including money laundering. In Uganda, the corruption and money laundering nexus is rampant in the tax collection body, the Uganda Revenue Authority (URA), where tax evaders collude with officials not to pay their levies on goods and to under-declare goods, not to mention the use of counterfeit currency and stealing from government funds. In fact, corruption is so entrenched that it has more or less become normal practice, notwithstanding the adoption of anti-corruption legislation[50] by the government. I suppose there are two reasons behind the prevalence of corruption in a country like Uganda: the arbitrary enforcement of engendered laws and the ingrained culture of corruption in various parts of society. As regards the arbitrary enforcement of laws, enforcement agencies should demonstrate a uniform application of laws and procedures to ensure that they are applied and enforced equally across the board. Where laws are rigorously enforced on the powerless or those who are potentially opposed to the cause of the ruling government, such as mavericks and members of the opposition, they will lose their effectiveness. As regards the later, there is a need for the ethical training to change the culture in various areas of society, as this is fundamental to developing an environment where anti-corruption laws or campaigns can flourish. At a corporate management level, there is also a need for the ethical training of managers and employees to demonstrate a high level of commitment to the required moral ethics, leadership and good corporate governance. Businesses should be encouraged to engage with employees and outside consultants to identify potential

47 Johnson, 'In Pursuit of Dirty Money'.

48 Rider, *Corruption: The Enemy Within,* p. 323.

49 Ibid.

50 The Leadership Code 2002, which aims at combating corruption on the part of public officials, requiring them to declare their assets every year. If there is a mismatch in the official's declared wealth, he/she may be asked to account for it. The Leadership Code empowers the Inspector General of the government to freeze accounts pending investigation and to prosecute offenders allegedly in breach of this statute.

areas of weakness to corruption and isolate them.[51] At a government level, there is a need to create policy platforms where important ethical decisions should be openly discussed. Laws should not only be created but enforced to foster good practice and to undertake necessary research on a forward-looking basis, but also to replicate success stories from other societies.[52]

There is also political meddling because of patronage and giving jobs as a token to politically well connected family members of the ruling elite.[53] Job allocation is sublimated to political whims, but the fundamental point is that this practice sidelines the market mechanism of the demand and supply for labour. It has generated a counter-productive effect on the local society's potential to compete favourably in the global market economy. Corruption has also undermines global anti-money laundering initiatives and other development initiatives locally. Money laundering and its predicate offences cannot be combated without fully harnessing the work of auditors, accountants, supervisors, engineers, lawyers, prosecutors, police officers, secretaries, administrators, etc. In short, corruption destroys local institutions and renders many economies susceptible to financial abuse, as shown by the boom in the number of money laundering cases.

It must be said that corruption is instrumental to undermining the rule of law – including laws designed to fight money laundering and the financing of terrorism.[54] In an inherently corrupt system, laws cannot work as envisaged as they are sidelined in the interests of corrupt officials. Corruption undermines national economies and is a threat to democratic institutions, fostering threats to human society such as transnational organized crime and terrorism.[55] Owing to corruption, 80 per cent of privatized enterprises in Russia are said to be controlled by criminals and their syndicates, and of these enterprises 40 per cent are currently owned by the Russian Mafia.[56] While privatization was initially designed to counter public sector corruption, in fact it has also created opportunities for the corrupt that did not previously exist under the state-controlled system.[57] This presumably explains the high incidence of cases of corruption in the majority of countries in transition such

---

51 The biggest problem, especially in developing countries, is for managers to overlook employees and to impose policies without consulting those that will be affected. The rationale for this is that managers cannot effectively manage unless they have the goodwill of their employees.

52 David Hess and Cristie L. Ford, 'Corporate Corruption and Reform Undertakings: A New Approach to an Old Problem', 41 *Cornell International Law Journal* (2008): p. 322.

53 In well-established cases, jobs are awarded for electioneering purposes, apparently being traded in return for support being given to particular candidates.

54 Money launderers or corrupt elements in society, whichever way one wants to put it, work outside or on the fringes of the prescribed rules or laws.

55 Kofi Annan, Secretary-General of the United Nations, 'Message to the Third Global Forum on Fighting Corruption and Safeguarding Integrity', 31 May 2003.

56 Hans Binnendijk (ed.), *Authoritarian Regimes in Transition* (Washington DC: Foreign Service Institute, 1987), p. 8.

57 Shams, 'Using Money Laundering Control to Fight Corruption'.

as Russia. The liberalization process in Russia introduced foreign actors into the domestic economy, which had initially been confined to national actors. It could be said that in an inherently corrupt system, privatization creates openings for criminal exploitation including money laundering. Criminals are known to thrive in an inherently corrupt environment where it is easy to manipulate or corrupt the system. Similarly, criminals will exploit weaknesses in macro-economic policies or will find it easy to infiltrate agencies that are responsible for the prudential supervision of financial institutions.[58] It is my contention that for anti-money laundering programmes such as CDD to work effectively, the system must be able to harness the skills of accountants, auditors, lawyers, supervisors and prosecutors. These people are essential in terms of servicing and keeping the system afloat with regard to its regulatory and supervisory imperatives.[59]

Challenges Posed by Corruption to the Efficacy of National Institutions

Corruption undermines countries by corroding the efficacy of local institutions such as the police and the judiciary. In many developing countries, the police, whose overriding function is to maintain law and order by fighting crimes, has been a veritable hindrance, aiding and abetting to a great extent the commissioning of crimes through corruption. Cases involving corruption have become intractable, either because of influence peddling or high-profile people being implicated in corruption scandals, making it difficult for anti-corruption provisions to be implemented. Similarly, in an inherently corrupt system, the cost of undertaking transactions is disproportionately high relative to what would be normal costs. To achieve his/her objective, the corrupt official will have to use the most sophisticated means to disguise the nature of the transaction. This is one of the *modus operandi* used by criminals in committing money laundering. It can therefore be inferred that firms which engage or collude in corruption can readily fall victim to extortion by people who take bribes – politicians, state officials, business managers, etc. Corruption destroys the integrity of company managers and employees if they collude in or turn a blind eye to corruption activities and criminality.[60]

Laws should always be implemented to demonstrate that the regulatory system is properly functioning. The lack of implementation of engendered laws not only undermines the system, it also creates openings that could potentially be exploited by money launderers. In the UK, money laundering laws (though laudable in

58 Walker, *International Banking Regulation: Law, Policy and Practice*, pp. 307–20.

59 The UK, Canada, Australia and New Zealand have all adopted skills-related immigration policies – for example, they all operate a 'points-based entry system' based on the immigrant's skills and education and whether these skills are required in the receiving country.

60 This was the concern expressed by Transparency International on its website at www.transparency.org/ (date accessed 3 December 2011).

theory) have been hamstrung in practice by the chronic lack of resources available for tackling money laundering, the disjointed handling of suspicious activities and the low priority given to money laundering prosecutions by the police.[61] In Uganda, corruption is increasingly becoming an issue for the government in the majority of government departments, for example, the judiciary (with regard to bribes solicited by court officials in the dispensation of justice),[62] the army (where army officers have been found to have inflated the size of the payroll in the form of 'ghost employees') and so on.[63] However, what is worthy of mention is that the dynamics of corruption make it a global issue, given that many foreign banks might have been used to transmit the illicit proceeds of corruption for safe custody abroad. There is another dimension that rapid privatization, encouraged by the reforms of the World Bank of the financial sector, was seen as an opportunity for corrupt leaders either to reward their cronies or to enrich themselves and members of their families. This has particularly been the case in many African countries, but the most obvious case of this typology of corruption is Kenya. Privatization presented opportunities for corrupt governments to take possession of assets formerly owned by the state and to reward their loyalists. The transfer of assets from the public sector to the private sector is what is technically known as privatization. Given that privatization was initially meant to minimize state intervention in market operations such as the use of subsidies, to relieve stretched government budgets and to instil discipline and stimulate the economy, as far as some economies were concerned, it did not go far enough in achieving this objective.[64] In Kenya, it is said that from simple cleaning contracts to airline business contracts, the privatization process was abused to reward government cronies or the associates of government officials for their loyalty.[65] In view of this, in 1997, the World Bank slammed lending conditions on Kenya whereby the government was asked to introduce concrete anti-corruption measures as a condition for borrowing from the Bank.[66] This was done as part of what had become the new guidelines issued by the IMF in response to corruption in 1997.[67] The guidelines specifically mention corruption as the cause of the diversion of public funds through misappropriation, fraud, money laundering, cronyism,

61 Taken from an article on money laundering in *The Guardian* newspaper (no date given).

62 *New Vision* (a daily newspaper), 26 April 2008.

63 *New Vision*, 27 March 2008.

64 Privatization was premised on the philosophy of the invisible hand of the market. This viewed the state as part of the problem rather than the solution and sought to minimize its influence by conjuring up this economic strategy.

65 C. Baylies, 'Political Conditionality and Democratisation', 65 *Review of African Political Economy* (1995): 321–34.

66 M. Stevens, 'The World Bank on Corruption', in *Governance*, January 1998, pp. 8–12.

67 Beare (ed.), *Critical Reflections on Transnational Organised Crime, Money Laundering and Corruption*, p. 115.

etc. Therefore, fighting corruption was viewed as part and parcel of supporting good governance in a country. However, singling out Kenya did not mean that other African governments did not take advantage of the privatization process to consolidate maladministration and perpetuate bad governance. In many countries, privatization was no longer seen as serving any good purpose as it diverted benefits from the public to corrupt government officials. In the private sector, services that were initially accessible under the old regime had their prices raised, leaving the poor at a disadvantage. Privatization impeded the delivery of essential services such as water in Kenya and hospitals in other parts of Africa, putting the delivery of these services exclusively beyond the reach of certain groups of in society. Conversely, privatization was viewed as responsible for accelerating high levels of unemployment, high infant mortality rates and increased death rates from minor curable diseases in many Third World countries.[68] Besides being abused as a result of corruption, the implementation of Structural Adjustment Programmes (SAPs) in many developing countries such as Uganda tragically tilted the political landscape towards that of simmering unpopularity and retrogressively resurrected the antipathy and despondence reminiscent of the old turbulent past.[69] This, coupled by the demobilization of civil servants, provided a fertile climate and a pool of resources (manpower) that fed and reinforced many rebel groups in the country, where disengaged soldiers were easily enlisted.[70] Donors have sometimes been more interested in markets, exports and political influence than they have in the long-term benefits to beneficiary countries.[71] As such, the market economy has undermined the tenets of self-determination with regard to the sovereign people's rights to determine their own destiny. It has reduced the power of the individual nation-states to shape and determine their destiny through participation in the democratic process. The ability of governments to bring about development, full employment or other national economic goals has been impaired by the power of capital to pick and leave.[72] Third World countries have been caught in a relentless downward spiral due to the SAPs and other economic vagaries.[73] While corruption is as old as mankind, in my view in countries like Uganda, corruption was exacerbated by the poor sequencing of reform programmes that were required

68 Mugarura, 'The Subdued Giant'.

69 People started conceptualizing Ugandan politics in terms of *The Animal Farm* by George Orwell (Harmondsworth: Penguin, 1954). In this book, the author dismisses the hype that greeted the overthrow of Snowball by Napoleon as nothing but a gimmick. Those who understand the history of Uganda will easily appreciate that Uganda has been embroiled in persistent political problems since its independence.

70 This position is well supported by the many Ugandans I contacted to corroborate some aspects of the manifestations of global market system in Uganda.

71 Mugarura, 'The Subdued Giant'.

72 J. Brecher and T. Costello, *The Race to the Bottom* (London: Verso, 1998), pp. 1–45.

73 Mugarura, 'The Subdued Giant'.

of the country under SAPs in the early 1980s.[74] For those who had been sidelined by the transition towards a liberalized market economy, corruption would be viewed literally as 'a means to justify an end', and for those in elevated official government positions, privatization presented an opportunity to own one of the formerly government properties. On a positive note, however, the liberalization of the economy in Uganda has started to demonstrate some signs of progress, such as generating a vibrant business environment, easy access to foreign currency and some conspicuous benefits to the economy.[75] Thus, I propose the need for the proper enforcement of existing anti-corruption regimes in order to consolidate the achievements of a liberalized market economy.

States have failed to work together in enforcing normative AML/CFT regimes created by the very same states. They have been prompt in creating laws at a global level, but when it comes to implementation, ironically they act in an individual manner. This would imply that unless a country anticipates some benefits – pecuniary or non-pecuniary – or is itself a victim of global exigencies, they tend to err on the side of caution and display a form of 'I don't care' attitude towards global regimes.[76] As such, the so-called global village is yet to constitute itself as a coherent, single, viable community subjected to a single set of rules.[77] Besides inter-state alliances, some states would not want to be seen as intrusive, paternalistic, imperialistic and disrespectful, charges that are often brought about whenever one state imposes its discretionary values upon another. Certainly, the majority of countries have not been given the opportunity to participate in the evolution of global regimes such as the FATF and the Basel Committee on Banking Supervision. However, it would seem prudent for a few countries to work together in initiating regimes, but progressively, as issues evolve, other countries, particularly those subject to the envisaged regulatory framework, should be consulted or even co-opted where necessary. This would serve to address any legitimacy issues creeping into the implementation of emerging global initiatives. Corruption has remained a serious problem because, despite all of the proliferated anti-corruption regimes, both at an individual government level with a extraterritorial reach and at an international level such as the EU and the UN, money accrued from corruption continues to flow into the financial centres of many countries unfettered. It is my contention that laws can work better if they are enforced through legitimate

74 Uganda was just recovering from the devastating war of 1979, which ousted the dictator Idi Amin, the whole economy was literally in disarray and the post-war environment was not conducive to sustaining meaningful reform programmes.

75 This has encouraged competition in businesses, improving the quality of goods and services, and some goods that were initially imported from outside countries are now manufactured at home, which is a good thing for the economy.

76 Any weaknesses in the global system are capable of being exploited to foster the insidious agenda of different criminal groups.

77 Steven R. Salbu, 'Extraterritorial Restriction of Bribery: A Premature Evocation of a Normative Global Village', 24 *Yale Journal of international Law* (1999): pp. 226–69.

institutions. Prescribing regimes without enacting measures to enforce them cannot go far in forestalling the twin threats of corruption and money laundering. Therefore, there must be affirmative action on corruption by denying corrupt leaders an opportunity to secure stolen assets in any country. There is also the need for affirmative action on corruption to stem its concomitant social effects and to ensure that essential information[78] is not fettered or diverted by corrupt officials to benefit criminals or criminal syndicates, but is used to benefit law enforcement authorities. Here globalization can play a significant role as an avenue to bring societies into the fold of prolific progressive societies[79] and providing leverage for poorer economies by bringing down transactional costs.[80]

The Role of the World Bank

The World Bank and the IMF have facilitated an environment which promotes good governance in the majority of borrowing member countries.[81] Good governance includes the promotion of transparency and accountability in member countries to ensure that borrowed funds are properly utilized.[82] Although the World Bank has a limited mandate[83] to enforce its will within a member country,

---

78 Globalization is information-driven as a result of the innovations in ICT, but if this information is not properly harnessed, it can go either way, that is, it can also allow criminals to access a society permeated by corruption in much the same that it has helped to bring down transaction costs. This is indeed the flipside of the globalization of world markets.

79 States can share resources such as intelligence and personnel, which are difficult to generate at national level. They can pool their limited resources on overlapping challenges that would otherwise be hard for an individual state to address. Besides the very fact that globalization transcends national boundaries, no country can unilaterally afford to face the threats created by the system alone.

80 Mugarura, 'The Subdued Giant', p. 355.

81 The IMF acts as an open forum for the discussion of corruption where corruption issues are not actively addressed by the borrower country. It can therefore make financial support conditional on reform when necessary to meet the IMF programme objectives. The IMF has in the past suspended financial assistance to a number of developing countries (for example, Kenya) due to concerns about macro-economic and programme implications of corruption and a lack of fiscal transparency. See 'Twenty-nine Countries Agree on OECD Anti-Corruption Convention and Other International Initiatives Progress', *13 Int'l Enforcement L. Rep.* (1997): pp. 510–512.

82 'IMF Adopts Guidelines regarding Governance Issues', 4 August, 1997, available at www.imf.org/external/np/sec/nb/1997/nb9715.htm (date accessed 3 December 2011).

83 Article 111(5)(b)–(c) of the Articles of Agreement. See also Ibrahim F.I. Shihata, 'Corruption – A General View with an Emphasis on the Role of the World Bank', 15 *Dick. J. Int'l* (1995): pp. 451–75.

it nevertheless ensures that soft law obligations are applied[84] in order to reduce the problem of corruption. In 1997, to demonstrate its commitment to fighting money laundering, the IMF went as far as warning member countries that funding could be withdrawn unless they adopted measures against corruption. It issued policy guidelines highlighting the dangers of corruption, such as the diversion of public funds through misappropriation, tax evasion, fraud, money laundering, the misuse of foreign exchange reserves, the abuse of power by bank supervisors and poor practices in regulating FDI.[85]

In the case of Mobutu Sese Seko discussed above, even though he was known to be diverting up to 50 per cent of the money borrowed for development assistance, the World Bank did little to stop it, and nor did it stop lending to his corrupt government until 1993.[86] The Articles of Agreement – the mandate of the World Bank's operations in member countries – imposes on the Bank the duty to ensure that the proceeds of its loans are spent only on designated purposes and that due attention is given to economy and efficiency.[87] Corruption diverts the proceeds of the Bank's loans from its designated purpose to private pockets. It therefore undermines the development efforts of the Bank, reduces public interest in the reform process – as I have already mentioned in relation to privatization – and causes the Bank's work to be perceived in a bad light, especially at a grassroots level in the country receiving the loans. Why would the World Bank literally acquiesce in corruption by lending to a country in the knowledge that money would be diverted from its intended purposes? It is sufficient to say that the World Bank and the IMF were not mandated to deal with matters involving corruption, as this was considered to be an internal matter for the individual state to deal with.[88] But again it needs to be noted that corruption has a huge economic impact on the economy, which brings it within the purview of the World Bank and

84 In July 1996, the Executive Director of the World Bank added a new section to its procurement guidelines on 'Fraud and Corruption'. This section allows it to cancel financing when corrupt practices are discovered and are not satisfactorily remedied by the borrower, to declare a consultant or supplier who engages in corrupt practices ineligible to bid in future contracts for a contract, to require the inclusion of contract provisions that allow the World Bank to inspect the accounts and records of contractors, suppliers and consultants and have them audited, to require disclosure of any payments made to local agents and to undertake large-scale audits of bank operations and a specific country by outside auditors.

85 Beare (ed.), *Critical Reflections on Transnational Organised Crime, Money Laundering and Corruption.*

86 Hawley, 'Exporting Corruption.

87 Shams, 'Using Money Laundering Control to Fight Corruption'.

88 Due to the fact that the World Bank does not have a sufficient mandate on corruption, the official of the Bank who witnesses corruption is not allowed to inform the government or to talk to the press directly about it. If he/she does, he/she will risk being deported out of the country for political meddling.

the IMF.[89] Bribes represent the illegal use of fees, taxes and access charges paid to public agents. These payments represent economic decisions and thus compel the World Bank and the IMF to address the issue of corruption resulting from such payments.[90] If the level of corruption in a country[91] is so high as to have an adverse impact on the effectiveness of the Bank's assistance and there is factual and objective analysis that the government is doing very little about it, the Bank will often take that into account in its lending strategy towards that country.[92] Given that corruption was viewed as a political matter, it was deemed to be an internal matter for which the Bank did not have jurisdiction. Until the 1990s, the Bank's work in relation to corruption was literally curtailed, but since then corruption was brought within the requirement of good governance to be addressed by a country as a condition for lending.[93] The Articles of Agreement was the major obstacle which made corruption an internal matter beyond the jurisdiction of the Bank. But while corruption was considered to be an internal matter, its prevalence is a sign of bad governance. In 1992, the Bank issued a report on good governance and development in which it established that good governance was central to creating and sustaining an environment which fosters strong, equitable development and good economic policies.[94] This marked a change in attitude towards corruption and henceforth the Bank would address corruption as a governance challenge to be addressed by a country seeking development assistance.[95]

In its efforts to fight corruption within its ranks, the World Bank enacted internal staff rules, requiring the annual financial disclosure of all assets and financial transactions by senior staff, the disclosure of family interests that affect the World Bank's dealings and providing guidelines on how employees are to behave in their dealings inside and outside of the Bank.[96] The IMF provides advice and technical assistance to foster good governance in areas within its mandate and expertise (mostly legal and institutional reforms), collaborating with other institutions, particularly the Work Bank, to coordinate their complementary areas

89 Shihata, 'Corruption – A General View with an Emphasis on the Role of the World Bank'.

90 Rose-Ackerman, *Corruption and Governments*, p. 30.

91 On a number of occasions, the Bank suspended funding on the development projects upon discovering evidence of corruption.

92 Shihata, 'Corruption – A General View with an Emphasis on the Role of the World Bank'.

93 Rose-Ackerman, *Corruption and Governments*.

94 Shihata, 'Corruption – A General View with an Emphasis on the Role of the World Bank'.

95 The fight on corruption was given more momentum with the appointment of James D. Wolfensohn as the new President of the World Bank in 1995. He strongly campaigned against corruption and as a result corruption was subsumed within a comprehensive World Bank strategy in delivering development assistance to member countries.

96 Shihata, 'Corruption – A General View with an Emphasis on the Role of the World Bank'.

of expertise.[97] It does this by assisting the economic policies of member countries through building policy-making institutions and improving the accountability of the public sector.[98]

The Bank's Potential Liability in Corruption Cases

It is possible that a bank accepting deposits accrued from corruption could be liable for assisting an offender in the transmission of the proceeds of crime. It could also be liable for dishonest assistance where it is proved that the bank acted dishonestly in accepting deposits after it had suspected or known that the deposits in question are accrued from corruption. However, the prosecution will have to prove that the bank by so doing acted dishonestly. Bearing in mind the Privy Council's decision in *Royal Brunei Airlines v Tan*,[99] acting dishonestly means 'not acting as an honest person would in the circumstances'.[100] It is an objective standard where the jury must demonstrate that by accepting deposits accrued from corruption, the bank fell below the ordinary standard of an ordinary honest man in those circumstances, that is, the bank's action would have been dishonest according to the ordinary standards of a reasonable honest person. This means that it must realize that its action by accepting deposits accrued from corruption had, by the standards of an ordinary honest person, fallen below what was expected of it.[101]

However, the bank can only be held liable for knowing receipt where there is compelling evidence that it had knowledge of the underlying breach of trusteeship. The knowing receipt concept is not based upon the receipt by the defendant of any trustee property (in this case, the tainted proceeds of corruption), but is said to be based on the participation in the trustee fraud by the defendant and for this chapter's purposes the bank.[102] For example, where the bank knowingly issues cheques, letters of credit or any other financial products to facilitate a person who is attempting to launder money generated from criminal activity, where established, the bank will be liable for knowing assistance. Likewise, where the bank accepts money knowingly from someone who has stolen government funds, it could be liable. This illustration helps to explain how the bank could be liable in cases of corruption, but it also raises another question: how is the bank deemed to have knowledge of the surrounding circumstances in relation to the money it receives from customers? Banking is a business and therefore the bank should not

97 Ibid.

98 'The Role of the IMF in Governance Issues', IMF News Brief No. 97/15, available at: www.imf.org/external/np/sec/nb/1997/NB9715.HTM (date accessed 5 August 2008).

99 [1995] 2 AC 378.

100 Pugh-Thomas, 'The Bank – An Attractive Deep Pocket Defendant (Part 2)', p. 50.

101 This illustration is based on the English case of *R v Ghosh* [1982] 2 All ER 689.

102 *Barnes v Addy* [1874] LR 9 Ch. App 244.

be invidiously made to act as a policeman apprehending thieves. As I have already mentioned, the test in relation to knowledge is objective and can also be inferred from objective factual circumstances. But, on the other hand, while banking is a business and is therefore profit-driven, the bank is bound by regulatory guidelines governing its operations.[103] As such, it should make necessary inquiries and satisfy itself that the money it is accepting is not the tainted proceeds of crime. In *Development Pty Ltd v DPC Estate Pty Ltd*,[104] knowledge is circumscribed by the following elements: (i) actual knowledge; (ii) wilfully shutting one's eyes to the obvious; (iii) wilfully and recklessly failing to make such inquiries as an honest and reasonable person would make; (iv) knowledge of the circumstances that would indicate the facts to an honest and reasonable person. If someone whose account has had persistent liquidity problems all of a sudden just splashes millions of dollars into his/her bank account, the bank should follow the required reporting guidelines.[105] But what if it takes a bribe and ignores the required anti-money laundering guidelines such as CDD, then it will be liable for knowing assistance.

Conclusion

Corruption is likened to a plague that undermines legal systems, impedes the implementation of laws, and destroys and undermines markets and the efficacy of local institutions in relation to their international law obligations. Corruption is insidious and has a wide range of corrosive effects on countries and governments. It undermines democracy and the rule of law, creates an environment conducive to violence and the violation of human rights, erodes markets and human rights and, worst of all, is exploited to feed and reinforce money laundering and its predicate crimes. Corruption therefore undermines the fabric of society and humanity. The environment created by corruption is likely to act in favour of criminals and their syndicates, providing access to countries targeted for criminal operations. While some countries, especially developing countries, have demonstrated the desire to fight corruption, their efforts are undermined by the local dynamics of development. In many countries in Africa, the system is too antiquated to respond to the fast-moving world and these countries will in my view take time to align

103 These guidelines are enunciated by many anti-money laundering oversight institutions, such as the Basel Committee, the FATF, the World Bank and the IMF, as I have already elucidated above.

104 (1975) 132 CLR 373.

105 Many banks which operate international standards must have a designated money laundering officer who should be notified when there are suspicions of money laundering. But again, the banks need to follow other guidelines, such as the threshold that the bank must accept from the customer. Where the transaction has been structured such that the deposits fall below reporting guidelines, it may also have to inform the money laundering officer so that he/she in turn can inform FIUs.

their economies to global required standards. It is perhaps also important to say that the term 'globalization' is a misnomer, because the concept assumes, albeit wrongly, that all countries have the potential to coexist. As necessary as it is, this coexistence – manifested by the cooperation of states – is not easy to generate.

Thus, I propose that two things should be undertaken to prevent regulatory shortcomings at a developing country level. There is a need for countries in developing countries to develop robust data registry centres equivalent of the National Audit Office in the UK in order to facilitate criminal reference checks[106] on both present and prospective bank clients.[107] This would go a long way towards creating profiles on criminals and criminal syndicates that could be accessed by all regulatory agencies. The generated information could help banks and other financial institutions to discover who the corrupt government officials are and to subject them to rigorous scrutiny before giving them access to sophisticated financial products such as the letter of credit or e-money, or even the electronic funds transfer. Unless there is sufficient information generated on bank customers as well as streamlined internal CDD mechanisms, the above innovative financial products can be exploited for criminal purposes. According to international banking regulatory standards, banks are required to know their customers.[108] However, in practicing the above standards, it would seem that corruption is never conceived as a money laundering predicate offence. In my view it is high time that this conception was changed in order to make corruption subject to global anti-money laundering laws. For this to happen, banks will have to first clean their acts up and lead the way with regard to local anti-corruption campaigns. In addition, it is important for countries to establish modalities for inter-state cooperation in areas of information exchange to overcome any potential information shortfalls. Models laws should be used as a framework for creating robust laws locally, particularly in economies with tenuous anti-money laundering regulatory frameworks. Model laws can work effectively once they have been modified to suit local conditions. For example, in Uganda Barclays Bank has established policy measures to close the regulatory failures resulting from ignorance of the market.[109]

The theory of globalization has in practice failed to crystallize into a viable regulatory framework capable of being enforced globally. There is no central authority (government) with jurisdiction over what global entities can and cannot do. I am sure we are in agreement that the 'invisible hand of the market' advocated

106 Undertaken at the Criminal Records Bureau, from which credit profiles of those seeking to borrow from banks are sought.

107 Banks in England collaborate in the exchange of information on prospective bank clients or those who seek to borrow from any individual bank or branch. In Uganda in particular, banks are vulnerable because even if an individual has defaulted in one bank, he/she can simply cross over to another bank and borrow without ever being cross-checked on his/her history.

108 I have already highlighted this challenge in the preceding sections of this chapter.

109 Barclays Bank, Africa Policy for the Prevention of Money Laundering (2001).

by Adam Smith has failed to deliver market discipline. Perhaps this is covered by the adage that freedom without safeguards creates chaos and lawlessness, as we have seen in the light of the recent global financial crisis. Therefore, there are glaring challenges in the enforcement of normative global regimes – whether the aforementioned regimes relate to corruption, money laundering or otherwise. Some countries tend to hover on the sidelines of global initiatives until they themselves fall victim to overlapping global exigencies. Given this, globalization has failed to constitute itself as a viable framework with a coherent set of rules. This kind of disunity and ambivalence does not augur well for the future of the whole globalization project. This ambivalence has prompted some scholars to dismiss the globalization of markets as a misnomer. As regards corruption, in developing countries, money laundering and corruption are embedded within each other and, in my view, corruption supersedes money laundering in terms of the damage it inflicts on societies. If one conceives money laundering to be part of the underground criminal enterprise perpetuated by criminals, this typology of money laundering is not as lethal in many developing countries as money laundering perpetuated by politicians in the form of corruption. Corruption is devouring economies and I wonder why it is never integrated into the development studies in many developing countries. The under-estimation of its effect is presumably part of the reason why it has been treated literally with soft hands and as something to be ignored. Therefore, money laundering and corruption offences should be accorded the same level of attention and subjected equally to rigorous global regulatory standards.

Chapter 6
Challenges to the Localization of Global Anti-Money Laundering Standards in Less Developed Economies

Introduction

The process of implementing normative AML/CFT regimes is dictated by varying dynamics of development in the majority of less developed economies. The UN Human Development Index (1996) defines less developed economies as those where each citizen survives on US$1 or less a day on average. However, in the context of this study, we define less developed countries as those which face the challenge of absolute systemic failure and are deficient in the necessary level of infrastructural development.

This chapter highlights the need for education, judicial reforms and the creation of robust anti-money laundering institutions as a prerequisite for the transposition of desired market changes. Undertaking the necessary reforms based on the above factors is essential to ease the ability of states to assimilate global AML/CFT standards into domestic society. It is unrealistic for states subject to different dynamics of development to be expected to adopt the same regulatory framework at the same time in the interest of the markets and not of the individual state concerned. For instance, some states are deficient in the requisite capacity to implement such a framework effectively and it is therefore unrealistic for them to be expected to harness normative anti-money laundering regimes. This chapter therefore underscores the challenges to the adoption of normative AML/CFT regimes across the board.

While the globalization of markets is endowed with the potential to foster domestic changes, the envisaged changes should be implemented bearing in mind the particularities of development in each individual country. Thus, the focus of this chapter is to underscore the challenges that inhibit the ability of some states to harness normative AML/CFT standards efficiently. This chapter has deconstructed the global market environment, articulating how the global AML/CFT regimes can robustly be harnessed as a global framework.

The Diversity and Regulation of Financial Markets

In a fragmented global economy fraught with inequalities, the regulation of financial markets has to reflect the diversity and complexity of the world, which in my view should be based on the equivalent of European mutual recognition principle, a principle that was exploited to enhance the integration of financial markets in Europe.[1] This principle is a non-centralized regulatory system combining home and host jurisdictions, and the recognition and harmonization of a managed regulatory system, as opposed to issuing hundreds of directives to achieve uniformity in EU Member States.

Mutual recognition, which was the central plank of the Second Banking Directive,[2] proposes that rather than emphasizing convergence of the system (which is not possible, given the different legal systems and cultural backgrounds of Member States), supervisory authorities should instead recognize systems operated by other Member States subject to the fulfilment of certain basic conditions.[3] The doctrine of mutual recognition, enunciated by the *Cassis de Dijon* case,[4] is used in the commercial sphere to overcome the hindrance of international movement of natural and juristic persons, goods and services that may be posed by the coexistence of multiple jurisdictions.[5]

The issue of multiple jurisdictions is characterized by different legal traditions and cultures, resulting in jurisdictional conflicts and a situation where compliance with international norms becomes a legal problem. The globalization of markets is yet to constitute itself as a viable global system with a single set of rules, and this challenge is compounded by multiple rules engendered by different regulatory regimes. This problem has rendered the global system complex and particularly in terms of transposing the engendered norms into substantive national laws. The alternative has been to encourage the harmonization of rules and cooperation among states, underscored by the mutual recognition principle in Europe. This

---

1 This was intended to foster a single market doctrine in banking and financial services, with no internal barriers to EU banks establishing branches in other parts of the EU or in providing cross-border services. A bank licensed in one EU Member State had a passport to establish branches or to provide services in other EU Member States. A single licence is required rather than licensing in each Member State. However, the licence does not apply to a branch of a bank established outside of the EU; the third bank must incorporate a subsidiary in the EU and be licensed in at least one jurisdiction there.

2 Directive 89/646/EEC.

3 Ibid.

4 The *Cassis de Dijon* doctrine has also expanded geographically outside the borders of the EU. Through the conclusion of the EEA (European Economic Area) Agreement and the EU–Turkey customs union, the principle of mutual recognition has, with some variations, now been extended to goods coming from Norway, Iceland and Liechtenstein (as EEA members) and Turkey. In order to implement this principle, the European Commission has insisted that EU Member States adopt a mutual recognition clause.

5 Case 120/78 [1979] ECR 649.

principle, propounded by the Second Banking Directive, is predicated on the realization that the integration of financial markets in Europe did not necessarily mean a 'one-size-fits-all' approach, but unity in diversity.

It has to be said that inter-state cooperation is necessary to avoid the adverse effects of the 'prisoner's dilemma', in which each participant is unsure of whether others will cooperate or engage in behaviour detrimental to the stability of the global economy. However, subscribing to global initiatives has proved problematic where societies are characterized by different local and developmental challenges which dictate the adaptability of the evolved global anti-money laundering regimes differently. There is the need for a common framework to ensure that evolving regimes in different jurisdictions complement each other in safeguarding against regulatory arbitrage[6] or regulatory failures.[7]

Regulatory arbitrage and regulatory failures are common features of an uncoordinated international system. In order for aspects of a large-scale regulation to be effective, it must be coordinated and perhaps formulated on a global basis.[8] Proliferating anti-money laundering regimes should be devised, taking into account the need to respond to dynamic changes in society (for example, changes in technology, the regulatory climate and the general business and criminal landscape). A proper sequencing is therefore necessary to guarantee the development of an adequate infrastructure and resources for the effective implementation of desired market changes. This view is proposed based on the fact that societies are different from each other in terms of infrastructural development and it is supposedly arbitrary for societies to adopt a common regulatory framework without first creating a requisite infrastructure.

While it is important for states to undertake necessary market reforms, these reforms should be engendered and implemented sequentially on a forward-looking basis. Mutual recognition as a model of regulating financial markets in Europe should be piloted and perhaps adopted globally because it provides a harmonization framework for the foreign and host regulatory systems without much conflict. EU Member States are characterized by different internal legal systems (in terms of contract and employment laws) and different regulatory environments coexisting within EU law.

6 This identifies and exploits any inconsistencies in the market and undermines the effectiveness of capital regulation. See Chris Mattens, 'Managing Capital Accord', 2000, p. 4, available at www.riskglossary.com/articles/regulatory_capital.htm (date accessed 4 December 2011).

7 Capital adequacy has been criticized in that the required eight per cent capital reserve is arbitrary, since it does not reflect the lows and highs of a business. In an ideal world, a well-designed regulatory system should see capital reserves rising during periods of high profitability and earnings for banks and falling in a recessionary period. See E.I. Altman and A. Saunders, 'An Analysis and Critique of the BIS Proposal of Capital Adequacy and Ratings', 25 *Journal of Banking and Finance* (2001): pp. 26–8.

8 Ibid.

Therefore, without mutual recognition, whereby states agree to surrender part of their sovereignty in order to coexist with the legal systems of different states, an integrated single European market would never have been achievable. Mutual recognition presupposes the equivalence of the objective of national legislation and the existence of similar public interest goals.[9] It also implies and requires mutual trust. Mutual trust in turn is fostered through the adoption of common rules. Mutual recognition and minimum harmonization are accompanied by other factors: home country control and the single banking licence.[10] With home country control, the home country undertakes to control and supervise its financial institutions as a substitute for host country supervision.[11]

In order for mutual recognition to function properly, domestic countries will have to adopt the different legal systems of other countries at home. However, this is difficult to apply in an environment where some countries have not defined money laundering as a distinct offence. This makes it nearly impossible to clamp down on potential money launderers because of the absence of laws and policies specifically created to deal with it.[12]

The absence of specific anti-money laundering legislation means that societies with tenuous anti-money laundering safeguards will have a regulatory advantage over those that have stringent laws (free-riding), but this is also counter-productive as far as attracting FDI in the host society is concerned. Small states are always reluctant to prosecute money laundering offences for fear that the negative publicity generated by such prosecutions (which are easily disseminated by the global media) could jeopardize the economy in terms of the flow of FDI.

It is my contention that this situation explains why many states choose to operate in secrecy and disguise the definition of certain crimes, even though they are being hurt by the prevalence of the same crimes at home.[13] This is supposedly why some (including Uganda) have preferred to operate on the fringes of the envisaged global anti-money laundering framework by delaying the creation of any distinct anti-money laundering legislation.

Making investment decisions entails aggregating the prevailing investment climate so as to ensure the security of the investment projects, and it can also be inferred that a sloppy system with ill-defined laws will not help in generating

9 Rosa M. Lastra, 'Law Reform in Emerging Economies', 3(2) *Journal of International Banking Law and Regulation* (2008): p. 419.

10 Ibid.

11 Ibid.

12 This renders societies an easy target for drug trafficking and money laundering, scaring off potential investors who usually prefer a sound regulatory regime to a lax one.

13 In Zambia, during the presidency of Fredrick Chiluba, journalists who reported on the prevalence of HIV/AIDS in the country would be imprisoned, allegedly for fear of engendering an anti-investment climate. In Uganda, during the early years of the leadership of President Yoweri Museveni, adopted the opposite approach without much impact on the FDI flow.

the much-desired positive investment climate. Equally, in the absence of robustly defined anti-money laundering laws, banks will be vulnerable and exposed to the risks of lawsuits and loss of trust if they breach confidentiality by reporting customers whose identities are then revealed.[14]

Bankers argue that, first and foremost, banking is a business and therefore a strict regulatory regime will scare off potential or existing customers. On many occasions, banks fail to enforce appropriate measures because they fear they will lose customers who may prefer to keep their money 'under the mattress' if to use banks means to bring out trouble in the form of rules, laws and procedures (which apparently customers do not understand).

Owing to the absence of robust laws and policies on money laundering in some jurisdictions, many foreign financial institutions adopt internal or sectoral measures to fill the vacuum in their internal anti-money laundering framework.[15] This has been possible through the macro-economic link to their parent home country institutions, whereby financial institutions domiciled in a foreign country are controlled by the policies of the parent authorities. Others have developed specific policies for preventing money laundering (such as Barclays Bank's Africa Policy for the Prevention of Money Laundering in 2001).[16] These measures are based on anti-money laundering legislation in the UK[17] and the Anti-Money Laundering Directives of the EU.[18]

As regards the courts, the absence of robust anti-money laundering legislation means one of two things. When the crime has not been recognized and defined by the national parliament, the courts can only prosecute on the grounds of customary international law.[19] It also means that the envisaged anti-money laundering regimes may not be effective, even though the state has ratified the necessary treaty. Where individual states do not feel the urgency of a particular law and yet the same law is deemed necessary for global cooperation, the state may either employ delaying tactics or circumvent its international obligations by failing to transpose the ratified treaties into domestic law.[20] Some states have passed implementing legislation that

---

14 This duty exists as a matter of contract between the customer and the bank, but also by virtue of the Data Protection Act 1998. See Cranston, *Principles of Banking Law*, p. 168; and also the frequently cited case of *Tournier v National Provincial and Union Bank of England* [1924] 1 KB 461.

15 I have already fully explored this point in Chapter 1.

16 Peter Edopu, 'Infrastructure to Detect and Control Money Laundering and Terrorist Funding in Uganda', available at www.iss.co.za/pubs/Monographs/No108/Chap3.pdf (date accessed 4 December 2011).

17 The Proceeds of Crime Act 2002 as amended.

18 Article 2(2) of the Second Anti-Money Laundering Directive.

19 There is a possibility of prosecuting money laundering and its predicate offences under customary law.

20 While Egypt ratified the Fourth Geneva Convention, it has never passed any implementing domestic legislation, which means in principle that it cannot implement the same Convention locally.

in fact restricts or narrows the scope of the grounds of jurisdiction laid down in international treaties.[21] For example, Uganda has not passed a law creating money laundering as a distinct offence. While crimes that generate proceeds that are laundered are punishable under the law, money is still a derivative crime.[22]

Latent and Infrastructural Deficiencies

Many nation-states or jurisdictions in developing countries are deficient in terms of infrastructural development and hence are likely to be slow in transposing the envisaged global anti-money laundering standards into domestic law. This problem is attributable to information asymmetries which curtail their capacity against the upsurge of overlapping global exigencies within their territories. Similarly, the global asymmetry of power has generally translated into ineffectiveness with regard to harnessing the proliferating regimes on money laundering. In relation to the FATF, this study has identified several drawbacks, which are given below.

Many aspects of anti-money laundering control (such as Recommendation 14 of the FATF) articulate the need for CDD to ensure the continuous monitoring of customers' accounts for money laundering purposes. A corollary of the duty to report suspicious transactions is the obligation of credit and financial institutions to demonstrate due diligence in their transactions. Credit and financial institutions are under a duty to examine with special attention any transactions which they regard as particularly likely, by their nature, to be related to money laundering. This duty extends the scope of cooperation beyond suspicious transaction reporting; according to the EU Commission it is a previous and necessary condition of reporting and therefore comes into play even when there is not yet specific suspicion of money laundering.[23]

The due diligence duty reflects the consideration behind Recommendations 14 (formerly 15) and 21 of the FATF. According to Recommendation 14, financial institutions should pay special attention to all complex or unusually large transactions or unusual patterns of transactions which have no apparent economic or visible lawful purpose. Recommendation 21, on the other hand, calls for special attention to be paid to business relations and transactions involving countries which

21 A case in point is the US legislation implementing the Fourth Geneva Convention. While the Geneva Convention lays down the 'universality principle' on all war crimes, this principle was replaced in the USA, in blatant breach of the Conventions, by the traditional principle of active and passive personality: see Antonio Cassese, *International Criminal Law* (Oxford: Oxford University Press, 2003), p. 306.

22 Edopu, 'Infrastructure to Detect and Control Money Laundering and Terrorist Funding in Uganda'.

23 Commission 1995, quoted in Mitsilegas, *Money Laundering Counter-Measures in the European Union.*

do not apply the FATF anti-money laundering standards or do so insufficiently.[24] In both cases, an attempt was made to establish the objective model of due diligence with the introduction of the concept of 'an unusual transaction'.[25] However, what constitutes unusual transactions caused a series of reactions related to the absence of legal certainty and the potential of the provision to impose a heavy burden on the institutions concerned.[26]

In fact, the FATF requires all countries' banks to keep account books and records of transactions for prudential supervision, statistics and tax records. The problems related to poor infrastructural development affect the effective administration of this paradigm; the system is either rudimentary in order to provide 'just-in-time' results or the information on which to make an instant judgement is patchy and unreliable. In many developing countries,[27] there is not only insufficient data generated on different crime typologies but also limited access to a centralized database of cases generated relating to the same crimes. A lack of data tends to inhibit the ability of local anti-money laundering institutions or agencies in internalizing the experiences of money laundering and its attendant predicate threats. Local money laundering experiences will enable societies to design a robust local anti-money laundering preventive strategy. It is my contention that unless there is sufficient data generated on different crime typologies, the respective agencies (police or otherwise) will be less effective in evolving robust policy measures on the threat of money laundering. This is compounded by the problem of corruption, where poorly paid civil servants are easily influenced to conspire with criminals to undermine the smooth operation of anti-money laundering laws. Low salaries for government officials, the need or desire to supplement the modest salaries of public sector officials and the use of clever business practices to mask the receipt of illicit payments are among the many problems that affect the proper functioning of global anti-money laundering laws in many societies.

With regard to customer account monitoring requirements, the challenge facing international regulators is that it is difficult for forex bureaux to know or generate customers' profiles. This is because many customers use forex bureaux on a one-off transaction basis, but also there are limited records to use for verification purposes. The transaction takes place at the counter and only patchy records on

24 Gilmore, 'International Action against Drug Trafficking', pp. 388–90.

25 Ibid.

26 In this context, the Economic and Social Committee called on banking practice to resolve the issues created by the article, while the parliament changed the wording slightly to include 'any unusual transaction and/or any transaction not having an apparent economic or visible lawful purpose'.

27 This problem has been voiced by the Anti-Money Laundering Committee in East Africa, which works under the auspices of the ESAAMLG. However, because of international pressure for the harmonization of local laws, there has been some improvement in terms of record keeping.

the transaction or the identity of the customer are kept or generated.[28] In Uganda, for example, the majority of Ugandans do not hold bank accounts and operate their businesses on a cash-only basis, making the regulation of a cash economy difficult. When people sell their produce (whatever this may happen to be) on the open market, they are paid cash, which they carry around in bags until it is spent. In the interim, some may prefer to keep the money 'under the mattress', since, for a large section of people, the concept of opening a bank account is still unfamiliar and not yet internalized into the society. In so doing, they miss out on the benefits of accessing essential facilities such as letters of credit, bonds and other financial instruments in securely effecting cash payments which are limited to bank-account holders. As this challenge highlights, tackling money laundering becomes more difficult where there is no clear distinction between 'tainted' and 'clean' cash. Therefore, the evolving anti-money laundering measures would succeed if the public was made aware not only of money laundering but also its far-reaching effects.

Ideally, the proposed institutional reforms should reflect the necessary market dynamics within the capacity of the society in question. Government-issued identification documents (such as passports, birth certificates and identity cards) should be appropriately used in verifying the identity of the bank's clients; however, in situations where this is not possible because of the tenuous infrastructure in some societies, an equivalent means of verification should be devised. Drawing on the experiences of Uganda, local leaders under the aegis of a local council system[29] are used to verify the identity of persons wishing to apply for Ugandan passports for the purpose of travelling abroad.[30] Banks should liaise with other agencies (such as the anti-fraud wing of the police) to ensure that the system of verification is streamlined and properly utilized for customer identification purposes.

In many societies, banks are susceptible to money laundering schemes because of insufficient information on present or prospective bank clients. The problem in relation to the poor dissemination of information has manifested itself into a lack of a robust system which banks could use to verify persons who are seeking to borrow money from local banks. To make matters worse, when a person has

28 Customers are simply asked to complete a foreign exchange transaction form indicating the amount of foreign currency that is being bought from or sold to a particular forex bureau. No other form of identity is required.

29 Lately, there have been instances where foreigners have given bribes to obtain Ugandan passports (for example, the case of the former Congolese rebels arrested in Belgium with Ugandan passports). If the system is streamlined by isolating the above anomalies, it has the potential to ease deficiencies in passport application checks.

30 The logic is that members of every household are either registered or known by local councillors and are therefore in closer proximity to the applicant than a government official somewhere else in a different district. The system has worked both effectively and well, except that it has recently been undermined by corruption (bribes). Record keeping at a local level is very poor and the majority of the local councillors are illiterate. As long as they are popular with the electorate, they will be elected.

defaulted in one bank, it is possible that he/she can simply walk across the road to the next bank and borrow money without ever being identified or detected as the defaulter in that previous bank.

Disparities in Technology and a Two-Lane System

It should be noted that since globalization is technologically embedded, the space within which global processes operate is dominated by the technologically advanced economies and is inimical to technologically less developed economies. First of all, the widespread availability of effective encryption technology undermines money laundering controls in countries which are 'driving in the slow lane' in terms of technological development.[31] The ICT world is developing very quickly, which presupposes that countries moving at a slower rate could be vulnerable to criminal exploitation. Criminals have demonstrated a high level of agility in exploiting weakness in the system, manipulating markets, undermining controls and doing whatever they do in a sophisticated manner that keeps them clear of detection. Criminals have robustly exploited enhanced technology to communicate with their sponsors and other syndicates with regard to activities like setting up schemes and liaising with local criminal groups. It is important to note that the pervasiveness of the Internet has not only engendered new crime typologies but has also drastically changed the landscape within which traditional crimes are conceptualized. Meanwhile, in developed countries, advances in technology mean that many business operations are impersonalized (for example, online and telephone banking), making the system prone to manipulation. Criminals are known to exploit advances in ICT not only to perpetuate money laundering but also to stay ahead of the game by circumventing state prudential and regulatory controls. In theory, globalization works as a means to transmit technological benefits from one place to another, helping to create a level playing field for all in the long run. However, the Internet provides an ideal opportunity for perpetuating money laundering-related crimes in technologically disadvantaged countries.

Specifically, the traditional KYC paradigm of AML/CFT control is being threatened by the innovative changes ushered in by advances in technology. Following the changed business landscape, criminals who would have been identified at the initial business stage take advantage of advances in technology to exploit the impersonalized nature of the modern business landscape. Thus, much as globalization in its economic context has generated economic opportunities for the business community,[32] the system is still skewed in favour of a handful of

31 Nigel Morris-Cotterill, 'The Use and Abuse of the Internet in Fraud and Money Laundering', 13(2) *International Law Review* (1999): pp. 211–12.

32 Some of these include the augmentation of domestic savings, the reduction in the cost of capital, the transfer of technology from advanced countries to developing

societies and is arguably less (or not at all) global as the system seeks to assert.[33] This is either explained by the sharp information asymmetries that exist between two societies or the fact that the global system needs to be customized locally by each society according to its development priorities. If societies fail to generate the requisite information, important policy issues may be misjudged, resulting in increased transactional costs and hence reduced profit margins.

The above predicament is associated with many developing countries where there are a host of problems, such as the absence of a centralized intelligence system, a confusing system of collation of information or a lack of investigatory capability to assess and prevent criminal activity. Equally, poor information undermines economies in pursuing the fight against organized crime groups. Therefore, the proponents of the global system have no choice but to take into consideration the local particularities in different countries of the global community in order for the envisaged framework to work. As far as African countries are concerned, the focus should be on establishing clear priorities to foster technological development, market-oriented education, the elimination of corruption and democratic governance.

Educational Shortcomings in Some Societies

There is a direct correlation between education and the stability of markets. This implies that a good education system generates a positive impact on markets and vice versa. In many developing countries, education is antiquated and not properly responsive to the imperatives of the global market system. Consequently, it can be argued that the majority of less developed economies are not able to engage meaningfully in global relations. Similarly, a less robust education system also means that some countries will not be able to cope with the speed and complexity at which the global system is moving. Thus, education creates a platform for awareness of market needs and challenges to markets posed by the interaction of national economies and global institutions. As an institution, education can be used to transmit change with regard to markets, crimes, politics, democracy, human rights, development, corruption and adapting society to the necessary changes accordingly.

Another obvious advantage created by a good education system is that it has the potential to generate the requisite skills and a stable knowledge base for markets and, when internalized nationally, it can engender market stability. Conversely, the absence of adequate information on proposed policy issues can

countries and the development of the financial sector. Indirect benefits include production specialization due to better management and improvements in macro-economic policies.

33 Developing countries are not yet able to reap the benefits which have been engendered by the global system because they currently lack technological competitiveness or edge.

result in serious policy misjudgements and can consequently derail or undermine the prospect of the integration of markets. Education has always been used as an avenue for implementing the requisite changes and meeting development goals. It produces a pool of skilled talent to facilitate the development of common markets between participating member countries. Banks and other financial institutions could be used to establish training programmes on markets, the fighting or prevention of corruption and other challenges. In some societies, financial market regulators have resorted to publishing information on markets in order to ensure that local stakeholders internalize the complexities of the market economy in their operations. This is equally significant in cautioning local markets from exposure to global externalities, whereby they could potentially be susceptible to events in other parts of the world.[34] Therefore, this would infer that policy makers have no choice but to forge partnerships with other global participants and to ensure that local policies are properly aligned to global imperatives. The benefits of a local–global partnership can be spread through the local media in tandem with the global media such as local radio stations, television programmes or local newspapers, academic think-tanks and most importantly the Internet. Consequently, the rich information that is generated from 'above' or at a global level may not trickle into areas where it is needed most if such features are not present in a particular society. As such, education should be ascribed a frontline role with a focus on overcoming some of the imperfections in society.[35] This chapter argues that fostering the envisaged global anti-money laundering standards will only be achievable in an environment where there is a robust educational system that integrates the needs of the local and global societies.

In advancing this argument, I have exploited the early experiences of countries like Japan of using education as a strategy of pursuing economic development. This could be used as a model for proposing desired changes in relation to desired global anti-money laundering regimes today. Japan was able to modernize in the twentieth century by evolving a policy of educating the populace in Western knowledge and practices.[36] To achieve this goal, the government launched an ambitious educational programme for all Japanese children, adopting systems principally from France, the UK and the USA.[37] Indeed, many Asian economies, such as South Korea, Taiwan, Hong Kong and Singapore, and more recently post-reform China, Thailand and other countries in East and South Asia, have

---

34 This can be achieved by disseminating information through newspapers and holding regular sessions on market sensitization on radio talk shows and television programmes.

35 B. Kinoue, 'From Individual Dignity to Respect for Jinkaku – Continuity and Change in the Concept of the Individual in Modern Japan', in Michael Likosky (ed.), *Transnational Legal Processes: Globalisation and Power Disparity* (London: Butterworths, 2002), pp. 295–6.

36 Ibid.

37 Ibid.

done remarkably well in spreading economic opportunities through adequately supportive social backgrounds, including high levels of literacy, numeracy and basic education.[38] The government of Japan also integrated moral ethics within the educational curriculum, as this was deemed to be crucial in the translation of the government's development programmes at a later stage.

Thus, if properly exploited, education can be an avenue for raising awareness of the existing anti-money laundering laws not only globally, but also of articulating the way in which laws are applied nationally. Education brings with it the rewards of knowledge and, where properly utilized, can encourage the development both of the individual and the wider society. Global awareness is not only necessary but is an imperative for policy makers, compliance officers, the police and other enforcement agencies to do their work properly within the framework of existing global anti-money laundering regimes. Regardless of whether a particular society is interested in subscribing to the global regimes on money laundering or otherwise, it is essential in these times to learn about globalization and how to harness the system for the benefit of the local society.

Education programmes, especially in tertiary institutions, should reflect and offer solutions to the novel development challenges facing societies. All university degree programmes at the national level should be integrated with ethics training tailored to the needs of an organized, stable and progressive society. Such a system should go a long way towards changing local attitudes and cultivating a development-oriented culture to enable the society to tackle challenges brought about development. Equally, all managers of enterprises should undergo a specific and perhaps also a tailored ethics training programme as part of a local strategic leadership initiative. In some parts of Africa, corruption is viewed as acceptable, perhaps due to the fact that it is a normal practice in almost every office.

In addition, if education is properly harnessed, it is a platform for launching public consciousness campaigns on pertinent global issues. This could be either by way of seminars, public enlightenment campaigns, workshops, conferences, press releases or training on the scourge of money laundering in society. There should be public outreach programmes geared towards helping members of the public to understand the potential problems of abuse inherent in financial systems by unscrupulous persons engaged in various illicit activities. One way of doing this could be to generate a portfolio of information, then making it freely accessible to the pubic (for example, handing out free newspapers) so that the public is conscious of the challenges faced by their society.[39]

The local anti-money laundering framework should be designed and disseminated in consultation with non-governmental organizations which are active in the area of globalization and financial crimes. Many national governments, especially in the South, are already constrained by limited resources and will be

38 Amartya Sen, *Development as Freedom* (Oxford: Oxford University Press, 2001), p. 91.

39 Kinoue, 'From Individual Dignity to Respect for Jinkaku'.

reluctant to create effective national programmes even if they are desirable. The benefits of training and sensitization programmes at a grassroots level cannot be under-estimated because citizens will have to be brought on board in relation to the campaign against corruption and money laundering.[40]

The public should be made aware of the ramifications of money laundering through various educational platforms like universities. This would help to easily transmit information on money laundering typologies to different sections of society. It also ought to be said that owing to the antiquated systems in many countries, record keeping is manual and of poor quality. In an attempt to tighten the loose ends in the fight against money laundering, financial institutions have adopted popular methods regarding the operations of forex bureaux, such as making announcements and stopping some banking businesses from operating wire transfers through certain banks.[41] At a more specific level, however, legal education in the faculties of law should integrate studies related to money laundering so that they serve as the flagship of development in society. There is a need for tailored educational programmes geared towards engendering an information portfolio necessary to encourage the regulation and supervision of financial markets in many countries.[42] Just as the educational institutions in the UK are used to translate the government's development objectives (such as research and development), other governments elsewhere should follow suit, ensuring that academics are equally utilized to deal with the development challenges in their society.

Arguably, the absence of adequate information on policy outcomes is capable of leading to serious policy misjudgements, subsequently helping to derail the adoption of existing or anticipated anti-money laundering initiatives. From an AML/CFT perspective, there is the need to generate a pool of comprehensive information that will facilitate a detailed investigation into alleged money laundering threats. This should be easily accessible by AML/CFT policy makers and other enforcement agencies. Equally, banks and other financial institutions should liaise with educational institutions to establish training programmes on the identification and prevention of corruption and money laundering predicate threats. This should be particularly aimed at employees in front offices who have direct contact with clients and compliance personnel. Employees should be kept up to date on major developments in the law on AML/CFT and be given regular training on identification techniques, particularly in response to changes in the modern banking environment. In small economies, financial market regulators (such as the Central Bank of Uganda) should ensure that local stakeholders are

40 Using Uganda as a case in point, a problem in the South is one of adoring the corrupt, as they are the ones who can afford to live a desirable, luxurious and ostentatious lifestyle.

41 Ibid.

42 This is well illustrated by the fact that many AML/CFT initiatives operate on the strength of the availability of information on both present and prospective bank clients.

made to appreciate the complexities of the global market economy and the way in which remote events are capable of impacting on regulatory measures in the local society. Therefore, regulators have to exploit different platforms and reach out to different market segments, either by way of the local media, academic think-tanks or other locally appropriate methods.

The individual government's educational curriculum should take into account the most pressing and pertinent needs of its society. As a prerequisite for harnessing the global market system, each and every society requires its technology-driven education to suit the contemporary global market imperatives. While not wanting to sound apocalyptic, it is my contention that unless that society is prepared to confront its most pertinent challenges, it will face enormous problems in keeping pace with the future, an objective that every forward-looking society should aspire to address.

In the absence of a clear policy direction through which societies can chart their future, perpetuate themselves or face up to their most pertinent challenges, there is no choice other than to hire experts, promoting over-dependence and its attendant failures. Societies must adopt a clear educational policy geared towards fostering their development needs; a failure to do so explains the reason why some societies have languished behind others in terms of domesticating the engendered anti-money laundering regimes. We can therefore infer that development (or a lack of it) is something that correlates to the ease with which the system adjusts and adapts itself in relation to its most pertinent challenges.

National authorities (through their various policy platforms) should initiate studies on money laundering with a view to establishing the particular money laundering typologies prevalent in that society. Once this knowledge is established, it should help to ensure two things: (i) that regulators are able to design an appropriate strategy capable of responding astutely to the externalities of the global economy; and (ii) that the civil society should play a crucial role in enlisting the goodwill of the people who are in close proximity with the criminals who plan and perpetuate these crimes.[43] Countries should make training of their judges (particularly in areas like international law, criminology, commercial arbitration and globalization) a priority.

There is a need for reform initiatives so that societies can adapt to the imperatives of the global market economy. If societies do not adjust in response to their external environment, laws will be surpassed, alienated and incomprehensible, and, above all, will generate a deterrent effect. Laws must bear a relationship with reality if they are to have a normative effect and to regulate conduct effectively, otherwise they will be circumvented and cast into the outer world of darkness.

43 This is essential in enhancing the work of intelligence and other authorities charged with the responsibility of fighting money laundering crimes.

The Corruption Factor

The challenges relating to a bad educational system, notwithstanding corruption,[44] in many developing countries[45] is now entrenched into almost every layer of society.[46] Corruption[47] is becoming an established work ethos in many societies, so much so that public offices are assiduously being used to further private business deals at the expense of the general public good. The abuse of office and corruption has been replicated at the local government level due to a lack of moral authority at the top. The lack of political will to combat bribery[48] and corruption is clearly demonstrated by political meddling in high-profile corruption cases.[49] There is a glaring need to strengthen ethical rules applicable to public officials. These rules should be broad enough to encompass standards that prevent conflicts of interest and streamline reporting procedures for proper accountability, as well as establish modalities for enforcing anti-corruption standards.

It is possible that money laundering may be almost interminable provided that there is no genuine will to counter and forestall corruption in public offices. Arguably, money launderers are capable of staying put because of bribes that the poorly paid or 'coerced' government officials employed to oversee the implementation of an anti-money laundering framework may find difficult to resist; as such, they can be exploited as an access route to integrating the ill-gotten proceeds of crime into the system. On the other hand, some officials who may be disinclined to accept bribes may also decide to give in for fear of jeopardizing their jobs if they blow the whistle on an inherently corrupt system where corrupt officials are venerated. Thus, prolific money launderers will have identified and exploited any glaring loopholes when devising their strategies before integrating

---

44 This is defined by Transparency International as 'the misuse of public power for private gain'. See Transparency International, *Global Corruption Report* (2004) p. 24, available at www.transparency.org/publications/gcr/gcr_2004 (date accessed 4 December 2011).

45 It is my contention that the causes of rampant corruption in Uganda and other developing countries are partly explained by competition for scarce resources.

46 This is underscored by the fact that leaders of some African states have collectively stolen up to $20 billion, depositing the monies in Swiss bank accounts. Haiti's 'Baby Doc' Duvalier is known to have channelled some $300–900 million into offshore banks, while President Marcos salted away well over $2 billion in Western banks.

47 For the World Bank, corruption is a product of bad governance and the weaknesses inherent in the public sector institutions. See 'Corruption Progress Report Since 1997 by the World Bank', available at www.worldbank.org (date accessed 4 December 2011).

48 Bribery, defined widely to include the direct or indirect giving of undue advantage of any kind for the official himself/herself or another person or entity in return for acting or refraining from acting in the exercise of his/her official duties, is made an offence under this convention.

49 Here many cases abound and they differ from place to place.

tainted funds into the mainstream financial system. This is one of the reasons why money laundering has proved hard to combat in developing countries.

Furthermore, corruption is instrumental in undermining market reforms and the rule of law.[50] It undermines national economies and is a threat to democratic institutions, fostering threats to society such as transnational organized crime and terrorism.[51] Therefore, in an inherently corrupt society, privatization creates openings for criminal exploitation, including money laundering. Criminals thrive in an inherently corrupt environment because they find it easy to manipulate the system. Similarly, criminals will find it easy to exploit weaknesses in macro-economic policies or to infiltrate agencies that are responsible for the prudential supervision of financial services.

Moreover, corruption in many developing countries has recently assumed a transnational dimension. Globalization has created opportunities for corrupt governments to exploit and benefit from, which is paradoxical since the system was earlier expected to engender an elaborate process of transferring what were formerly state-owned assets into private ownership. Kickbacks, commissions or representation fees are sought in return for rigging bids (that is, manipulating the laws adopted to govern the privatization process).[52]

The growth of offshore financial centres in the name of privatization has created opportunities for laundering dirty money. In the mid-1980s, a Morgan Guaranty Trust study of 'Capital Flight from Third World Countries' revealed that in one year alone, a total of $198 billion disappeared offshore from 18 developing countries.[53] This, apart from weakening support for deregulation and market reforms, also causes laxity in creating laws to govern the transition towards a market economy.[54] Corruption has distracted law makers and law enforcers from setting a socially comparative context of corruption, and economic liberalization has been viewed as a panacea to the problem.[55] Lax financial regulations have attracted money launderers because, to a large extent in such an environment, the authorities do not fully cooperate with international efforts aimed at reducing the threat of money laundering. Thus, new means must be found, and economic deregulation and liberalization offer such opportunities when pursued in a non-transparent manner. It is important to prescribe measures to combat the scourge of

50 Money launderers or corrupt elements in the society, whichever way one wants to put it, work outside or on the fringes of the prescribed rules or laws.

51 Kofi Annan, Secretary-General of the United Nations, 'Message to the Third Global Forum on Fighting Corruption and Safeguarding Integrity', 31 May 2003.

52 Ackerman, *Corruption and Governments*, p. 27.

53 F. Vogl, 'The Supply Side of Global Bribery', 1998, p. 11, available at www.imf.org/external/pubs/ft/fandd/1998/06/vogl.htm (date accessed 4 December 2011).

54 Ackerman, *Corruption and Governments*.

55 D. Hobbs, 'Professionals and Organised Crime in Britain', in M. Maguire, R. Morgan and R. Reiner (eds), *The Oxford Handbook of Criminology* (Oxford: Oxford University Press, 1994), pp. 441–68.

money laundering, but these measures should be preceded by creating a positive policy environment in the recipient society to sustain the implementation of the anticipated measures.

In a situation where the educated are pushed to the sidelines of the employment market, their potential would not be harnessed by societies suffering from skills shortages. This subsequently creates a brain drain as skilled individuals flee poorly managed economies for greener pastures elsewhere. In order for anti-money laundering paradigms (for example, the enhanced CDD provisions under the revised FATF recommendations and the Third Anti-Money Laundering Directive (2005)) to work effectively, the system will need to harness the skills of accountants, auditors, lawyers, supervisors and prosecutors. These same people are essential to service and keep the system compliant with its regulatory and supervisory imperatives. It is conceivably a huge loss for society when its educated talent end up in foreign countries as immigrants instead of making a direct contribution to their societies of origin. Equally, societies that are serious about fighting money laundering (as a prerequisite for harnessing global market opportunities) have left no stone unturned in attracting the best workforce. To stave off a potential shortfall in the supply of labour, attenuated by an ageing population, many Western countries now link immigration policies to skills that particular immigrants bring. The more educated, skilled and experienced the applicant is, the higher his/her chances of gaining easy entry into developed countries.

Economic Structural Issues

Emerging AML/CFT regimes are largely focused on the formal financial sector,[56] and this approach fails to address the work of the underground shadow economy which operates informally, particularly in a liberalized market environment. Financial liberalization denotes a process whereby the government relaxes managerial controls on commercial activities. On many occasions this entails reducing commercial interest rates and discontinuing selective lending.[57] In short, liberalization has been defined as 'the process of transferring formerly state-owned enterprises to private ownership'.[58] This makes it easy for institutions to enter and leave, as they deem fit, and equally easy for institutions to circumvent state prudential and regulatory controls.

In order to close the regulatory gap between the formal and informal sectors,[59] I propose the importance of a well-coordinated information gathering geared

56 It is largely the formal sector that is regulated, but in the case of the work of the informal sector, the authorities need to be more proactive if its activities are to be forestalled.

57 Rondo Cameron (ed.), *Banking and Economic Development: Some Lessons of History* (New York: Columbia University Press, 1997), p. 7.

58 Ibid.

59 Ibid.

at establishing the degree of criminal activity, in particular money laundering-related crimes, in individual societies. Therefore, there is a strong rationale for the state to take a centre-stage position in the regulation of financial markets because withdrawal by the state undermines intelligence gathering through its security institutions such as the police.[60] State intervention is also essential in restoring stability to the domestic financial system. As regards foreign banking establishments, there should be a mechanism to ensure that certain institutions act as a lender of last resort for all foreign banks. This should ensure a safety net for foreign banking establishments in the event of financial distress and its attendant moral hazards on financial institutions, thus stabilizing the global economy as a whole in the long run.

With regard to foreign banking establishments, I propose that domestic regulators adopt and apply the fundamental principles of the Basel Committee on Banking Supervision because these principles are comprehensive and necessary. The principles are as follows: (i) domestic regulators need to ensure that no foreign banking establishment escapes supervision; and (ii) they also need to ensure that supervision should be adequate and comprehensive.[61] Adequate supervision is that in which the host authorities are responsible for the supervision of the foreign banking establishments (subsidiaries)[62] operating in their territories as individual institutions, while the parent authorities are responsible for them as part of the larger banking group.[63] The parent authorities should be informed by the host authorities of any serious problems which arise in a parent bank's foreign establishment and, similarly, they should inform the host authorities when problems arise in the parent bank which are likely to affect parent-bank foreign operations.[64] Bank supervisors must be competent to practise consolidated supervision, in which case the parent banks or banking groups should be responsible for the supervision as well as the adequacy of their capital on the basis of the business wherever conducted.[65]

Many less developed countries are cash-based economies, thus creating a difficult environment in which to conduct an effective anti-money laundering

60 This partly explains why failed states, for example, Somalia, Iraq, the Congo and Afghanistan, have become havens for drug trafficking and small arms trafficking.

61 Following the collapse of the BCCI in July 1992, the Basel Committee published the minimum standards for the supervision of the international banking group and their cross-border established subsidiaries. The full account of these principals can be found at www.bis.org/publ/bcbsc004.htm (date accessed 4 December 2011).

62 Subsidiaries are independent legal entities under the laws of the country of incorporation (host country) as opposed to branches, which are legally dependent units controlled by the parent licensing authorities.

63 Rosa M. Lastra, 'Cross-Border Bank Insolvency: Legal Implications in the Case of Banks Operating in Different Jurisdictions in Latin America', 6(79) *Journal of International Economic Law* (2003): p. 9.

64 Ibid.

65 Consolidated supervision is based on the assumption that financial groups form a single economic entity.

regime. This is particularly so in relation to generating requisite information to build an effective money trail. Cash (as a means of payment) is used in effecting almost every transaction, even when transactions involve huge sums of money. Buyers simply go to their banks, withdraw whatever amount of money they want and make cash payments to their creditors. The use of cash transactions are the norm rather than an exception in most African countries. Introducing threshold cash reporting requirements is often proposed but is difficult to implement in practice because of the structural problems within these societies. Then there is also the challenge of the cross-border transportation of cash and other criminal proceeds. In Africa, it is easy for criminals of all shapes and sizes to move money about across national borders without coming to the attention of the authorities because of the porous nature of the land borders.[66] This problem has been compounded by corrupt officials who collude with businessmen to make as much money in a short space of time as they possibly can.

The problems raised by a cash economy curtail a bank's efforts to distinguish between dirty and clean money.[67] Recommendation 1 of the FATF imposes obligations on countries to take measures to stop terrorists and criminals from using cash carriers to finance their activities.[68] Banks have to rely only on the verbal information provided by the customer, which may be inaccurate, exaggerated or hard to corroborate. The absence of data registry centres on customer profiles regarding things like bank loans poses serious market risks. For example, the absence of customer credit profiles implies that both defaulters and non-defaulters are treated in the same way and are subjected to the same assessment benchmarks. This has made the major banks in Uganda embark on a pilot project to test the possibility of creating a credit reference bureau. This project aims to build a database of cases on both present and prospective bank clients which would be drawn upon in order to check customer credit profiles. The engendered information profiles would be exchanged across banks to generate the required information on bank customers.[69]

The KYC mandate[70] provides that institutions must require the identification of their customers when entering into business relations, such as opening bank accounts. This applies to all cases of entering into a business relationship,

66 Commonwealth Secretariat, *A Model of Best Practice for Combating Money Laundering in the Financial Sector* (London: Commonwealth Secretariat, 2000), p. 9.

67 Rhys Bollen, 'The International Financial System and Future Global Regulation', 23(9) *Journal of International Banking and Financial Law Regulation* (2008): p. 467.

68 Humphrey Moshi, 'Fighting Money Laundering: Challenges in Africa', *East African Human Rights Law Journal* (2007): pp. 1–7.

69 The Ugandan daily newspaper, the *New Vision*, 11 August 2008.

70 This paradigm presupposes that if you know your customer, then you are likely to know when they are trying to launder money using financial institutional services. The problem is that banks have millions of customers who benefit from banking services, making them stretched or short-staffed, and are virtually overwhelmed by the sheer scale of financial institution operations.

especially when opening a savings account or when offering a safe custody facility. The KYC requirement applies to any transactions involving sums of €15,000/£10,000 or more. When the institution does not know the sum involved at the time of the transaction, it must proceed with the identification procedure as soon as it knows this and has established that the amount involved meets the threshold requirement. Even in cases where the amount of the transaction is less than €15,000, the institution must require identification if it suspects money laundering.[71] Identification procedures for personal customers when opening accounts may need to be customized depending on whether the individual is a resident or non-resident.[72] Different considerations may apply in relation to the opening of 'trust accounts'. An even greater range of possibilities will need to be considered in relation to the opening of accounts for legal persons.[73] The identification duty is complemented by the obligation of credit and financial institutions to keep records of the following so that they may be used as evidence in any money laundering investigation:

a. in the case of identification, a copy or the reference of the evidence should be produced;
b. in the case of transactions, the supporting evidence and records (consisting of the original documents or copies) should be admissible in court proceedings under the applicable national legislation.

There are situations, however, where identification requirements are relaxed, for example, in cases involving insurance policies written by insurance undertakings within the meaning of the EU Anti-Money Laundering Directive,[74] where the annual periodic premium amounts paid do not exceed €15,000 or £10,000. EU Member States may waive the identification requirement for insurance policies in respect of certain pension schemes.[75] On the other hand, where there is doubt that the customer is operating on their own behalf or where it is certain they are not, credit and financial institutions are required to take reasonable measures to obtain information so as to ascertain the true identity of the persons on whose behalf the customers are acting.[76]

The KYC paradigm of anti-money laundering control in many jurisdictions is likely to suffer the following shortcomings. It is the contention of this chapter that the KYC ideal as an anti-money laundering paradigm is too onerous to implement in developing countries given the structural bottlenecks that characterize such societies. There are no robust central registries from where data relating to

71 Lastra, 'Cross-Border Bank Insolvency'.
72 Ibid.
73 Ibid.
74 Directive 79/267/EEC.
75 Ibid.
76 Ibid., Article 4.

prospective bank customers can be drawn and used for verification purposes. This challenge is compounded by the fact that very few residents would have their physical addresses registered, let alone known, by the authorities. Even if this is not much of a problem, it is still difficult to verify and authenticate data in relation to people's land registrations because land registries in many developing countries are too antiquated to respond astutely to the twenty-first-century era of globalization. This is in contrast to developed countries, where technology has advanced to ease customer identification so much so that customer profiling would simply take a matter of minutes, if not seconds. Thus, this situation delineates the sharp disparities in infrastructural development which causes dissonance in the way in which regimes created globally are harnessed locally.

In the administration of the KYC campaign as a paradigm of money laundering control in developed countries, some bank officials have misused or overused this tool to discriminate against certain disadvantaged groups in society.[77] It is within this cohort that many people are refused banks accounts either because they are unable to produce the required information in relation to birth certificates[78] or to satisfy any other requirements, such as those relating to the residence and work profiles of the prospective person who wants to open a bank account in the host country. This has given way to the proliferation of Alternative Remittance Systems (ARSs)[79] of sending money to their countries of origin, as this is often considered to be less cumbersome and more easily accessible.

In the ARS, the sending customer (the originator of the money/value transfer) pays or hands over funds to the ARS operator. The sender also specifies the recipient or beneficiary of the transaction along with his/her location. The funds can be paid in cash, cash equivalent, cheques, other monetary instruments or stored value cards. In certain situations, the sender can pay cash directly into a bank account operated by the ARS operator. In large ARS networks, the customers generally have access to the ARS through local agents (sub-agents). The sender usually receives a unique reference to identify the transaction, which is then passed on to the beneficiary. The sender's only remaining role will be to follow up and relay the information to the ARS operator if there is any problem with regard to the receipt of the money.[80]

---

77 I appreciate that the above measures are prudent and necessary for the proper functioning of financial institutions, but equally the administration of these measures has a tendency to affect one particular group or section of the society as opposed to others.

78 Many societies where immigrants come from may never have recorded births, deaths or other vagaries of life, largely due to the slow pace of the rudimentary system.

79 This means any system used for transferring money from one location to another and generally operating outside the banking channels. ARSs include either money or value transfers, regardless of their legal status in particular jurisdictions and regardless of whether or not they are currently covered in part or in total by national regulatory systems.

80 The aforementioned method is popular for sending money home among the Ugandans residents in London.

These informal channels have proliferated in many parts of the world, not only in response to the problem highlighted above but also because of the favourable market conditions generated by globalization. More often, remittance channels will be infiltrated or misused by those planning to launder the illicit proceeds of crime.[81] The use of false identities and structuring are common techniques to which ARSs are vulnerable. The risks associated with ARSs will vary from country to country. For example, a developing country relying heavily on domestic ARSs but without the infrastructure to verify the identity of the sender will face different regulatory challenges compared to a country with a developed formal sector.[82]

While cognisant of the need for a robust global anti-money laundering framework capable of responding to the complexities of the modern global system, the evolution of the global system should take into account the local specifics and particularities of money laundering challenges in individual countries or regions.[83] Some of the paradigms espoused by the FATF (embodied in its 40+9 recommendations) are apparently not feasible in many developing countries, given the lack of economic and legal infrastructure compared to many developed countries. At a more specific level, if we take the case of Recommendation 12 of the FATF, which provides guidelines to banks with regard to KYC[84] prior to transacting business together, this thesis argues that this paradigm is too onerous to undertake in many developing countries for the following reasons. There is no centralized registry system where information about nationals of the country is generated, collated and corroborated by institutions seeking to do business with certain individuals. This has rendered financial institutions vulnerable in situations where they have to rely on the authenticity of this information. The asymmetry in the way in which information is created and disseminated has inhibited the ability of some societies to make well-informed policy choices necessary to protect the system against the exigencies of the global business environment. Obviously, this is not to mention the fact that the absence of a robust economic and legal infrastructure has inhibited the development of a robust database necessary to enhance the proper decision-making processes.

Land registries, which would serve to fill the information void in many developing countries, suffer from the following shortcomings: the existing registries are either antiquated, disorganized or staffed with underpaid and/or corrupt public officials.[85] This is compounded by the fact that many countries are structurally deficient compared to developed countries, where every prospective

81 See the Interpretative Note to the FATF Special Recommendation VI: Alternative Remittance Systems issued in February 2003.

82 FATF, 'Money Laundering and Terrorist Financing Typologies', 10 June 2005.

83 To successfully achieve this, it is important to launch tailored research studies so as to properly inform the decision-making process.

84 See Appendix 1.

85 In any case, very few people bother to register their land titles and as such there are no records capable of being used for verification purposes.

bank account holder can be verified in a split second by way of verifying his/her address through the postcode system. As such, the regulatory system in developing countries is susceptible to manipulation. It can therefore be said that in order for developing countries to adopt an organized proactive regulatory regime based on global standards, they will have to give priority to infrastructural development so as to withstand the perverse features of the modern global system.

While the FATF acknowledges the dynamics of development in different countries, it is nevertheless essential for the global anti-money laundering framework to be preceded by a development climate comparable to that in the G10 countries. As such, measures aimed at eradicating poverty and corruption, the two apparent impediments to development in developing countries, should be given utmost priority. This contention is supported by the fact that poverty destroys a society's potential and deprives that same society of its capabilityto manage itself efficiently. It is evident that with widespread poverty, coupled with tenuous infrastructure, those in developing countries are predisposed to a life of misery and capability deprivation. In such an environment, money laundering might be viewed not as a choice but as an imperative. Thus, we can infer that the above societies are likely to remain prone and unstable, at least insofar as developing a robust local anti-money laundering infrastructure is concerned. It can equally be said that the ability of societies to manage their apparent development threats has been undermined by the precarious economic environment highlighted above.[86]

The Resource Constraint Effect on the Sequencing of Financial Sector Reforms

The ability of any country to fight crimes generally and money laundering in particular is dictated by the availability of resources. This is necessary in order to facilitate the creation of laws and procedures, while also ensuring that global anti-money laundering laws are transposed into substantive domestic laws. Thus, resource constraint effects have become an apparent challenge for countries when developing a comprehensive policy framework against corruption and its attendant social evils. It is also an incontestable fact that fighting crimes and money laundering in particular has been constrained by a lack of sufficient resources in individual national governments. The three East African countries of Uganda, Tanzania and Kenya have all contended that their efforts to participate fully in regional initiatives and to implement the UN Conventions on cross-border crimes (such as the Palermo Convention)[87] are often derailed or constrained by a lack of sufficient resources.

In some countries, local institutions such as the police, whose overriding mandate is to fight crime, are dysfunctional and in any case are often compromised

86 Sen, *Development as Freedom*, p. 87.

87 It was in Italy that the United Nations Convention on Transnational Organized Crime convened on 15 December 2000.

(to a great extent aiding and abetting the commissioning of crimes) through corruption. Cases involving corruption have become vexatious and intractable, either because of influence peddling or high-profile individuals being implicated in corruption scandals, making it difficult for anti-corruption provisions to be implemented.

Local capacity building in many developing countries has been derailed by the following factors: the post-independence period in Africa has been marked by wars either between countries or within individual countries in the form of civil wars or by proxies fighting the wars of others.[88] The internal problems in Africa vary, but include inherited colonial legacies (including the illogicality of many borders) and the transition from colonialism towards undemocratic and often corrupt, militarized neo-colonial regimes.[89] The devastating effect of this has sadly been to divert resources away from areas such as education, industrialization and the building of a stable economic and social infrastructure to support development. When this situation is compounded by a lack of civil liberties, gender discrimination, a lack of freedom of expression, bad education and a failure to promote education, this leads to what (in my view) can be summed up as a 'poverty of opportunities and ideas' to turn things around. In effect, such a situation inhibits the development potential of individual countries with regard to boosting the development of the potential of the local human resources. The irony is that banks rely on supervisors, auditors, policy makers, legal experts and other skilled people to plan and pursue their development and strategic plans. In order for international technical experts to be effective in the delivery of much-needed technical assistance in developing countries, they will have to work in partnership with local experts who are endowed with local familiarity and knowledge in relation to ongoing and prospective local projects.[90]

Many developing countries have been depleted of their human resource capital not only through perpetual wars and the ravages of malaria and HIV/AIDS, but also through economic vagaries such as the globalization of the market economy, where they have become marginal participants.[91] Developing countries have lost people of all ranks and ages to HIV/AIDS, many of whom were highly skilled and not easily replaced by the affected societies. This plight needs to be analysed

88 All the elements mentioned above are encapsulated in the present war currently taking place in the Democratic Republic of Congo.

89 This was true in the case of Uganda under the dreaded Idi Amin era (1971–1979).

90 This is vividly illustrated by the bungled sale of the Ugandan Commercial Bank and its shortcomings, such as corruption, insider dealing and a lack of transparency.

91 According to International Labour Organization (ILO) estimates, Zimbabwe is said to have lost 100,000 of its skilled workers in the last two years and it is therefore estimated to be losing an average of 50,000 people per year. AIDS is also taking its toll due to poverty and limited access to retroviral drugs. While I have used Zimbabwe as an example, the United Nations Development Programme (UNDP) estimates that Africa is losing its skilled workers at the rate of 200,000 every year.

against the backdrop that conditions across the whole of the southern African region deteriorated in the 1990s to their worst ever recorded levels, including mortality rates for those under five years old (140 per 100,000 children), the incidence of deadly diseases such as malaria (5,500 per 100,000 people), tuberculosis (149 per 100,000 people) and HIV/AIDS (30 per 100,000 people and a 12 per cent prevalence for adults under 49 years of age in 1995).[92] While social suffering worsened, the capacity of nations to increase expenditure on health and education declined. Therefore, many developing countries subsequently found themselves in the predicament where they were constrained in terms of resources and unable to implement the desired anti-money laundering standards, or any other development initiatives for that matter. It has to be said that the predicament of poverty creates conditions which predispose a society to a life of suffering and misery. Poverty deprives the society of its capacity to harness global initiatives, including those aimed at combating money laundering and its predicate threats.

The above analysis suggests that unless radical reforms are undertaken to reverse the economic and social trends of under-development in poor countries, an environment prone to financial instability and abuses such as money laundering will continue to exist.[93] Certainly, no society can secure and foster a positive anti-money laundering climate locally in the absence of a well-trained police force to foster a climate of law and order. There is a need to set up a special fund to facilitate the training of police officers in criminal and cross-border legal issues. Of course, a well-trained police force is essential in fighting local crimes, not to mention crimes in relation to money laundering. Equally, police training at a local level can go a long way in enhancing local consciousness on non-local crime specifics and devising effective strategies for tackling money laundering and its predicate threats. States must appreciate that every crime control strategy at a national level must involve the police, whose constitutional mandate is to enforce law and order.

Similarly, it is important for states to subscribe for membership of the International Criminal Police Organization (Interpol) for membership, so that in the event of crimes transcending national boundaries, they can draw on the resources of Interpol to pursue alleged criminals wherever they are. Interpol as an organization was established to pursue two objectives: first, to promote and ensure mutual legal assistance between police authorities in different countries and in the sprit of the Universal Declaration of Human Rights;[94] and, secondly, to promote public policing so as to enhance the fight against ordinary crimes. Each Interpol member is required to nominate an office for communication with the Lyon headquarters, the National Central Bureau, being the mechanism through

92 Patrick Bond, *Against Global Apartheid: South Africa Meets the World Bank, IMF and International Finance* (Cape Town: University of Cape Town Press, 2001), p. 26.

93 For the provision in relation to international peace and security, see Article 39 of the UN Charter 1945.

94 M. Anderson and E. Bort (eds), *The Frontiers of Europe* (London: Pinter, 1998), p. 45.

which all of Interpol's enquiries are channelled.[95] Indeed, this is essential in order to generate information on the movement and laundering of the proceeds of crime. With the availability of adequate information on crime typologies, it will help to enhance law enforcement agencies in initiating criminal or even civil proceedings against money laundering fugitives, wherever they may be hiding.

Conclusion

There is need for the harmonization of global AML/CFT laws so as to bring countries into line with expected global standards. However, due to varying dynamics of development in individual countries, harmonization should be preceded by sequenced structural reforms. Undertaking reforms should not only be influenced by global market imperatives but should also be realistic, taking into account conditions of development in a country. For example, the UK has refused to join the euro, even though it was initially deemed essential to enhance and strengthen the proper functioning of the single European market. It is no wonder that the UK is seemingly vindicated because there are so many crises in the Eurozone area. This example can be used to show that countries should where possible defer the implementation of normative changes until they have built a requisite framework to pursue such changes. Reforms should be comprehensive, encapsulating all areas where global AML/CFT regimes are to be implemented. It is my contention that the globalization of laws at various levels of society should see national governments undertaking the desired national reforms accordingly.[96] The global AML/CFT regimes are an essential platform for the harmonization of differences and approaches on money laundering-related challenges.[97] Since societies are different in culture, dynamics and development interests, these variables cannot be ignored in the name of globalization. Therefore, the localization of global anti-money laundering laws in the absence of the necessary reforms

95 Ibid.

96 Global institutions have demonstrated that speaking with one voice is far from realistic in reducing disparities in power relations. On the contrary, the prevalence of policy platforms, for example, the World Trade Organization (WTO), to which many countries have subscribed, should essentially give them leverage to voice their concerns, which is apparently not the case in reality.

97 There is a need for the adoption of harmonized rules and conventions governing trade, capital flows and foreign investment. Transition and emerging market economies need to improve their business environment by implementing far-reaching economic and reform programmes that include – but are not limited to – providing monetary and fiscal discipline, improving the efficiency of their public sector, implementing privatization programmes to increase the efficiency of state-owned and state-operated assets, modernizing regulatory codes, reforming and liberalizing their financial systems, reducing the level of public and private sector corruption, promoting trade liberalization and regional integration, eliminating barriers to FDI and adopting unified and competitive exchange rate regimes.

cannot work, and if it does, it will debase economies in the long run. Global laws must be harmonized to suit local conditions, otherwise clustering states together, irrespective of their differences is metaphorically to liken 'elephants to goats and obviously this paradigm cannot work'.[98] For the adoption of a global AML/CFT framework to work, domestic governments should be given technical assistance to ensure some level of parity in terms of their ability to harness global AML/CFT regimes. At the moment, there is a significant gap between developed and developing countries in terms of the necessary infrastructure. Therefore, it cannot be practical for countries at varying levels of development to harness the anticipated global changes at the same time. As has already been noted, laws at whatever level they are envisaged must be realistic bearing in mind the local circumstances if they are to regulate undesired conduct effectively. Otherwise laws which create unrealistic standards are likely to be overlooked and ignored. The use of model laws such as the global AML/CFT regimes proposed at various levels in countries with tenuous legal systems is necessary, but they *must* be modified to suit local conditions, or else the implementation of robust laws in a tenuous legal system by a country without due regard to its development dynamics could potentially debase the system. This presumably explains why the World Bank reforms have failed to have a substantial impact in many countries where they were introduced.

The challenges to local financial institutions with regard to internalizing CDD (as a core element of the global AML/CFT framework) measures are many and are perhaps too numerous to cover comprehensively here. I think a one-size-fits-all approach is unrealistic because it might not reflect the varying sizes of those for whom it is intended. While financial institutions which apply global AML/CFT regimes are required to implement robust CDD programmes, it might prove costly for banks to undertake. Banking is a business and like all businesses, banks must control their operational costs to generate profits and stay afloat financially. This infers that CDD is more easily implementable in banks with abundant resources than in those which without such funds, an issue that underscores the challenges of adopting a uniform regulatory framework in conditions of economic and power disparities. It is very important for banks to safeguard against the dangers of money laundering and the financing of terrorism and how they can be used to transmit the illicit proceeds of crime. This means that financial institutions must assess the risks posed by their customers both at the inception of the customer relationship and continuously thereafter. However, financial institutions must be realistic in ensuring that the implementation of CDD standards and other core programmes are sustainable. For banks in less developed countries, it might not be impractical to apply robust CDD standards. It is my contention that they should tailor their CDD and other risk assessment procedures of their customers to their imperatives. In the pragmatic approach underscored by Exemption 17 of South African Banking Act 2002. Exemptions under this provision were negotiated

98 Janet Dine, *Companies, International Trade and Human Rights* (Cambridge: Cambridge University Press, 2005) pp. 1–40.

and agreed by banks in implementing CCD programmes in South Africa in order not to discriminate against vulnerable groups who could not have verifiable residential addresses and other CDD requirements. Indeed, this chapter has also underscored how other challenges in some countries, such as the lack of requisite education, the lack of resources, the lack of robust local AML/CFT institutions, the absence of infrastructural development and the high prevalence of corruption, can derail efforts to implement robust CCD programmes. Therefore, it is my belief that implementing the envisaged anti-money laundering regimes such as CDD should be done sequentially, bearing in mind the environment in which global financial institutions operate. Global AML/CFT regimes can work as long as they are aligned to the particularities or dynamics of local development. It is therefore imperative before a state countenances the adoption of such measures that it first harmonizes its laws and systems as a framework for normative societal changes.

Chapter 7
Harmonization of Global Anti-Money Laundering Laws

Introduction

The challenges underscored in the preceding chapters can be overcome through realigning the state so that it is able to transpose its envisaged international obligations. The realignment of the state is possible through the process of the harmonization of global anti-money laundering initiatives at an individual state level. Harmonization is a process or a mechanism of internalizing various policy changes at a local level. Some of the aforementioned mechanisms are generated by specialist institutions such as the harmonization of private international law, coordinated by the International Institute for the Unification of Private Law (UNIDROIT).[1] UNIDROIT is an independent intergovernmental organization with its seat in Rome. Similarly, there is the United Nations Commission on International Trade Law (UNCITRAL) with its seat in Vienna.[2] UNCITRAL is a core legal body within the UN system in the field of international trade law. It was established in 1966 by the General Assembly with the mandate to further the progress of the harmonization and unification of international trade law. These two institutions are specifically created in order to harmonize a specialized area of law. There are other bodies specifically created to foster the harmonization of global anti-money laundering laws such as those that have evolved under the auspices of the FATF, the Basel Committee and the FSF. These bodies provide a platform for inter-state cooperation on the issues of AML/CFT. This chapter examines the institutional mechanisms for the harmonization of global anti-money laundering laws and the ease with which global anti-money laundering laws are harnessed locally.

Harmonization is implemented in many and perhaps different ways, not least a state adopting soft law norms enunciated by AML/CFT oversight institutions. Soft laws are non-binding obligations which are created to plug gaps in the international legal system with regard to the envisaged regulatory issue. Soft law norms are initially issued as 'guidelines', but with the intention of crystallizing them into hard law in the future. These soft law norms can help to define standards

1 See its official website at www.unidroit.org (date accessed 10 December 2011).

2 See its official website at www.uncitral.org (date accessed 10 December 2011).

of normative practice.[3] In addition, harmonization can take place through the adoption of hard laws such as treaties. Treaties create binding legal obligations, such as the Directives of the EU, which the state will have to introduce into domestic law within a stipulated timeframe. This can either be done through a state adopting enabling legislation or through the interpretative role of national courts. Moreover, harmonization can be encouraged through the reform process of national economies such as those encouraged by the World Bank and the IMF.[4] IFIs have always played a significant role in engineering financial sector reforms in many countries. They are mandated to make countries translate global anti-money laundering standards, such as those envisaged by the Basel Committee on Banking Supervision and the FATF recommendations, into their internal operational policies on a forward-looking basis. This chapter examines the process of internalizing global anti-money laundering laws locally, but also highlights the challenges created by attempts to achieve the full harmonization of laws both nationally and internationally.

Money laundering is a complex process that is not easy to combat within the realm of an individual state, however powerful that state is.[5] This is illustrated by the fact that the USA has engineered the creation of multilateral AML/CFT institutions, notwithstanding that it is a powerful economy.[6] It recognizes its limits as a state and the challenges posed by the global threat of money laundering. The schemes through which money laundering is committed have become sophisticated due to the instrumentalities of globalization, such as the sophisticated methods of moving illicit proceeds of crime about.[7] This situation is underscored by the following complexity: money laundering could be hypothetically committed in the UK by an American citizen who channels the money to Uganda in South African currency, in a matter of minutes if not seconds.[8] When this complexity is coupled with differences in and the fragmentation of national anti-money laundering laws, it is capable of being exploited to facilitate the spread of money laundering and predicate threats. Thus, the complexity of money laundering crimes and the fluidity of the current global climate can offer criminals the latitude to commit money laundering and stay put. Criminals have also gained access to the new markets by

3 As such, soft law norms tend to have echoes of customary law which states agree to adopt because they see it as important and necessary for society.

4 These reforms may be dictated by different reasons, targeting different areas of the economy.

5 The USA has robust anti-money laundering laws but it is also at the forefront of encouraging the creation of specialized anti-money laundering bodies to coordinate the fight on money laundering and its predicate threats.

6 The USA engineered the adoption of the Basel Committee on Banking Supervision in 1974 and it was also influential in the establishment of the FATF in Paris in 1989.

7 In relation to this, many methods abound, such as telegraphic money transfers, e-money methods and letters of credit, not to mention traditional methods such as currency smuggling.

8 Shams, *Legal Globalization.*

exploiting the discrepancies between the legal systems of countries in different parts of the world.[9] Such a view seems to justify the need for the harmonization of global anti-money laundering laws so that they can be applied easily within the borders of different countries.

It has to be said that harmonization is needed not only in order for countries to work together on overlapping global issues but also to ease conflict of laws and regulatory extraterritoriality.[10] The integration of financial markets must be supported by the application of a uniform framework on which the anticipated global changes can be implemented. In addition, the conflict of laws issue, where different countries apply different laws and legal systems, has the potential to undermine the regulation of financial institutions that are offering cross-border financial services within the same legal framework. This issue was regarded as a major challenge by representatives of the FATF in their efforts to create a harmonized framework in the delivery of financial services.[11] Perhaps it should also worth mentioning the potential challenge of forum shopping, otherwise known as the race to the bottom, which occurs when state parties to the same market domain (such as the European single market) adopt different regulatory standards – one adopting a rigorous regime and the other not. This apparently justifies why FATF member countries and regional trading partners are required to introduce national laws based on international standards on money laundering and its underlying predicate threats.

The adoption of the FATF's 40+9 recommendations by member countries created a platform for global anti-money laundering standards to be applied internationally. Global AML/CFT regimes have encouraged inter-state cooperation by way of evolving guidelines for the implementation of the envisaged global initiatives such as the FATF recommendations and the supervisory standards under the Basel Committee. The globalization of markets has also encouraged reforms within individual member countries, as demonstrated by the work of the World Bank and the IMF in many developing countries. It should be noted that if the policy environment is conducive, globalization[12] has the potential to generate more synergies for development in less developed countries than it removes. In the first place, multilateral banking institutions can provide invaluable forums

9 United Nations Office of Drug Control and Crime Prevention (UNDCCP), available at www.undccp.org (date accessed 16 December 2006).

10 Shams, *Legal Globalization.*

11 Recommendation 21 of the FATF. This recommendation calls on financial institutions to give special attention to business relations and transactions with persons, including companies and financial firms from countries which do not apply the FATF 40+9 recommendations or do so in an insufficient manner.

12 Globalization is not inherently bad, but what countries ought to do prior to subscribing to the system is to remove the domestic impediments that inhibit the adoption of global initiatives.

for information exchange.[13] Multilateral initiatives have the potential to promote more open-ended and creative discussions among governments as well as to provide effective channels for citizen input, both domestically and at the level of international institutions.[14] Moreover, harmonization regimes such as soft law norms can be instrumental in developing and enforcing international standards. While existing international banking organizations have no formal legislative or enforcement power, they do have the authority to issue and promote supervisory and best practice guidelines. These guidelines, though far from binding, can assume the status of 'soft law'[15] and help guide countries struggling with design and implementation problems to establish cooperative arrangements. Furthermore, globalization can bring about the benefit of impartiality and legitimacy. For example, the world's central banking organization, the Bank for International Settlements (BIS), embodies the opinion of its world members. When the BIS adopts a particular set of standards (as it did through the adoption of the Basel Capital Accord), it is seen as embodying the interests of the international banking community as a whole. In doing so, it maintains the legitimacy and neutrality respected by banking supervisory authorities worldwide.[16] In addition, countries that do not have the necessary physical or human resources to develop their own systems can draw upon the expertise and experience that other members with whom they conduct business bring. Multilateral banks in Uganda have led the way in spearheading the development of anti-money laundering procedures and policies over their local counterparts.[17] This is because the parent supervisory authorities are responsible for the supervision of their home branches and subsidiaries operating in foreign jurisdictions, and will therefore supervise them in the same effective way as their home counterparts.[18] This is necessitated by the fact that the parent is responsible for the supervision of branches and subsidiaries under consolidated supervision. Consolidated supervision is undertaken by the single regulator of both the parent and subsidiaries or branches of the bank.[19] The

13 This enhances the sharing of valuable information, best practices of risk management methodologies and monitoring.

14 Dinah Shelton, 'Commitment and Compliance: The Role of Non-Binding Norms in International Legal Systems', 2 *Journal of International Law* (2000): p. 413.

15 Soft law can generally be adopted more rapidly because it is non-binding. It can also be quickly amended or replaced if it fails to meet current challenges. It extends to implementation and compliance, where the dynamic interaction of the various actors can play a crucial role.

16 Shelton, 'Commitment and Compliance'.

17 Barclays Bank has put in place guidelines to prevent money laundering and the Standard Chartered Bank has also formulated anti-money laundering guidelines to use in conjunction with minimum group standards.

18 This is the required approach under the Basel Committee consolidated supervision of banks' international activites model.

19 Jose de Luna Martinez and Thomas A. Rose, 'International Survey of Integrated Financial Sector Supervision', World Bank Policy Research Working Paper 3096, available

rationale for consolidated supervision is that a single supervisor or regulator, as it is sometimes called, is more effective than multiple supervisors in monitoring risks across financial institutions. In the UK, the consolidated supervision of banks and other financial institutions is the responsibility of the Financial Services Authority (FSA).

A uniform AML/CFT framework is an imperative to prevent criminal organizations from abusing the financial system, but it is also essential to contain the threat of money laundering. The global framework will certainly help to address weaknesses inherent in the local regulatory system. Foreign banks which operate in Uganda have managed to circumvent the absence of AML/CFT laws by exploiting the parent-grown banking policies, which have to be applied to all international branches. It has to be said that if the home and foreign laws are not aligned by way of enabling legislation, there is the likelihood of regulatory arbitrage to the disadvantage of foreign banks.[20]

International Harmonization Processes

Harmonization provides a working platform where the envisaged global anti-money laundering standards are implemented nationally.[21] The essential feature of harmonization is that states agreeing to apply harmonization instruments take them seriously and internalize them into the national legal system.[22] As already noted, for the envisaged global standards to work across different countries, they have to be harmonized with the laws of countries where they are to be applied. This is intended to bring about the convergence of anticipated international norms and substantive national law. The convergence of the two legal systems is intended to minimize the potential conflict of laws and its negative effects. Through harmonization processes, different regulators are able to apply different laws differently, especially when they belong to different legal jurisdictions.[23]

---

at: http://info.worldbank.org/etools/docs/library/154465/supervisors2004/pdf/martinez_rose.pdf (date accessed 10 December 2011).

20 If foreign banks are tightly regulated when their local rivals are not, they will not be able to compete with their local rivals.

21 The harmonization of private international law is coordinated by UNIDROIT. This is an independent intergovernmental organization with its seat in Rome. It work is to examine ways of harmonizing and coordinating the private law of states, and of groups of states, and gradually to prepare for the adoption of uniform private laws by states. Then we have other bodies such as the International Chamber of Commerce (ICC) which is based in Paris. For more information, see: www.iccwbo.org (date accessed 10 December 2011).

22 Kern Alexander, 'The Role of Soft Law in the Legalisation of International Banking Supervision: A Conceptual Approach', 2000, ESRC Centre for Business Research, University of Cambridge, Working Paper No. 168.

23 Shams, *Legal Globalization*, p. 13.

Laws may take the form of model laws[24] or soft laws, for example, laws issued by the European Bank for Reconstruction and Development (EBRD) on economic development through private sector investment in Eastern Europe.[25] The adoption of soft law norms by a country is essential in paving the way for their crystallization into hard law both nationally and internationally.[26] International soft law norms can arise from agreements that would not be possible in a treaty or other enforceable agreements because of fundamental differences among states and the concomitant reluctance by specific legal obligations of these regimes to undermine national interests.[27] This chapter demonstrates the challenges inherent in the harmonization of laws – due to asymmetries in the international system, varying legal cultures and the multiplicity of different global laws. Some of the envisaged global anti-money laundering laws may come in the form of model laws on money laundering, such as the third Anti-Money Laundering Directive in Europe and those created under the auspices of the Palermo Convention (2000) and its predecessor the Vienna Convention (1988).[28] These laws would have been transposed nationally in order to generate a normative effect on money laundering locally. The transposition of global anti-money laundering standards locally would see governments making policy adjustments to reflect the state's obligations under the treaty.

It would seem that subscribing to global regimes necessitates a move away from state centrism as this undermines the adoption of a uniform global framework.[29] The UK's accession to the EU demonstrates that individual Member States were made to adjust or dispense with some of their national laws to promote a functional European single market. To achieve the effective functioning of the EU in relation to its envisaged objectives, three sources of law are created at an EU policy level, namely regulations, directives and decisions. These laws are designed literally to level the playing field in the application of EU law within all participating Member States because of their varying legal and economic backgrounds. Regulations have a normative force as well as direct applicability in all participating Member States irrespective of national interest. Directives are transposed in a flexible manner,

24 These are set by bodies such as UNCITRAL and UNIDROIT, which were created specifically for harmonizing a specialized area of the law. For an overview of these two bodies, see ibid.

25 Christel Bourbon-Seclet, 'Cross-Border Security Interests in Movable Property: An Attempt at Rationalizing the International Patchwork: Part 2', 20(10) *Journal of International Law Review* (2005): pp. 501–13.

26 Alexander, 'The Role of Soft Law in the Legalisation of International Banking Supervision'.

27 Ibid., p. 5.

28 For more detailed information on the global anti-money laundering framework, see the 40+9 recommendations of the FATF available at www.fatf-gafi.org (date accessed 10 December 2011).

29 This position is popular among sceptics of the global system, for example, former communist countries, but also in countries that do not seem to have benefited much from the global market system.

whereby Member States are given a stipulated timeframe in transpose the desired EU changes into their national law. They are legislative measures binding Member States to the result to be achieved. However, Member States are given the mandate to decide the mode of implementing these targets.[30] Decisions, which are issued by the European Court of Justice (ECJ), require all Member States to comply with the decisions of the ECJ pursuant to Article 226 of the EC Treaty.[31] Harmonizing existing differences between states such as varying legal backgrounds and cultures has the potential to generate inter-state cooperation and to create a level playing field on which to harness the envisaged global standards.

The court as an institution provides the desired interface to implement the envisaged global anti-money laundering regimes. Courts elaborate rules and offer guidelines on global AML/CFT regimes helping to foster their adoption across jurisdictions.[32] The engendered norms are then widely disseminated through local institutions to ease the process of internalizing global AML/CFT standards into society.[33] The internalization of soft law norms can also be achieved through the legal processes whereby soft laws are voluntarily incorporated before they can be applied nationally. The ECJ, for example, plays a normative role in bringing about the harmonization of different laws in Europe. When the ECJ's intervention is sought on an issue of EU law in relation to a Member State, it will offer guidelines on the contentious issue. When it comes to the decisions of the court with regard to the issue of EU law, the respective Member State has no choice but to apply the decisions passed by the ECJ in its entirety. But this is at the EU level, where EU institutions have enhanced the domestication of EU law into the laws of individual Member States. The downside in translating the desired global regimes through the domestic court system is that in some regions, where judges are poorly trained or corrupt and courts are overloaded and struggling to retain experienced prosecutors, there will be backlogs, delays and hence the prevalence of corruption in some organizations as a quick fix.[34] It is also possible that ensuring that national rules conform to global standards will be sidelined in the absence of harmonization initiatives to align different regulatory systems. In this regard local institutions should undertake the necessary adjustments based on the exigencies of the market, such as money laundering and its predicate threats.

---

30 Paul Craig and Graine DeBurca, *EU Law: Text, Cases, Materials*, 3rd edn (Oxford: Oxford University Press, 2002), p. 105.

31 Craig and DeBurca, *EU Law: Text, Cases, Materials.*

32 There are many examples of such cases, but in the UK we have witnessed cases where the court through its interpretative has clarified the law on money laundering. See for instance the case of *R v Gibson* [2000] Crim LR 479.

33 This is indeed bad news for those countries which have been advocating the further expansion of the EU, such as France and Germany, and could spell doom for the wider European integration of economies such as Turkey (now on the waiting list) into Europe.

34 Mugarura, 'The Subdued Giant', p. 322.

In harnessing global anti-money laundering regimes, individual national governments should be afforded the opportunity to determine the extent of their participation.[35] The national legal systems should be used to plug weaknesses inherent in the system by evolving mechanisms or modalities for national participation.[36] This can be done through the courts and other policy platforms such as universities and national think-tanks in disseminating the desired national policies. It is in this respect that societies must be dynamic in response to changes ushered in by the imperatives of the global market economy. Its shortcomings notwithstanding, the global system has also created opportunities for national development.[37] It would therefore seem that if the global system is properly managed through the harmonization of existing differences, it has the potential to generate synergies for development nationally and internationally.

Furthermore, harmonization could also be impeded by the undemocratic manner in which some global regimes emerge vis-à-vis local economies.[38] Global regimes have demonstrated on a number of occasions the propensity to sideline local economies by competing for the sovereign space in which societies manifest themselves. I suppose in this regard that developed countries have had to surrender more of their sovereign space and independence than their less developed counterparts.[39] All countries subject to the same regulatory framework, based on the envisaged global AML/CFT standards, will have to incorporate the desired changes into substantive national law. As already noted, developed countries, which have robust systems in place, would have had a lot to surrender compared to their counterparts in developing countries. I also feel very strongly that in order to foster the harmonization process, countries subject to global regulatory regimes should be given the opportunity to contribute to the evolving anti-money laundering standards. This form of indirect participation in global standard-setting would make emerging regimes legitimate and correspondingly states would be more than willing to internalize them into substantive national laws. The apparent challenge with the Basel Committee's supervisory standards is that they are more inclined to favour the G10 economies than other countries, especially less

35 Some of the 40+9 recommendations (for example, Recommendation 12) of the FATF are conspicuously inapplicable in developing countries because they are largely oriented to the market environment in developed countries. I suppose this is an issue which reflects the asymmetric composition of the committees that propose the creation of AML/CFT recommendations.

36 Mugarura, 'The Subdued Giant'.

37 No country today can afford to run a closed economy, however big or privileged it is.

38 The FATF 40+9 recommendations on money laundering and predicate offences are introduced into domestic law through the back door using the World Bank and the IMF lending conditionalities.

39 It is my contention that although developed countries may have to surrender much of their sovereign space when compared to developing countries, they have the capacity to absorb the shock, while developing countries will literally be disorientated.

developed economies.[40] The Basel Committee should be reconstituted to ensure that other financial centres subject to the same regulatory regimes are able to field representatives on anti-money laundering committees. This would afford state parties the leverage to participate directly in the evolution of global anti-money laundering or the wider banking regulatory standards to which the countries in question are subject. The broader participation of states is essential to ensure the legitimacy of the Basel Committee and to overcome the criticism levelled against it that, in its current form, it is not representative of all countries and as such is less legitimate.[41]

In many less developed economies, courts as institutions are not as powerful as they are in developed economies because of the dynamics of economic development. In any case the intermediation of courts as far as global AML/CFT regimes are concerned is sidelined, either by the absence of well-trained judges, the prevalence of corruption or a lack of a requisite infrastructure to protect society against threats, including money laundering offences. Therefore, national courts need to have a far-reaching mandate to deal with contemporary threats, not least to deal with money laundering and its related predicate threats such as corruption. In this way, the courts would play a crucial role in the translation of desired anti-money laundering norms within the framework of internationally agreed standards. Unfortunately, in some jurisdictions, the role of the courts is undercut by the obduracy of governments, which treat them as conduits for their wishes. Traditionally, courts have always been mere accessories of the state, primarily interpreting laws to foster the will of parliament.[42] Courts undertake this function by interpreting and applying the law created by parliament and other organs of the state through delegated legislation. They have always played a primary role in the translation of normative standards into domestic law. Where it is deemed necessary, they may go as far as referring statutes back to parliament so that any anomalies in the law can be resolved or removed.[43] Laws should be introduced to reflect the necessary changes in dynamic society, as I have already elucidated by way of alluding to the European Communities Act 1972 and the Human Rights Act 1998 in the UK. There are situations where states have ratified international treaties, such as the Palermo Convention in 2000, but subsequently dither when it

40 I am sure that this would undermine the potential of the Basel Committee on Banking Supervision to crystallize into an international global framework.

41 Some of the allegations have been that the G10 is a reconfiguration of a colonial structure, providing a platform to perpetuate neo-colonial policy and its tendencies.

42 Mugarura, 'The Subdued Giant'.

43 This scenario is captured by the case of *Fisher v Bell* [1961] 1 QB 394, which was based on the Restriction of Offensive Weapons Act 1959. The law was deemed to be so vaguely structured that it had to be referred back to Parliament for the anomaly to be removed the following year.

comes to translating engendered obligations into policy and practice at a national level.[44]

Furthermore, national courts provide an interpretative function in deciding cases brought before them by disputing parties. Decisions generated at the court level are consolidated as guidelines for future policy development purposes. In addition, the court is in a reciprocal relationship with other decision-making bodies such as parliament in giving direction on how society should be governed.[45] The reciprocal relationship is manifested in the fact that parliament creates laws through its legislative process and the courts interpret them, offering direction on the engendered norms. In dualist countries, governments must pass legislation to provide direction on how anticipated global initiatives are to be domesticated.[46]

The adoption of the European Communities Act 1972 in the UK is significant in demonstrating the fact that countries must be prepared to surrender part of their sovereign space in order to accommodate envisaged market changes.[47] I have always viewed the European Communities Act as an instrument of harmonization which enabled the UK to internalize EU law at a national level. By embracing the EU, the UK had demonstrably compromised its national self-interest for the common good of a fully functioning European single market. Similarly, the adjustment of national laws happens to be the case with all emerging global regimes, including SAPs introduced by the World Bank and the IMF in many economies. With regard to the latter, it is now a settled fact that through the international monitoring and surveillance of national economies under Article 1V of the Articles of Agreement,[48] the independence of national governments has been sidelined by the operation of IFIs in many countries. The only difference between the EU and the aforementioned institutions is that the EU treaties are ratified and given primacy in all Member States by way of incorporation into the substantive national law. By contrast, the World Bank and the IMF reforms are largely viewed in some countries as intrusive and paternalistic of national economies as they are adopted through lending conditionalities.[49] The World Bank conditionalities, such as financial sector adjustment reforms, is what one would call 'soft law obligations' as

44 Uganda is a signatory to the above anti-money laundering instrument, but it has delayed implementing it through its national parliament. This means that at present, the courts cannot apply this law as a framework for prosecuting money laundering locally. If they are to prosecute money laundering, they can do so on the basis of other anti-money laundering regimes such as the Leadership Code (2002), but not the Palermo Covention as of yet.

45 The relationship between courts and other organs of government is constitutional under the principle of the tripartite separation of powers.

46 Mugarura, 'The Subdued Giant', p. 332.

47 Is it a form of quid pro quo?

48 The legal basis on which the World Bank Group operates in executing its mandate worldwide.

49 These regimes are designed and imposed to maintain the economic stability of borrowing countries.

opposed to soft law.[50] In the World Bank's view, undertaking structural adjustment reform programmes helps to strengthen institutional capacity and subsequently to ensure that societies are properly governed. However, it should be noted that much as soft law obligations are not legally binding, countries are nevertheless expected to undertake the required adjustment measures as prudential measures at an institutional level.[51] Thus, in relation to the World Bank and IMF regimes and courts, the courts are sidelined because traditionally, based on the doctrine of separation of powers, they always work in tandem with the executive and the legislature to foster national interests. They have literally had to act as the shock absorbers in translating the global regimes on any issue area domestically.[52] They are in a predicament whereby they are relegated to applying pre-existing laws whenever it is deemed right and necessary to do so in settling cases brought by the disputing parties. Save for situations where the law passed by parliament is so bad that applying it would amount to an absurdity, as I have already demonstrated, courts have a constitutional obligation to work in tandem with parliament in evolving a legal framework on the basis of the inherent traditions and customs of that particular society.[53]

Given the limits of national courts in relation to overlapping matters of international law, I propose the creation of a global AML/CFT court constituted with a global mandate. This court should be designed with a specialist division on money laundering and its predicate threats.[54] Thus, the proposed anti-money laundering court should proceed along the lines of the ECJ in its relationship with EU Member States on matters of EU law.[55] In the dispensation of the EU law, the interaction between the ECJ and national judges provides a platform for incorporating EU law into national law and of diffusing within the national legal order modes of reasoning and decision making developed by the court. Therefore, it should be noted that national judges are active participants in translating desired

50 Soft law is non-binding, but soft law obligations, although not binding in an explicit sense, require states to make the necessary adjustments to implement them. A failure to comply with soft law obligations may trigger sanctions on a non-complying member country.

51 Francois Gianviti, 'The Evolving Role and Challenges for the International Monetary Fund', *International Lawyer* (2001): pp. 8–12.

52 Courts as institutions are expected to provide the required interface on the future direction of a country. They are used as a platform to internalize the will of parliament in their decision-making process. However, where parliament is literally pushed into a corner, the courts will have to absorb part of that pressure as the two are constitutionally expected to work together in tandem.

53 Mugarura, 'The Subdued Giant'.

54 The creation of a global court would reinforce the enforcement mechanisms of global anti-money laundering regimes.

55 Under Article 68 of the EC Treaty, there are restrictions on national courts to submit cases to the ECJ. Only courts of last resort are required to seek a preliminary ruling from the ECJ.

changes into the mainstream legal system. This is exemplified by the fact that in the event of a conflict involving Member States in the application of EU law, national judges will where necessary file for a preliminary reference to the ECJ for the issue to be resolved. In so doing, the judges provide the required interface between two policy domains and foster the traditions and fundamentals on which the EU is founded while incorporating changes into society at the same time. It is therefore the case that the EU legal system is equipped with the capacity to generate policy outcomes and structure future policy processes, both at a national and a supranational level.[56] These connections are organized and sustained by the preliminary reference procedure established by Article 234 (formerly 177) of the EC Treaty.[57] Article 234, combined with the development of the doctrines of supremacy and direct effect, constitutes a decentralized means of enforcing EU law, connecting supranational and national governance.[58]

The third instrument for harmonization is the adoption of soft laws such as those on a capital adequacy framework for the regulation of international banks.[59] Capital adequacy was negotiated under the auspices of the Basel Committee, otherwise known as 'Basel II', to provide a capital measurement baseline of all internationally active banks.[60] Under the capital adequacy framework, all internationally active banks must hold assets to a value of at least eight per cent of their risk-weighted assets plus off-balance sheet commitments.[61] The capital adequacy framework was initially intended as a caution for international banks

56 If judges refused to give effect to EU law by refusing to file preliminary references, the EU legal system would have been stillborn. Therefore, national judges have been active participants in the development of the EU and this should be a model for national legal systems on how to proceed in relation to supranational regimes.

57 This article mandates Member States to refer a contentious issue of EU law to the ECJ, which is the highest court. However, for this to happen, the litigant would have to have exhausted the available domestic remedies.

58 Alec Stone Sweet, 'Integration and Europeanisation of the Law', Queen's Paper on Europeanisation (No. 2/2002), Nuffield College, University of Oxford.

59 It was motivated by a couple of factors. First, bank regulators were interested in enhancing the capital position of banks in order to enhance their ability to absorb losses due to less-developed-country debt and other risks. Secondly, there was a need to forestall possible competition in regulatory laxity in terms of the capital adequacy standards of banks.

60 Bagheri and Nakajima, 'Optimal Level of Financial Regulation under the GATS', p. 517.

61 Paul R. Krugman and Maurice Obstfeld, *International Economics: Theory and Policy*, 5th edn (London: Pearson, 2000), pp. 659–67. The Basel Accord goes further to divide capital into two tiers. Tier 1 capital defined as paid share capital/common stock and published reserves from post-tax retained earnings, which must comprise of at least 5 per cent of the bank's capital base. Tier 2 is defined as undisclosed reserves, asset revaluation reserves, general provisions/general loan loss reserves and subordinated debts being limited to 10 per cent of Tier 1 and, combined with Tier 1, must comprise 8 per cent of the bank's risk-weighted assets.

with regard to various types of risk: credit, market and operational. There is also liquidity risk, which is the temporary inability to meet payments, and then market or positional risk, and systemic risk.[62]

Bank illiquidity could potentially lead to financial distress and cause demand for withdrawals from depositors. This causes bank runs as panic grips depositors trying to get ahead of each other.[63] This challenge, coupled with macro-economic factors, has been a potential trigger for financial crises by way of changing asset prices and increasing interest rates.[64] This can potentially trigger a contagious effect as investors lose confidence in the system, affecting not only the single region involved but also other regions, including even those that are performing well.[65] Therefore, capital adequacy was intended not only to secure the international banking institutions against the aforementioned risks but also to create a 'level playing field' by requiring uniform capital regulation so as to prevent the race to the bottom as competitors outprice each other on international markets.[66] Supervisors would be able to apply the same standards and prevent free-riding off of the reputation of less heavily regulated international banks.

The Proposed Regulatory Changes under the Basel III Framework

It has become apparent that the Basel Committee Principles on Banking Supervision and the FATF 40+9 recommendations are not sufficient in cautioning countries against the exigencies of global financial markets.[67] As a matter of fact, the recent global financial crisis (2007–2010) highlighted the challenges to economies in regulating global regulatory exigencies. Furthermore, it has also become a tradition for new regimes to emerge in response to global crises. However, while this is acceptable, on a negative note, it also highlights the inability of the current regulatory regimes to stop crises from happening in the first place. It is time states became more proactive to ensure that crises do not even have to happen, which seems to justify the need for a more robust Basel III. However, it should be noted that the adoption of global regulatory regimes cannot be sufficient in the absence of clear mechanisms to enforce engendered rules. This has prompted 27 central bank governors from different countries to propose the

62 The East Asian crisis of 1997/1998 demonstrated the way in which impaired bank assets are adjusted downwards and the ability of the central bank to act as a lender of last resort to illiquid but solvent banks.

63 M. Brownbridge and C. Kirkpatrick, 'Financial Sector Regulation: The Lessons of the East Asian Crisis', 17 *Development Policy Review* (1999): pp. 243–66.

64 Ibid.

65 Ibid.

66 Daniel E. Ho, 'Compliance and International Soft Law: Why Do Countries Implement the Basel Accord?', 5 *Journal of International Economic Law* (2002): p. 647.

67 *Financial Times*, 26 June 2010.

adoption of Basel III. This new framework is intended to compel banks to hold more capital reserve as a precaution against future financial crises. Basel III as a regulatory model will include a minimum core 'Tier 1' of somewhere between 7 and 9 per cent of their risk-bearing assets, including a 'capital conservation buffer'. 'Tier 1' refers to the bank's capital reserves, which are intended to absorb shocks more robustly, as opposed to the core level of two per cent under existing rules, which was deemed too inadequate to protect economies against financial shocks in the event of a financial crisis. Basel III will include a minimum Tier 1 ratio of 4.5 to 6 per cent, with the additional capital reservation buffer of 2–3 per cent. One expected outcome of the Basel III regulatory framework is that any bank that fails to keep above this buffer would have to curb payouts such as bonuses and dividends.[68] However, it would seem that the highly capitalized banks will have a disproportionate advantage over less well-capitalized banks and this is likely to become the potential area of contention for the proposed regulatory measures to work across the board. Less well-capitalized banks may face a long road to recovery and an increase in capital – both the Tier 1 and capital conservation buffers would undercut the amount of money which banks can lend out to companies. Thus, less well-capitalized banks will be less inclined to support the Basel III proposals because, much as it is necessary to provide a more robust framework attuned to overlapping challenges, in practice this might not be easy to implement due to the inequalities in the global financial system. Banks that might not be in a position to meet the proposed requirements under Basel III would most likely be less inclined to implement it. It is my contention that Basel III cannot be an effective global framework unless it internalizes the wider regulatory challenges in the global financial economy so that it has a global appeal in the eyes of all stakeholders. It also needs to be noted that Basel III is still a proposal and we hope that when it is finally adopted as a regulatory framework, the mistakes of the past Basel regulatory regimes (for example, a lack of adequate representation of stakeholder countries) will not be repeated.[69]

The Legal Status of Soft Laws

International soft laws encompass the whole range of legal norms, principles, codes of conduct and transaction rules of the state practice that are recognized either in formal or informal multilateral agreements.[70] The use of soft law in multilateral agreements generally implies the consent of the state to apply them, but there is no *opinion juris* to make them legally binding as rules of customary international law.

68 Ibid.

69 More detailed information on Basel III can be found in the consultative paper of the BIS, available at www.bis.org (date accessed 10 December 2011).

70 Ho, 'Compliance and International Soft Law'; see also Alexander, Dhumale and Eatwell, *Global Governance of Financial Systems*, pp. 138–40.

Customary law is the presentation of those conditions in the form of law; in other words, setting the terms of the future coexistence of society members in the form of legal relations. The space of consent in customary law is subtle and is not made by any specific act of will on the part of its subjects. Their assent is manifested in their participation in the day-to-day struggle of social self-ordering, knowing that some aspect of that self-ordering may come to be universalized as law.[71]

While soft law norms are not legally binding on states,[72] they nonetheless create guidelines to deal with certain business exigencies. They contribute to the development of international rules, standards and legal principles that can as time goes on metamorphosize into hard law.[73] It therefore has to be said that countries gain immensely from adopting soft law norms such as the guidelines of the Basel Committee on Banking Supervision and the FATF's 40+9 recommendations. In a sense, the adoption of soft law norms is driven by the need to have a working framework capable of applying to different countries. In theory, a failure to observe soft law does not amount to a breach of international law norms, but in practice it may generate some tensions with other countries. Jurisdictions that refuse to cooperate and comply with the recommendations of the FATF are publically blacklisted ('named and shamed') by the FATF and economic sanctions may be imposed against them. When the non-cooperative jurisdiction is a dependent territory, then the blacklisting applies to that territory.[74] In the same respect, the World Bank and the IMF have co-opted the Basel and the FATF supervisory standards in their monitoring framework of national economies.[75] Therefore, countries seeking to use the resources of the World Bank and the IMF are expected to adjust their national economic systems as a precondition for lending. Soft law norms should be introduced to close gaps inherent in some sources of public international law.[76] For instance, state parties will be required to apply anti-money laundering standards regardless of whether they have already transposed the provisions of the treaty or not.[77] States should also bring their laws into harmony with international anti-money laundering standards by adopting legislative measures on concealment and the laundering of the proceeds of crime.[78] Soft law could also be utilized to plug

71 Philip Alliot, 'The Concept of International Law', 3 *European Journal of international Law* (1999): pp. 30–31.

72 International law should be enforced to demonstrate that the law works to maintain sanity in society by punishing offenders.

73 Alexander, 'The Role of Soft Law in the Legalisation of International Banking Supervision'.

74 Gianviti, 'The Evolving Role and Challenges for the International Monetary Fund'.

75 William E. Holder, 'The International Monetary Fund's Involvement in Combating Money Laundering and the Financing of Terrorism', p. 384.

76 Alexander, 'The Role of Soft Law in the Legalisation of International Banking Supervision'.

77 Article 1 of the Vienna Convention 1988.

78 Ibid., Article 3(1).

loopholes in existing law so that there is a framework for the uniform application of global anti-money laundering standards across the board.

If the global anti-money laundering framework is to work effectively, there should be a mechanism for the extradition of culprits apprehended in one country to the jurisdiction of another country for trial.[79] Thus, each country should recognize money laundering as an extraditable offence,[80] accepting to extradite its own nationals or, where it does not do so solely on the grounds of nationality, at the request of another seeking extradition, to submit the case without delay to its competent authorities for the purpose of prosecution of the offence set forth in the request.[81] In this regard, all states should ratify the Palermo Convention in order to have a uniform policy framework for dealing with aspects of money laundering, particularly cross-border jurisdictional issues. The Palermo Convention should be ratified by all states to ensure the application of a uniform policy approach on drug trafficking and money laundering. Signing up to global anti-money laundering regimes would afford state parties the benefit of mutual legal assistance with regard to investigations, prosecutions and judicial proceedings in relation to money laundering offences. Similarly, the Palermo Convention provides modalities for extradition in respect of money laundering offences alleged by the jurisdictions that make a formal extradition request.[82] The extradition request should only be declined where there are reasons to believe that compliance would facilitate the prosecution or punishment of any person on account of his/her religion, race, nationality or political opinion, or would cause prejudice for any of those reasons to any persons affected by the request.[83]

What is worthy of mention is that treaties such as the Palermo Convention are only effective when state parties ratify and subsequently internalize them into substantive national laws.[84] If the state does not ratify the Convention,[85] it cannot generate binding legal effect at home. Once the treaty has been transposed, it forms part of national law, reflecting the proposed changes internally.[86] This is in contrast to customary law, which is a product of dialectic of practice but not dialectic of ideas as legislation.[87] Therefore, different forms of law generate different obligations in different societies. The need for national sovereignty notwithstanding, it is a common state practice for civilized states to transpose

79 In the absence of a global court, money laundering can only be tried in the country where the offence was committed.

80 Recommendation 3 of the FATF.

81 Ibid., Recommendation 39.

82 Article 7(1) of the Palermo Convention 2000.

83 Article 6(6) of the Vienna Convention 1988.

84 In monist countries, after treaties are ratified, they form part of the national law.

85 Mugarura, 'The Subdued Giant'.

86 The foregoing is particularly the case with dualist economies such as the UK, but in the case of monist economies like France, once treaties have been ratified, they form part of the national law without any recourse to national parliaments being necessary.

87 See Alliot, 'The Concept of International Law', p. 14.

international treaties and to ensure international harmony.[88] However, the issue of national self-interests may create ambivalence in some states, which choose to stay on the sidelines in the domestication of international anti-money laundering regimes. Given this possibility, some countries may ratify international treaties but literally drag their feet in translating the envisaged standards into domestic law for the reasons elucidated above. For example, some countries may not be inclined to protect depositors' assets when they are themselves exposed in terms of their net outflows to service the national debt.[89]

The need for countries to adopt a global anti-money laundering framework is essential to ensure that fugitive offenders are pursued and prosecuted wherever they are hiding. Individual states should work together to ensure that they have a framework to respond astutely to the exigencies of globalization and its related challenges. It should be pointed out that whenever a law is created in a society, the purpose would be to close the disparity gap in the existing legal framework, obviously in keeping with local realities.[90] It is improbable that laws created in a different social setting will have resonance in other jurisdictions, where the problems may be informed by a different set of factors.[91] Besides, law as an institution is capable of engendering values and traditions that translate the requisite changes into society. States usually undertake a cost-benefit analysis and seriously assess the implications of anticipated global regimes on local development interests. This rather cautious approach notwithstanding, there is no country, even if it is a developed powerful country, that can afford to be ambivalent as all countries must work together on overlapping global issues. Countries which were initially on the sidelines of global initiatives with regard to the WTO, such as Russia and China,[92], have been clamouring to join as they have acknowledged that they cannot afford to stay out and be sidelined. Staying on the sidelines of global initiatives will undercut the influence of these same countries on issues of global importance.[93] The analysis of international law and its dynamics is essential to underscore the parameters within which global AML/CFT laws are harnessed nationally. It should be highlighted that the realm of implementing global anti-money laundering framework is international law.

88 See, for example, the Vienna Convention 1988 and the Palermo Convention 2000.

89 Jeffrey Frieden, *Banking on the World: The Politics of American International Finance* (London: HarperCollins, 1988), p. 188. Frieden argues that the debt burden in less developed countries led to international bankers being blamed rather than courted.

90 Mugarura, 'The Subdued Giant'.

91 Ibid.

92 Actually, China has already joined the WTO, although Russia has yet to join.

93 This explains why China, which has more or less operated a closed economy, has began to open up, not to mention that it has been clamouring to join multilateral trade initiatives such as the WTO.

International Financing Institutions

The World Bank and the IMF are among the cohort of international financial institutions that are active in facilitating the fight against money laundering and its predicate offences.[94] These two institutions were created in the aftermath of the Second World War to facilitate the recovery of countries that had been devastated by the War.[95] In the final stages of the War, a series of conferences took place to discuss how to prevent the reoccurrence of the economic conditions that led to the worldwide depression and the rise of the Nazis in Germany.[96] The 1944 Articles of Agreement of the World Bank and the IMF were adopted a few months before the submission of the Dumbarton Oaks Proposal establishing a General International Organization – the future UN – in the same year. The arrangements for international cooperation in the Dumbarton Oaks Proposal were limited to the facilitation of international economic, social and humanitarian problems and the promotion of respect for human rights and fundamental freedoms. The proposal did not intend to found the UN as an organization, which would have to deal first and foremost with human development. Its main purpose was supposed to be the maintenance of peace and security, the mandate that was given to the Security Council based on the sovereign equality of its members.[97] The international economic and social cooperation in the UN Charter differs from the Dumbarton Oaks Proposals in that it was meant to promote:[98]

a. higher standards of living, full employment and higher conditions of economic and social progress and development;
b. solutions for economic, social, health and related problems, and international cultural and educational cooperation; and
c. universal respect for, observance of, human rights and fundamental freedoms for all without distinction as to race, sex, language or religion.

The World Bank and the IMF and were created for different economic purposes. The Articles of Agreement of the IMF limited the purposes of the Fund to facilitating the expansion and balanced growth of international trade, and contributing to the promotion and maintenance of high levels of employment, real income and the development of the production resources of all members as

94 Other financial institutions which are active in fighting money laundering and the financing of terrorism include regional banks and FATF-affiliated regional bodies in Asia, the Caribbean, South America and Africa.

95 Andreas F. Lowenfeld, *International Economic Law*, International Economic Law series (Oxford: Oxford University Press, 2003), p. 500.

96 Ibid.

97 P. van Dijck and G. Faber (eds.) *Challenges to the New World Organisation* (The Hague: Kluwer Law International, (1996), pp. 13–16.

98 Article 55 of the UN Charter 1945.

primary objectives of economic policy.[99] The Articles of Agreement also obliges the IMF to impose legal obligations on member countries not to engage in the kind of practices that had contributed to the great depression of the early 1930s and the outbreak of the Second World War.[100] On the other hand, the main purpose of the World Bank was to promote the long-term balanced growth of international trade and the maintenance of equilibrium in the balance of payments in order to assist its members in raising productivity, the standards of living and labour conditions in their territories.[101] To facilitate the achievement of that end, both the World Bank and the IMF adopted the so-called structural adjustments facilities whereby countries seeking to use their facilities would be asked to undertake certain reforms as conditions. These reform adjustments were deemed essential in order to stimulate economic growth in countries suffering from financial difficulties, to generate revenues through increased international trade and to enable countries to be able to meet their borrowing obligations.[102] As far as the World Bank is concerned, the list of borrower countries is confined to governments of developing and former communist countries. As for the IMF, even though its facilities are available to all member governments, very few OECD member countries can be made subject to conditions.[103] While this might seem to be a one-sided application of policy measures on weak developing countries, it is justified in a way by the fact that adjustment programmes were initially intended to strengthen capacity in such countries. It would also seem to be justified that countries with strong functioning institutions do not necessarily have to be subjected to structural adjustment measures.[104] These measures were also justified so as to inject a measure of flexibility and predictability into the international economic systems and thus to minimize the risk and uncertainties invariably faced by major financial centres in the form of systemic risks.[105]

---

99 Article 1 of the IMF Articles of Agreement 1947.

100 Before 1945, there was international monetary system. States and their enterprises traded with one another, currencies were exchanged and states held monetary reserves – in gold, silver and foreign currencies. At the dawn of the Second World War, no international legal regime governed the conduct of states. The currency market was literally in a state of what one would call 'to whom it may concern'.

101 Article 1(iii) of the IBRD Articles of Agreement; see also Lowenfeld, *International Economic Law*, p. 502.

102 These reform adjustment programmes were prescribed in many developing countries since they were the countries that needed to borrow most from the World Bank and the IMF reserves.

103 David Henderson, 'International Agencies and Cross-Border Liberalization: The WTO in Context', in Anne O. Krueger, *The WTO as an International Organization* (Chicago: Chicago University Press, 1998), p. 97.

104 Heather Marquette, *Corruption, Politics and Development: The Role of the World Bank* (Basingstoke: Palgrave Macmillan, 2003).

105 Beare (ed.), *Critical Reflections on Transnational Organised Crime, Money Laundering, and Corruption*, p. 107.

The World Bank and the IMF contributed enormously to the global fight against money laundering through their work in promoting stronger financial, economic and legal systems internationally.[106] Both encourage financial institutions to adopt robust supervisory standards and legal and institutional frameworks to prevent abuse in the financial sector. The IMF surveillance function under Article IV of the Articles of Agreement involves intensive exchange with each member country on its economic and financial systems.[107] The IMF staff will examine the country's economic and legal system to identify potential vulnerabilities and advise the country to take corrective measures and polices. The IMF has adopted several discrete initiatives designed to strengthen the financial stability and to prevent global crises.[108] In 1999, the IMF, together with the World Ban,k adopted Financial Sector Assessment Programmes (FSAPs) as a centrepiece for inquiring into the health and stability of member countries. The mandate of both the World Bank and the IMF will cover the banks, securities, money markets, foreign exchange and payment systems of countries, whilst also assessing the regulatory, supervisory and legal frameworks of financial institutions.[109] It is this work which has relevance for fighting money laundering. By undertaking the regulatory assessment programme, any vulnerabilities in the system would be identified and states would subsequently be advised to take corrective measures.

The WTO as a Harmonization Platform

The WTO as a multilateral forum provides a platform for harmonization as it was founded on the negotiation of trade rounds in the interests of its member countries. It was created in 1995 to provide a rule-based trading system built on the principles of non-discrimination and liberalization, openness and free trade: to forbid discrimination in favour of national producers while also regulating national behaviours on the part of exporters (for example, dumping).[110] It was also to reduce tariffs and to prohibit other forms of quantitative restrictions, including overt forms such as quotas and unfair practice concealed by unfounded health or administrative regulations.[111] The WTO as a global institution provides a platform for negotiating agreements but also settling trade disputes. It subsumed the work of the General Agreement on Tariffs and Trade (GATT) which was the vehicle

106 Frieden, *Banking on the World.*

107 Holder, 'The International Monetary Fund's Involvement in Combating Money Laundering and the Financing of Terrorism', p. 383.

108 Ibid.

109 Ibid.

110 Mugarura, 'The Subdued Giant'.

111 Ibid.

for negotiating trade agreements between countries.[112] The weakness of GATT had been that, much as it provided a vehicle for negotiating trade agreements in relation to goods, these negotiations did not cover negotiations in relation to the trade in services.[113]

The General Agreement on Trade in Services (GATS) provides a framework for trade in cross-border financial services, including financial markets.[114] The GATS regime is founded on the premise that enhanced competition in financial services will lead to healthier financial institutions and will improve the quality of financial services.[115] It incorporates four modes of trade in services: cross-border; consumption abroad; commercial presence; and temporary movement of natural persons.[116] Given the focus of this chapter, the aforementioned areas will be analysed in relation to banking services. The cross-border supply of services would have taken place when consumers of goods in one country are allowed to obtain loans in another across the border.[117] Consumption of banking services of banking services abroad would have taken place when purchasing banking services such as a letter of credit or e-money when travelling abroad. Commercial presence is highlighted by a situation where a bank is allowed to establish a branch or a subsidiary in another country. The movement of natural persons would have taken place when a financial institution registered in one country is allowed to send its executives, managers and other banking personnel to another country in order to deliver services.[118] GATS has important implications, especially for the regulation of banks. Its specific provisions and general principles are most favoured nations and market access.[119] The most favoured nations (MFNs) treatment connotes the treatment of WTO members equally on the principle of non-discrimination.[120] In banking, if a concession is made to a country's bank, then similar concession under the MFN provision should also be given to foreign banks. This is important to make sure that there is no discrimination against foreign banks, as this would be inimical to the full integration of financial services. Under GATS, if a country allows foreign competition in a sector such as banking, equal opportunities in that sector should be given to other service providers from all other WTO member countries. GATS also provides a flexible approach based on an adaptable set

112 More information on the WTO can found on its website at www.wto.org (date accessed 10 December 2011).

113 GATS was agreed in 1947 but took effect two years later.

114 Alexander, Dhumale and Eatwell, *Global Governance of Financial Systems*, pp. 100–104.

115 Alexander, 'The Role of Soft Law in the Legalisation of International Banking Supervision'.

116 James R. Barth, Gerard Capiro, Jr. and Ross Levine, *Rethinking Bank Regulations* (Cambridge: Cambridge University Press, 2006), p. 169.

117 Ibid.

118 Ibid.

119 Ibid.

120 Article 11 of GATS 1947.

of rules for members to negotiate specific commitments on the nationality and market access principles.[121] The principle of national treatment under Article XVI forbids discrimination based on the origin of products.[122]

National treatment (Article XVII) requires that any conditions or qualifications are negotiated and become a schedule of commitment, prohibiting home regulators from treating foreign banks less favourably than they treat domestic banks.[123] This also means that under the nationality principle, member countries cannot erect barriers to entry or operate policies that discriminate against foreign banks as compared to domestic banks. In so doing, the WTO promotes the harmonization or approximate national domestic policies to the free flow of international trade in services.[124] The WTO Council for Trade in Services has responsibility for issuing a legally non-binding interpretation of GATS. It fulfils this function by acting upon recommendations generated as a result of examinations of various WTO committees in particular sectors.[125] The internalization of financial services signifies that a country's prudential regulatory and supervisory regimes should promote sound banking practices.[126] It is this function that has particular relevance in fighting money laundering as it replicates the same principle put forward by the Basel Committee on Banking Supervision. As regards market access, there are certain commitments in the GATS schedule that are incorporated, and the extent of market access being given to those sectors specified in the schedule. For example, if a government commits itself to allow foreign banks to operate in its domestic market, that is a market access commitment.[127] The principles of national treatment and market access work in such a way that a member country would indicate in its negotiated schedule of commitment that it is granting market access and national treatment to foreign banks from other member countries.[128] The country would then list in its schedule all restrictions on market access and national treatment that would be imposed on foreign banks.[129] The market access principle prohibits five types of types of limitations, unless they have been incorporated by a member in its schedule of commitment.[130] The following are the prohibited limitations: limitations on the number of suppliers; limitations on the total value of service transactions or assets; limitations on the total number of natural persons that may

121 Alexander, 'The Role of Soft Law in the Legalisation of International Banking Supervision'.

122 Article 11 of GATTS 1947, which sought to eliminate quantitative restrictions on imported products.

123 Arie Reich, *WTO Legal Text: The Results of the Uruguay Round of Multilateral Trade Negotiation* (Cambridge: Cambridge University Press, 1999), p. 418.

124 Ibid.

125 See the WTO website at www.wto.org (date accessed 10 December 2011).

126 Ibid.

127 Reich, *WTO Legal Text*.

128 Ibid.

129 Ibid.

130 Ibid.

be employed; measures which restrict or require specific types of legal entities or joint ventures; and limitations on the introduction of foreign capital.[131] The specific commitment by financial services is made in accordance with the annex on financial services in GATS, which compliment the basic rules and definitions of GATS, taking into account the specific characteristic of financial services.[132] In particular, para. 2(a) states that: 'Notwithstanding any other provisions of the agreement, a member shall not be prevented from taking measures for prudential reasons. These measures would include but are obviously not limited to protection of investors; depositors; policy holders or persons to whom a fiduciary duty is owed by the financial services supplier; or to ensure the integrity and stability of financial system.' However, this list of prudential measures would have to be incorporated into a member's schedule of commitment, as they are not regarded as limitations on market access or national treatment.[133] Nevertheless, it should be noted that para. 2(a) does not specifically define or provide any indicative list of what prudential measures are. Measures that are consistent with prudential measures would seem to encompass the following: capital adequacy ratios, the restriction of credit concentration, portfolio allocation, disclosure and reporting requirements, as well as licence criteria which are not more burdensome than is necessary.[134] It is para. 2(a) that seems to have particular relevance to societies in relation to measures adopted by the financial institution against money laundering and its predicate threats.

Similarly, the principles of nationality and market access can be limited when a member country enters into economic integration such as the EU or the East African Community (EAC). Certain concessions decided upon as a result of regional agreements which are not applicable to non-member countries. This exemption also allows a country to apply more favourable treatment than that guaranteed by GATS commitment on a non-MFN basis, but it does not permit less favourable treatment. In addition, Article XIX provides that developing countries may attach to their market opening conditions designed to increase their participation in the services trade – for example, the transfer of technology.[135] In view of this, the WTO is a more harmonizing institution than its counterparts, the World Bank and the IMF, given that it provides a negotiation platform and a dispute settlement mechanism. However, the WTO as a global institution replicates the principles of good regulatory standards in much the same way as the FATF and

131 Aaditya Matto, 'Financial Services and the WTO: Liberalization in Developing and Transition Economies', presented at the WTO, 2007, paper 154, available on the WTO website at www.wto.org (date accessed 15 December 2011).

132 Ibid.

133 Ibid.

134 Ibid.

135 The service industry is an area where developing countries lack a competitive advantage and Article XIX is actually meant to give concessions so as to enhance their market access.

the Basel Committee on Banking Supervision – created to champion prudential regulation and supervision of financial institutions.

The Challenges Created by IFIs

The biggest challenge created by the involvement of IFIs in many developing countries is one of ignoring the dynamics of local development in a recipient country. Legislation in developing countries has been substantially affected by SAPs: debtor states have been coerced into passing legislation that is pernicious when judged by the standards of such economies.[136] This has indeed consigned many countries subject to adjustment policy measures to a downward spiral of development challenges.

The plausible role played by IFIs in many economies notwithstanding, the SAPs are perceived as intrusive with regard to internal state sovereignty and the concept of self-determination. Self-determination presupposes the decolonization of the state (external), as per UN Resolution 1514 (XXV) of 1960, but also that people within the sovereign state determine their destiny (internal), as prescribed by UN Resolution 1541.[137] For example, the introduction of financial sector reforms in developing countries is blamed for the downward spiral of many economies. As such, there is a growing disenchantment with and hostility towards the market economy.[138] A familiar example that demonstrates the impact of SAPs[139] is the situation in Uganda, where the army was restructured in the 1990s, then the government succumbed to pressure from the donor agencies to reduce the number of public sector employees.[140] When this was compounded by the demobilization of other public sector workers, it created a fertile climate that fed and reinforced different fighting groups in the country, in which the disengaged soldiers were easily enlisted.[141] One wonders why many governments have followed the World Bank and IMF SAPs since they were first introduced in 1970s and yet are still facing significant challenges to development. This would infer that in order to

136 Mugarura, 'The Subdued Giant'.

137 These two resolutions were passed within 24 hours of each other, one setting out the rights and duties of a state and the other giving people the right of self-determination.

138 Mugarura, 'The Subdued Giant'.

139 These programmes, designed by the World Bank and the IMF, proliferated in the early 1980s, as one country after another was afflicted by a lethal combination of high interest rates and falling commodity prices.

140 Mugarura, 'The Subdued Giant'.

141 Under the required SAPs, Uganda was to reduce its civil service to one-sixth of its original size from 320,000 people to 55,000 between 1995 and 1997. In 1998 the Ugandan government was required to undertake further large-scale civil service reform, including lay-offs and the merging of ministries within six months. These figures were tendered by the Ministry of the Civil Service when setting guidelines to improve privatization on 13 May 1998.

generate any meaningful effect, the World Bank/IMF reform programmes should be specifically tailored to local development specific conditions. In Africa, where more than 30 countries adopted SAPs, average incomes fell by 20 per cent during the 1980s, open unemployment quadrupled, investment fell to levels which were lower than in the 1970s and the region's share of the world markets fell by half, to two per cent.[142] This development climate is exploited by criminals such as money launderers, who establish themselves in disintegrating states. In addition, the weakness left as a result of this has generated a negative environment that is adverse to the domestication of anticipated anti-money laundering obligations within a country. Therefore, many IFIs regimes[143] are either too onerous on weak vulnerable states to be implemented or their programmes are incompatible with the political, economic and social environment in the recipient states.[144] While I appreciate that IFIs have the right to design prudential measures to ensure that loans are paid, they should do so bearing in mind the need to promote social welfare standards and enhance the economic stability of the countries receiving development assistance. If reform programmes work in an adverse manner to their intended purpose – the stability of national economies – it becomes difficult to justify their importance. This is supposedly the reason why some critics of the IFI-led reform programmes have argued that SAPs are often motivated by a hidden agenda.[145]

Furthermore, some of the G10 countries can flatly disregard global standards whenever they deem it desirable to do so,[146] while requiring non-G10 countries to make adjustments for implementing global standards irrespective of the prevailing economic conditions.[147] This problem is compounded by the absence of a robust supervisory infrastructure[148] in some countries to enhance the adoption of global anti-money laundering standards locally. Many less developed countries are deficient in terms of the requisite human resource capabilities to oversee the implementation of desired anti-money laundering global standards compared to

---

142 Oxfam Policy Department, *A Case for Reform: Fifty Years of the IMF and the World Bank* (London: Oxfam, 1995), p. 5.

143 By IFIs, I mean the World Bank, the IMF and other lending institutions such as regional banks.

144 For much of this paragraph, see Mugarura, 'The Subdued Giant'.

145 Stiglitz, *Globalization and Its Discontents*, p. 53.

146 This causes accountability problems, creates chaos in the administration of the system as well as resentment on the part of countries that are coerced into adopting these standards.

147 This runs counter to the WTO principle of MFNs.

148 This encompasses both economic and legal infrastructure necessary to carry out the proposed reforms or changes in the local systems. Because these reforms are cosmetic and are undermined by a precarious economic environment (wars, poverty in its various manifestations, lack of good education, etc.), it usually does not take long before the system develops cracks and subsequently crumbles.

their counterparts in developed countries – a problem which is tangential to under-development and all its attendant shortcomings.

In terms of a harmonization platform, the WTO is accused of saying one thing in theory but doing exactly the opposite in practice – literally being two-faced.[149] This is always a vivid manifestation of poor leadership because the leader is deemed to be the holder of great vision. This vision cannot be clearly articulated by putting across conflicting messages. There is superficial equality which masks serious inequality in both the approach and reality of power in this institution.[150] Its claim to defend fair competition is far from justified as it is subservient to the multinational corporations (MNCs).[151] It has been described as the most opaque institution imaginable, meeting in secret in the shadow of the International Chamber of Commerce (a club comprising the biggest transnational organizations).[152] Not surprising then is the fact that the WTO is oblivious to issues of sustainable development, which are confined to debates in other forums. It is equally oblivious to environmental issues, protesting, at the expense of the future, against any regulation of the mining industry.[153] The deregulation recommended by GATT-WTO is simply intended to benefit transnational monopolies by reducing the space in which states (and particularly Third World states) can exercise management to nothing. The conduct of the WTO as a multilateral forum has provoked a range of arguments that cannot be easily compartmentalized as only economic in nature. Not only do these arguments over the objectives and pace of liberalization cover both the economic and political spaces, it is also clear that the WTO replicates the structural imbalance in world power between the developed and the developing world.[154] Therefore, the WTO will have to refocus its attention to its initial mandate of addressing the embedded weaknesses that plagued it under the GATT arrangement.

The Need for Robust National Institutions

Law in the sense of formal written rules will be largely irrelevant if the emerging rules are not incorporated into an institutional framework. Therefore, as local societies make efforts towards implementing the envisaged anti-money laundering

---

149 The dispute settlement mechanism has been frequently used and could progressively engender a change in attitude within the WTO. This is again why I am strongly arguing for a global court on money laundering. Laws must be enforced in order to generate a sense of the issue being taken seriously at a local level.

150 S. Amin, *Capitalism in the Age of Globalisation* (London: Zed Books, 1994).

151 Mugarura, 'The Subdued Giant'.

152 Amin, *Capitalism in the Age of Globalisation.*

153 Ibid.

154 F. Macmillan, 'International Economic Law and Public International Law', 6 *International Trade Law and Regulation* (2004): pp. 115–24.

regimes, the challenge remains one of creating fully-fledged local institutions to translate the engendered norms locally. These institutions are essential not only to ease the translation of anti-money laundering regimes locally but also to engender an institutional ethos based on the envisaged norms. Policy-making institutions should initiate regional studies with regard to understanding the global typologies of money laundering, cross-border jurisdictional issues and forging a working partnership with other sectors of government that will be affected by the envisaged global regimes. It is equally important for globalizing countries to institute a committee of experts (based on the model of something like the committee of wisemen under Lamfalussy in the integration of financial markets in Europe) to filter through the proposed policy measures and expedite the implementation of anticipated reforms. Institutional mechanisms should be imbued with checks and balances in order to minimize errors at the initial policy formulation stage.

The creation of the Inspector General of Government (IGG) in Uganda as a specialist anti-corruption institution has been applauded as a step in the right direction.[155] This institution is premised on the UNCAC 2005 framework which provides that where there is a significant increase in the assets of a public official for which no reasonable explanation in relation to his/her lawful income is provided, an offence of illicit enrichment is committed.[156] The UN's commitment to fighting corruption is further illustrated by Article 24 of the UNCAC, which deals with the concealment of the proceeds of corruption. It also provides that where an individual who has not participated in corruption conceals or retains property which he/she knows is a result of corruption, he/she will be committing the offence of concealment.[157] The IGG translates the UNCAC in Uganda. Indeed, the IGG has recently demonstrated that it is capable of performing correctly in investigating corruption-related cases and subsequently ensuring that corrupt public officials are prosecuted.

However, much as the proliferating anti-corruption initiatives are well intentioned, given their mandate, their concomitant capacity to stem or control corruption has been hamstrung by the fact that they are created in a manner that makes them subordinate to the appointing authority (the executive) and hence susceptible to manipulation. The IGG in Uganda has been criticized for targeting political mavericks (politicians who have fallen out of grace with the government)

155 Under Article 19 of the UNCAC, where there is a significant increase in the assets of a public official for which no reasonable explanation in relation to his/her lawful income is provided, an offence of illicit enrichment is committed. Article 24 deals with the concealment of the proceeds of corruption. Where an individual who has not participated in the corrupt activity conceals or retains property which he/she knows is the result of an offence committed under the UN Convention, he/she will have committed the offence of concealment.

156 Article 28 of the UNCAC.

157 Article 24 of the UNCAC relates to those who aid and abet the commission of acts of corruption under Article 28.

and members of the opposition.[158] On many occasions, local institutions in developing countries are not independent when executing their mandate and this is worse in situations when they are investigating public officials on allegations of corruption. The anti-corruption institutions are accused of literally being the 'launderette', whereby they are used to cleanse government officials of corruption allegations and even to suppress any investigations against state officials – the same officials they are supposed to hold to account.[159]

It would be prudent for officials who are appointed to lead anti-money laundering agencies to be vetted by non-affiliated independent bodies to avoid the possibility of duplicity and conflicts of interests, which tend to undermine the underlying objectives of local anti-money laundering institutions. There must be established mechanisms for the enforcement of emerging anti-money laundering laws, otherwise laws which are not enforced cannot be taken seriously, as they do not generate any binding effect. In any case, the anti-corruption institutions should have an autonomous mandate so that they can bring their weight to bear on corrupt government officials whenever it is deemed necessary to do so. This will help to counter a situation involving conflicts of interests and duplicity where the accuser is the judge, jury and executioner.

It is my contention that anti-money laundering institutions at a national level should be created with a monitoring mechanism, for example, on-site visits for system verification, and should focus on placating societies with regard to practical, desirable change.[160] It would seem that some governments merely create dysfunctional local institutions for the sake of appeasing the international donor community. The monitoring process should encourage continuous review assessments and civil society participation.[161] This should go a long way towards cultivating a culture of seriousness and ensuring that institutions do not eventually veer off the path charted in their initial objectives. There should be a clear set of rules and procedures to monitor the adaptation of the system to proposed changes.

The challenges faced in Europe with regard to the integration of financial markets[162] signify that the global governance of international finance is more

---

158 This corruption typology is common in much of Africa: see Ugandan daily newspaper *The Monitor*, 15 July 2007.

159 Some local anti-money laundering institutions are widely viewed in some countries as undemocratic because of the way officials in these institutions are appointed and also because they work under the direct influence of ruling governments.

160 This is precisely the reason why it is important to have bodies such as the FATF. However, it can do much better by addressing some of its weaknesses, such as a lack of accountability.

161 This is proposed based on the World Bank procedure, but in a manner that is oriented towards local societies.

162 Despite efforts at integration, financial markets are still divided, something that is highlighted by minimum harmonization initiatives and mutual recognition to achieve some level of market convergence.

easily said than done.[163] While the EU is a successful integration story with four functional institutions to coordinate EU policy details nationally, the European single market is far from realistic and is still fragmented. Policy guidelines are coordinated through any of the four institutions of the EU – the Parliament, the Commission, the Council and the Court – constituting it as a quasi-European super state in default. However, the integration of financial markets is far from practical, as demonstrated by the fact that member countries are allowed to maintain their national regimes alongside the EU regimes and are only required to adopt a minimum level of conformism through the principles of home country control and minimum harmonization.[164] Thus, the concept of global governance without fully-fledged global institutions such as a global parliament to legislate on policy details has become a pertinent issue in the integration of global markets. This environment could potentially cultivate conditions for criminal exploitation such as money laundering and market abuse. The local financial institutions should be developed bearing in mind the need to accommodate the envisaged global standards. However, these institutions should be created after wide consultation have been undertaken to ensure that the proposed institutional framework is appropriate and adaptable to the local imperatives of development.

NGOs

The action of international NGOs has contributed to the enunciation of soft law norms regarding the regulation of many global issues, including money laundering and corruption.[165] The role of NGOs in fostering global initiatives and in filling the void created by the reduced role of the state cannot be under-estimated. Perhaps it needs to be said that NGOs[166] have traditionally been accorded the legal status of individuals – they generally exist under the national law of a place where they have been created, as well as the law of the place where they are active. The state is in the predicament where it has either lost or ceded its traditional powers to non-state actors as it reconstituted itself at a supranational level.[167]

NGOs have the potential to create a platform for the participation of citizens directly in the affairs of the national interest, promoting issues of governance, government accountability, judicial reform, electoral reform and generally

---

163 This contention is further strengthened by the regulatory failure highlighted in the recent global financial crisis (2008).

164 See e.g. Directive 91/308/EEC.

165 Pierre-Marie Dupuy, 'Soft Law and the International Law of the Environment', *Michigan Journal of International Law* (1991): pp. 422–3.

166 The ICJ decision in the *Barcelona Traction* case has the nationality of the place of incorporation. See the case of *Belgium v Spain,* International Court of Justice (1970), pp. 42–3.

167 Dupuy, 'Soft Law and the International Law of the Environment'.

improving the institutional framework of governments. With regard to corruption and money laundering, Transparency International has played a vital role, generating data on corruption, disseminating it to various stakeholders and often pressurizing some governments to reform their policies. In the case of the UK, for instance, several articles in the press echoed the Transparency International working group's assessment and put pressure on the government to introduce some legislation changes. In France, just before the parliamentary election in 2007, Transparency International highlighted the fact that a provision in the draft legislation expressly excluded ongoing corrupt arrangements. The ensuing public pressure contributed to the deletion of the provision.[168]

Likewise, civil society organizations (for example, the International Criminal Court and Transparency International) have been instrumental in changing attitudes in the business community. They have made some organizations change their internal procedures and develop compliance mechanisms in accordance with the OECD guidelines and recommendations.[169] In addition, Transparency International, as well as various business associations, assists companies that want to learn about successful models of codes of conduct and compliance programmes.[170] Civil society organizations have provided analyses and organized debates on corruption and political party funding as a means of fighting private sector corruption.[171] Therefore, these organizations have played an influential role in enhancing the capacity of societies to combat money laundering and its attendant evils including corruption. They are not affiliated to any government and will therefore not be inhibited by the campaign against any corrupt practices and money laundering. Some governments have adopted strict licensing laws to undercut the work of NGOs, especially those organizations that are viewed as being critical of the government. However, this study contends that all development-minded societies should embrace the role of civil society organizations.

Interpol

Interpol, which has been augmented by the creation of other regional police agencies, has also played a central role in the fight against money laundering

168 Transparency International, *Global Corruption Report* (London: Pluto Press, 2004).

169 The OECD issues guidelines for multinational enterprises operating in or from adhering countries. These provide voluntary principles and standards for responsible business conduct, including on combating corruption and bribery.

170 Transparency International, *Global Corruption Report.*

171 In October 2000, Transparency International organized a seminar in La Pietra in Italy. The meeting concluded with the issuing of recommendations to the OECD on how to extend the Convention to cover the bribery of foreign political parties and party officials, which they submitted to the OECD Working Group.

by exchanging essential information to ensure that money launderers as well as other cross-border criminals are prosecuted. Its ethos as a multilateral police organization gives it the mandate of a global policing institution.

The idea of an international police institution was first mooted in 1914 but only materialized in 1923 with the composition of 176 member states, of which 46 European member states account for 80 per cent of its communication traffic.[172] The move to create a transnational police force was prompted by the growing concern over the internationalization of certain crimes which could not be confined to a single state, such as terrorism, drug trafficking offences and money laundering.[173] The creation of an international police force was also prompted by common social influences of people in Europe who objected to everyday crimes and the inadequacies of national criminal justice systems.[174] Another reason was the need for a common definition of crimes, as some of the problems were understood far more than either recent criminological orthodoxy or common sense would expect.[175] There was also a further reason underpinned by the scholarship that points to the absence of a reliable and valid method of evaluating the scope of transnational crimes. This scholarship contends that there is little hard data on recorded cross-border crimes in Europe and thus there is an absence of information about the economic cost of such activity.[176]

Interpol operates at three levels: first, at the macro-level, which entails constitutional and international legal agreements and the harmonization of national laws and regulation; secondly, at the meso-level, which focuses on the operation, structure practices and procedures of police and law enforcement agencies; and, thirdly, at the micro-level, which entails the investigation of specific offences and the control and prevention of particular forms of crime.[177] At the macro-level, government ministers take decisions on matters relating to rights of entry and exit from sovereign states (extradition procedures, asylum policies and visa harmonization) and on legal issues about operational powers across borders in respect of arrest, detention, investigation and surveillance.[178]

Interpol was created to undertake two fundamental functions. It promotes and ensures mutual legal assistance between criminal police authorities within the legal limits laid down in different countries and in the sprit of the Universal Declaration of Human Rights. Secondly, it is created to promote public policing that is likely to

---

172 J. Anderson et al., *Policing Across National Boundaries* (London: Pinter, 1995), p. 15.

173 Ibid.

174 Ibid.

175 L. Johnson, *Policing Britain: Risk, Security and Governance* (London: Longman, 2000), p. 154.

176 Ibid.

177 Anderson, *Policing the World*, p. 11.

178 Ibid.

contribute to the prevention and suppression of ordinary crimes.[179] Each Interpol member is required to nominate an office (the National Central Bureaux (NCBs)) to communicate with the Lyon headquarters as the mechanism through which Interpol enquiries are channelled. Police information is circulated between NCBs on international notices, which contain photographs, fingerprints and physical descriptions of persons colour coded according to the nature of the enquiry. Clearly, Interpol's role as a communication network restricts it to the exchange of information on a case-by-case basis, and partly because of this, its capacity to promote greater police cooperation in Europe as elsewhere is limited.[180] Its work is also limited in another respect: Article 3 of the Convention adopted under the Council of Europe (1949), mindful of the sensitivities surrounding national sovereignty, defined the organization's mission as the efficient prosecution of common law crimes and offences to the exclusion of other matters of a political, religious and racial character.[181] It was largely because of the exclusion of political crime from Interpol's operation brief that following terrorist acts in the 1960s and early 1970s, the European Council of Ministers instigated the creation of TREVI.[182]

Specifically, in relation to money laundering, Interpol has a specialist branch (FOPAC) which cooperates with police departments and multilateral organizations in gathering and disseminating information on the movement and laundering of the proceeds of crime.[183] It has developed model legislation designed to make it easier to obtain the kind of evidence needed in criminal investigations and proceedings aimed at the confiscation of the proceeds of crime and is working with the UN agencies to complete an automated compendium of information on the status of legislation and law enforcement in different countries.[184] However, the problem with Interpol is that, just as with other international agencies, it is an institution inclined towards developed countries, which account for 80 per cent of its communication traffic.

179 M. Anderson, and E. Bort (eds), *The Frontiers of Europe* (London: Pinter, 1998), p. 45.

180 Ibid.

181 Ibid.

182 TREVI operates at three levels. There is TREVI 1, with the mandate to combat terrorism, as well as to address the problem of drug trafficking; TREVI 2 is concerned with scientific and technical knowledge and police training; and TREVI 3 was set up to address the question of security, such as civilian air travel, a role which was later assumed by TREVI 1.

183 Anderson, *Policing the World.*

184 Johnson, *Policing Britain*, p. 154.

The Schengen Agreement

The Schengen Agreement provides the most complete modal of European cooperation in fighting European-wide crimes. It was signed in 1985 by Belgium, France, Germany, Italy, Luxembourg, and the Netherlands, Spain and Portugal in 1991 and Greece in 1992.[185] The Agreement acknowledged the need to remove all internal frontiers between Member States in order to facilitate the free movement of workers, goods and capital, but ensuring at the same time that the borders were strengthened to control the unnecessary entry of aliens.[186] According to the Agreement, non-European immigrants would need to acquire a visa normally of three months' duration to enter in any of the Schengen member countries, while any decision reached on asylum applications made in one Member State would be binding in all other states.[187] The Agreement stipulates a number of measures including increased border surveillance, the right of pursuit of criminals across borders and the coordination and sharing of information between the police forces of Member States. The last of these is underpinned by the establishment of a computerized data exchange, the Schengen Information System (SIS), which is intended to act as a common database shared by all members containing eight million personnel and seven million records on objects. The SIS is regarded as a compensatory measure for the removal of frontier checks, enabling police agencies in different countries to have identical information on wanted persons, 'undesirable persons', asylum seekers and those extradited or under surveillance.[188]

Just like TREVI and Interpol, the Schengen Agreement also works at three levels: macro-level agreement, deciding policies such as the pursuit of criminals; macro-level policing, which involves the cooperation of states on cross-border security matters; and meso-level structures, such as the SIS being put into place to facilitate micro-level policing. The work of the Agreement is immune to judicial and overall parliamentary accountability to European institutions, an issue which has particular implications on human rights, data protection and the issue of sovereignty.[189] It has been argued that Schengen Agreement members are prepared to surrender some issues of sovereignty in return for an enhanced capability to combat crime, limit clandestine immigration and enable internal border controls

185 Ibid.

186 Ibid.

187 These concerns were reflected in the Maastricht Treaty 1992 of the EU whose so-called Third Pillar (Title IV) contained a series of provisions on cooperation in the field of justice and home affairs. As such, Member States would regard the following as areas of common interest: preventing and combating terrorism, asylum policy; rules on the crossing of external borders of the Member States and the exercise of control thereon; immigration policy; policy regarding nationals of third countries; and judicial cooperation in criminal matters.

188 J. Sheptycki, (ed.), *Issues in Transnational Policing* (London: Routledge, 1998), pp. 39–47.

189 Ibid.

to be removed.[190] However, the success of such endeavours depend upon members adopting a common policy on matters such as immigration.[191]

The above institutions are augmented by Europol which was created in 1991 with the mandate to collect and analyse data on drug trafficking, money laundering and related criminal activities, together with the facilitation of intelligence exchange between law enforcement agencies in Member States.[192] The mandate of Europol[193] extends to the prevention of illicit trafficking in motor vehicles, nuclear and radioactive substances and the trafficking of illegal immigrants.

Conclusion

In order to work globally, the putative global anti-money laundering regimes must be preceded by harmonization to ensure that engendered norms are internalized locally. In this regard, there is a need for the involvement of specialist organizations and agencies[194] in local economies but based on agreed rather than coercive terms – a fundamental tenet of contractual agreements. The intervention of IFIs has assisted fledging national economies in building local institutions based on international standards by offering technical assistance, facilitating information exchange and launching initiatives to close the disparity gap between the local and global societies. Chiefly, the World Bank and the IMF have played a pivotal role in fostering local capacity building by way of encouraging financial sector reforms and funding many local initiatives on financial crimes, something that local fledging economies would not to afford on their own. However, it would seem that the relationship between the World Bank and the IMF and borrowing countries is based on consent and should be subjected to the principles of international loan agreements. It is well known that the World Bank and the IMF do not have the mandate to interfere in the domestic politics of a country in which they operate, but it would nevertheless seem that their operations are political, since they are involved in all manner of political issues in countries in which they operate. In some countries, the operations of these institutions have caused problems for the

190 Ibid.

191 In January 2008, Italy's decision to grant political asylum to the Iraqi Kurds fleeing persecution led to demands for de-linking from the common immigration arrangement with the French and German ministers for fear of opening the immigration floodgates to Northern Europe.

192 Johnson, *Policing Britain.*

193 This organization is similar to the Federal Bureau of Investigation (FBI) in the USA.

194 Some of these organizations have been criticized for being driven by their own motives rather than the interests of recipient local governments in overcoming over-dependence and development problems. Civil society organizations have taken credit for engaging at a grassroots level in tackling development problems in local society.

ruling governments, such as a loss of popularity and widespread unemployment, issues which have huge political consequences for national governments.

The work of the civil society organizations such as Transparency International has assisted local economies in information gathering and engaging with governments in terms of fighting corruption and money laundering. It is my contention that fighting the global threat of money laundering would be greatly enhanced by the introduction of the global court based on the model of the ECJ in the EU. The proposed court, through its influence and mandate, would engender a change in social attitudes, engendering a positive anti-crime ethos in many societies. The court would also be used as a forum for dispute settlement (like the WTO), elaboration on and enforcing compliance with emerging global anti-money laundering norms. Although the majority of anti-money laundering regimes are imbued with the mechanism for sanctions, the fact that sanctions are invoked in a coercive manner has not helped in fostering compliance among member countries. What states do instead is to express their resentment in a subtle way by circumventing the engendered obligations under the ratified treaties.[195] The court, through the elaboration process, would help reduce resentment against the emerging anti-money laundering regimes, thus causing the engendered norms to be internalized. Apparently, the issue of prosecuting money laundering crimes in national courts signifies that the culprit (who often has significant financial resources) can exploit weaknesses in the national legal system to stay put. In any case, those who commit corruption as another predicate of money laundering are often people in elevated government positions and would be protected by the system. However, with the proposed global court, extradition treaties and mutual legal assistance in place, it is possible that some headway could be made in terms of fighting overlapping money laundering offences. The global court would help to plug weaknesses in the global enforcement regimes of anti-money laundering laws, which are capable of being exploited by the launderers to further their criminal activities. If this is not done, money laundering is bound to remain a challenge for the international community for many years to come.

195 States may have to enter into an arrangement to sign the treaty subject to certain reservations, which may constrain the implementation of the treaty in the state.

Chapter 8

The Proposed Reforms to Transpose Global Anti-Money Laundering Regimes into some Countries

Introduction

The thrust of this chapter is to propose the desired reforms that will have to be undertaken as a condition of harnessing the global anti-money laundering regimes in some countries. Reforms are essential to align local institutions to the envisaged global AML/CFT standards. The World Bank and the IMF have played a key role in initiating reform programmes in individual countries. However, it is my contention that reforms should reflect the development imperatives at a local society level. For example, the World Bank/IMF financial sector reforms have not gone very far in placating some local economies, supposedly because the proposed reforms are not locally oriented as much as they would need to be.[1] In addition, the anticipated reform programmes should be comprehensive so as to encompass all local institutions, for example, education institutions, local courts and financial institutions, through which national governments manifest themselves. The proposed reform package identified in this chapter will create an environment where it is easy to fight the threat of money laundering and its underlying predicate offences.

Education Reforms

While education reforms are essential, they should have a clear focus in order to overcome some imperfections in the system. Empirical studies[2] have shown that education can provide a platform to transmit information with regard to anti-corruption tailored programmes. Similarly, the public can be sensitized through education, by way of seminars, public enlightenment campaigns, workshops,

1 A detailed account of challenges facing the domestication of the envisaged anti-money laundering norms has already discussed earlier in this book.

2 B. Kinoue, 'From Individual Dignity to Respect for Jinkaku – Continuity and Change in the Concept of the Individual in Modern Japan', in Michael Likosky (ed.), *Transnational Legal Processes: Globalisation and Power Disparity* (London: Butterworths, 2002), pp. 295–6.

conferences, press releases and training in order to rid society of criminal activities such as corruption. Through training and sensitization programmes, citizens can easily be brought on board in the fight against corruption and other forms of crime. It is equally my contention that a good education system should be localized by way of making it society-oriented (specialized)[3] and adapted to its cultural, social and economic needs if it is to correlate with the development interests of the society in question.

The education system in societies (especially in less developed countries) needs to be adjusted in terms of its development imperatives if it is to serve a robust development purpose and to remain relevant. This was clearly demonstrated by Japan, which was able to modernize in the twentieth century by evolving a policy of educating the populace in Western knowledge and practices.[4] To achieve this goal, the government launched an ambitious educational programme for all Japanese children, adopting systems principally from France, the UK and the USA.[5]

Indeed, many Asian economies (such as Hong Kong, Singapore, South Korea and Taiwan, and later post-reform China and Thailand among others) have done remarkably well in spreading economic opportunities through adequately supportive social backgrounds, achieving high levels of literacy, numeracy and basic education.[6] The government of Japan also integrated moral ethics within its educational curriculum, as this was deemed to be essential for the translation of the government's development programme at a later stage.

Today, China, which has overtaken many economies economically, dominates the international student market (both in the USA and the EU) and is accordingly producing more than 5,000 engineers, not to mention other graduates, every year, emulating the Japanese model discussed above.[7] Thus, education provides and helps to boost the skills requirement to foster development of local economies, but it also raises awareness about the attendant challenges of the global system to society and how to tackle them.

As opposed to developed countries, the population in developing countries is less educated and less able to access education. Since societies are becoming more globalized, there is a need to ensure that ordinary citizens acquire the requisite knowledge on globalization and its influence vis-à-vis on their societies. This is an essential element to ensure that citizens have a say in relation to changes in society and are able to influence policy decisions at a higher government level. As for

3 Foreign-oriented education is geared towards foreign systems and often has very little correlation to development problems that saddle the local society. Sustainable development needs to be feasibly adjusted to the imperatives of the local environment.

4 Kinoue, 'From Individual Dignity to Respect for Jinkaku', pp. 295–6.

5 Ibid.

6 Sen, *Development as Freedom*, p. 91.

7 The CBI report on 'The Role of Education in Economic Development', *The Guardian*, 2 August 2008.

infrastructural and technical capacity deficiencies in the regulatory and security agencies, education could play a significant role by ensuring the continuous training of both the regulators and other agencies of financial institutions. This is necessary in order to strengthen the fight against economic and other financial crimes by ensuring adequate capacity building and the conduction of programmes at national and international levels. The training of accountants, supervisors, engineers, lawyers and teachers (all core skills in society) should be integrated with ethics to enhance global market needs.

The character of the desired educational reform[8] should be designed to reflect the development imperatives of the progressive market-oriented economy. Much as globalization and its attended philosophies may be resented by some societies, its spill-over effects can be well managed through a robust local education system. Modern educational needs should focus on science, commercially related subjects and research and development studies – for example, on globalization and the law, the impediments to development today. Abstract education, apparently a predicament by which many societies (particularly former colonial countries) are marred, has added to the spectre of under-development that clouds the image of many African economies.

Changes in the education curriculum are essential because the current system (being a vestige of a colonial past) is inadequate in a putative global era and has been superseded by changes in the world economy, thus resulting in bad education.[9] The need to study a globalization-related curriculum would also entail the need for a student exchange programme, resulting in enhanced shared experiences with other students, particularly those from developed countries. Graduates with international exposure are more receptive to change and will provide a positive influence when introducing normative changes into the domestic economy. The spectre of poor sequencing of priority development needs in some societies has sacrificed development at the altar of a system that is incompatible with the development priorities of the society.[10]

Judicial Reforms

The need for necessary legal reforms should be preceded by the process of creating laws designed according to anticipated market needs and the use of engendered

8 The move to introduce universal primary education, launched in 2002, is a step in the right direction, being a positive measure designed to overcome the challenges of illiteracy in Uganda.

9 In law, when the case is overruled and no longer applicable, it cannot be invoked as a precedent. Equally, a system which is no longer applicable with respect to the imperatives of the society is a bad system.

10 No country can ever develop without first developing an infrastructure to support the anticipated development initiatives.

norms in ordering the system. This would presuppose that certain legal traditions in countries will have to be dispensed with in order to reflect such novel changes and challenges that the society in question is experiencing. For example, for the UK to accommodate the paradigmatic changes ushered in by the European Economic Community (EEC) in 1973, which mutated into what is now the EU in 1997,[11] it acceded to the EEC by the European Communities Act in 1972. Henceforth, the UK traditions with regard to the interpretation and application of laws would change to reflect the changes that had been ushered in by EEC law. Besides the benefits of subscribing to the EU, the flipside was that the emerging EU institutions engendered a new paradigm and created a countervailing authority to the British Parliament at Westminster, diminishing the autonomy of the state by derogating legislative powers away to Brussels.

The EU will legislate in all areas of national importance, except where a Member State has derogated or entered into a reservation on some or all aspects of a particular treaty.[12] Section 3 of the European Communities Act 1972 articulates that in the event of a potential conflict between national and EU laws in the UK, the latter has to take precedence. Lord Denning, decrying the erosion of British sovereignty as a result of the pervasive character of EU treaties, likened it to 'an impending estuary'.[13] In the case of *Bulmer v Bollinger* (1974),[14] Lord Denning had this to say: 'Parliament has decreed that the treaty henceforward to be part of our law. It is in force to any Statute.' Indeed, as highlighted above, traditionalists like Lord Denning viewed the accession of the UK to the EEC as an erosion of national sovereignty. However, it should be appreciated that accommodating global regimes or changes at home entails a move away from statism.[15]

The proposed global anti-money laundering laws can easily be implemented locally by exploiting the legislative process of parliament. The requisite legal reform process should ensure that the engendered decisions are legitimately and democratically aligned to national interests.

There should be a clear framework for the legislative process, encompassing the way in which laws are proposed, enacted and updated.[16] Members of the opposition should be fully utilized to ensure that the proposed laws are not motivated by grandiose political interests but are necessary and proportionate.[17] In jurisdictions where members of the opposition are denied a voice (either as a result

11 By the Treaty of Amsterdam.

12 Any EU Member State may exercise its right to stay out of any treaty arrangements in its national self-interest under the principle of subsidiarity.

13 *R v Secretary of State for Transport, ex parte Factortame Ltd* [1988] 2 AC 85.

14 [1974] Ch 401.

15 Mugarura, 'The Subdued Giant'.

16 Rosa M. Lastra, 'Financial Law Reform', 23(9) *Journal of International Banking Law and Regulation* (2008): p. 413.

17 Proportionality is used to denote whether measures taken were appropriate and necessary.

of corruption, intimidation or coercion), the created laws will be lopsided, dictated by political interests of the incumbent government and will not necessarily foster the interests of the wider society.

Similarly, introducing necessary changes into society (not least those relating to money laundering) should be accompanied by the proper dissemination of information to ease the adoption of the desired changes. This should encapsulate the way in which laws, regulations and court decisions are recorded, authenticated and disseminated to government bodies, courts of justice, lawyers, academics, the business community, NGOs and the general public.[18]

Laws must not just be passed – they also need to be widely known, applied and enforced. Local society needs to be educated about the law and its role in fostering the required market changes.[19] To help achieve these overriding objectives, countries should develop local institutions that efficiently support the proposed changes through courts of justice, regulatory agencies, private bar group associations and specialist research institutions.[20] With regard to developing countries, local radio (remembering of course that access to television and the Internet is limited) and perhaps free local newspapers[21] should be utilized to bring the public on board with regard to the envisaged programmes on a wider national level.

The public and the business community need to be educated about the rule of law in a market economy.[22] It is my contention that it is a huge mistake to suppose that the law is the preserve of the executive and the legal profession. Citizens should be able to conceptualize what the laws are and their attendant responsibilities so as to assert them as leverage for the development of society.[23] Legal education in tertiary institutions of learning should be designed with an ethos that accommodates the envisaged market changes.

Education as culture embodies certain values and traditions, and therefore cannot remain immutable in the face of changes in society; indeed, must be dynamic in response to changes in the global society. Therefore, it is my contention that the global legal framework should be dictated by the interplay of global and local changes or challenges, depending on how much change each society would have absorbed.

The teaching of law in universities and other tertiary institutions should place emphasis on globalization and markets to make the local society competitive within global markets. First, the whole legal curriculum should focus on the

---

18 Lastra, 'Financial Law Reform'.

19 Ibid.

20 A detailed discussion of the role of local institutions in harnessing AML/CFT regimes has already been discussed in Chapter 7.

21 The government should subsidize the cost of radios and establish ways of handing out free local newspapers for the purpose of informing the public.

22 Lastra, 'Financial Law Reform'.

23 Mugarura, 'The Subdued Giant'.

challenges within the local society. A proper sequencing of legal reform is required, guaranteeing that an adequate infrastructure (as a basis for the effective implementation of the required changes) is created first and foremost.[24] Given this, legal methodologies in law schools and the training of lawyers and government officials on new laws are all important facets in translating envisaged changes into society. Secondly, the introduction of a number of student exchange programmes with other countries into the university curriculum is recommended to ensure that students are given international exposure.[25] This is desirable to blend local educational needs with an ethic of international experience to ease the adoption of the envisaged market changes.[26] Thirdly, the training of judges should focus on international law and criminology, arbitration, mediation and negotiation, so that it is easy to translate a transnational legal order into the domestic context. Although globalization and its wider market dynamics may be resented within some societies, there is no society today which can afford to operate a closed economy.[27]

Financial Sector Reforms

Legal reforms should be undertaken to harmonize the introduction of desired changes into the local economy.[28] Monetary and financial reform must also reflect the particular economic and political circumstances of individual countries that are subject to the proposed reforms.[29] The early years of transition, especially in Eastern European countries, tended to concentrate on basic infrastructural development within the banking and capital markets, strengthening financial supervision and building appropriate skills in the commercial sector and administrative authorities.[30] Once an effective foundation for reform was established, it helped to launch the anticipated market changes.

---

24 Lastra, 'Financial Law Reform'.

25 Where resources may not generally allow this in some societies, it should be implemented in phases according to which needs should have priority.

26 For this, see the Japanese model of education, already covered in Chapter 6.

27 This is demonstrated by countries like China and Russia, which have been clamouring to join Western-led institutions such as the WTO. Countries which are economically vibrant cannot compete favourably in the global market unless they also open up their economies to other economies.

28 European Bank for Reconstruction and Development, 'Competition, Law and Policy: Enhancing Enforcement and Cooperation', *Law in Transition*, 2004, www.ebrd.com/downloads/research/law/lit041.pdf (date accessed 10 December 2011).

29 Steven Fries and Anita Taci, 'Banking Reform and Development in Transition Economies', European Bank for Reconstruction and Development, 2002, www.ebrd.com/downloads/research/economics/workingpapers/wp0071.pdf (date accessed 10 December 2011).

30 Lastra, 'Financial Law Reform'.

The blanket approach of propping up necessary reform initiatives by the World Bank has not been compatible because these reforms are initiated without recourse to local development specifics in different societies. This problem was highlighted by the failure of SAPs to stimulate development wherever they have been introduced, as discussed in the previous chapter. In Uganda, for instance, the adoption of SAPs served as a catalyst in bringing about the current political and development malaise in the country.[31] Some political leaders ruthlessly exploited this environment to consolidate their dictatorial tendencies, both at the expense of their constituents and of development. The financial sector reforms introduced in 1987 by the World Bank, in total disregard of Uganda's capacity to accommodate such reforms, were exploited for criminal purposes, not least through the use of counterfeit currency within the Ugandan economy.

In Uganda, the banking industry is regulated by the Financial Institutions Act 1993.[32] This law was enacted following the financial sector reform programme, which began in 1991 with the support of the World Bank Financial Sector Adjustment Credit Project.[33] The enactment of this statute was meant to lay down a sound legal framework for the regulation of banking business in a new environment, while its adoption o was designed to control the legislative deficiencies which the banking sector experienced under the Banking Act 1969. However, the resulting use of counterfeit currency was a result of poorly managed reforms embedded in the introduction of this legislation.[34]

Therefore, implementing financial sector reforms should where necessary be deferred until the respective government/state is capable of managing the envisaged market changes. As such, any reforms should be oriented towards the local society in question. However, in some societies, where insufficient resources would inhibit the reform process, local initiatives should be supported and facilitated by IFIs. If IFIs are to remain relevant, they should work together to reduce global crises by serving as quasi-lenders of last resort to troubled international banks. The top-down reform approach by the World Bank and the IMF[35] for local economies has elicited anger in some societies over what is widely viewed as the use of lending conditionalities to impoverish recipient economies. While I do not share the viewpoint that the World Bank should be abolished, the source and the reason

---

31 I have already dicussed how many developing countries were caught up in this unpalatable situation.

32 Nyanduga Mukinya, 'Evolution of Banking Systems in East Africa: A Comparative View', Central Bank of Kenya, 2002.

33 Ibid.

34 Ibid.

35 There are advantages to the global nature of the IMF's surveillance and technical assistance activities, not least that it offers opportunities for raising awareness on the need for a robust anti-money laundering system. The IMF provides extensive policy and technical assistance to central banks and other national institutions around the world in building up their supervisory capabilities.

for the anger in those voices should be acknowledged. If IFIs supported reform work counter to their anticipated objective of stimulating development, it becomes very difficult to justify their importance and raises the charge of them having a hidden agenda.

There are two issues worthy of mention with regard to a non-locally-based approach to financial sector regulation. First, it would seem that a global anti-money laundering approach based on the recommended anti-money laundering standards would create a level playing field. However, in practice this has not been the case, for the reasons set out in chapter 2. Secondly, if reforms are not local society-oriented, they may be sidelined by politicians using the proposed reforms as a cloak to consolidate their dictatorship. The same reform programmes may also be exploited for criminal purposes, as this text has already illustrated with regard to the issue of counterfeit currency in Uganda.

The intervention of IFIs in local societies is sometimes necessary, but should always be dictated by the prevailing local circumstances.[36] Each society subscribing to global regimes should have the opportunity to influence the evolving anti-money laundering regimes to which it is subject. This should be done either by way of regional representation or by the individual societies themselves. By the same contention, it is wrong for IFIs to coerce countries to adopt a uniform global framework when these same countries have not been given the opportunity to develop the requisite infrastructure to support the envisaged changes.

With regard to the World Bank and the IMF, while work they have done in building local capacity cannot be denied, it is important to ensure that individual countries are co-opted in the evolution and implementation of the engendered norms. Therefore, it is my contention that the above agencies should instead engineer training and support local experts in deficient technical areas.[37] In other words, there is the need for home-grown solutions rather than extraneous measures which are capable of externalizing the problem in terms of adapting the same solutions to local development imperatives. In so doing, the proliferating anti-money laundering regimes will not only be seen to be legitimate but will also go a long way towards solving development challenges, not least the absence of a suitable workforce at a local society level.

With its vast resources, the World Bank should work in partnership with local NGOs in fostering local solutions to tackle the challenges of the global system (such as financial sector abuse and money laundering). Local NGOs are more adept at fostering local solutions compared to Washington-based agencies. It is equally essential to utilize local NGOs as a platform for sensitizing the local population against the dangers of money laundering and financial market abuse. With regard to money laundering committed by people in elevated official positions, there is a

36 The World Bank and the IMF should be reformed to reflect contemporary changes since their inception in the immediate post-Second World War period.

37 This is covered by the adage 'Give a man a fish, he eats for a day, teach him how to fish, he eats for life'.

need for institutional safeguards to ensure checks and balances on those holding high office positions.[38]

Financial Sector Supervision

This chapter contends that countries should come together regionally or otherwise to evolve an effective framework within which to respond to the threats posed by money laundering and its related exigencies. This is because however well resourced a state is, as a result of the transnational character of global crimes, no single state can afford to act unilaterally in the present era of globalization.

Any effective global anti-money laundering framework should be legitimate and accountable to local institutions, where the emerging regimes are to be implemented after all. All AML/CFT regimes should be backed by a multilateral treaty, affording states the opportunity to have a say by way of ratifying and internalising the treaty provisions domestically. It would seem that some anti-money laundering regimes (for example, the FATF and the Basel Committee Supervisory Standards) are superimposed because, notwithstanding their broad mandate, they are created by a few countries (the G10) without fully consulting all countries that the engendered regimes are intended to regulate. This is unlike treaty-based regimes (such as the Vienna Convention), because these are agreed, ratified and domesticated by states, fostering the spirit of international law.

While this chapter advocates the need to regulate foreign financial institutions at a domestic level to overcome the inherent imperfections of international supervision, as demonstrated by the BCCI saga, any anticipated national regimes should clearly focus on transcending national interests. There should be a global framework to enable domestic regulators to discharge this function without discrimination.[39] The current global anti-money laundering regimes are desirable because their presence demonstrates that the financial community is alert and united as regards the threat of money laundering. However, experience has clearly demonstrated that certain aspects of the evolving anti-money laundering regimes have remained beyond the reach of some local societies, particularly those from developing countries.[40]

Likewise, the international financial community should focus on strengthening local regulatory institutions so that societies are properly equipped to translate

38 Many regimes (for example, the FATF and EU anti-money laundering regimes) have sought to close this loophole to make sure that people in elevated positions (including politically exposed persons) are also subjected to disclosure requirements.

39 Thomas Oatley, 'The Dilemmas of International Financial Regulation', 23(4) *Regulation* (1999): pp. 36–9.

40 I have already demonstrated how a lack of sufficient information on different crime typologies can engender a negative climate for an effective global anti-money laundering framework.

the envisaged global anti-money laundering standards into the domestic context. The use of local private regulators[41] is essential in enhancing and propping up home-grown expertise, not to mention providing the leverage for generating local experience and familiarity to sustain the proposed initiatives. There is also the benefit that local regulators are responsible and accountable to local institutions. However, the supervision and regulation approaches of the private financial institutions should be closely monitored to ensure their effectiveness and efficiency, and that the overall institutional development objectives are met.[42]

Government-owned financial institutions (like Northern Rock in the UK) should be privately regulated to counter any conflicts of interest, whilst privately-owned financial institutions should be closely monitored by the government, perhaps under the auspices of the central bank. There is a correlation that indicates that government-owned financial institutions tend to suffer higher levels of corruption than privately-owned financial institutions.[43] While the open private sector approach to supervision and regulation tends to spur on development, cases have already been discussed that highlight situations where criminals have cleverly manipulated the proliferating financial institutions to consolidate their criminal underground industry. As such, early governmental intervention in privately-owned financial institutions should be encouraged to prevent a repeat of the abuse of the financial systems by those masquerading as highly sought-after investors. Financial liberalization and market abuse are often accompanied by problems such as the counterfeit currency issue in Uganda and the BCCI scandal in the UK.

However, where local regulators are conservative and impregnable with corrupt tendencies (the 'cancer' afflicting many developing societies), the adoption of a single local regulation (perhaps under the auspices of the central bank) may not go far enough in achieving its predetermined objectives. There is a need for affirmative action on corruption, not only to stem its concomitant social effects but also to ensure that essential information[44] is not fettered or diverted by corrupt officials to benefit criminals or criminal syndicates. Here, globalization can play a significant role by bringing some societies into the fold of prolific progressive societies,[45] enabling poorer countries by bringing down transactional costs.

41 I strongly believe that 'global' regulators might find the environment unpalatable for them to properly execute their mandate.

42 Oatley, 'The Dilemmas of International Financial Regulation'.

43 Ibid.

44 Globalization is information-driven as a result of innovations in ICT, but if this information is not properly harnessed, it can go either way – that is, in much the same way that it has helped to bring down transaction costs, it can also increase the opportunities for criminals in a society permeated by corruption.

45 It can share in the resources of other countries, such as intelligence and personnel (which are difficult to instantly generate at a national level) or the countries can pool their limited resources together to facilitate what would otherwise be hard for any individual country to undertake.

Conclusion

In conclusion, the question of states being required to undertake reforms is the only way forward in order for states to take advantage of the globalization of markets. While Uganda, along with its five counterpart SADC member countries, has not passed a law defining money laundering as a distinct offence, it was able through the World Bank financial sector reforms to enact the Financial Institutions Act 1993.[46] To make banks more robust with regard to fighting money laundering related offences, the Foreign Exchange Bill 2004[47] was passed and clause 8(3) of this Bill halts forex bureaux from dealing in money transfers to or from the country. It was envisaged that if forex bureaux were allowed to operate in a relaxed regime, it would undermine financial institutions contrary to the Basel[48] Committee on Banking Supervision and regulatory practices. These guidelines were transposed through the Financial Institutions Act 1993. The issue of counterfeit currency in 2000 exposed weaknesses in the Ugandan financial services regulatory framework. It put the government under pressure from the US authorities[49] to volunteer information on Ugandans arrested abroad with fake foreign currency in various denominations.

In Uganda, as part of the reform process, there was the need to introduce the Criminals Records Bureau (CRB) which could be accessed by banks in relation to the requisite data on the credibility of potential bank clients. This is essential to ease the process of corroborating information on bank clients and to deter potential criminals from infiltrating the system for criminal purposes. Unless the desired reforms are undertaken in the financial sector, banks will still be exposed to regulatory risks which could be transmitted through the global system.

I have already demonstrated that there is no state that can afford to operate a closed economy and therefore common initiatives are essential. This presupposes a need for reform to align economies to their international obligations. It also needs to be said that the issue of reforms – either based on World Bank/IMF conditionalities or other global initiatives relating to AML/CFT – has proved to be controversial. The initial stages of implementation of financial sector reforms in Uganda disorientated the economy in two ways. First, there was widespread unemployment as a result of recommendations imposed by the SAPs especially in the public sector. Secondly, the proposed reform initiatives also changed the dynamics of corruption in the country. While corruption is as old as humanity,

---

46 Mukinya, 'Evolution of Banking Systems in East Africa: A Comparative View'.

47 *The Monitor*, Kampala, 5 August 2004, p. 4.

48 It should be noted that the 'Basel guidelines' are not a treaty capable of producing a binding effect on signatory states, but merely a 'soft law' constituting a statement of good policy practices.

49 Some Ugandans were arrested in Boston and for the purposes of prosecution, the prosecutor sought Ugandan cooperation with regard to gathering evidence and essential information.

individuals in high political positions would either through their families or proxies manipulate the privatization process to buy formerly state-owned enterprises at throwaway prices. On the contrary, it seems that the implementation of the World Bank reforms helped to put the Ugandan economy back on the development path. The economy has subsequently registered a high persistent gross domestic product (GDP) growth of more than 6 per cent on average since the 1990s and this has conspicuously transformed the image of the Ugandan economy. In a nutshell, blanket reforms can disorientate the economy since they might not reflect the local dynamics of development, but individual country-oriented reforms are imperative in order to support and foster a stable environment for financial markets.

Chapter 9

A Glimpse into Law and Global Markets

Introduction

It is impossible to harness the global AML/CFT framework in any country in the absence of a proper functioning[1] legal system. This chapter articulates that law as an instrument of social change should provide a framework in which to order a meaningful global economy. Global cooperation is necessary to avoid the adverse effect of the prisoner's dilemma, in which each participant is unsure of whether others will cooperate or engage in behaviour that is detrimental to the stability of the global economy.[2] However, a common legal framework is particularly essential to ensure that different jurisdictions complement each other in safeguarding against regulatory arbitrage[3] or regulatory failures.[4] Regulatory arbitrage and regulatory failures are common features of an uncoordinated international system. In order for some aspects of a large-scale regulation to be effective, they must be coordinated and perhaps formulated on a global basis.[5] This would seem to justify, as already demonstrated earlier in this book, the importance of the global AML/CFT framework. However, globalization is just a misnomer as it is a lopsided process that is fraught with inequalities. It is presented as an extension of the

1 Proper functioning in this respect is simply supposed to mean a system where laws are applied equally and in a non-discriminatory fashion – a system that is not inclined to favour one side against the other.

2 R. Bollen, 'The International Financial System and Future Global Regulation', 23(9) *Journal of International Banking Law and Regulation* (2008): p. 468.

3 This identifies and exploits any inconsistencies in the market and undermines the effectiveness of capital regulation. See C. Mattens, 'Managing Capital Accord', 2000, p. 4, available at www.riskglossary.com/articles/regulatory_capital.htm (date accessed 15 June 2006).

4 Capital adequacy has been criticized that the required eight per cent capital reserve is arbitrary, since it does not reflect the lows and highs of a business. In an ideal world, a well-designed regulatory system should see capital reserves rising during periods of high profitability and earnings for banks and falling during a recessionary period. See E.I. Altman and A. Saunders, 'An Analysis and Critique of the BIS Proposal of Capital Adequacy and Ratings', 25 *Journal of Banking and Finance* (2001): pp. 26–8.

5 M. Bagheri and C. Nakajima, 'Optimal Level of Financial Regulation under the GATS: Regulatory Competition and Co-operation Framework for Capital Adequacy and Disclosure of Information', 5(2) *International Journal of Economic Law* (2002): p. 157.

reach of one local condition or entity[6] across the globe and, by doing so, develops the capacity to designate a rival social condition or entity as global.[7] Arguably, what masquerades as a global AML/CFT framework is a set of laws developed in various policy domains and introduced locally as global laws.

In the current global climate, states have lost their sovereign space as market competition intensifies. The fact that law is subordinate to power in the event of conflicting interests connotes that law alone cannot help to salvage global relations and, in addition, the global system is prone to abuse since it is characteristically contingent upon the dynamics of power and the tendency for the powerful states to assert their leverage to dominate global regimes.[8]

The domestication of global AML/CFT initiatives should be preceded by tailored reforms at a local level to harmonize differences between the systems and hence enhance the coexistence of the global community. Using Uganda as a reference point, the tenuous nature of developing economies, which are often deficient in infrastructural development and prone to the vagaries of the putative global era, is highlighted. In light of the above, many developing economies have become marginal participants in the global economy because of the dictates of the global market economy. The systemic global failures are aggregated by the fact that human rights and the environment – the embodiments of human life – have been subordinated to rapacious global capitalism.[9] Most importantly, law needs to be ascribed a frontline position because wherever there is the rule of law, development follows.

The twin challenges of under-development and its effect have significantly curtailed the potential of local societies to create robust national institutions to bring about the adoption of necessary global initiatives.[10] Moreover, the global asymmetries of power and its dynamics have not helped in creating a level playing field for an effective economic and political environment in global relations.[11] I

---

6 Janet Dine argues that the concept of transnational corporations is in fact a fallacy because these so-called corporations would have been created as American or British companies in their home countries in accordance with their home laws and the fact that they operate in foreign countries does not necessarily make them transnational. See Dine, *Companies, International Trade and Human Rights*, pp. 1–40. See also K. Siew, 'Regulatory Challenges in the Development of a Global Securities Market', 173 *Singapore Journal of Legal Studies* (2004): pp. 179–80.

7 B. De Sousa Santos, *Towards the New Legal Common Sense: Law, Globalisation and Emancipation* (London: Butterworths, 2002), p. 14.

8 Vividly captured by the phrase that 'power tends to corrupt and absolute power corrupts absolutely'.

9 This situation is covered by demonstrations that have been witnessed in almost every part of the globe over what is seen as the perpetuation of injustice in the name of trade.

10 Oxfam, *World Development Report: Fifty Years of the World Bank and IMF* (Milton Keynes: Open University Press, 2001).

11 This has had wide implications for every aspect of human life.

agree entirely with the exposition of Rosalyn Higgins[12] that if the legal system of a society is robust enough, disputes are to a large extent avoided.[13] Thus, I hasten to conveniently infer that a distorted legal system is a recipe for chaos, abuse of power and fragrant violation of basic human rights and is overly retrogressive. This analysis is essential for us in order to fathom the meaning of law and its efficacy in the management of society. Law is conceptualized as 'a body of regularised procedures and normative practices that are considered justiciable, that is, susceptible of being enforced by a judicial authority in a given society, and contribute to the creation and prevention of disputes, as well as to their settlement through an argumentative discourse coupled by the threat of force'.[14] Law, including international law, has a threefold social function: first, it carries the structures and systems of society through time; secondly, it inserts the common interests of society into the behaviour of the members of society; and, thirdly, it establishes possible futures for society in accordance with the particular society's theories, values and purposes. It is a presence of social past, an organizing of social present and a conditioning of social future.[15] In simple terms, 'law' represents, in the end, a set of events whose common property is sanctioned regularity.[16]

The legal system of a society is supposed to provide an operational framework for securing good values that are commonly regarded as normative by the society – peace, security, freedom within which the society can function – being ordered or organized. Hence, this chapter argues that without law to foster fundamental freedoms, chaos would be unleashed upon societies – cars would not safely move on the roads, children would not safely go to school, people would not safely live with one another, aeroplanes would not safely fly and land – and without it, perhaps it should also be added that life would literally stall.[17] Law should not be misconceived as only necessary for deterring proscribed behaviours or solving disputes in society, as many may wish to suppose, but fundamentally law is also about preventing disputes from happening in the first place. Law as culture engenders a change in social attitudes and if the engendered cultural ethos is properly internalized into society, disputes are to a great extent minimized.

In addressing the interaction of globalization and the law, there are two distinct issues worthy of mention. First, there is the adoption and implementation across large swathes of the globe of what are now widely accepted as valuable legal

---

12 R. Higgins, *Problems and Process: International Law and How We Use it* (Oxford: Oxford University Press, 1994), Chapter 1.

13 Ibid.

14 De Sousa Santos, *Towards the New Legal Common Sense*.

15 P. Allott, 'The Concept of International Law', 3 *European Journal of International Law* (1999): pp. 31–3.

16 R. Falk, 'The Role of Law in World Society: Present Crisis and Future Prospects', in M.S. McDougal, W.M Reisman and B.H. Weston (eds), *Toward World Order and Human Dignity: Essays in Honor of Myres S. McDougal* (New York: Free Press, 1976), p. 133.

17 Higgins, *Problems and Process*.

norms and approaches. Secondly, there is the increasing number of areas of the law which are now subject to international agreements that are more or less binding on the states that are party to them. Most obvious are trade laws and the international sale of goods (which cover a range of issues from tariffs to contract enforcement and intellectual property rights). Therefore, there is a need to protect those legal specificities that express and define the values and attitudes of local and national communities.

The same is true of national parliaments (governments), courts, human rights, democracy, the environment or global institutions. Globalization should work for all to globalize benefits by addressing the embedded weaknesses of the system. Suffice it to say that a badly managed global system not only helps to fuel resentments against proliferating global regimes but also fosters an environment that undermines the potential synergies crystallized by the system. It is in respect of this that law – both as a system of rules and as a culture – should be seen to take a leading position in curing the ills of the global system.

It would seem that a good law should evolve by taking into account changes and challenges in the dynamic society and therefore international law cannot remain immutable in the face of challenges if it is to play its stabilizing role in the ever-changing society. When a law is superseded by time or circumstances, one would always expect another law to be promulgated and enacted in its place. The advocates of law as rules from a sovereign command and who therefore contend that violations of established norms should invoke sanctions are disenchanted by the failure of international law in its duty to bring aberrant states to order. No person of whatever status is above the law if one takes Dicey's tenets on the rule of law seriously. According to Dicey (1885),[18] the rule of law is conceptualized as having three pillars: (i) the absolute supremacy or predominance of regular law as opposed to arbitrary power and which excludes the existence of arbitrariness of the prerogative wider discretionary powers of the government; (ii) equality before the law, which supposes that nobody is exempt from it, and equal subjection of all to the ordinary law of the land administered by the courts of law; and (iii) that rules which in foreign countries form part of the constitutional codes are not the source but the consequence of law and order within a community. Hence, the system governed by rules precludes conduct that creates anarchy, warfare and constant aggression of other societies by other states. Thus, it remains to be seen whether the tenets of the law underscored by Dicey's theoretical exposition have been achieved.[19]

18 In his book, *The Introduction to the Study of the Constitution* (1885), in 'Constitution of the United Kingdom', Institute for Public Policy Paper (1991).

19 A.W. Bradley and K.D. Ewing, *Constitution and Administrative Law* (London: Longman, 1997), Chapter 1.

The State and Contemporary Crimes

As demonstrated in Chapter 1, the role of the contemporary state has changed drastically to include inter-state practice rather than just inter-state interaction because of the changing nature of international law.[20] National boundaries are gradually becoming less significant, becoming increasingly permeated by large and rapidly growing flows of trade, investment and technology, and this has wide ramifications to the rule of law both nationally and internationally. The UN system suffers from many shortcomings, not least the fact that since its inception, it has been characterized by the asymmetries of power, making it increasingly prone to abuse[21] and slow in coping with the dynamics of the challenging and changing world. Furthermore, the UN system functions through sovereign states which are vested with strategic national interests. Therefore, when it comes to less powerful actors, such as small states, international law is taunted as slack and an instrument of oppression. Is this surprising, given that international law has always been shaped by a cynical form of double standards in which one side is always legally right and an adversary is always denigrated as being engaged in unacceptable lawlessness? The above sentiments, which came about as a result of divided loyalties, the inability to harness law as a platform for change and to create a level playing field for all in which society can be ordered, has become the apparent threat to international peace and security.[22] According to Kofi Annan[23] while addressing the UN General Assembly, 'international law as a framework is riddled with gaps and weaknesses. Too often, international law is applied selectively and enforced arbitrarily'. As such, international law is accused of lacking the teeth to turn a body of laws into an effective legal system.

There are many ways to create international norms,[24] including ratifying treaties at an inter-state level which are subsequently legislated through national parliaments in order to domesticate[25] the envisaged obligations within an agreed

---

20 R. Falk and A. Kosovar, 'World Order and the Future of International Law', 93 *American Journal International Law* (1999): pp. 847–53.

21 As I have already mentioned, the UN as a system has been dominated by powerful states and a lack of a level playing field when it comes to the interests of small states.

22 What constitutes a threat to international peace and security in international law is envisaged by Article 39(a) of the UN Charter.

23 The former UN Secretary-General.

24 Article 38(1) of the Statute of the International Court of Justice provides that there are four sources of international law: (i) international conventions, whether general or particular, establishing rules expressly recognized by the contesting states; (ii) international Custom as evidence of a general practice accepted as law; (iii) the general principles of law recognized by civilized nations; and (iv) subject to the provisions of Article 59, judicial decisions and the teaching of the most highly qualified publicists of the various nations as a subsidiary means of creating norms of international law.

25 Transposition is only necessary for dualist countries whereby the agreed convention will produce effect after they have been incorporated into the domestic legal

timescale.[26] In the EU law-making process, the creation of laws takes two forms, namely by way of Regulations and Directives.[27] Regulations have a normative force and generate direct effect in all Member States irrespective of national interests, while Directives are transposed in a Member State within a stipulated timescale and usually take into account national considerations. Directives are legislative measures binding Member States as to the result to be achieved. They determine certain targets that usually relate to certain economic and regulatory matters. National governments, however, choose the form of how these targets are to be implemented.[28] Conventions (treaties) are implemented by state governments when they ratify and agree to implement them by way of passing enabling legislation in the case of dualist states. If a state does not ratify the convention, to a large extent, it will not generate a binding effect locally. Conventions are not law at all, but signify that states are contemplating their adoption, and will not generate any binding effect until they have been transposed into substantive national law.

The process of domesticating or transposing[29] (the two words are usually used interchangeably) of international law is important to ensure that the new laws are harmonized with substantive national laws to reflect a state's envisaged obligations under the treaty. The second source of international law is by way of customs. Customary law, including customary international law, is the product of dialectic of practice, as opposed to legislation, which is the product of dialectic of ideas. Society members produce the conditions of their ordering social coexistence through the practice of orderly coexistence. Customary law is the presentation of those conditions in the form of law; in other words, setting the terms of the future coexistence of society members in the form of legal relations. The space of consent in the making of customary law is subtle and is not made by any specific act of will on the part of its subjects. Their assent (*opinio juris*) is manifested, in the

---

system – for example, in the case of the UK, this is usually done by adopting enabling legislation to transpose the ratified treaties. Nevertheless, for monist countries such as France, conventions are effective as soon as these countries have signed up to international treaties.

26 However, even if the state does not sign up to the treaty, the respective treaty can still generate a binding effect on the state if the majority of countries internalize it as a norm of international law, as a result of which it automatically acquires the status of customary international law.

27 The third source of EU law is a Decision, which has direct applicability to all Member States, but for the purposes of this chapter, I will only discuss Regulations and Directives.

28 Craig and DeBurca, *EU Law: Text, Cases, Materials*. Also pursuant to Article 226 of the EC Treaty, the Commission has to deliver a reasoned opinion to a Member State which it considers to have failed to implement a Directive.

29 This is usually the case with dualist countries, for example, the UK, where international treaties must be domesticated by the passing of enabling legislation through which they are implemented. However, in monist countries like France, once treaties have been ratified, they automatically become part of national law.

first place, in their participation in the day-to-day struggle of social self-ordering, knowing that some aspect of that self-ordering may come to be universalized as law.[30]

It seems to me that the putative globalization is a paradigm shift because it is fundamentally opposed to the concept of self-determination. Because of the dynamics of the global market system, many national governments have not only surrendered their sovereign autonomy but have also been sidelined to the fringes in their economies. Sovereign states have, for example, lost their voice on issues of national development and on other aspects of self-determination such as national polity.

International law has played a significant role in justifying initiatives in the international arena that are controversial, to mobilize support for such policies at home and particularly as a legal club with which to strike adversaries.[31] This has been compounded by the vacuum which has been created by the reconfiguration of the world space from bipolarism to unipolarism.[32] The unipolarist discourse contends that the proponents of the global system have failed to adopt a legal framework in which to harness globalization as a system. Therefore, international law should provide the space for inter-state relations – and thus the de-territorialization where the state loses its legitimate space has not helped in consolidating state sovereignty. The state has been relegated either to the regions or to other supranational institutions where policy decisions are reached without recourse to individual state interests, as illustrated in the relationship between the UK and the EU. Certainly, the absence of an effective global government within which to manage the challenges of the global system has also engendered significant challenges for the state, not least allowing criminals to exploit the vacuum created by the vanquished or sidelined societies in order to consolidate their mandate.

In the words of Wolf Heydebrand,[33] ‘the implementation of international rules is left to a precarious balance between their perceived legitimacy, periodically renegotiated working agreements among dominant states, and the desire among corporate and non-corporate actors to reap the benefits of ongoing co-operative relations rather than being ensnared in costly and disruptive disputes’. The emergence of quasi-legal regimes such as commercial arbitration or international economic regulation operating beyond the conventional boundaries of national sovereignty has debased the state in the following context. The reproduction of

---

30 Allot, ‘The Concept of International Law’.

31 Falk, ‘The Role of Law in World Society’.

32 These words are used to highlight the transition from the ‘Old World Order’ characterized by the East/West, North/South divide to a one-world market-driven economy free of border controls, where the space in which humans see themselves seems to be contracting as each day goes by.

33 Wolf Heydebrand, *Globalisation and the Rule of Law at the End of US Advocacy of Labour Protectionism*, Antroposotica, (2005), pp. 111–20.

transnational social order in the context of new legal forms underscores how the notion of the rule of law has been transformed and possibly bypassed by economic globalization.[34] The notion of governance without government has also not helped in enhancing cooperation between governments, which presumably explains why there are echoes of anarchy in the fostering of globalization of markets.[35]

The innovations in technology and transport systems have transformed the whole business landscape,[36] but equally these instruments have also been exploited for criminal purposes. As such, the conspicuous development in many states as a result of their participation in the global market economy is at the verge of being dashed or obliterated by the parallel leverage that has been accorded to criminals in fostering their criminal objectives. In both developed and developing countries alike, the state as an entity of international law has been sidelined by the deregulation and derogation of power to non-state actors from areas formerly performed by the state. The state has lost its economic power to the global market and has lost its political power to regional or global institutions. This is 'a new authoritarianism' that has displaced or banished the authority of the state to the sidelines.[37] The international context of the state has exerted a particularly strong influence in the field of legal regulation of the economy and commercial law as the state is always required to change the existing laws to accommodate interests of transnational cooperations operating in the country. Legislation in developing countries has been substantially affected by SAPs: debtor states have been coerced into passing legislation on the privatization of public enterprises and financial contributions from parents for the education of their children in countries like Kenya, Tanzania and Uganda.[38] Neoliberal policies imposed on many African countries by the World Bank and the IMF, particularly in the 1980s, crystallized into the downward spiral of many African economies. The implementation of SAPs in Uganda, apart from engendering the aforementioned climate, also precipitated a clash between leaders and their constituents. President Yoweri Museveni's[39] then enormous popularity (who was idolized by the people and widely cherished as a liberator) burst,[40] deteriorating into near-political anarchy, a development that has

34 Ibid., p. 120.

35 The failed WTO trade talks and the recent refusal of Ireland to ratify the Treaty of Lisbon are two cases that underline the above point.

36 Improvements in ICT has increased the speed and volume of international transactions. Payments can be effected by electronic mediums in a split second and this along with other innovations has changed the whole business landscape.

37 Shelley, 'Transnational Organised Crimes: A New Authoritarianism', pp. 25–48.

38 S. Adelman, *The Debt Crisis, Underdevelopment and the Limits of the Law* (Oxford: Oxford University Press, 1998), p. 182.

39 He was ushered into power as the President of Uganda in 1986 after a five-year protracted guerrilla war.

40 This shows the role of non-state actors in dictating the course and outcome of certain events in some societies.

continued to grip the Ugandan political climate to date.[41] So what this portends is that the sovereignty of states is being directly threatened as a result of global localism that is being unleashed by a torrent of pervasive global forces, which threatens or challenges the autonomy of the domestic state. It is therefore not possible to isolate the impact of outside influence, legal or otherwise, in influencing the course of events in other countries. This asymmetry, a result of the structural power imbalance between lenders and borrowers, imposes severe austerity on the people of the borrowing country [42] in order to help the lender to come out on top.[43]

Perhaps it also needs to be mentioned that international financial agencies such as the World Bank and the IMF can be seen as playing a normative role in shaping the global economy. Through economic surveillance and monitoring of the world's national economies, the IMF seeks to control national monetary policies. Pauly[44] argues that international economic involvement thus ultimately entails political adjustment. There is no word about law and democracy, but the policy clearly envisages global economic growth and stability as independent variables, and politics and law as dependent variables. While I appreciate that the IMF, like any other financial institution, must follow prudential guidelines in lending, experience has shown that this has sometimes gone too far, eliciting accusations of a hidden agenda from some quarters.[45]

A familiar example that demonstrates the impact of SAPs in Uganda was the restructuring of the army[46] in the 1990s, which culminated in the demobilization of a sizeable number of soldiers from the armed forces. The government, yielding to pressure from donor agencies (which was bound up in a package of SAPs reforms required of the country),[47] undertook restructuring programmes, especially

41 While the current National Resistance Movement (NRM) government under the leadership of President Museveni is credited with bringing about the development climate that Uganda is enjoying, corruption has spiralled out of control. In addition, the government seems bent on undermining the democratic values it initially embodied, such as using the police to deny the opposition a platform to demonstrate and express their views. This is a glaring departure from the virtues and democratic values that NRM government embodied and professed to champion in its early years.

42 Unemployment has been high following public sector reforms as a result of the liberalization and deregulation of the domestic state.

43 Tabb, *The Amoral Elephant*, p. 87.

44 Ibid.

45 Stiglitz, *Globalization and its Discontents*, p. 53. Stiglitz contends that the World Bank and the IMF are well aware that conditionalities have failed to produce any tangible results on the ground and are largely there to serve the interests of Northern-dominated transnational corporations.

46 This saw a sizeable number of soldiers demobilized without adequate termination benefits and was allegedly responsible for the explosion in gun crime and armed robberies in Kampala City and elsewhere.

47 Under the Washington Consensus, many developing countries were required to cut public expenditure, to stimulate the development of the economy and to be competitive

in the public sector. Undoubtedly, some aspects of the SAPs were inimical to the economic environment, the implementation of which at the time tragically tilted the political landscape towards that of disenchantment, and perhaps retrogressively resurrected the antipathy and despondence reminiscent of the old turbulent past.[48] This, coupled with the demobilization of civil servants, provided a fertile climate and a pool of resources (manpower) that fed and reinforced many rebel groups in the country, where the disengaged soldiers were easily enlisted.[49] Donors have sometimes been more interested in markets, exports and political influence than they have in long-term benefits to beneficiary countries. As such, the market economy has undermined the tenets of self-determination with regard to the sovereign people's rights to determine their own destiny. It has reduced the power of the individual nation states to shape and determine their destinies through participation in the democratic process. The ability of governments to pursue development, full employment or other national economic goals has been impaired by the power of capital to pick and leave.[50]

As the aforementioned Ugandan example in relation to financial liberalization highlights, neoliberalism[51] in developing countries has translated into chaos and a development crisis, and many states have lost the power to legitimately make decisions on issues of national polity. Many countries in Africa have followed the prescribed SAPs and yet are increasingly in great economic difficulty. This has taken place despite the earlier optimism that reform would stimulate development through a set of guidance policies under the SAPs. As a result, there is a growing disenchantment with and hostility towards the market economy. The World Bank and the IMF-driven reforms have not proved successful and have also proved incompatible with the development needs of the countries they are designed to help.[52] I suppose the startling failure of the blanket World Bank/IMF-guided

as a condition for further borrowing from donor agencies. Stiglitz argues that the above policies were not plausibly the best in a situation of low economic growth, a position in which many developing countries currently find themselves, because they potentially 'rub salt into the wound', creating more misery.

48 People started conceptualizing Ugandan politics in terms of George Orwell's *Animal Farm* (Harmondsworth: Penguin, 1954).

49 This position is supported by many of the Ugandans I have contacted to corroborate some aspects of the global system in Uganda.

50 Brecher and Costello, *The Race to the Bottom*, pp. 1–45.

51 This has been defined as policies and processes where a handful of private interests are permitted to control as much as possible of social life in order to maximize their personal profit. See N. Chomsky, *Profit Over People* (New York: Seven Stories Press, 1998), p. 24.

52 This is underpinned by two factors: (i) some of the above policies are adopted based on the countries performance by way of its GDP. According to Samir Amin, the highly-paid World Bank or IMF officials have never been on the ground to corroborate how this information is arrived at. In any case, their point of interface, as far as gathering this information goes, are the highly-placed government officials, for example, ministers

policies is explained by the fact that every individual problem has its own specifics and particularities, which should dictate the method of solving it. Why does the doctor carry out diagnostic tests before prescribing a drug to a patient and why would donor agencies ignore the diagnostic approach to problem solving? This explains why the cherished SAP reform programmes espoused by the World Bank and the IMF have perhaps not gone far enough in helping to alleviate the economic plight in the South as had previously been anticipated. It is my contention that any reform initiatives should be specific problem-oriented and, as regards SAPs, they should capably generate a positive impact if they are tailored to the social, economic and political environment of the locality concerned. Far from the optimism that was earlier associated with the liberalization of markets, many economies have experienced the exact opposite, which is precisely why they are a bit cagey whenever the topic of globalization is floated.[53] Instead of the anticipated acceleration of market integration, many countries have disintegrated with the result that per-capita income has slackened[54] to all-time low relative to that in the 1960s and 1970s.[55] The rapid mobility of people and capital can not only result in gainful commercial transactions but can also spread corruption and organized crime in their various manifestations. These problems transcend national boundaries and

---

of finance, the same officials presiding over the ailing and mismanaged governments; (ii) another apparent reason for conditionalities is the need to stimulate the national economy by undertaking public sector reforms so that respective economies are made vibrant and able to sustain their payments on borrowed loans, which seems acceptable from the lender's point of view. But conditionalities have wrecked governments, precipitated conditions for wars and genocide, for example, the former Yugoslavia, where SAPs induced nationwide unemployment, and also in Uganda with regard to the restructuring of the army in the early 1990s. Sixty years of the World Bank and the IMF regime in funding and coordinating development policies in developing countries have done much to alleviate the plight of the countries they profess to help. See Amin, *Capital in the Age of Globalisation*, pp. 17–26.

53 Small nations accuse the world economic powerhouses – the USA, the EU, India, Australia and Brazil – of deliberately delaying progress as the complex negotiations, involving 153 countries, lurched towards another crisis. See *The Times*, 30 July 2004.

54 I wish to reiterate that if properly harnessed, globalization can be a formidable force for good – for example, it can help to narrow inequalities in income, spreading improvements in basic hygiene, vaccination against communicable diseases and the lower rate of mortality rate as per the UNDP World Development Report (1997). However, there is the flipside that equally needs to be factored into assessing the benefits of the system. The current globalization trends fuel cross-border crimes such as terrorism, small arms trafficking and money laundering, as criminals position themselves to take advantage of global markets.

55 I appreciate that the fact that the population has been growing since the 1960s has contributed to keeping GDP figures low, but nevertheless it is my contention that population growth in the modern era is not a sufficient excuse for the level of under-development in Uganda. In any case, if the increase in size of the population is properly managed, it can be counted upon as a significant development resource, since it creates a market and boosts labour supply.

call for collective and coordinated action at the international level. Laws have been employed to confine the actions of the state – for example, national governments must transpose laws to accommodate neoliberal policies and its concomitant SAPs in many countries.

The WTO and Liberalization

The WTO as a multilateral forum provides a platform for liberalization, as it was founded on the premise of the negotiation of trade rounds in the interest of its member countries. The WTO was founded in 1995 to provide a rule-based trading system built on the edifice of non-discrimination and liberalization, openness and free trade: to forbid discrimination in favour of national producers while also regulating national behaviours on the part of exporters (such as dumping).[56] It was also to reduce tariffs and prohibit other forms of quantitative restrictions, including overt forms such as quotas and unfair practice concealed by unfounded health or administrative regulations.[57] In relation to financial markets, GATS provides a framework for dealing with the trade in cross-border financial services, including financial services.[58] The principle of national treatment forbids discrimination based on the origin of products.[59] In so doing, the WTO promotes harmonization or approximate national domestic policies for the free flow of international trade.[60] The WTO Council for Trade in Services has responsibility for issuing a legally non-binding interpretation of GATS. It fulfils this function by acting upon recommendations generated as a result of examinations of various WTO committees in particular sectors.[61] The internalization of financial services signifies that a country's prudential regulatory and supervisory regimes should promote sound banking practices.[62] It is this function that has particular relevance to fighting money laundering as it replicates the same principle put forward by the Basel Committee on Banking Supervision. For example, if a government commits itself to allow foreign banks to operate in its domestic market, that is a market access commitment.[63] In my view, the WTO is a more harmonizing institution than its counterparts, the World Bank and the IMF, given that it provides a negotiation platform and a dispute settlement mechanism. However, in my view, the WTO

56 Mugarura, 'The Subdued Giant'.

57 Ibid.

58 Alexander, Dhumale and Eatwell, *Global Governance of Financial Systems*, pp. 100–104. For more information on GATS, see Chapter 7.

59 Article X1 of GATTS, which sought to eliminate quantitative restrictions on imported products.

60 Reich, *WTO Legal Text*.

61 See the WTO website at www.wto.org (date accessed 14 December 2011).

62 Ibid.

63 Ibid.

replicates some of the principles of good supervisory standards put forward by the FATF and the Basel Committee on Banking Supervision – bodies created to champion the prudential regulation and supervision of financial institutions.

However, it should be noted that like its sister international financial institutions, the WTO encroaches on the sovereign areas of national economic life whereby the economic sovereignty of states is undermined. In crucial areas such as agriculture, intellectual property rights (IPRs) and the regulation of foreign investment and services, sovereign powers have been relocated from Third World states and peoples to the WTO through *inter alia* the adoption of uniform global standards.[64] Thus, for example, be it Uganda, the UK or Japan, the same IPR regimes are to be adopted by all under the agreement on Trade Related Apspects of Intellectual Property Rights.[65]

While law can potentially be exploited to promote some semblance of economic and social order, the use of international law has proved problematic because of state-based opportunisms, hegemonic arrogance or posturing at a regional level. As such, it is seen as slack, only effectively being used to protect and promote[66] the grandiose interests of powerful states. An example of this is where a few states have gone out of their way to manipulate multilateral institutions for national self-interest (*ex post opportunism*), without regard to the objectives of the system they profess to champion.[67] In relation to the WTO, individual state posturing has threatened to rupture the ethos of trade multilateralism that was the embodiment of the 1994 Uruguay trade talks.[68] The WTO is a practical manifestation of the globalization in trade and commercial aspects in that it makes scant (indeed only oblique) reference to the principle of human rights.[69] For certain sections of the global society,[70] such as developing countries, the WTO is a veritable nightmare, although, superficially, it is described as a democratic institution because it adopts

64 B.S. Chimni, 'International Institutions Today: An Imperial, Global State in the Making', 15(1) *European Journal of International Law* (2004): pp. 7–10.

65 For TRIPS and other agreements, see the WTO, 'The Result of the Uruguay Round of Multilateral Trade Negotiations: The Legal Texts', 1995, available at www.wto.org/english/docs_e/legal_e/ursum_e.htm (date accessed 14 December 2011).

66 Laws should be predictable, clear and certain, but this is rarely the case with the current globalization trajectory.

67 Talks collapsed in acrimony in Cancun, Mexico in September 2004, after poor countries walked out having disagreed over farming subsidies that virtually locked out poor developing countries from accessing markets in developed countries.

68 The focus was primarily on reducing tariff barriers between industrialized countries. Developing countries were for the most part marginalized participants and equally marginalized beneficiaries.

69 Chomsky, *Profit Over People*.

70 There is lots of talk that the world community today has literally contracted into the form of a 'village' and the word 'society' in some circles is used to denote a section of this putative 'global village'.

the principle of 'one man, one vote'; its decisions are based on a consensus and together allow for a more equitable outcome.

Arguably, the WTO as a multilateral forum has added impetus to the ranging globalization crisis – its role and mandates are changing, often in a manner that lacks transparency and inequity.[71] This was responsible for the stalled Ministerial Conferences in Seattle, Cancun and most recently Geneva, not to mention the acrimonious demonstrations that have taken place in almost every part of the globe over what is conceived by demonstrators to be bad trade policies and practices. The failed Seattle Ministerial Conference helped to expose the underhanded spirit in which WTO meetings are conducted. The existence of Quad[72] – the quadrilateral group of trade ministers formed in 1981 – was discovered by the delegates and some of the demonstrators for the first time. Under this arrangement, representatives of Canada, the EU, Japan and the USA meet first in private boardrooms to work out the preliminaries for discussion. This acts as an informal committee guiding the trade regime, but, as illustrated by the above composition, no representatives of small countries are invited even when the issues to be discussed concern them.[73] Once the Quad reaches agreement on key decisions without the participation of other representatives of the global community, a select group of 20–30 delegates are invited to come together for informal meetings. Only after that are the remaining 153 members invited to discuss what at this point has already been decided upon – *faits accomplis*.

According to Chomsky,[74] the poor countries of the world are forced to fall into line by the pressure of the economic and political muscles of the developed countries arrayed against them. In other words, weak states are bullied into voting on a framework that is not representative of their interests. Another serious charge made by Chomsky is that officials who represent the Quad are closely linked to corporations, which poses the potential for conflicts of interests.[75] The WTO as a multilateral institution is also undermined by the obduracy of some states that

71 According to Noam Chomsky, the WTO cynically provides the USA with an avenue for exporting free market values to other. It also provides it with the new tools of foreign policy by empowering the WTO to go inside the borders of 148 countries that have signed up to it; believe it or not, international institutions can work as long as they keep to the demands of the powerful.

72 Much of this work in relation to the WTO draws from W.K. Tabb, *Globalization and the Struggle for Social Justice in the Twenty-First Century* (Berkeley, CA: Monthly Review Press, 2001), Chapter 1.

73 This fact was decried by Julius Nyerere, where he said that in 1989 Tanzania had produced a lot of cotton and as such he had projected many programmes based on returns from the bumper cotton produce. He woke up one night and heard over the radio that the price of cotton had been slashed on the world market by more than half. He was irked by this prospect because Tanzania as the biggest cotton producer should at least have been consulted.

74 Chomsky, *Profit Over People*.

75 Ibid.

have sought to use it as a platform for consolidating their hegemonic positions. It is supposedly ironic for some countries that masquerade[76] as the father figures of the market doctrine to become statist in total disregard of the causes they profess to champion. The inference from this is the suggestion that 'globalization is good for you but not for me', a posture that undermines the cause for the globalization of the market economy. This development has not gone down well with some sceptics.

In relation to settling international trade disputes, international commercial arbitration as a preferred method[77] of dispute resolution in international business transactions is far more complicated. The application of national, substantive or non-legal standards is far more complicated than the application of national law by judges.[78] The arbitrator may have no access to the applicable national law, unlike the national judges, who normally apply[79] the law in which they have been trained for years. According to Dr Loukas Mistelis,[80] arbitration deals predominantly with international trade disputes, while national courts deal predominately with national cases for which knowledge of national law and state interests is often called upon. Thus, when selecting the standard to apply, parties or arbitrators may nationalize or internationalize the dispute.[81]

In the final analysis, given the antecedents of the WTO[82] and the fact that it was adopted to strengthen the trading system with regard to the problems that plagued it under GATS it epitomizes the fact that prescribing laws to order the system is one thing, but translating them so that they may work effectively is indeed another.

---

76 It is predicated on Washington-led policies under what came to be known as 'Washington Consensus'. See John Williamson, 'From Reform Agenda to Damaged Brand Name', 40(3) *Finance and Development* (2003): pp. 10–13, available at www.imf.org/external/pubs/ft/fandd/2003/09/pdf/williams.pdf (date accessed 14 December 2011).

77 In London alone, there are more than 4,500 arbitration and alternative dispute resolution proceedings annually.

78 L. Mistelis, 'Is Harmonisation a Necessary Evil?: The Future of Harmonisation and New Sources of International Trade Law', in Ian Fletcher, Loukas Mistelis and Marise Cremona (eds), *Foundations & Perspectives* (London: Sweet & Maxwell, 2001), p. 3.

79 J. Stone, *Foundations and Perspectives of International Trade Law* (London: Sweet & Maxwell, 2001), pp. 1–5.

80 L. Mistellis, 'International Trade and Investment Dispute Settlement', School of International Arbitration, Queen Mary, University of London, 2004.

81 Ibid.

82 The changes from GATT to the WTO was intended to strengthen the existing GATT principles rather than to change the underpinning GATT principles themselves. This was expected to improve the compliance of WTO members with WTO law and to reduce the use of unilateral trade measures. One of the changes was the establishment of the dispute settlement panel, and the adoption of the panel report can no longer be blocked by one of the parties to the dispute as was formerly the case under GATT. Because of this, the number of disputes submitted to the dispute settlement panel has literally exploded since the creation of the WTO, reflecting greater confidence in the new system by its members.

The problem with international law – the thesis that this chapter has sought to establish – is the fusion of law and politics, and it is now a settled fact that in the event of conflict, the rule of power prevails. Thus, the question whether the WTO as an institution has achieved its initial mandate remains an open one.

Law and Markets in Uganda

The globalization of laws is always aimed at bringing about the convergence of different legal systems to level the playing field for stakeholders to forge together on overlapping global challenges. The vivid example of this is the FATF's 40+9 recommendations. However, any meaningful globalization of laws should be implemented within an institutional framework,[83] in which the system can be organized and called to order.[84] There are those who oppose this idea, contending that the harmonization of laws is far from realistic, given that societies have different cultures and it is therefore impossible to liken 'elephants to goats'.[85] The concept of transnationalism has also been dismissed[86] as nothing but a misnomer: all we have are American, Japanese or UK companies operating in Uganda or elsewhere. These companies would have been created in accordance with the laws of their home countries, laws that may be alien to their host countries, which begs the question of why these companies are called transnational corporations.

Paradoxically, in countries that have just become committed to the free market economy (including Uganda), laws governing the free market either do not exist[87] or are vague, contradictory or badly structured. Judges may have little experience or training in resolving the legal problems arising out of private business deals and

83 Global institutions have demonstrated that speaking with one voice is far from realistic given the disparities in power relations. On the contrary, the prevalence of policy platforms, for example, the WTO, to which many countries have subscribed should essentially give them leverage to voice their concern – although apparently this is not the case.

84 There is a need for the adoption of harmonized rules and conventions governing trade, capital flows and foreign investment. Transition and emerging market economies need to improve their business environment by implementing far-reaching economic and reform programmes that include – but are not limited to – providing monetary and fiscal discipline, improving the efficiency of their public sector, implementing privatization programmes to increase the efficiency of state-owned and operated assets, modernizing regulatory codes, reforming and liberalizing financial systems, reducing the level of public and private sector corruption, promoting trade liberalization and regional integration, eliminating barriers to direct investment, and adopting unified and competitive exchange rate regimes.

85 Dine, *Companies, International Trade and Human Rights*, pp. 1–40.

86 Ibid.

87 The apparent failure to prosecute Union Carbide in Bhopal due to the fact that there was no framework within which to bring legal proceedings is a good example that underpins this point.

in applying new regulatory and taxation statutes. Besides, laws in the book may not mean much or may be difficult to comprehend.[88] For laws to have legitimacy, they must be internalized and the public should be brought on board in the law-making process.[89] It is a huge mistake[90] to suppose that law is the monopoly of the legal profession and the executive – citizens will have to conceptualize what their rights and responsibilities are in order to assert them as leverage for the development of society.[91] Laws must not be created for the sake of it; they must be disseminated and known for the good of society.

In some jurisdictions such as Uganda, the judicial system is less robust, supposedly for the following reasons: first, very few judges are highly trained and in any case they are appointed to the bench if they are sympathetic to the government's political cause;[92] secondly, Uganda, like many developing countries, is not yet fully independent at least as far as the process of creating laws is concerned. When this problem is coupled with a poor economic and social infrastructure, it leaves law weak and fraught with deterrent effects. This implies that people will avoid bringing disputes in the local courts of law and will prefer to circumvent them by offering bribes or taking the law in their own hands. The foregoing institutional challenge does not augur well for cultivating the system based on the rule of law. Laws must bear some relationship with reality if they are to be obeyed and to regulate conduct effectively, because laws that set unrealistic standards are likely to be overlooked and ultimately pushed aside. Law is a very sensitive product of any culture as it is intimately bound up with rule and legitimacy, and to have legitimacy, rules need to be internalized into the society. The use of model laws in fledgling legal systems is necessary but *must* be modified to suit local conditions – a failure of do so will generate adverse consequences with regard to encouraging local development.

Many developing countries are caught up in the dilemma where the existing legal systems are less robust in stimulating development but are also inadequate in cushioning society against the challenges brought about by the globalization of

---

88 Rose-Ackerman, *Corruption and Government*, p. 152.

89 This can take the form of elected representatives as voices of the masses, but a situation where voters are coerced either through intimidation to vote for a particular candidate or corruption through the use of money undermines the participatory influence of the public in the legal process.

90 Law requires that society have theories which explain and justify law within social consciousness (the public mind) and within individual consciousness (the private mind, including the social consciousness of subordinate societies) – such theories reflect the society's values and purposes.

91 Ignorance is partly responsible for the frequent violations of human rights in some societies. Some cynical regimes exploit these to consolidate their dictatorships and maladministration.

92 First there is the problem of corruption in the judiciary, but, secondly, the independence of the judiciary is undermined by political meddling and resource constraints, making it less robust in fostering the development priorities of the society.

markets. As such, some individual governments have been marginalized insofar as delivering social services and other development programmes is concerned. While globalization and its negative effects is an issue, Ugandan society in particular is also plagued by corruption.[93] Corruption where job allocation is sublimated to political whims implies that the skilled labour force will be under-utilized by the society, which is likely to be constrained by skills shortages. It is absurd to say the very least that many developing countries are consciously creating an environment that pushes away the badly needed skilled workers.[94] As such, it has not been possible for such societies to compete favourably in the global market, let alone implement national development programmes. Many societies have enacted laws but have fallen short in terms of implementing the created laws. In Uganda, the implementation of anti-corruption legislation like the Leadership Code (2002) has been rendered worthless through non-implementation. This brings us to the conclusion that creating laws to run the system is good, but implementing them is better because this shows that the system is working effectively.

The adoption of global initiatives is important, but it needs to be qualified in order to enhance local development interests and not to alienate local societies. Alienating local development interests can come about in many ways, not least where global initiatives are adopted without recourse to tailored local reforms in relation to how the evolved initiatives are to be adapted and implemented.[95] This argument is forwarded based on the fact that when a law is enacted in a society, it would have been spurred on by the need to close loopholes or weaknesses in the existing framework in that particular society. It is unlikely that the same laws, unless as a matter of mere coincidence, would have congruence or resonance with a set of problems in a different jurisdiction, where the problems may be informed by a different set of factors.

The advantages of subscribing to global regimes should enhance the global fight against organized crimes and other forms of global exigencies. Certainly, nobody can dispute the need for a common framework in order for markets to operate properly. In terms of stemming the threat of money laundering, every internationally active bank is under an obligation to create an environment where continuous CDD measures are applied and implemented. These anti-money laundering measures are designed to ensure that banks are able to monitor

---

93 Corruption in many societies takes two forms: internal, which is engendered by the dynamics of the domestic society; and external, which is induced by the exigencies of the market economy. See the Report of the Commission for Africa (2005), available at www.commissionforafrica.info/2005-report (date accessed 14 December 2011), pp. 142–8.

94 According to International Labour Organization (ILO) estimates, Zimbabwe is said to have lost 100,000 of its skilled workers in the last two years and this exodus seems far from over.

95 The economic predicaments of many developing countries make it hard in practice to undertake long-term system implementation tests to ensure their feasibility and sustainability.

a customer's account throughout the relationship he/she has initiated with a particular bank. If the bank fails to do so, as we have already demonstrated, it could face punitive measures. Indeed, the majority of banks will have to internalize the evolved anti-money laundering standards to ensure a normative environment for markets to function. It is my contention that self-regulatory rules should be overseen by separate oversight agencies to ensure that there is no conflict of interests, mimicking the concept of the separation of powers in relation to the rule of law. This conflict of interest issue would explain why, despite the evolution of a plethora of anti-money laundering laws, money laundering continues to be a troublesome issue in the international banking system. In corrupt regimes, banking officials will either merely look away from the obvious, creating an avenue for exploitation, or they will be complicit in money laundering for the obvious short-term gains that are reaped in the process. In other jurisdictions, banks might simply be deficient in terms of a requisite infrastructure to ensure a proper dispensation of normative anti-money laundering standards, while other banks, especially those from developed countries with a developed infrastructure and the leverage to bolster the global anti-money laundering system, might simply choose not lend their support for obvious opportunistic reasons. In so doing, they deliberately undermine the effective functioning of global anti-money laundering laws.

It would seem that the global system (no matter what the issue in question is) is based on a false premise that countries can potentially harness the same system regardless of their individual development dynamics. Perhaps we need to remind ourselves that the evolved global regimes, in this case the global AML/CFT regimes, are implemented in individual countries and are prone to the dynamics of development at a local level. In other words, it is possible for the dynamics of development at a local societal level to resonate in the internal banking system accordingly. This leaves us to wonder whether the term 'global anti-money laundering system' is created to signpost international political posturing or whether it actually helps in fostering a robust anti-money laundering environment globally. Whatever the answer, one thing that cannot be discounted is fact that the absence of a functional global jurisdiction, government or even institutions can engender an environment that is conducive to money laundering.

The integration of markets has played a fundamental role in promoting market discipline. For instance, through the creation of regional and global initiatives, not least the emergence of the regional police initiatives such as Europol and Interpol, alleged criminals can be pursued no matter where they are hiding and brought to justice.[96] These initiatives are created with the mandate to transcend national or territorial boundaries of other states, and thus criminals in their different shapes and sizes will have nowhere to hide. There are also mutual legal

96 Usually through security agencies which have jurisdiction over cross-border crimes, such as Interpol, Europol, TREVI and other policing arrangements in different parts of the world.

assistance treaties signed between states to provide modalities for circumventing hurdles which criminals may exploit to stay put. As such, once criminals are aware that there are no safe havens anywhere, they will usually think twice before they commit crimes. Similarly, globalization has enhanced the potential of states to come together on global problems, as underpinned by the catchphrase that 'global problems require global engagement'.

The challenges raised by globalization can be managed by adjusting economies efficiently to global changes. The mandate of some global institutions should be changed to reflect the contemporary changes in the global community. At an African level, there is a need to ensure that African governments are more adaptable to global challenges by creating an effective infrastructure to enable them to compete favourably. The huge endowment of physical and human resources in the continent should be properly exploited to enhance the welfare standards of its people but obviously not corrupt leaders. The 'blame game' must stop, much as this chapter acknowledges that the enhancement of resource endowment has become the precursor for instability, ultimately obscuring the image of the continent. The proponents of the global system should ensure that greed and profiteering do not undermine the need for a shared framework of understanding about rights, but how these rights are enforced should not necessarily lead to homogenization, to a one-size-fits-all approach to legal cultures, and indeed should express the features of the communities out of which they have grown.

Regional initiatives in Africa such as the EAC and the SADC, which were often created with good intentions, have not stimulated development[97] in the same effective way as the EU and the North American Free Trade Agreement (NAFTA) have done in generating development opportunities for their respective regions. Implausibly, some of the African problems are not global but local. Ever since Africa fell prey to colonialism, largely due to internal bickering and disorganization, many African leaders have learned nothing from history – they are corrupt, self-centred, removed from their societies and some are not fit to govern.[98] This has added to the array of problems that have beset the continent and impeded its much-needed development. If properly harnessed – which apparently has not been the

97 The problem with regional integration has always been that of the asymmetric distribution of accrued benefits, which subsequently creates disunity within the system. The collapse of the first East African Community (EAC) in 1977, where Uganda was dissatisfied with the disproportionate distribution of the benefits accruing to the Community, underscores this. A failure to agree a framework for the proportionate distribution of the accrued benefits among the three east African countries of Kenya, Uganda and Tanzania infuriated Uganda, and it decided to pull out. Kenya was allegedly claiming more than 50 per cent of the accrued benefits, leaving Tanzania and Uganda to share the remaining 50 per cent.

98 Whoever learns how to shoot a gun aspires to shoot himself to power, as was evidently the case in many parts of Africa.

case – globalization has the potential to generate more development opportunities than it takes away.

There is a need for affirmative action on corruption to stem its concomitant social effects and to ensure that essential information[99] is not fettered away or diverted by corrupt officials to benefit criminals or criminal syndicates, but is instead used to benefit law enforcement authorities. Here globalization can play a significant role by bringing some societies into the fold of prolific progressive societies[100] and improving the situation for poor countries by bringing down transactional costs. Nevertheless, where the country feels the need to safeguard local interests, globalization notwithstanding, it should stay out of global initiatives – for example, in the name of national-self interest, the USA has refused to sign the Kyoto Protocol on climate change[101] or to submit to the jurisdiction of the ICC. With the ICC, the USA[102] has tried to negotiate bilateral immunity agreements with other state parties to safeguard its forces serving in foreign missions. Ostensibly this means that where the need for multilateralism conflicts with national self-interests, the latter should prevail. This should only be the case where staying out of global initiatives does not generate any spill-over effects on other states.

In relation to education reforms, it is my contention that education should be given a frontline role with a clear focus to overcome imperfections in society. In effect, this would be one way of reaching out to the populace with regard to the measures aimed at corruption and its predicate offences. Through education, the public will be sensitized, for instance, by way of seminars, public enlightenment campaigns, workshops, conferences, press releases and training in order to rid society of criminal activities such as corruption. Apparently the majority of Ugandans do not regard corruption as a crime as such.[103] Through training and sensitization programmes, citizens can easily be brought on board in the campaign

99 Globalization is information-driven as a result of the innovations in ICT, but if this information is not properly harnessed, it can go either way, that is, in much the same way as it has helped to bring down transaction costs, it can also assist criminals in a society permeated by corruption. This seems to be one of the flipsides of globalization.

100 It can share in the resources of other countries, such as intelligence and personnel (which are difficult to instantly generate at a national level) or the countries can pool their limited resources together to facilitate what would otherwise be hard for any individual country to undertake. Besides, the very fact that globalization transcends national boundaries means that no country can unilaterally afford to go it alone in facing the threats created by the system.

101 The USA refused to sign the 1997 Kyoto Protocol, citing out that it was fatally flawed because it failed to include developing countries as participants in the required action to correct the 'emission problem'.

102 Perhaps the USA is justified in this because it is called upon more than any other nation to send its troops overseas, making them vulnerable to prosecution, including malicious prosecution, for their misdeeds overseas.

103 This is supposedly because corruption is justified as a sign of being successful which is compounded by the fact that the masses in developing societies are sidelined to

against corruption and other forms of crimes. It is also my submission that a good education system should be localized by way of making it society-oriented (that is, specialized)[104] and adapted to its cultural, social and economic needs if it is to correlate with the development interests of the local society.

The need for education system reform notwithstanding, a high proportion of the population in some societies in developing countries is not educated or able to access education. Since societies are becoming more globalized, it is imperative that ordinary citizens appreciate the implications of global influence vis-à-vis their societies and how to best influence policy decisions at a higher government level. This is possible by strengthening the role of civil society. As for infrastructural and technical capacity deficiencies in the regulatory and security agencies, education could play an important role by ensuring continuous training of both the regulators and other agencies of financial institutions. This could go a long way in assisting the fight against economic and other financial crimes by ensuring adequate capacity building by conducting programmes at national and cross-country levels.

The character of the education reform[105] package envisaged by this chapter is one tailored to the development imperatives of the progressive market-oriented economy. The modern education needs should focus on science, research and development studies, for example, globalization and the law, the impediments to development today.[106] The issue of less robust education, apparently the predicament faced by many societies, adds to the spectre of under-development that obscures the image of many African economies. Changes in the education curriculum are necessary because the current system – bearing the vestiges of colonial past in a putative global era – is not only inadequate to cope with these changes but has similarly been superseded by developments in the world economy and thus is bad education.[107] There is a need to mobilize local resources, including the use of local languages that have the potential to harness more than 50 per cent of the workforce in the mainstream development process.

---

the fringes of politics. In many developing countries, the masses are disenfranchised and programmes are superimposed.

On the contrary, the masses in developed countries are part and parcel of governments as regards influencing mainstream policy decisions.

104 Foreign-oriented education systems will not help to foster the development challenges the local society faces. Robust education should be tailored to the development imperatives of the local society if it is to foster development.

105 The establishment of universal primary education in 2002 under the leadership of President Museveni was a step in the right direction as a positive measure designed to resolve the issue of illiteracy in Uganda.

106 N. Mugarura, 'The Effects of Torture on Democracy and Development: An African Perspective', unpublished paper (2001): p. 16.

107 In law, when the case is overruled and no longer applicable, it cannot be invoked as a precedent. Equally, the system, which is no longer applicable with respect to the imperatives of the society, is a bad system.

The efficacy of law with regard to creating a working framework in response to money laundering and other market exigencies has presumably been weakened by the powers of the state being whittling down in areas where it needs to maintain its presence. The state's powers have been reduced through deregulation, which has been compounded by the reconstitution of the state at the regional and global institutional levels. Invidiously, not all the powers ceded by the state are reconstituted – this has not only undermined state regulatory controls, but has also handed individual actors – for instance, criminals – the opportunity to consolidate their activities in the void created as a result. Nevertheless, the fact that law is contingent upon power would suggest that law is a de facto instrument of powerful states to confirm and consolidate existing asymmetric power relations.

Chapter 10
Conclusion

In the final analysis, the globalization of laws (including laws on money laundering and its predicate crimes) is endowed with the potential to level the playing field with regard to asymmetries in information and development in diverse stakeholder countries. The engendered benefits should provide developing countries with resources such as the ability to share information on the fight against organized crime. For example, through the creation of regional and international initiatives such as Europol and Interpol, culprits who fleece economies of their assets will be pursued and brought to justice. Also, the creation of these initiatives can enhance cooperation between societies and transcend the limitations of national or territorial boundaries that criminals would wish to exploit in order to remain at large. This ensures some parity in relation to the adoption of a common framework on the definition, criminalization and dimensions of money laundering as a crime. The standards that evolve at a multinational level would help to fill the void in the law, countering the challenges of regulatory arbitrage or forum shopping (where weakly regulated regimes are exploited at the expense of those with rigorous regulatory systems).

However, if the policy environment is conducive, globalization (in its multifaceted contexts)[1] has the potential to generate development synergies, particularly in less developed countries. In the first place, multilateral banking institutions can provide invaluable forums for the exchange of information.[2] Multilateral initiatives have the potential to promote more open-ended and creative discussions among governments, as well as to provide effective channels for citizen input, both domestically and at the level of international institutions.[3] Secondly, they can be instrumental in developing and enforcing international norms. While existing international banking organizations have no formal legislative or enforcement power, they do have the authority to issue and promote supervisory and best practice guidelines. These guidelines, though far

1 Globalization is not inherently bad, but what countries ought to do prior to subscribing to the system is to remove the impediments that might compromise the adoption of global initiatives.

2 This enhances the sharing of valuable information and best practices of risk management methodologies and monitoring.

3 Dinah Shelton, 'Commitment and Compliance: The Role of Non-Binding Norms in International Legal Systems', 2 *Journal of International Law* (2000): p. 413.

from binding, can assume the status of 'soft law'[4] and assist in helping countries struggling with design and implementation problems to establish cooperative arrangements. Thirdly, globalization can bring about the benefit of impartiality and legitimacy. For example, the BIS, the world's central banking organization, embodies the opinions of its global members. When the BIS adopts a particular set of standards (as it did through the Basel Capital Accord), it is seen as embodying the interests of the international banking community as a whole. In so doing, it maintains the legitimacy and neutrality respected by banking supervisory authorities worldwide.[5] Fourthly, countries that do not have the physical or human capacity to develop their own systems can draw upon the expertise and experience possessed by other members with whom they conduct business. Multilateral banks in Uganda have led the way in spearheading the development of anti-money laundering procedures and policies over their local counterparts.[6] This is because the parent supervisory authorities are responsible for the supervision of their home branches and subsidiaries operating in foreign jurisdictions and will therefore run them in the same effective way as their home counterparts. However, if there is no reciprocal enabling measure in the host country, a strict regulatory regime could harm foreign business establishments by handing the competitive advantage to their local rivals.

The current globalization trends have facilitated the activities of criminals in laundering the proceeds of their crimes anywhere in the world. The large volume of legitimate capital moving at any one time in the world and the rapidly reduced regulatory controls on such movements have made it possible for large amounts of the proceeds of crime to enter the global financial markets unnoticed.[7] The increased need for criminal enterprises to use international fund transfers has also made them aware of the benefits of moving funds internationally in a disguised way,[8] effectively disrupting audit trails as law enforcement is impeded by jurisdictional and legal boundaries. In addition, the growing diversification of international financial instruments and the differences in controls and regulations

4 Soft law can generally be adopted more rapidly because it is non-binding. It can also be quickly amended or replaced if it fails to meet current challenges. It extends to implementation and compliance, where the dynamic interaction of the various actors can play a crucial role.

5 Shelton, 'Commitment and Compliance'.

6 Barclays has put in place guidelines to prevent money laundering; the Standard Chartered Bank has also formulated anti-money laundering guidelines to use in conjunction with minimum group standards.

7 The FATF Asia Secretariat, 'Disposal of Proceeds of Crime Money Laundering Methods', Workshop Report of the Expert Group in Hong Kong, 14 November 1996.

8 See the demise of the BCCI, which closed down in 1991 following the discovery of massive fraud and money laundering by US regulators. The chief victim of the bank malpractices were depositors and governments in developing economies. For further details on this case, see Walker, *International Banking Regulation*, Chapter 1.

between countries has provided those wishing to conceal and disguise funds with ample opportunities to do so.[9]

In view of the increased trends in organized crime activities, states *must* come together when evolving the robust legal framework necessary to accommodate the exigencies of a global system.[10] This presumably explains why the majority of states have acknowledged the need for a multilateral approach as a response to the increasing threat of money laundering.[11] Equally, banks should also adopt consolidated supervision based on the model of the Basel Committee, where both the parent and the branches should be supervised.[12] It has to be appreciated that a well-designed global anti-money laundering framework should be premised on the principles of practicability, democracy, legitimacy, transparency and accountability if it is to generate an effective impact and to be sustainable, legitimate and global.

As already noted, the international cooperation of states is essential in generating mechanisms such as mutual legal assistance in criminal and civil matters. Mutual legal assistance treaties are signed between countries to provide modalities for circumventing the hurdles which criminals currently exploit to remain at large. As such, once criminals are aware that there are no safe havens anywhere, they may think twice before they decide to commit crimes. Similarly, globalization also has the potential to bring countries together on global challenges underpinned by the catchphrase 'global problems require global engagement'. In terms of money laundering, the global system has played a major role in evolving an international AML/CFT framework to govern and improve modalities to ensure that financial institutions are not used for money laundering purposes.[13] As such, this book has paid particular attention to the role played by the FATF, the BIS, the IMF, World Bank and the EU in bringing about global anti-money laundering regimes. However, there remains the problem of over-regulation by multiple regulatory regimes and the possibility of the duplication of rules governing financial markets.

It can conveniently be argued that if the globalization of markets (manifested by inter-state relations at various levels) is properly harnessed, it is endowed with the potential to generate more synergies to level the playing field with regard to asymmetries in information and development than it takes away. The advantages of subscribing to global regimes should assist the global fight against organized crime and other forms of global exigencies. For instance, through the creation of regional and global initiatives, not least the emergence of regional police initiatives such as Europol and Interpol, alleged criminals can be pursued no matter where

9 Ibid.

10 We live in a world that is interconnected as never before – one in which groups and individuals interact more and more directly across frontiers, often without involving the state at all.

11 More than 100 countries have now signed the Palermo Convention 2000.

12 This prompts a need for regulators, either from the FATF or elsewhere, to monitor and regulate the system.

13 See Appendix 2.

they are hiding and be brought to book.[14] These initiatives are created with the mandate to transcend national or territorial boundaries of other states, and thus criminals in their different shapes and sizes will have nowhere to hide. As such, once criminals are aware that there are no safe havens anywhere, they will usually think twice before they commit crimes.

However, in order for countries (particularly those with tenuous legal system and infrastructure) to benefit from proliferating global initiatives, they need to be realistic so that they are not debased by the dynamics of globalization. In reality, many developing countries are economically at a disadvantage as far as the process of creating global AML/CFT regimes is concerned. When this challenge is coupled with a poor economic and social infrastructure, it makes the majority of developing countries vulnerable to global exigencies. This cannot augur well for the cultivation of a functional global system that accommodates the needs of the local and global economies. It is necessary to reiterate that laws in its various manifestations must bear a relationship with reality to in order regulate undesired conduct effectively. Normative anti-money laundering standards should also be harmonized to reflect the cultural imperatives in the societies into which they are introduced. As has already been demonstrated, law is a sensitive product of any culture as it is intimately bound up with rule and legitimacy, and to have legitimacy, rules need to be internalized into the society. The use of model laws in tenuous legal systems is necessary but *must* be modified to suit local conditions – a failure of which generates adverse consequences with regard to encouraging local development. This presupposes the need for tailored legal reforms to adapt economies efficiently to desired global changes. For example, the implementation of AML/CFT in developing countries will require substantial legal reform that further limits the potential for control over the pricing schemes of companies.[15] There are a range of issues involved, such as the repealing, enactment and adoption of national laws and policies to bring existing structures into line with desired changes. The absence of a robust legal system presumably explains why some countries have been marginalized in terms of harnessing global markets, delivering social services and other development programmes. Certainly, liberalization has also created avenues for corruption where initially government-owned assets are sold to state officials and their cronies. As such, it has not been possible for these societies to compete favourably in the global market, let alone implement national development programmes. Many societies have enacted laws but have fallen short in implementing these laws. It should be noted that states have very little choice but to coexist in the pursuit of global initiatives such as AML/CFT regimes.

14 Usually through security agencies, which have a transnational remit over cross-border crimes, such as Interpol, Europol, TREVI and other policing arrangements in different parts of the world.

15 See, for instance, the WTO Ministerial Conference on the TRIPS Agreement and Public Health at the Doha Ministerial Conference, WT/MIN (01)/Dec/W/2, 14 November 2001.

However, they need to defer accession to global initiatives until they have created a system that is compatible with the imperatives of the global market. This should entail, among other things, the need to develop a requisite infrastructure before they accede to global regimes. This argument is based on the fact that acceding to global regimes should not be adopted for the sake of it but for the sake of enhancing development of economies.

This chapter has articulated that a lack of development opportunities creates a suitable environment for criminals to perpetuate money laundering. For example, those who are unemployed can more easily be lured into drug dealing in return for lucrative pay and banking officials might not be able to resist bribes or be keen on reporting suspicious transactions in line with anti-money laundering requirements espoused by many self-regulatory regimes (such as the FATF or the Basel Committee) if they are poorly paid or work in poor conditions. Hungry people are vulnerable and prone to money laundering-related crimes – they will easily avert their eyes from the obvious or succumb to bribes if they are not properly remunerated or have not been given the proper education to sensitize and equip their society against corrupt practices.

In addition, the fact that less developed states are sidelined at a global level with regard to the process of evolving global anti-money laundering regimes means that they are at a double disadvantage in terms of harnessing the evolved regimes. Hence, it is currently not possible to have a level playing field either in relation to the ability of states to harness global standards or the process of global standard-setting at a supranational level.

Prescribing normative global standards is one thing, but ensuring that global standard setters should always take into account the varying economic dynamics in evolving normative AML/CFT regimes is quite another. Ensuring that such dynamics are taken into consideration should go a long way towards guaranteeing that the proliferating regimes are suited to the local development conditions and hence are easily adaptable. There should also be a clear mechanism whereby individual states are able to participate directly in the committees or bodies charged with the responsibility of creating global standards. In my view, it would make more sense if the adoption of global anti-money laundering laws is preceded by a feasibility study designed to reflect the dynamics between the local and the global. While the FATF asks countries to transpose the anti-money laundering framework, taking into account their varied levels of development, some of the 40+9 FATF recommendations are far from realistic for many countries at present.[16] Thus, the adoption of global anti-money laundering regimes should only be introduced in a country when the prevailing climate is favourable to ensuring that these regimes are capable of being harnessed at a local level. If this is not done, coercing states

16 For example, CDD, which has become a paradigm of money laundering control by all major anti-money laundering initiatives, is too onerous to implement in the financial centres of developing countries.

to adopt global regimes in circumstances where they are deficient could not only have a corrosive effect but could also debase their economies.

Coercing states to adopt global regimes could be perceived negatively in relation to internal state sovereignty. The case of the Seychelles (where the government was reprimanded by the FATF for passing a law[17] that would encourage money laundering) underscores the fact that the independence of countries in making decisions in the name of national self-interest has been lost through global governance to national economies. According to the government of the Seychelles, the Economic Development Act 1996 was deemed essential to attract much-needed FDI, while from the FATF's perspective the Act was capable of being exploited to encourage money laundering and had to be withdrawn. These kinds of clashes can always be avoided when there a working partnership between regulators of international financial regimes and the individual countries concerned. As highlighted by this, unless inter-state cooperation is properly managed, it can engender tensions between sovereign states.

The willingness of states to embrace the fight against money laundering or any other form of organized transnational crime is dictated by the prevailing economic and political environment in the particular society concerned.[18] Perceptions towards crimes (and money laundering in particular) are shaped by the prevailing environment in some countries and this is the reason why some societies do not see money laundering as a problem.[19] Some societies see themselves as being so overwhelmed by problems that they would not turn away laundered money, which is needed to plug shortfalls in funding development programmes in the economy.[20] Global standards will be resented if they show signs of having a hidden agenda (for example, interfering with the free flow of capital in the country) or are used covertly to promote the interests of other countries in the domestic state. These tensions postulate the need for globalization to generate a platform where countries cooperate fully on overlapping development challenges. Many countries have ratified anti-money laundering treaties (such as the Palermo Convention in 2000) but have failed to translate them into substantive domestic law.

Money laundering and its predicate crimes can have a corrosive effect and can potentially destroy the lives of millions of poor people, and yet the perpetrators

---

17 The law offered to protect whoever invested more than US$10 million in the country, except if that money was the subject of criminal investigations in the Seychelles itself.

18 This point is supported by the fact that poorer countries are more likely to become complicit to money laundering because of their physical infrastructural deficiencies in terms of combatting money laundering.

19 Some banks have been aiding and abetting money laundering through corresponding banking, as illustrated in the case of Sani Abacha in Chapter 5.

20 Given this discussion, globalization should help to transmit the benefits of development through the global system, but should not to be used to strangulate small countries.

of these crimes often get away scot-free or are venerated in society. This does not set a good precedent for an effective system based on the rule of law. It is just as criminal as any other form of violation of human rights to kill millions of people by depriving them of their means of livelihood. As such, perpetrators of political corruption should be brought within the jurisdiction of the International Criminal Court[21] for trial. This could be one way of ensuring that leaders who preside over regimes carrying out gross violations of human rights (either unwittingly or intentionally through corrupt practices) are made answerable for those crimes.

In relation to the global governance of international finance, there are two issues worthy of mention. First, on the issue of legitimacy of evolved global anti-money laundering standards, it should be noted that the G10 countries often come together in response to situational emergencies and create a framework to combat the situation. This framework is initially disguised in the form of soft law norms but is eventually used to bind other countries.[22] This has manifested itself in relation to regimes evolving under the auspices of the Basel Committee and the FATF. Irrespective of whether the respective regime has been endorsed by individual national governments, experience has shown that such a regime will be imposed on some governments, particularly less developed countries, which in any case are vulnerable and have to borrow money to fund development programmes. Financial institutions have conditioned lending in such a way that countries will be required to embrace financial sector reforms locally. This is deemed essential to ensure that the economy is restructured and vibrant to guarantee that the borrowed funds are paid back. The second point is that of the glaring lack of accountability, where governments that create global regimes are accountable to nobody but themselves. In this case, where developed countries (particularly the G10 countries) believe it is not in their interests to implement global standards, they will not do so.[23] On the other hand, non-compliance on the part of small states is unacceptable and will generate condemnation and, where possible, sanctions. Therefore, to overcome such tensions, the global anti-money laundering norms should only be created through multilateral treaties to overcome legitimacy and accountability deficiencies.

The legitimacy of international policy making should recognize that states which are subject to international norms on money laundering or similar global regimes should be given the opportunity to influence the form that the engendered norms will assume. This would be one way of fostering a political willingness to implement and enforce the proliferating global standards. As such, the World Bank and the IMF should always co-opt local economies on evolving regimes, a move that would ease tensions between these institutions and those at a local level.

21 Established by the Rome Statute in 1998, with jurisdiction over three serious categories of international crimes: genocide, war crimes and crimes against humanity.

22 The Basel Committee Supervisory Standards have now been co-opted by the World Bank and the IMF as conditions for lending to borrowing states.

23 Stigliz, *Globalization and its Discontents*.

Countries subject to varying dynamics of development cannot easily coexist as differences tend to reverberate throughout the system, generating tensions and challenges to fostering a shared framework of purpose. It is essential for the global anti-money laundering framework to be supported by a development environment that is nearly comparable across the board. As such, measures aimed at eradicating poverty and corruption, the two apparent impediments to development in developing countries, should be given the greatest priority. This contention is supported by the fact that the problem of poverty has the potential to destroy societies and to deprive them of their capabilities to manage themselves efficiently. It is evident that as a result of widespread poverty, coupled with tenuous infrastructure, those in developing countries are predisposed to a life of misery and capacity deprivation. In such an environment, money laundering might be viewed not as a choice but as an imperative. Thus, it can be inferred that developing countries are likely to remain vulnerable and sidelined as far as developing a robust local anti-money laundering infrastructure is concerned. The state's ability to manage its apparent development challenges is undermined by a hostile global economic environment over which it has very little control.[24]

Finally, much as this book has articulated the inherent challenges caused by the globalization of markets, it has to be said that globalization is a fact of life and is the way forward. States must find ways of repositioning themselves efficiently to global changes. There is no state that can afford to posture and indeed there is no state that can afford to operate a closed economy – not anymore. AML/CFT institutions with oversight responsibilities should allow countries the flexibility of implementing their AML/CFT obligations to reflect the varying levels of development across regions. Countries will have to first develop a requisite infrastructure to enable them to compete favourably in the global market. On a very positive note, if properly harnessed, which has apparently not been the case thus far, the globalization of markets in its various manifestations is endowed with the potential to enhance economies in many respects, not least creating employment opportunities for local economies and easing access to requisite information instead of leveraged information. It can help to bring less developed economies into the fold of prolific progressive societies[25] through the leverage of reduced transactional costs.

---

24 Sen, *Development as Freedom*, p. 87.

25 It can share in the resources of other countries, such as intelligence and personnel (which are difficult to instantly generate at a national level) or the countries can pool their limited resources together to facilitate what would otherwise be hard for any individual country to undertake. Besides, the very fact that globalization transcends national boundaries means that no country can unilaterally afford to go it alone in facing the threats created by the system.

Appendix 1
The Financial Action Task Force (FATF)

Introduction

The Financial Action Task Force (FATF) on money laundering is an intergovernmental body whose purpose is the development and promotion of policies to combat money laundering – the process of criminal proceeds in order to disguise their illegal origin.

The 40 recommendations set out the basic framework for anti-money laundering efforts and they are designed to be of universal application. They cover the criminal justice system and law enforcement, financial system and regulation, and international cooperation.

A. General Framework of the Recommendations

Recommendation 1

Each country should take immediate steps to ratify and to implement fully the United Nations Convention against Illicit traffic in Narcotic Drug and Psychotropic Substances (hereinafter the Vienna Convention).

Recommendation 2

Financial institution secrecy laws should be conceived so as not to inhibit implementation of these recommendations.

Recommendation 3

An effective money laundering enforcement program should include increased multilateral cooperation and mutual legal assistance in money laundering investigations and prosecutions and extradition in money laundering cases, where possible.

B. Role of National Legal Systems in Combating Money Laundering

Scope of the Criminal Offence of Money Laundering

Recommendation 4

Each country should take such measures as may be necessary, including legislative ones, to enable it to criminalise money laundering as set forth in the Vienna Convention. Each country should extend the offence of drug money laundering to one based on serious offences. Each country would determine which serious crimes would be designated money laundering. (See Interpretative Note)

Recommendation 5

As provided in the Vienna Convention, the offence of money laundering should apply at least to knowing money laundering activity, including the concept that knowledge may be inferred from objective factual circumstances.

Recommendation 6

Where possible, corporation themselves – not only their employees – should be subject to criminal liability.

Provisional Measures and Confiscation

Recommendation 7

Countries should adopt measures similar to those set forth in the Vienna Convention, as may be necessary, including legislative ones to enable their competent authorities to confiscate property laundered, proceeds from, instrumentalities used in or intended for use in the commission of any money laundering offence, or property of corresponding value, without prejudicing the rights of bona fide third parties.

Such measures should include the authority to: (i) identify, trace and evaluate property which is subject to confiscation; (ii) carry out provisional measures, such as freezing and seizing, to prevent any dealing, transfer or disposal of such property; and (iii) take any appropriate investigative measures.

C. Role of The Financial System In Combating Money Laundering

Recommendation 8

Recommendations 10 to 29 should apply not only to banks, but also to non-bank financial institutions. Even for those non-bank financial institutions which are not subject to a formal prudential supervisory regime in all countries, for example, bureaux de change, governments should ensure that these institutions are subject to the same anti-money laundering laws or regulations as all other financial institutions and that these laws or regulations are implemented effectively. (See Interpretative Notes)

Recommendation 9

The appropriate national authorities should consider applying Recommendations 10 to 21 and 23 to the conduct of financial activities as commercial undertaking by business or professions, which are not financial institutions, where such conduct is allowed or not prohibited. Financial activities include, but are not limited to, those listed in the attached annex. It is left to each country to decide whether special situations should be defined where the application of anti-money laundering measures is not necessary, for example, when a financial activity is carried out on an occasional or limited basis. (See Interpretative Note)

Customer Identification and Record-Keeping Rules

Recommendation 10

Financial institutions should not keep anonymous accounts or accounts in obviously fictitious names: they should be required (by law, by regulations, by agreements between supervisory authorities and financial institutions or by self-regulatory agreements among financial institutions) to identify, on the basis of an official or other reliable identifying document, and record the identity of their clients, either occasional or usual, when establishing business relations or conducting transactions (in particular opening accounts or passbooks, entering into fiduciary transactions, renting of safe deposit boxes, performing large cash transactions).

Recommendation 11

Financial institutions should take reasonable measures to obtain information about the true identity of the persons on whose behalf an account is opened or a transaction conducted if there are any doubts as to whether these clients or customers are acting on their own behalf, for example, in the case of domiciliary companies (i.e. institutions, corporations, foundations, trusts, etc. that do not conduct any commercial or manufacturing business or any other form of commercial operation in the country where their registered office is located). (See Interpretative Note)

Recommendation 12

Financial institutions should maintain, for at least five years, all necessary records on transactions, both domestic and international, to enable them to comply swiftly with information requests from the competent authorities. Such records must be sufficient to permit reconstruction of individual transactions (including amounts and types of currency involved if any) so as to provide, if necessary, evidence for prosecution of criminal behaviour.

Financial institutions should keep records on customer's identification (e.g. copies or records of official identification documents like passports, identity cards, driving licences or similar documents), account files and business correspondence for at least five years after the account is closed.

Recommendation 13

Countries should pay special attention to money laundering threats inherent in new or developing technologies that might favour anonymity, and take measures, if needed, to prevent their use in money laundering schemes.

Increased Diligence of Financial Institutions

Recommendation 14

Financial institutions should pay special attention to all complex, unusual large transactions, and all unusual patterns of transactions, which have no apparent economic or visible lawful purpose. The background and purpose of such transactions should, as far as possible, be examined, the findings established in writing, and be available to help supervisors, auditors and law enforcement agencies. (See Interpretative Note)

Recommendation 15

If financial institutions suspect that funds stem from a criminal activity, they should be required to report promptly their suspicions to the competent authorities. (See Interpretative Note)

Recommendation 16

Financial institutions, their directors, officers and employees should be protected by legal provisions from criminal or civil liability for breach of any restriction on disclosure of information imposed by contract or by any legislative, regulatory or administrative provisions, if they report their suspicions in good faith to the competent authorities, if they did not know precisely what the underlying criminal activity was, and regardless of whether illegal activity actually occurred. (See Interepatative Note 16)

Recommendation 17

Financial institutions, their directors, officers and employees should not, or, where appropriate, should not be allowed to, warn their customers when information relating to them is being reported to the competent authorities. (See Interpretative Note)

Recommendation 18

Financial institutions reporting their suspicions should comply with instructions from the competent authorities. (See Interpretative Note)

Recommendation 19

Financial institutions should develop programs against money laundering. These programs should include, as a minimum:
(i) the development of internal policies, procedures and controls, including the designation of compliance officers at management level, and adequate screening procedures to ensure high standards when hiring employees;
(ii) an ongoing employee training programme;
(iii) an audit function to test the system.

Measures to Cope with the Problem of Countries with No or Insufficient Anti-Money Laundering Measures

Recommendation 20

Financial institutions should ensure that the principles mentioned above are also applied to branches and majority owned subsidiaries located abroad, especially in countries which do not or insufficiently apply these recommendations, to the extent that local applicable laws and regulations permit. When local applicable laws and regulations prohibit implementation, competent authorities in the country of mother institutions should be informed by the financial institutions that they cannot apply these recommendations.

Recommendation 21

Financial institutions should give special attention to business relations and transactions with persons, including companies and financial institutions, from countries which do not or insufficiently apply these recommendations. Whenever these transactions have no apparent economic or visible lawful purpose, their background and purpose should, as far as possible, be examined, their findings established in writing, and be available to help supervisors, auditors and law enforcement agencies.

Other Measures to Avoid Money Laundering

Recommendation 22

Countries should consider implementing feasible measures to detect or monitor the physical cross-border transportation of cash and bearer negotiable instruments, subject to strict safeguards to ensure proper use of information and without impeding in any way the freedom of capital movements. (See Interpretative Note)

Recommendation 23

Countries should consider the feasibility and utility of a system where banks and other financial institutions and intermediaries would report all domestic and international currency transactions above a fixed amount, to a national central agency with a computerised data base, available to competent authorities for use in money laundering cases, subject to strict safeguards to ensure proper use of the information.

Recommendation 24

Countries should further encourage in general the development of modern and secure techniques of money management, including increased use of checks, payment cards, direct deposit of salary checks, and book entry recording of securities, as a means to encourage the replacement of cash transfers.

Recommendation 25

Countries should take notice of the potential for abuse of shell corporations by money launderers and should consider whether traditional measures are required to prevent unlawful use of such entities.

Implementation and the Role of Regulatory and Other Administrative Authorities

Recommendation 26

The competent authorities supervising banks of other financial institutions or intermediaries should ensure that the supervised institutions have adequate programmes to guard against money laundering. These authorities should cooperate and lend expertise spontaneously or on request with other domestic judicial or law enforcement authorities in money laundering investigation and prosecutions. (See Interpretative Note)

Recommendation 27

Competent authorities should be designed to ensure that an effective implementation of all these recommendations, through administrative supervision and regulation, in other professions dealing with cash as defined by each country.

Recommendation 28

The competent authorities should establish guidelines which will assist financial institutions in detecting suspicious patterns of behaviour by their customers. It is understood that such guidelines will primarily serve as an educational tool for financial institutions personnel.

Recommendation 29

The competent authorities regulating or supervising financial institutions should take the necessary legal or regulatory measures to guard against control or acquisition of a significant participation by criminal or their confederates. (See Interpretative Note)

D. Strengthening of International Cooperation

Exchange of General Information

Recommendation 30

National administrations should consider recording, at least in the aggregate, international flows of cash in whatever currency, so that estimates can be made of cash flows and reflows from various sources abroad, when this is combined with central bank information.

Recommendation 31

International competent authorities, perhaps Interpol and the World Customs Organisation, should be given responsibility for gathering and disseminating information to competent authorities about the latest development in money laundering and money laundering techniques. Central banks and bank regulators could do the same on their network. National authorities in various spheres, in consultation with trade associations, could disseminate this to financial institutions in individual countries.

Exchange of Information Relating to Suspicious Transactions

Recommendation 32

Each country should make efforts to improve spontaneous or upon request international information exchange relating to suspicious transactions, persons and cooperation involved in those transactions between competent authorities. Strict safeguards should be established to ensure that this exchange of information is consistent with national and international provisions on privacy and data protection.

Other Forms of Cooperation

Basis and Means of Cooperation in Confiscation, Mutual Legal Assistance and Extradition

Recommendation 33

Countries should try to ensure, on a bilateral or multilateral basis, that different knowledge standards in national definitions – i.e. different standards concerning the intentional element of the infraction – do not affect the ability or willingness of countries to provide each other with mutual legal assistance.

Recommendation 34

International cooperation should be supported by a network of bilateral and multilateral agreements and arrangements based on generally shared legal concepts with the aim of providing practical measures to affect the widest possible range of mutual assistance.

Recommendation 35

Countries should be encouraged to ratify and implement relevant international conventions on money laundering such as the 1990 Council of Europe Convention on Money Laundering, Search, Seizure and Confiscation of the Proceeds from Crime.

Recommendation 36

Cooperative investigations among countries' appropriate competent authorities should be encouraged. One valid and effective investigative technique in this respect is controlled delivery related to assets known or suspected to be the proceeds of crime. Countries are encouraged to support this technique, where possible. (See the Interpretative Note)

Recommendation 37

There should be procedures for mutual legal assistance in criminal matters regarding the use of compulsory measures including the production of records by financial institutions and other persons, the search of persons and premises, seizure and obtaining of evidence for use in money laundering investigations and prosecutions and in related actions in foreign jurisdictions.

Recommendation 38

There should be authority to take expeditious action in response to requests by foreign countries to identify, freeze, seize and confiscate proceeds or other property of corresponding value to such proceeds, based on money laundering or crimes underlying money laundering activity. (See Interpretative Note)

Recommendation 39

To avoid conflicts of jurisdiction, consideration should be given to the devising and applying mechanisms for determining the best value for prosecution of defendants in the interest of justice in cases that are subject to prosecution in more than one country.

Recommendation 40

Countries should have procedures in place to extradite, where possible, individuals charged with money laundering offences or related offences. With respect to its national legal system, each country should recognise money laundering as an extraditable offence. Subject to these legal frameworks, countries may consider simplifying extradition by allowing direct transmission of extradition requests between appropriate ministries, extraditing persons based only on warrants of arrests or judgements, extraditing their nationals, and/or introducing a simplified extradition of consenting persons who waive formal extradition proceedings.

Annex to Recommendation 9: List of Financial Activities Undertaken by Business or Professions which are not Financial Institutions

1. Acceptance of deposits and other repayable funds from the public.
2. Lending.[1]
3. Financial leasing.
4. Money transmission services.
5. Issuing and managing means of payment (e.g. credit and debit cards, cheques, traveller's cheques and bankers' drafts).
6. Financial guarantees and commitments.
7. Trading for account of customers (spot, forward, swaps, futures, options) in:
   a. money market instruments;
   b. foreign exchange;
   c. exchange, interest rate and index instruments;
   d. commodity future trading.
8. Participation in securities issues and the provision of financial services related to such issues.
9. Individual and collective portfolio management.
10. Safekeeping and administration of cash or liquid securities on behalf of clients.
11. Life insurance and other investment related insurance.
12. Money changing.

1 Including, *inter alia*, consumer credit, mortgage credit, factoring, with or without recourse, and finance of commercial transactions including forfeiting.

Appendix 2: The Nine FATF Recommendations

Recognising the vital importance of taking action to combat the financing of terrorism, the FATF has agreed these Recommendations, which, when combined with the FATF Forty Recommendations on money laundering, set out the basic framework to detect, prevent and suppress the financing of terrorism and terrorist acts.

Special Recommendation I: Ratification and implementation of UN instruments

Each country should take immediate steps to ratify and to implement fully the 1999 United Nations International Convention for the Suppression of the Financing of Terrorism. Countries should also immediately implement the United Nations resolutions relating to the prevention and suppression of the financing of terrorist acts, particularly United Nations Security Council Resolution 1373.

Special Recommendation II: Criminalising the financing of terrorism and associated money laundering

Each country should criminalise the financing of terrorism, terrorist acts and terrorist organisations. Countries should ensure that such offences are designated as money laundering predicate offences.

Special Recommendation III: Freezing and confiscating terrorist assets

Each country should implement measures to freeze without delay funds or other assets of terrorists, those who finance terrorism and terrorist organisations in accordance with the United Nations resolutions relating to the prevention and suppression of the financing of terrorist acts. Each country should also adopt and implement measures, including legislative ones, which would enable the competent authorities to seize and confiscate property that is the proceeds of, or used in, or intended or allocated for use in, the financing of terrorism, terrorist acts or terrorist organisations.

Special Recommendation IV: Reporting suspicious transactions related to terrorism

If financial institutions, or other businesses or entities subject to anti-money laundering obligations, suspect or have reasonable grounds to suspect that funds are linked or related to, or are to be used for terrorism, terrorist acts or by terrorist organisations, they should be required to report promptly their suspicions to the competent authorities.

Special Recommendation V: International co-operation

Each country should afford another country, on the basis of a treaty, arrangement or other mechanism for mutual legal assistance or information exchange, the greatest possible measure of assistance in connection with criminal, civil enforcement, and administrative investigations, inquiries and proceedings relating to the financing of terrorism, terrorist acts and terrorist organisations.

Countries should also take all possible measures to ensure that they do not provide safe havens for individuals charged with the financing of terrorism, terrorist acts or terrorist organisations, and should have procedures in place to extradite, where possible, such individuals.

Special Recommendation VI: Alternative remittance

Each country should take measures to ensure that persons or legal entities, including agents, that provide a service for the transmission of money or value, including transmission through an informal money or value transfer system or network, should be licensed or registered and subject to all the FATF Recommendations that apply to banks and non-bank financial institutions. Each country should ensure that persons or legal entities that carry out this service illegally are subject to administrative, civil or criminal sanctions.

Special Recommendation VII: Wire transfers

Countries should take measures to require financial institutions, including money remitters, to include accurate and meaningful originator information (name, address and account number) on funds transfers and related messages that are sent, and the information should remain with the transfer or related message through the payment chain.

Countries should take measures to ensure that financial institutions, including money remitters, conduct enhanced scrutiny of and monitor for suspicious activity funds transfers which do not contain complete originator information (name, address and account number).

Special Recommendation VIII: Non-profit organisations

Countries should review the adequacy of laws and regulations that relate to entities that can be abused for the financing of terrorism. Non-profit organisations are particularly vulnerable, and countries should ensure that they cannot be misused:

(i) by terrorist organisations posing as legitimate entities;
(ii) to exploit legitimate entities as conduits for terrorist financing, including for the purpose of escaping asset freezing measures; and
(iii) to conceal or obscure the clandestine diversion of funds intended for legitimate purposes to terrorist organisations.

Special Recommendation IX. Cash couriers

Countries should have measures in place to detect the physical cross-border transportation of currency and bearer negotiable instruments, including a declaration system or other disclosure obligation. Countries should ensure that their competent authorities have the legal authority to stop or restrain currency or bearer negotiable instruments that are suspected to be related to terrorist financing or money laundering, or that are falsely declared or disclosed. Countries should ensure that effective, proportionate and dissuasive sanctions are available to deal with persons who make false declaration(s) or disclosure(s). In cases where the currency or bearer negotiable instruments are related to terrorist financing or money laundering, countries should also adopt measures, including legislative ones consistent with Recommendation 3 and Special Recommendation III, which would enable the confiscation of such currency or instruments.

Appendix 3: United Nations Convention Against Illicit Traffic in Narcotic Drugs And Psychotropic Substances

Adopted in Vienna, 19 December 1988 (excerpts)

The Parties to this Convention,

Deeply concerned by the magnitude of and rising trend in the illicit production of, demand for and traffic in narcotic drugs and psychotropic substances, which pose a serious threat to the health and welfare of human beings and adversely affect the economic, cultural and political foundations of society,

Recognizing the links between illicit traffic and other related organized criminal activities which undermine the legitimate economies and threaten the stability, security and sovereignty of States,

Recognizing also that illicit traffic is an international criminal activity, the suppression of which demands urgent attention and the highest priority,

Aware that illicit traffic generates large financial profits and wealth enabling transnational criminal organizations to penetrate, contaminate and corrupt the structures of government, legitimate commercial and financial business, and society at all its levels,

Determined to deprive persons engaged in illicit traffic of the proceeds of their criminal activities and thereby eliminate their main incentive for so doing, ...

Article 3

Offences and Sanctions

1. Each Party shall adopt such measures as may be necessary to establish as criminal offences under its domestic law, when committed intentionally:

...

(a) (v) The organization, management or financing of any [drug trafficking] offences;

(b) (i) The conversion or transfer of property, knowing that such property is derived from any [drug trafficking] offence, or from an act of participation in such offence or offences, for the purpose of concealing or disguising the illicit origin of the property or of assisting any person who is involved in the commission of such an offence or offences to evade the legal consequences of his actions;

(ii) The concealment or disguise of the true nature, source, location, disposition, movement, rights with respect to, or ownership of property, knowing that such property is derived from an offence or offences established in accordance with subparagraph (a) of this paragraph or from an act of participation in such an offence or offences;

(c) Subject to its constitutional principles and the basic concepts of its legal system:
(i) The acquisition, possession or use of property, knowing, at the time of receipt, that such property was derived from an offence or offences established in accordance with subparagraph (a) of this paragraph or from an act of participation in such offence or offences;

...

Article 5

Confiscation

1. Each Party shall adopt such measures as may be necessary to enable confiscation of:

(a) Proceeds derived from offences established in accordance with article 3, paragraph 1, or property the value of which corresponds to that of such proceeds;
(b) Narcotic drugs and psychotropic substances, materials and equipment or other instrumentalities used in or intended for use in any manner in offences established in accordance with article 3, paragraph 1.

2. Each Party shall also adopt such measures as may be necessary to enable its competent authorities to identify, trace, and freeze or seize proceeds, property, instrumentalities or any other things referred to in paragraph 1 of this article, for the purpose of eventual confiscation.

3. In order to carry out the measures referred to in this article, each Party shall empower its courts or other competent authorities to order that bank, financial or commercial records be made available or be seized. A Party shall not decline to act under the provisions of this paragraph on the ground of bank secrecy.

4. (a) Following a request made pursuant to this article by another Party having jurisdiction over an offence established in accordance with article 3, paragraph l, the Party in whose territory proceeds, property, instrumentalities or any other things referred to in paragraph l of this article are situated shall:
(i) Submit the request to its competent authorities for the purpose of obtaining an order of confiscation and, if such order is granted, give effect to it; or
(ii) Submit to its competent authorities, with a view to giving effect to it to the extent requested, an order of confiscation issued by the requesting Party in accordance with paragraph l of this article, in so far as it relates to proceeds, property, instrumentalities or any other things referred to in paragraph l situated in the territory of the requested Party.
(b) Following a request made pursuant to this article by another Party having jurisdiction over an offence established in accordance with article 3, paragraph

1, the requested Party shall take measures to identify, trace, and freeze or seize proceeds, property, instrumentalities or any other things referred to in paragraph 1 of this article for the purpose of eventual confiscation to be ordered either by the requesting Party or, pursuant to a request under subparagraph (a) of this paragraph, by the requested Party.
(c) The decisions or actions provided for in subparagraphs (a) and (b) of this paragraph shall be taken by the requested Party, in accordance with and subject to the provisions of its domestic law and its procedural rules or any bilateral or multilateral treaty, agreement or arrangement to which it may be bound in relation to the requesting Party.
(d) The provisions of article 7, paragraphs 6 to 19 are applicable mutatis mutandis. In addition to the information specified in article 7, paragraph 10, requests made pursuant to this article shall contain the following:
(i) In the case of a request pertaining to subparagraph (a) (i) of this paragraph, a description of the property to be confiscated and a statement of the facts relied upon by the requesting Party sufficient to enable the requested Party to seek the order under its domestic law;
(ii) In the case of a request pertaining to subparagraph (a)(ii), a legally admissible copy of an order of confiscation issued by the requesting Party upon which the request is based, a statement of the facts and information as to the extent to which the execution of the order is requested;
(iii) In the case of a request pertaining to subparagraph (b), a statement of the facts relied upon by the requesting Party and a description of the actions requested.
(e) Each Party shall furnish to the Secretary-General the text of any of its laws and regulations which give effect to this paragraph and the text of any subsequent changes to such laws and regulations.
(f) If a Party elects to make the taking of the measures referred to in subparagraphs (a) and (b) of this paragraph conditional on the existence of a relevant treaty, that Party shall consider this Convention as the necessary and sufficient treaty basis.
(g) The Parties shall seek to conclude bilateral and multilateral treaties, agreements or arrangements to enhance the effectiveness of international cooperation pursuant to this article.

5. (a) Proceeds or property confiscated by a Party pursuant to paragraph 1 or paragraph 4 of this article shall be disposed of by that Party according to its domestic law and administrative procedures.
(b) When acting on the request of another Party in accordance with this article, a Party may give special consideration to concluding agreements on:
(i) Contributing the value of such proceeds and property, or funds derived from the sale of such proceeds or property, or a substantial part thereof, to intergovernmental bodies specializing in the fight against illicit traffic in and abuse of narcotic drugs and psychotropic substances;
(ii) Sharing with other Parties, on a regular or case-by-case basis, such proceeds or property, or funds derived from the sale of such proceeds or property, in accordance

with its domestic law, administrative procedures or bilateral or multilateral agreements entered into for this purpose.

6. (a) If proceeds have been transformed or converted into other property, such property shall be liable to the measures referred to in this article instead of the proceeds.
(b) If proceeds have been intermingled with property acquired from legitimate sources, such property shall, without prejudice to any powers relating to seizure or freezing, be liable to confiscation up to the assessed value of the intermingled proceeds.
(c) Income or other benefits derived from:
(i) Proceeds;
(ii) Property into which proceeds have been transformed or converted; or
(iii) Property with which proceeds have been intermingled
shall also be liable to the measures referred to in this article, in the same manner and to the same extent as proceeds.

7. Each Party may consider ensuring that the onus of proof be reversed regarding the lawful origin of alleged proceeds or other property liable to confiscation, to the extent that such action is consistent with the principles of its domestic law and with the nature of the judicial and other proceedings.

8. The provisions of this article shall not be construed as prejudicing the rights of bona fide third parties.

9. Nothing contained in this article shall affect the principle that the measures to which it refers shall be defined and implemented in accordance with and subject to the provisions of the domestic law of a Party.

United Nations Convention Against Transnational Organized Crime

Adopted by the General Assembly on 15 November 2000 (excerpts)

Article 2

Use of terms

For the purposes of this Convention:

(a) "Organized criminal group" shall mean a structured group of three or more persons, existing for a period of time and acting in concert with the aim of committing one or more serious crimes or offences established in accordance

with this Convention, in order to obtain, directly or indirectly, a financial or other material benefit;
(b) "Serious crime" shall mean conduct constituting an offence punishable by a maximum deprivation of liberty of at least four years or a more serious penalty;
(c) "Structured group" shall mean a group that is not randomly formed for the immediate commission of an offence and that does not need to have formally defined roles for its members, continuity of its membership or a developed structure;
(d) "Property" shall mean assets of every kind, whether corporeal or incorporeal, movable or immovable, tangible or intangible, and legal documents or instruments evidencing title to, or interest in, such assets;
(e) "Proceeds of crime" shall mean any property derived from or obtained, directly or indirectly, through the commission of an offence;
(f) "Freezing" or "seizure" shall mean temporarily prohibiting the transfer, conversion, disposition or movement of property or temporarily assuming custody or control of property on the basis of an order issued by a court or other competent authority;
(g) "Confiscation", which includes forfeiture where applicable, shall mean the permanent deprivation of property by order of a court or other competent authority;
(h) "Predicate offence" shall mean any offence as a result of which proceeds have been generated that may become the subject of an offence as defined in article 6 of this Convention;
(i) "Controlled delivery" shall mean the technique of allowing illicit or suspect consignments to pass out of, through or into the territory of one or more States, with the knowledge and under the supervision of their competent authorities, with a view to the investigation of an offence and the identification of persons involved in the commission of the offence;
(j) "Regional economic integration organization" shall mean an organization constituted by sovereign States of a given region, to which its member States have transferred competence in respect of matters governed by this Convention and which has been duly authorised, in accordance with its internal procedures, to sign, ratify, accept, approve or accede to it; references to "States Parties" under this Convention shall apply to such organizations within the limits of their competence.
...

Article 6

Criminalisation of the laundering of proceeds of crime

1. Each State Party shall adopt, in accordance with fundamental principles of its domestic law, such legislative and other measures as may be necessary to establish as criminal offences, when committed intentionally:

(a) (i) The conversion or transfer of property, knowing that such property is the proceeds of crime, for the purpose of concealing or disguising the illicit origin of the property or of helping any person who is involved in the commission of the predicate offence to evade the legal consequences of his or her action;
(ii) The concealment or disguise of the true nature, source, location, disposition, movement or ownership of or rights with respect to property, knowing that such property is the proceeds of crime;
(b) Subject to the basic concepts of its legal system:
(i) The acquisition, possession or use of property, knowing, at the time of receipt, that such property is the proceeds of crime;
(ii) Participation in, association with or conspiracy to commit, attempts to commit and aiding, abetting, facilitating and counselling the commission of any of the offences established in accordance with this article.

2. For purposes of implementing or applying paragraph 1 of this article:

(a) Each State Party shall seek to apply paragraph 1 of this article to the widest range of predicate offences;
(b) Each State Party shall include as predicate offences all serious crime as defined in article 2 of this Convention and the offences established in accordance with articles 5, 8 and 23 of this Convention. In the case of States Parties whose legislation sets out a list of specific predicate offences, they shall, at a minimum, include in such list a comprehensive range of offences associated with organized criminal groups;
(c) For the purposes of subparagraph (b), predicate offences shall include offences committed both within and outside the jurisdiction of the State Party in question. However, offences committed outside the jurisdiction of a State Party shall constitute predicate offences only when the relevant conduct is a criminal offence under the domestic law of the State where it is committed and would be a criminal offence under the domestic law of the State Party implementing or applying this article had it been committed there;
(d) Each State Party shall furnish copies of its laws that give effect to this article and of any subsequent changes to such laws or a description thereof to the Secretary-General of the United Nations;
(e) If required by fundamental principles of the domestic law of a State Party, it may be provided that the offences set forth in paragraph 1 of this article do not apply to the persons who committed the predicate offence;
(f) Knowledge, intent or purpose required as an element of an offence set forth in paragraph 1 of this article may be inferred from objective factual circumstances.
Article 7 Measures to combat money-laundering

1. Each State Party:

(a) Shall institute a comprehensive domestic regulatory and supervisory regime for banks and non-bank financial institutions and, where appropriate, other bodies particularly susceptible to money-laundering, within its competence, in order to deter and detect all forms of money-laundering, which regime shall emphasise requirements for customer identification, record-keeping and the reporting of suspicious transactions;
(b) Shall, without prejudice to articles 18 and 27 of this Convention, ensure that administrative, regulatory, law enforcement and other authorities dedicated to combating money-laundering (including, where appropriate under domestic law, judicial authorities) have the ability to cooperate and exchange information at the national and international levels within the conditions prescribed by its domestic law and, to that end, shall consider the establishment of a financial intelligence unit to serve as a national centre for the collection, analysis and dissemination of information regarding potential money-laundering.

2. States Parties shall consider implementing feasible measures to detect and monitor the movement of cash and appropriate negotiable instruments across their borders, subject to safeguards to ensure proper use of information and without impeding in any way the movement of legitimate capital. Such measures may include a requirement that individuals and businesses report the cross-border transfer of substantial quantities of cash and appropriate negotiable instruments.

3. In establishing a domestic regulatory and supervisory regime under the terms of this article, and without prejudice to any other article of this Convention, States Parties are called upon to use as a guideline the relevant initiatives of regional, interregional and multilateral organizations against money-laundering.

4. States Parties shall endeavour to develop and promote global, regional, sub regional and bilateral cooperation among judicial, law enforcement and financial regulatory authorities in order to combat money-laundering.
...

Article 10

Liability of legal persons

1. Each State Party shall adopt such measures as may be necessary, consistent with its legal principles, to establish the liability of legal persons for participation in serious crimes involving an organized criminal group and for the offences established in accordance with articles 5, 6, 8 and 23 of this Convention.

2. Subject to the legal principles of the State Party, the liability of legal persons may be criminal, civil or administrative.

3. Such liability shall be without prejudice to the criminal liability of the natural persons who have committed the offences.

4. Each State Party shall, in particular, ensure that legal persons held liable in accordance with this article are subject to effective, proportionate and dissuasive criminal or non-criminal sanctions, including monetary sanctions.

Article 11

Prosecution, adjudication and sanctions

1. Each State Party shall make the commission of an offence established in accordance with articles 5, 6, 8 and 23 of this Convention liable to sanctions that take into account the gravity of that offence.

2. Each State Party shall endeavour to ensure that any discretionary legal powers under its domestic law relating to the prosecution of persons for offences covered by this Convention are exercised to maximise the effectiveness of law enforcement measures in respect of those offences and with due regard to the need to deter the commission of such offences.

3. In the case of offences established in accordance with articles 5, 6, 8 and 23 of this Convention, each State Party shall take appropriate measures, in accordance with its domestic law and with due regard to the rights of the defence, to seek to ensure that conditions imposed in connection with decisions on release pending trial or appeal take into consideration the need to ensure the presence of the defendant at subsequent criminal proceedings.

4. Each State Party shall ensure that its courts or other competent authorities bear in mind the grave nature of the offences covered by this Convention when considering the eventuality of early release or parole of persons convicted of such offences.

5. Each State Party shall, where appropriate, establish under its domestic law a long statute of limitations period in which to commence proceedings for any offence covered by this Convention and a longer period where the alleged offender has evaded the administration of justice.

6. Nothing contained in this Convention shall affect the principle that the description of the offences established in accordance with this Convention and of

the applicable legal defences or other legal principles controlling the lawfulness of conduct is reserved to the domestic law of a State Party and that such offences shall be prosecuted and punished in accordance with that law.

Article 12

Confiscation and seizure

1. States Parties shall adopt, to the greatest extent possible within their domestic legal systems, such measures as may be necessary to enable confiscation of:

(a) Proceeds of crime derived from offences covered by this Convention or property the value of which corresponds to that of such proceeds;
(b) Property, equipment or other instrumentalities used in or destined for use in offences covered by this Convention.

2. States Parties shall adopt such measures as may be necessary to enable the identification, tracing, freezing or seizure of any item referred to in paragraph 1 of this article for the purpose of eventual confiscation.

3. If proceeds of crime have been transformed or converted, in part or in full, into other property, such property shall be liable to the measures referred to in this article instead of the proceeds.

4. If proceeds of crime have been intermingled with property acquired from legitimate sources, such property shall, without prejudice to any powers relating to freezing or seizure, be liable to confiscation up to the assessed value of the intermingled proceeds.

5. Income or other benefits derived from proceeds of crime, from property into which proceeds of crime have been transformed or converted or from property with which proceeds of crime have been intermingled shall also be liable to the measures referred to in this article, in the same manner and to the same extent as proceeds of crime.

6. For the purposes of this article and article 13 of this Convention, each State Party shall empower its courts or other competent authorities to order that bank, financial or commercial records be made available or be seized. States Parties shall not decline to act under the provisions of this paragraph on the ground of bank secrecy.

7. States Parties may consider the possibility of requiring that an offender demonstrate the lawful origin of alleged proceeds of crime or other property

liable to confiscation, to the extent that such a requirement is consistent with the principles of their domestic law and with the nature of the judicial and other proceedings.

8. The provisions of this article shall not be construed to prejudice the rights of bona fide third parties.

9. Nothing contained in this article shall affect the principle that the measures to which it refers shall be defined and implemented in accordance with and subject to the provisions of the domestic law of a State Party.

Article 13

International cooperation for purposes of confiscation

1. A State Party that has received a request from another State Party having jurisdiction over an offence covered by this Convention for confiscation of proceeds of crime, property, equipment or other instrumentalities referred to in article 12, paragraph 1, of this Convention situated in its territory shall, to the greatest extent possible within its domestic legal system:

(a) Submit the request to its competent authorities for the purpose of obtaining an order of confiscation and, if such an order is granted, give effect to it; or
(b) Submit to its competent authorities, with a view to giving effect to it to the extent requested, an order of confiscation issued by a court in the territory of the requesting State Party in accordance with article 12, paragraph 1, of this Convention insofar as it relates to proceeds of crime, property, equipment or other instrumentalities referred to in article 12, paragraph 1, situated in the territory of the requested State Party.

2. Following a request made by another State Party having jurisdiction over an offence covered by this Convention, the requested State Party shall take measures to identify, trace and freeze or seize proceeds of crime, property, equipment or other instrumentalities referred to in article 12, paragraph 1, of this Convention for the purpose of eventual confiscation to be ordered either by the requesting State Party or, pursuant to a request under paragraph 1 of this article, by the requested State Party.

3. The provisions of article 18 of this Convention are applicable, mutatis mutandis, to this article. In addition to the information specified in article 18, paragraph 15, requests made pursuant to this article shall contain:

(a) In the case of a request pertaining to paragraph 1 (a) of this article, a description of the property to be confiscated and a statement of the facts relied upon by the requesting State Party sufficient to enable the requested State Party to seek the order under its domestic law;
(b) In the case of a request pertaining to paragraph 1 (b) of this article, a legally admissible copy of an order of confiscation upon which the request is based issued by the requesting State Party, a statement of the facts and information as to the extent to which execution of the order is requested;
(c) In the case of a request pertaining to paragraph 2 of this article, a statement of the facts relied upon by the requesting State Party and a description of the actions requested.

4. The decisions or actions provided for in paragraphs 1 and 2 of this article shall be taken by the requested State Party in accordance with and subject to the provisions of its domestic law and its procedural rules or any bilateral or multilateral treaty, agreement or arrangement to which it may be bound in relation to the requesting State Party.

5. Each State Party shall furnish copies of its laws and regulations that give effect to this article and of any subsequent changes to such laws and regulations or a description thereof to the Secretary-General of the United Nations.

6. If a State Party elects to make the taking of the measures referred to in paragraphs 1 and 2 of this article conditional on the existence of a relevant treaty, that State Party shall consider this Convention the necessary and sufficient treaty basis.

7. Cooperation under this article may be refused by a State Party if the offence to which the request relates is not an offence covered by this Convention.

8. The provisions of this article shall not be construed to prejudice the rights of bona fide third parties.

9. States Parties shall consider concluding bilateral or multilateral treaties, agreements or arrangements to enhance the effectiveness of international cooperation undertaken pursuant to this article.

Article 14

Disposal of confiscated proceeds of crime or property

1. Proceeds of crime or property confiscated by a State Party pursuant to articles 12 or 13, paragraph 1, of this Convention shall be disposed of by that State Party in accordance with its domestic law and administrative procedures.

2. When acting on the request made by another State Party in accordance with article 13 of this Convention, States Parties shall, to the extent permitted by domestic law and if so requested, give priority consideration to returning the confiscated proceeds of crime or property to the requesting State Party so that it can give compensation to the victims of the crime or return such proceeds of crime or property to their legitimate owners.

3. When acting on the request made by another State Party in accordance with articles 12 and 13 of this Convention, a State Party may give special consideration to concluding agreements or arrangements on:
(a) Contributing the value of such proceeds of crime or property or funds derived from the sale of such proceeds of crime or property or a part thereof to the account designated in accordance with article 30, paragraph 2 (c), of this Convention and to intergovernmental bodies specialising in the fight against organized crime;
(b) Sharing with other States Parties, on a regular or case-by-case basis, such proceeds of crime or property, or funds derived from the sale of such proceeds of crime or property, in accordance with its domestic law or administrative procedures.

Article 15

Jurisdiction

1. Each State Party shall adopt such measures as may be necessary to establish its jurisdiction over the offences established in accordance with articles 5, 6, 8 and 23 of this Convention when:
(a) The offence is committed in the territory of that State Party; or
(b) The offence is committed on board a vessel that is flying the flag of that State Party or an aircraft that is registered under the laws of that State Party at the time that the offence is committed.

2. Subject to article 4 of this Convention, a State Party may also establish its jurisdiction over any such offence when:
(a) The offence is committed against a national of that State Party;
(b) The offence is committed by a national of that State Party or a stateless person who has his or her habitual residence in its territory; or
(c) The offence is:
(i) One of those established in accordance with article 5, paragraph 1, of this Convention and is committed outside its territory with a view to the commission of a serious crime within its territory;
(ii) One of those established in accordance with article 6, paragraph 1 (b) (ii), of this Convention and is committed outside its territory with a view to the commission

of an offence established in accordance with article 6, paragraph 1 (a) (i) or (ii) or (b) (i), of this Convention within its territory.

3. For the purposes of article 16, paragraph 10, of this Convention, each State Party shall adopt such measures as may be necessary to establish its jurisdiction over the offences covered by this Convention when the alleged offender is present in its territory and it does not extradite such person solely on the ground that he or she is one of its nationals.

4. Each State Party may also adopt such measures as may be necessary to establish its jurisdiction over the offences covered by this Convention when the alleged offender is present in its territory and it does not extradite him or her.

5. If a State Party exercising its jurisdiction under paragraph 1 or 2 of this article has been notified, or has otherwise learned, that one or more other States Parties are conducting an investigation, prosecution or judicial proceeding in respect of the same conduct, the competent authorities of those States Parties shall, as appropriate, consult one another with a view to coordinating their actions.

6. Without prejudice to norms of general international law, this Convention does not exclude the exercise of any criminal jurisdiction established by a State Party in accordance with its domestic law.

...

Article 27

Law enforcement cooperation

1. States Parties shall cooperate closely with one another, consistent with their respective domestic legal and administrative systems, to enhance the effectiveness of law enforcement action to combat the offences covered by this Convention. Each State Party shall, in particular, adopt effective measures:

(a) To enhance and, where necessary, to establish channels of communication between their competent authorities, agencies and services in order to facilitate the secure and rapid exchange of information concerning all aspects of the offences covered by this Convention, including, if the States Parties concerned deem it appropriate, links with other criminal activities;

(b) To cooperate with other States Parties in conducting inquiries with respect to offences covered by this Convention concerning:

(i) The identity, whereabouts and activities of persons suspected of involvement in such offences or the location of other persons concerned;

(ii) The movement of proceeds of crime or property derived from the commission of such offences;

(iii) The movement of property, equipment or other instrumentalities used or intended for use in the commission of such offences;
(c) To provide, when appropriate, necessary items or quantities of substances for analytical or investigative purposes;
(d) To facilitate effective coordination between their competent authorities, agencies and services and to promote the exchange of personnel and other experts, including, subject to bilateral agreements or arrangements between the States Parties concerned, the posting of liaison officers;
(e) To exchange information with other States Parties on specific means and methods used by organized criminal groups, including, where applicable, routes and conveyances and the use of false identities, altered or false documents or other means of concealing their activities;
(f) To exchange information and coordinate administrative and other measures taken as appropriate for the purpose of early identification of the offences covered by this Convention.

2. With a view to giving effect to this Convention, States Parties shall consider entering into bilateral or multilateral agreements or arrangements on direct cooperation between their law enforcement agencies and, where such agreements or arrangements already exist, amending them. In the absence of such agreements or arrangements between the States Parties concerned, the Parties may consider this Convention as the basis for mutual law enforcement cooperation in respect of the offences covered by this Convention. Whenever appropriate, States Parties shall make full use of agreements or arrangements, including international or regional organizations, to enhance the cooperation between their law enforcement agencies.

3. States Parties shall endeavour to cooperate within their means to respond to transnational organized crime committed through the use of modern technology.
...

Article 29

Training and technical assistance

1. Each State Party shall, to the extent necessary, initiate, develop or improve specific training programmes for its law enforcement personnel, including prosecutors, investigating magistrates and customs personnel, and other personnel charged with the prevention, detection and control of the offences covered by this Convention. Such programmes may include secondments and exchanges of staff. Such programmes shall deal, in particular and to the extent permitted by domestic law, with the following:

(a) Methods used in the prevention, detection and control of the offences covered by this Convention;
(b) Routes and techniques used by persons suspected of involvement in offences covered by this Convention, including in transit States, and appropriate countermeasures;
(c) Monitoring of the movement of contraband;
(d) Detection and monitoring of the movements of proceeds of crime, property, equipment or other instrumentalities and methods used for the transfer, concealment or disguise of such proceeds, property, equipment or other instrumentalities, as well as methods used in combating money-laundering and other financial crimes;
(e) Collection of evidence;
(f) Control techniques in free trade zones and free ports;
(g) Modern law enforcement equipment and techniques, including electronic surveillance, controlled deliveries and undercover operations;
(h) Methods used in combating transnational organized crime committed through the use of computers, telecommunications networks or other forms of modern technology; and
(i) Methods used in the protection of victims and witnesses.

2. States Parties shall assist one another in planning and implementing research and training programmes designed to share expertise in the areas referred to in paragraph 1 of this article and to that end shall also, when appropriate, use regional and international conferences and seminars to promote cooperation and to stimulate discussion on problems of mutual concern, including the special problems and needs of transit States.

3. States Parties shall promote training and technical assistance that will facilitate extradition and mutual legal assistance. Such training and technical assistance may include language training, secondments and exchanges between personnel in central authorities or agencies with relevant responsibilities.

4. In the case of existing bilateral and multilateral agreements or arrangements, States Parties shall strengthen, to the extent necessary, efforts to maximise operational and training activities within international and regional organizations and within other relevant bilateral and multilateral agreements or arrangements.

Article 30

Other measures: implementation of the Convention through economic development and technical assistance

1. States Parties shall take measures conducive to the optimal implementation of this Convention to the extent possible, through international cooperation, taking

into account the negative effects of organized crime on society in general, in particular on sustainable development.

2. States Parties shall make concrete efforts to the extent possible and in coordination with each other, as well as with international and regional organizations:
(a) To enhance their cooperation at various levels with developing countries, with a view to strengthening the capacity of the latter to prevent and combat transnational organized crime;
(b) To enhance financial and material assistance to support the efforts of developing countries to fight transnational organized crime effectively and to help them implement this Convention successfully;
(c) To provide technical assistance to developing countries and countries with economies in transition to assist them in meeting their needs for the implementation of this Convention. To that end, States Parties shall endeavour to make adequate and regular voluntary contributions to an account specifically designated for that purpose in a United Nations funding mechanism. States Parties may also give special consideration, in accordance with their domestic law and the provisions of this Convention, to contributing to the aforementioned account a percentage of the money or of the corresponding value of proceeds of crime or property confiscated in accordance with the provisions of this Convention;
(d) To encourage and persuade other States and financial institutions as appropriate to join them in efforts in accordance with this article, in particular by providing more training programmes and modern equipment to developing countries in order to assist them in achieving the objectives of this Convention.

3. To the extent possible, these measures shall be without prejudice to existing foreign assistance commitments or to other financial cooperation arrangements at the bilateral, regional or international level.

4. States Parties may conclude bilateral or multilateral agreements or arrangements on material and logistical assistance, taking into consideration the financial arrangements necessary for the means of international cooperation provided for by this Convention to be effective and for the prevention, detection and control of transnational organized crime.
...

Article 32

Conference of the Parties to the Convention

1. A Conference of the Parties to the Convention is hereby established to improve the capacity of States Parties to combat transnational organized crime and to promote and review the implementation of this Convention.

2. The Secretary-General of the United Nations shall convene the Conference of the Parties not later than one year following the entry into force of this Convention. The Conference of the Parties shall adopt rules of procedure and rules governing the activities set forth in paragraphs 3 and 4 of this article (including rules concerning payment of expenses incurred in carrying out those activities).
3. The Conference of the Parties shall agree upon mechanisms for achieving the objectives mentioned in paragraph 1 of this article, including:
(a) Facilitating activities by States Parties under articles 29, 30 and 31 of this Convention, including by encouraging the mobilization of voluntary contributions;
(b) Facilitating the exchange of information among States Parties on patterns and trends in transnational organized crime and on successful practices for combating it;
(c) Cooperating with relevant international and regional organizations and non-governmental organizations;
(d) Reviewing periodically the implementation of this Convention;
(e) Making recommendations to improve this Convention and its implementation.

4. For the purpose of paragraphs 3 (d) and (e) of this article, the Conference of the Parties shall acquire the necessary knowledge of the measures taken by States Parties in implementing this Convention and the difficulties encountered by them in doing so through information provided by them and through such supplemental review mechanisms as may be established by the Conference of the Parties.

5. Each State Party shall provide the Conference of the Parties with information on its programmes, plans and practices, as well as legislative and administrative measures to implement this Convention, as required by the Conference of the Parties.
...

Article 34

Implementation of the Convention

1. Each State Party shall take the necessary measures, including legislative and administrative measures, in accordance with fundamental principles of its domestic law, to ensure the implementation of its obligations under this Convention.

2. The offences established in accordance with articles 5, 6, 8 and 23 of this Convention shall be established in the domestic law of each State Party independently of the transnational nature or the involvement of an organized criminal group as described in article 3, paragraph 1, of this Convention, except to the extent that article 5 of this Convention would require the involvement of an organized criminal group.

3. Each State Party may adopt more strict or severe measures than those provided for by this Convention for preventing and combating transnational organized crime.

Political Declaration And Action Plan Against Money Laundering

adopted at the Twentieth Special Session of the United Nations General Assembly devoted to "countering the world drug problem together", New York, 10 June 1998 (excerpts)

Political Declaration

Drugs destroy lives and communities, undermine sustainable human development and generate crime. Drugs affect all sectors of society in all countries; in particular, drug abuse affects the freedom and development of young people, the world's most valuable asset. Drugs are a grave threat to the health and well-being of all mankind, the independence of States, democracy, the stability of nations, the structure of all societies, and the dignity and hope of millions of people and their families; therefore:
We, the States Members of the United Nations,
Concerned about the serious world drug problem, having assembled at the twentieth special session of the General Assembly to consider enhanced action to tackle it in a spirit of trust and cooperation,

1. Reaffirm our unwavering determination and commitment to overcoming the world drug problem through domestic and international strategies to reduce both the illicit supply of and demand for drugs;
...
15. Undertake to make special efforts against the laundering of money linked to drug trafficking and, in that context, emphasize the importance of strengthening international, regional and sub regional cooperation, and recommend that States that have not yet done so adopt by the year 2003 national money-laundering legislation and programmes in accordance with relevant provisions of the United Nations Convention against the Illicit Traffic in Narcotic Drugs and Psychotropic Substances of 1988, as well as the measures for countering money-laundering, adopted at the present session;

16. Undertake to promote multilateral, regional, subregional and bilateral cooperation among judicial and law enforcement authorities to deal with criminal organizations involved in drug offences and related criminal activities, in accordance with the measures to promote judicial cooperation, adopted at

the present session, and encourage States to review and, where appropriate, to strengthen by the year 2003 the implementation of those measures;

...

20. Call upon all States to take into account the outcome of the present session when formulating national strategies and programmes and to report biennially to the Commission on Narcotic Drugs on their efforts to meet the above-mentioned goals and targets for the years 2003 and 2008, and request the Commission to analyse these reports in order to enhance the cooperative effort to combat the world drug problem.

These are new and serious promises which will be difficult to achieve, but we are resolved that such commitments will be met by practical action and the resources needed to ensure real and measurable results; Together we can meet this challenge.

Countering Money-Laundering

The General Assembly,

Recognizing that the problem of laundering of money derived from illicit trafficking in narcotic drugs and psychotropic substances, as well as from other serious crimes, has expanded internationally to become such a global threat to the integrity, reliability and stability of financial and trade systems and even government structures as to require countermeasures by the international community as a whole in order to deny safe havens to criminals and their illicit proceeds,

Recalling the provisions of the United Nations Convention against Illicit Traffic in Narcotic Drugs and Psychotropic Substances of 1988, according to which all parties to the Convention are required to establish money-laundering as a punishable offence and to adopt the measures necessary to enable the authorities to identify, trace and freeze or seize the proceeds of illicit drug trafficking,

Recalling Commission on Narcotic Drugs resolution 5 (XXXIX) of 24 April 1996, (21) in which the Commission noted that the forty recommendations of the Financial Action Task Force established by the heads of State or Government of the seven major industrialized countries and the President of the European Commission remained the standard by which the measures against money-laundering adopted by concerned States should be judged, as well as Economic and Social Council resolution 1997/40 of 21 July 1997, in which the Council took note with satisfaction of the document entitled "Anti-drug strategy in the hemisphere", approved by the Inter-American Drug Abuse Control Commission of the Organization of American States at its twentieth regular session, held at Buenos Aires in October 1996 and signed at Montevideo in December 1996, and urged the international community to take due account of the anti-drug strategy in the hemisphere as a significant contribution to the strengthening of the Global

Programme of Action adopted by the General Assembly at its seventeenth special session,(22)

Recognizing the political will expressed by the international community, especially as reflected in such initiatives as the Convention on Laundering, Search, Seizure and Confiscation of the Proceeds from Crime, adopted in 1990 by the Committee of Ministers of the Council of Europe, the Ministerial Communiqué of the Summit of the Americas Conference Concerning the Laundering of Proceeds and Instrumentalities of Crime, held at Buenos Aires in December 1995, and by such bodies as the Inter-American Drug Abuse Control Commission of the Organization of American States, the Asia/Pacific Group on Money Laundering, the Caribbean Financial Action Task Force, the Offshore Group of Banking Supervisors and the Commonwealth, all of which are well-recognized multilateral initiatives aimed at combating money-laundering and constitute legal or policy frameworks within which concerned States are defining and adopting measures against money-laundering,

Aware that the proceeds of illicit drug-trafficking and other illicit activities, which are laundered through banks and other financial institutions, constitute an obstacle to the implementation of policies designed to liberalize financial markets in order to attract legitimate investment, in that they distort those markets,

Emphasizing that there is a need to harmonize national legislation with a view to ensuring appropriate coordination of policies for combating money-laundering, without prejudice to the action each State is undertaking within its own jurisdiction to combat this form of criminality,

Recognizing the need to promote and develop effective mechanisms for the pursuit, freezing, seizure and confiscation of property obtained through or derived from illicit activities, so as to avoid its use by criminals,

Recognizing that only through international cooperation and the establishment of bilateral and multilateral information networks such as the Egmont Group, which will enable States to exchange information between competent authorities, will it be possible to combat effectively the problem of money-laundering,

Emphasizing the enormous efforts of a number of States to draw up and apply domestic legislation that identifies the activity of money-laundering as a criminal offence,

Realizing the importance of progress being made by all States in conforming to the relevant recommendations and the need for States to participate actively in international and regional initiatives designed to promote and strengthen the implementation of effective measures against money-laundering,

1. Strongly condemns the laundering of money derived from illicit drug trafficking and other serious crimes, as well as the use of the financial systems of States for that purpose;

2. Urges all States to implement the provisions against money-laundering that are contained in the United Nations Convention against Illicit Trafficking in Narcotic

Drugs and Psychotropic Substances of 1988 and the other relevant international instruments on money-laundering, in accordance with fundamental constitutional principles, by applying the following principles:
(a) Establishment of a legislative framework to criminalize the laundering of money derived from serious crimes in order to provide for the prevention, detection, investigation and prosecution of the crime of money-laundering through, inter alia:
(i) Identification, freezing, seizure and confiscation of the proceeds of crime;
(ii) International cooperation; and mutual legal assistance in cases involving money-laundering;
(iii) Inclusion of the crime of money-laundering in mutual legal assistance agreements for the purpose of ensuring judicial assistance in investigations, court cases or judicial proceedings relating to that crime;
(b) Establishment of an effective financial and regulatory regime to deny criminals and their illicit funds access to national and international financial systems, thus preserving the integrity of financial systems worldwide and ensuring compliance with laws and other regulations against money-laundering through:
(i) Customer identification and verification requirements applying the principle of "know your customer", in order to have available for competent authorities the necessary information on the identity of clients and the financial movements that they carry out;
(ii) Financial record-keeping;
(iii) Mandatory reporting of suspicious activity;
(iv) Removal of bank secrecy impediments to efforts directed at preventing, investigating and punishing money-laundering;
(v) Other relevant measures;
(c) Implementation of law enforcement measures to provide tools for, inter alia:
(i) Effective detection, investigation, prosecution and conviction of criminals engaging in money-laundering activity;
(ii) Extradition procedures;
(iii) Information-sharing mechanisms;

3. Calls upon the United Nations Office for Drug Control and Crime Prevention to continue to work, within the framework of its global programme against money-laundering, with relevant multilateral and regional institutions, organizations or bodies engaged in activities against money-laundering and drug trafficking and with international financial institutions to give effect to the above principles by providing training, advice and technical assistance to States upon request and where appropriate.

International Convention for the Suppression of the Financing of Terrorism

Preamble

The States Parties to this Convention,

Bearing in mind the purposes and principles of the Charter of the United Nations concerning the maintenance of international peace and security and the promotion of good-neighbourliness and friendly relations and cooperation among States,
Deeply concerned about the worldwide escalation of acts of terrorism in all its forms and manifestations,
Considering that the financing of terrorism is a matter of grave concern to the international community as a whole,
Noting that the number and seriousness of acts of international terrorism depend on the financing that terrorists may obtain,
Noting also that existing multilateral legal instruments do not expressly address such financing,
Being convinced of the urgent need to enhance international cooperation among States in devising and adopting effective measures for the prevention of the financing of terrorism, as well as for its suppression through the prosecution and punishment of its perpetrators,
Have agreed as follows:

Article 1

For the purposes of this Convention:

1. "Funds" means assets of every kind, whether tangible or intangible, movable or immovable, however acquired, and legal documents or instruments in any form, including electronic or digital, evidencing title to, or interest in, such assets, including, but not limited to, bank credits, travellers cheques, bank cheques, money orders, shares, securities, bonds, drafts, letters of credit.

2. "A State or governmental facility" means any permanent or temporary facility or conveyance that is used or occupied by representatives of a State, members of Government, the legislature or the judiciary or by officials or employees of a State or any other public authority or entity or by employees or officials of an intergovernmental organization in connection with their official duties.

3. "Proceed" means any funds derived from or obtained, directly or indirectly, through the commission of an offence set forth in article 2.

Article 2

1. Any person commits an offence within the meaning of this Convention if that person by any means, directly or indirectly, unlawfully and wilfully, provides or collects funds with the intention that they should be used or in the knowledge that they are to be used, in full or in part, in order to carry out:
Money Laundering and the Financing of Terrorism:
(a) An act which constitutes an offence within the scope of and as defined in one of the treaties listed in the annex; or
(b) Any other act intended to cause death or serious bodily injury to a civilian, or to any other person not taking an active part in the hostilities in a situation of armed conflict, when the purpose of such act, by its nature or context, is to intimidate a population, or to compel a government or an international organization to do or to abstain from doing any act.

2. (a) On depositing its instrument of ratification, acceptance, approval or accession, a State Party which is not a party to a treaty listed in the annex may declare that, in the application of this Convention to the State Party, the treaty shall be deemed not to be included in the annex referred to in paragraph 1, subparagraph (a). The declaration shall cease to have effect as soon as the treaty enters into force for the State Party, which shall notify the depositary of this fact;
(b) When a State Party ceases to be a party to a treaty listed in the annex, it may make a declaration as provided for in this article, with respect to that treaty.

3. For an act to constitute an offence set forth in paragraph 1, it shall not be necessary that the funds were actually used to carry out an offence referred to in paragraph 1, subparagraphs (a) or (b).

4. Any person also commits an offence if that person attempts to commit an offence as set forth in paragraph 1 of this article.

5. Any person also commits an offence if that person:
(a) Participates as an accomplice in an offence as set forth in paragraph 1 or 4 of this article;
(b) Organizes or directs others to commit an offence as set forth in paragraph 1 or 4 of this article;
(c) Contributes to the commission of one or more offences as set forth in paragraphs 1 or 4 of this article by a group of persons acting with a common purpose. Such contribution shall be intentional and shall either:
(i) Be made with the aim of furthering the criminal activity or criminal purpose of the group, where such activity or purpose involves the commission of an offence as set forth in paragraph 1 of this article; or
(ii) Be made in the knowledge of the intention of the group to commit an offence as set forth in paragraph 1 of this article.

Article 3

This Convention shall not apply where the offence is committed within a single State, the alleged offender is a national of that State and is present in the territory of that State and no other State has a basis under article 7, paragraph 1, or article 7, paragraph 2, to exercise jurisdiction, except that the provisions of articles 12 to 18 shall, as appropriate, apply in those cases.

Article 4

Each State Party shall adopt such measures as may be necessary:
(a) To establish as criminal offences under its domestic law the offences set forth in article 2;
(b) To make those offences punishable by appropriate penalties which take into account the grave nature of the offences.

Article 5

1. Each State Party, in accordance with its domestic legal principles, shall take the necessary measures to enable a legal entity located in its territory or organized under its laws to be held liable when a person responsible for the management or control of that legal entity has, in that capacity, committed an offence set forth in article 2. Such liability may be criminal, civil or administrative.

2. Such liability is incurred without prejudice to the criminal liability of individuals having committed the offences.

3. Each State Party shall ensure, in particular, that legal entities liable in accordance with paragraph 1 above are subject to effective, proportionate and dissuasive criminal, civil or administrative sanctions. Such sanctions may include monetary sanctions.

Article 6

Each State Party shall adopt such measures as may be necessary, including, where appropriate, domestic legislation, to ensure that criminal acts within the scope of this Convention are under no circumstances justifiable by considerations of a political, philosophical, ideological, racial, ethnic, religious or other similar nature.

Article 7

1. Each State Party shall take such measures as may be necessary to establish its jurisdiction over the offences set forth in article 2 when:
(a) The offence is committed in the territory of that State;
(b) The offence is committed on board a vessel flying the flag of that State or an aircraft registered under the laws of that State at the time the offence is committed;
(c) The offence is committed by a national of that State.
2. A State Party may also establish its jurisdiction over any such offence when:
(a) The offence was directed towards or resulted in the carrying out of an offence referred to in article 2, paragraph 1, subparagraph (a) or (b), in the territory of or against a national of that State;
(b) The offence was directed towards or resulted in the carrying out of an offence referred to in article 2, paragraph 1, subparagraph (a) or (b), against a State or government facility of that State abroad, including diplomatic or consular premises of that State;
(c) The offence was directed towards or resulted in an offence referred to in article

2, paragraph 1, subparagraph (a) or (b), committed in an attempt to compel that State to do or abstain from doing any act;
(d) The offence is committed by a stateless person who has his or her habitual residence in the territory of that State;
(e) The offence is committed on board an aircraft which is operated by the Government of that State.

3. Upon ratifying, accepting, approving or acceding to this Convention, each State Party shall notify the Secretary-General of the United Nations of the jurisdiction it has established in accordance with paragraph 2. Should any change take place, the State Party concerned shall immediately notify the Secretary-General.

4. Each State Party shall likewise take such measures as may be necessary to establish its jurisdiction over the offences set forth in article 2 in cases where the alleged offender is present in its territory and it does not extradite that person to any of the States Parties that have established their jurisdiction in accordance with paragraphs 1 or 2.

5. When more than one State Party claims jurisdiction over the offences set forth in article 2, the relevant States Parties shall strive to coordinate their actions appropriately, in particular concerning the conditions for prosecution and the modalities for mutual legal assistance.

6. Without prejudice to the norms of general international law, this Convention does not exclude the exercise of any criminal jurisdiction established by a State Party in accordance with its domestic law.

Article 8

1. Each State Party shall take appropriate measures, in accordance with its domestic legal principles, for the identification, detection and freezing or seizure of any funds used or allocated for the purpose of committing the offences set forth in article 2 as well as the proceeds derived from such offences, for purposes of possible forfeiture.

2. Each State Party shall take appropriate measures, in accordance with its domestic legal principles, for the forfeiture of funds used or allocated for the purpose of committing the offences set forth in article 2 and the proceeds derived from such offences.

3. Each State Party concerned may give consideration to concluding agreements on the sharing with other States Parties, on a regular or case-by-case basis, of the funds derived from the forfeitures referred to in this article.

4. Each State Party shall consider establishing mechanisms whereby the funds derived from the forfeitures referred to in this article are utilized to compensate the victims of offences referred to in article 2, paragraph 1, subparagraph (a) or (b), or their families.

5. The provisions of this article shall be implemented without prejudice to the rights of third parties acting in good faith.

Article 9

1. Upon receiving information that a person who has committed or who is alleged to have committed an offence set forth in article 2 may be present in its territory, the State Party concerned shall take such measures as may be necessary under its domestic law to investigate the facts contained in the information.

2. Upon being satisfied that the circumstances so warrant, the State Party in whose territory the offender or alleged offender is present shall take the appropriate measures under its domestic law so as to ensure that person's presence for the purpose of prosecution or extradition.

...

Article 10

1. The State Party in the territory of which the alleged offender is present shall, in cases to which article 7 applies, if it does not extradite that person, be obliged,

without exception whatsoever and whether or not the offence was committed in its territory, to submit the case without undue delay to its competent authorities for the purpose of prosecution, through proceedings in accordance with the laws of that State. Those authorities shall take their decision in the same manner as in the case of any other offence of a grave nature under the law of that State.

2. Whenever a State Party is permitted under its domestic law to extradite or otherwise surrender one of its nationals only upon the condition that the person will be returned to that State to serve the sentence imposed as a result of the trial or proceeding for which the extradition or surrender of the person was sought, and this State and the State seeking the extradition of the person agree with this option and other terms they may deem appropriate, such a conditional extradition or surrender shall be sufficient to discharge the obligation set forth in paragraph 1.

Article 11

1. The offences set forth in article 2 shall be deemed to be included as extraditable offences in any extradition treaty existing between any of the States Parties before the entry into force of this Convention. States Parties undertake to include such offences as extraditable offences in every extradition treaty to be subsequently concluded between them.

2. When a State Party which makes extradition conditional on the existence of a treaty receives a request for extradition from another State Party with which it has no extradition treaty, the requested State Party may, at its option, consider this Convention as a legal basis for extradition in respect of the offences set forth in article 2. Extradition shall be subject to the other conditions provided by the law of the requested State.

3. States Parties which do not make extradition conditional on the existence of a treaty shall recognize the offences set forth in article 2 as extraditable offences between themselves, subject to the conditions provided by the law of the requested State.

4. If necessary, the offences set forth in article 2 shall be treated, for the purposes of extradition between States Parties, as if they had been committed not only in the place in which they occurred but also in the territory of the States that have established jurisdiction in accordance with article 7, paragraphs 1 and 2.

5. The provisions of all extradition treaties and arrangements between States Parties with regard to offences set forth in article 2 shall be deemed to be modified as between States Parties to the extent that they are incompatible with this Convention.

Article 12

1. States Parties shall afford one another the greatest measure of assistance in connection with criminal investigations or criminal or extradition proceedings in respect of the offences set forth in article 2, including assistance in obtaining evidence in their possession necessary for the proceedings.

2. States Parties may not refuse a request for mutual legal assistance on the ground of bank secrecy.

3. The requesting Party shall not transmit nor use information or evidence furnished by the requested Party for investigations, prosecutions or proceedings other than those stated in the request without the prior consent of the requested Party.

4. Each State Party may give consideration to establishing mechanisms to share with other States Parties information or evidence needed to establish criminal, civil or administrative liability pursuant to article 5.

5. States Parties shall carry out their obligations under paragraphs 1 and 2 in conformity with any treaties or other arrangements on mutual legal assistance or information exchange that may exist between them. In the absence of such treaties or arrangements, States Parties shall afford one another assistance in accordance with their domestic law.

Article 13

None of the offences set forth in article 2 shall be regarded, for the purposes of extradition or mutual legal assistance, as a fiscal offence. Accordingly, States Parties may not refuse a request for extradition or for mutual legal assistance on the sole ground that it concerns a fiscal offence.

…

Article 18

1. States Parties shall cooperate in the prevention of the offences set forth in article 2 by taking all practicable measures, inter alia, by adapting their domestic legislation, if necessary, to prevent and counter preparations in their respective territories for the commission of those offences within or outside their territories, including:

(a) Measures to prohibit in their territories illegal activities of persons and organizations that knowingly encourage, instigate, organize or engage in the commission of offences set forth in article 2;

(b) Measures requiring financial institutions and other professions involved in financial transactions to utilize the most efficient measures available for the identification of their usual or occasional customers, as well as customers in whose interest accounts are opened, and to pay special attention to unusual or suspicious transactions and report transactions suspected of stemming from a criminal activity. For this purpose, States Parties shall consider:
(i) Adopting regulations prohibiting the opening of accounts the holders or beneficiaries of which are unidentified or unidentifiable, and measures to ensure that such institutions verify the identity of the real owners of such transactions;
(ii) With respect to the identification of legal entities, requiring financial institutions, when necessary, to take measures to verify the legal existence and the structure of the customer by obtaining, either from a public register or from the customer or both, proof of incorporation, including information concerning the customer's name, legal form, address, directors and provisions regulating the power to bind the entity;
(iii) Adopting regulations imposing on financial institutions the obligation to report promptly to the competent authorities all complex, unusual large transactions and unusual patterns of transactions, which have no apparent economic or obviously lawful purpose, without fear of assuming criminal or civil liability for breach of any restriction on disclosure of information if they report their suspicions in good faith;
(iv) Requiring financial institutions to maintain, for at least five years, all necessary records on transactions, both domestic or international.

2. States Parties shall further cooperate in the prevention of offences set forth in article 2 by considering:
(a) Measures for the supervision, including, for example, the licensing, of all money-transmission agencies;
(b) Feasible measures to detect or monitor the physical cross-border transportation of cash and bearer negotiable instruments, subject to strict safeguards to ensure proper use of information and without impeding in any way the freedom of capital movements.

3. States Parties shall further cooperate in the prevention of the offences set forth in article 2 by exchanging accurate and verified information in accordance with their domestic law and coordinating administrative and other measures taken, as appropriate, to prevent the commission of offences set forth in article 2, in particular by:
(a) Establishing and maintaining channels of communication between their competent agencies and services to facilitate the secure and rapid exchange of information concerning all aspects of offences set forth in article 2;
(b) Cooperating with one another in conducting inquiries, with respect to the offences set forth in article 2, concerning:
(i) The identity, whereabouts and activities of persons in respect of whom

reasonable suspicion exists that they are involved in such offences;
(ii) The movement of funds relating to the commission of such offences.

4. States Parties may exchange information through the International Criminal Police Organization (Interpol).

Annex

1. Convention for the Suppression of Unlawful Seizure of Aircraft, done at The Hague on 16 December 1970.

2. Convention for the Suppression of Unlawful Acts against the Safety of Civil Aviation, done at Montreal on 23 September 1971.

3. Convention on the Prevention and Punishment of Crimes against Internationally Protected Persons, including Diplomatic Agents, adopted by the General Assembly of the United Nations on 14 December 1973.

4. International Convention against the Taking of Hostages, adopted by the General Assembly of the United Nations on 17 December 1979.

5. Convention on the Physical Protection of Nuclear Material, adopted at Vienna on 3 March 1980.

6. Protocol for the Suppression of Unlawful Acts of Violence at Airports Serving International Civil Aviation, supplementary to the Convention for the Suppression of Unlawful Acts against the Safety of Civil Aviation, done at Montreal on 24 February 1988.

7. Convention for the Suppression of Unlawful Acts against the Safety of Maritime Navigation, done at Rome on 10 March 1988.

8. Protocol for the Suppression of Unlawful Acts against the Safety of Fixed Platforms located on the Continental Shelf, done at Rome on 10 March 1988.

9. International Convention for the Suppression of Terrorist Bombings, adopted by the General Assembly of the United Nations on 15 December 1997.

Resolution 1373 (2001): Adopted by the Security Council at its 4385th meeting, on 28 September 2001

The Security Council,
Reaffirming its resolutions 1269 (1999) of 19 October 1999 and 1368 (2001) of 12 September 2001,
Reaffirming also its unequivocal condemnation of the terrorist attacks which took place in New York, Washington, D.C. and Pennsylvania on 11 September 2001, and expressing its determination to prevent all such acts,
Reaffirming further that such acts, like any act of international terrorism, constitute a threat to international peace and security,
Reaffirming the inherent right of individual or collective self-defence as recognized by the Charter of the United Nations as reiterated in resolution 1368 (2001),
Reaffirming the need to combat by all means, in accordance with the Charter of the United Nations, threats to international peace and security caused by terrorist acts,
Deeply concerned by the increase, in various regions of the world, of acts of terrorism motivated by intolerance or extremism,
Calling on States to work together urgently to prevent and suppress terrorist acts, including through increased cooperation and full implementation of the relevant international conventions relating to terrorism,
Recognizing the need for States to complement international cooperation by taking additional measures to prevent and suppress, in their territories through all lawful means, the financing and preparation of any acts of terrorism,
Reaffirming the principle established by the General Assembly in its declaration of October 1970 (resolution 2625 (XXV)) and reiterated by the Security Council in its resolution 1189 (1998) of 13 August 1998, namely that every State has the duty to refrain from organizing, instigating, assisting or participating in terrorist acts in another State or acquiescing in organized activities within its territory directed towards the commission of such acts,
Acting under Chapter VII of the Charter of the United Nations,

1. Decides that all States shall:
(a) Prevent and suppress the financing of terrorist acts;
(b) Criminalize the wilful provision or collection, by any means, directly or indirectly, of funds by their nationals or in their territories with the intention that the funds should be used, or in the knowledge that they are to be used, in order to carry out terrorist acts;
(c) Freeze without delay funds and other financial assets or economic resources of persons who commit, or attempt to commit, terrorist acts or participate in or facilitate the commission of terrorist acts; of entities owned or controlled directly or indirectly by such persons; and of persons and entities acting on behalf of, or at the direction of such persons and entities, including funds derived or generated from property owned or controlled directly or indirectly by such persons and associated persons and entities;

(d) Prohibit their nationals or any persons and entities within their territories from making any funds, financial assets or economic resources or financial or other related services available, directly or indirectly, for the benefit of persons who commit or attempt to commit or facilitate or participate in the commission of terrorist acts, of entities owned or controlled, directly or indirectly, by such persons and of persons and entities acting on behalf of or at the direction of such persons;

2. Decides also that all States shall:
(a) Refrain from providing any form of support, active or passive, to entities or persons involved in terrorist acts, including by suppressing recruitment of members of terrorist groups and eliminating the supply of weapons to terrorists;
(b) Take the necessary steps to prevent the commission of terrorist acts, including by provision of early warning to other States by exchange of information;
(c) Deny safe haven to those who finance, plan, support, or commit terrorist acts, or provide safe havens;
(d) Prevent those who finance, plan, facilitate or commit terrorist acts from using their respective territories for those purposes against other States or their citizens;
(e) Ensure that any person who participates in the financing, planning, preparation or perpetration of terrorist acts or in supporting terrorist acts is brought to justice and ensure that, in addition to any other measures against them, such terrorist acts are established as serious criminal offences in domestic laws and regulations and that the punishment duly reflects the seriousness of such terrorist acts;
(f) Afford one another the greatest measure of assistance in connection with criminal investigations or criminal proceedings relating to the financing or support of terrorist acts, including assistance in obtaining evidence in their possession necessary for the proceedings;
(g) Prevent the movement of terrorists or terrorist groups by effective border controls and controls on issuance of identity papers and travel documents, and through measures for preventing counterfeiting, forgery or fraudulent use of identity papers and travel documents;

3. Calls upon all States to:
(a) Find ways of intensifying and accelerating the exchange of operational information, especially regarding actions or movements of terrorist persons or networks; forged or falsified travel documents; traffic in arms, explosives or sensitive materials; use of communications technologies by terrorist groups; and the threat posed by the possession of weapons of mass destruction by terrorist groups;
(b) Exchange information in accordance with international and domestic law and cooperate on administrative and judicial matters to prevent the commission of terrorist acts;
(c) Cooperate, particularly through bilateral and multilateral arrangements and agreements, to prevent and suppress terrorist attacks and take action against

perpetrators of such acts;
(d) Become parties as soon as possible to the relevant international conventions and protocols relating to terrorism, including the International Convention for the Suppression of the Financing of Terrorism of 9 December 1999;
(e) Increase cooperation and fully implement the relevant international conventions and protocols relating to terrorism and Security Council resolutions 1269 (1999) and 1368 (2001);
(f) Take appropriate measures in conformity with the relevant provisions of national and international law, including international standards of human rights, before granting refugee status, for the purpose of ensuring that the asylum-seeker has not planned, facilitated or participated in the commission of terrorist acts;
(g) Ensure, in conformity with international law, that refugee status is not abused by the perpetrators, organizers or facilitators of terrorist acts, and that claims of political motivation are not recognized as grounds for refusing requests for the extradition of alleged terrorists;

4. Notes with concern the close connection between international terrorism and transnational organized crime, illicit drugs, money-laundering, illegal arms-trafficking, and illegal movement of nuclear, chemical, biological and other potentially deadly materials, and in this regard emphasizes the need to enhance coordination of efforts on national, sub regional, regional and international levels in order to strengthen a global response to this serious challenge and threat to international security;

5. Declares that acts, methods, and practices of terrorism are contrary to the purposes and principles of the United Nations and that knowingly financing, planning and inciting terrorist acts are also contrary to the purposes and principles of the United Nations;

6. Decides to establish, in accordance with rule 28 of its provisional rules of procedure, a Committee of the Security Council, consisting of all the members of the Council, to monitor implementation of this resolution, with the assistance of appropriate expertise, and calls upon all States to report to the Committee, no later than 90 days from the date of adoption of this resolution and thereafter according to a timetable to be proposed by the Committee, on the steps they have taken to implement this resolution;

7. Directs the Committee to delineate its tasks, submit a work programme within 30 days of the adoption of this resolution, and to consider the support it requires, in consultation with the Secretary-General;

8. Expresses its determination to take all necessary steps in order to ensure the full implementation of this resolution, in accordance with its responsibilities under the Charter.

Appendix 4: Basel Committee Newsletter, 11 May 2008

Last October the Committee restructured its subcommittees to better reflect its strategic objectives going forward. These objectives seek to:

- promote a strong capital foundation at banks;
- strengthen supervision and risk management practices in the face of rapid financial innovation;
- promote understanding of the links between risk management, disclosure and accounting practices; and
- strengthen outreach to non-member countries, industry participants and other constituents.

For further information regarding the work of the Committee and its subcommittees please visit www.bis.org/bcbs.

This Newsletter discusses the Committee's recent progress and new initiatives to achieve these objectives.

Progress on Basel II implementation

Implementation of the Basel II Framework continues to move forward around the globe. A significant number of countries and banks already implemented the standardised and foundation approaches as of the beginning of this year. In many other jurisdictions, the necessary infrastructure (legislation, regulation, supervisory guidance, etc) to implement the Framework is either in place or in process, which will allow a growing number of countries to proceed with implementation of Basel II's advanced approaches in 2008 and 2009. This progress is taking place in both Basel Committee member and non-member countries. The Committee's Accord Implementation Group (AIG) and its working groups on validation, operational risk and trading book issues continue to actively share supervisory experiences in Basel II implementation, thereby promoting consistency across jurisdictions.
Supervisors also have made strong progress to coordinate home-host implementation issues at the level of individual banks, particularly for Pillar 1 (minimum capital requirements). The Committee's AIG is now focusing its attention on Pillar 2 (supervisory review process) and it also will begin work on Pillar 3 (market discipline). Many of the home-host issues that are under review by the AIG are not new but have come to the fore as a result of the rapid globalisation of the banking sector. Basel II has served as a catalyst to encourage greater cooperation and communication between jurisdictions and the industry. The input, both formal and informal, from industry groups, individual firms, and other constituents is particularly helpful in guiding this process.

Pillar 1

The Basel Committee and its AIG have concluded that supervisory coordination efforts are working well in practice to address institution-specific implementation issues. The Committee notes that the *High-level principles for the cross-border implementation of the New Accord* have been particularly helpful in shaping the discussions among supervisors and with the industry.

Supervisory and industry feedback about the workings of the colleges of supervisors, which are tailored to the circumstances of individual institutions, has been positive. Other forums involving bilateral discussions among supervisors have also proven to be beneficial in addressing Basel II home-host issues. Supervisors have been sharing information in an effective manner to minimise burden on the industry and themselves. Banks have found the process to be helpful and reports from participants in supervisory colleges have been positive. Both home and host supervisors report that they have achieved practical approaches to sharing the type of information needed to meet their responsibilities. Host supervisors report that banks' local managements are improving their ability to provide information concerning the institutions' Basel II implementation.

The AIG continues to monitor progress at supervisory colleges. It regularly reports such progress and results to the Committee.

Pillar 2

The challenges of coordination between home and host supervisors go beyond Pillar 1 and have clear Pillar 2 implications, particularly around topics like global risk management, diversification effects and the treatment of risks beyond those captured in Pillar 1 (e.g. risk concentrations and interest rate risk). The Committee and its AIG are now devoting significant resources to the Pillar 2 implementation process. While there are differences in supervisory approaches across countries, it is not yet clear how these will impact individual institutions in practice. In an important measure for promoting communication and transparency, a large and growing number of countries have put in place and made available to the public their Pillar 2 evaluation processes for a bank's internal capital adequacy and assessment process (ICAAP).

Basel Committee members approach these identified issues and challenges in various ways. These include:

- Sharing various ICAAP approaches across countries;
- Supervisory sharing of case studies on how these approaches are applied in practice at the level of individual institutions;
- Improving coordination and communication with non-member countries;
- Sharing case studies of firms' internal approaches;
- Focusing on the treatment of specific topics such as concentrations,

diversification, stress testing and the treatment of interest rate risk;
- Discussing different approaches to validation;
- Working on home-host coordination of the advanced measurement approaches for operational risk implementation and supervisory considerations in the assessment of allocation methodologies.

The Basel Committee believes these processes provide a sound framework to ensure a balanced implementation of Pillar 2. It notes that the discussions around Pillar 2 have been particularly beneficial for both firms and supervisors to discuss emerging risk management and internal capital issues.
While these efforts have focused on addressing Basel II-related coordination issues, they also help reinforce supervisory cross-border relationships more generally, with longer term benefits in areas such as crisis management during less benign financial market conditions.

Liquidity risk

After a sound capital foundation, strong liquidity risk management practices are a key element of a resilient banking system. The Basel Committee recently initiated a review of jurisdictions' approaches to supervising and regulating funding liquidity risk. Its Working Group on Liquidity is currently conducting a survey of regulatory and supervisory practices and will present its findings to the Committee for consideration. The survey also will assess how liquidity risk is being managed under the assumption of stressed market conditions. Based on the results of the project, the Basel Committee will determine what, if any, further action is needed.

Definition of capital initiative

In recent years, there have been remarkable advances in banks' economic capital management frameworks as well as the development of the markets for various capital instruments, notably hybrid capital products. In light of these developments the Basel Committee has launched an initiative to review the definition of regulatory capital across jurisdictions. The Committee's Definition of Capital subgroup is initially starting with a stock-take of the current definition of capital in member jurisdictions as well as fact-finding on how market participants, including rating agencies, perceive and value the equity-like characteristics of various capital instruments. This fact finding work will focus on the fundamental aspects of capital such as its loss absorbency. The subgroup will also look at the role of accounting in the calculation of regulatory capital and the relationships between regulatory definitions and firms' own definitions of capital in their internal economic capital models. Upon completion of its work, the subgroup will present its findings to the Committee for its discussion.

Economic capital initiative

At its March meeting, the Basel Committee gave its Risk Management and Modelling Group the mandate to assess the range of practice of banks' approaches to economic capital measurement and management. This effort supports supervisors' objective to stay on top of evolving risk management techniques and reinforces the AIG's work on Pillar 2. Areas of potential emphasis include:

- new measurement approaches for credit risk,
- the treatment of diversification effects,
- the assessment of complex counterparty credit risks,
- the treatment of interest rate risk, and
- firms' approaches to validation of internal capital assessments.

Accounting and auditing work

The Basel Committee's Accounting Task Force (ATF) focuses on promoting high quality international accounting and audit standards, which support sound risk management practices. The ATF currently is engaged in several areas of work related to accounting and audit standards, which have a potentially large impact on financial institutions. The ATF is initiating work with the Committee's Risk Management and Modelling Group to evaluate practices related to fair value estimates that rely on models.

The ATF recently reviewed a discussion paper on fair value measurements issued by the International Accounting Standards Board (IASB). In its comment, it noted that as internationally active banks continue to increase their cross border activities, it is important that the IASB and the FASB develop consistent fair value measurement guidance. The ATF also reviewed an exposure draft related to audits of accounting estimates, which includes fair value estimates, issued by the International Auditing and Assurance Standards Board. In its comment, the Committee noted that the current exposure draft does not sufficiently address the need for additional audit guidance for fair value estimates, particularly those derived through the use of models.

Outreach to non-member countries and the industry

The Basel Committee continues to expand its cooperation with the broader supervisory community and the industry. The combined effects of rapid globalisation of banks, the pace of financial innovation and changes in risk management practices require a redoubling of efforts to deepen outreach to non-member supervisors and the industry.

Outreach to non-member countries

The Committee recently established the International Liaison Group (ILG) to provide a forum for deepening its engagement with supervisors around the world on a broad range of issues. It provides a platform for non-member countries to contribute to new Committee initiatives early in the process and to develop new proposals that are of particular interest to ILG members.

The ILG has initiated new workstreams on the following:

- a project to assess the range of practice on approaches to risk-based supervision;
- an information exchange on jurisdictions' approaches to achieving sound provisioning and reserving practices; and
- an assessment of how the rapidly growing area of microfinance fits into existing supervisory frameworks.

In addition, the Committee is in the process of identifying practical ways to increase participation of non-member countries in the work of its other subcommittees.

Outreach to industry

The Committee has derived important benefit in seeking input from industry participants on its workstreams and proposed supervisory or regulatory initiatives. It will engage the industry on financial market, risk management, supervisory, and regulatory developments that are forward looking and of common interest to supervisors and industry. Input from a range of constituents on these issues is an important contribution to shaping the Committee's future agenda.

Bibliography

Articles/chapters

Ehrlich, T.H., 'To Regulate or Not? Managing the Risk of E-Money and its Potential Application in Money Laundering Schemes' (1998) 11(3) *Harvard Journal of Law and Technology*: pp. 833–63.

Allott, Philip, 'The Concept of International Law' (1999) *European Journal of International Law*: pp. 33–50.

Arora, A., 'Money Laundering Regulation: Finance and Credit Law' (2004) *Journal of Business Law*: pp. 332–56.

Bassiouni Cherif, M., 'The International Narcotics Control Scheme', in M. Bassiouni Cherif (ed.), *International Criminal Law*, vol. 1. New York: Transnational Publishers, 1986, pp. 507–24.

Bell, R.E, 'Prosecuting the Money Launderers Who Act for Organised Crime' (1999) 3(2) *Journal of Money Laundering Control*: pp. 104–12.

Chimni, B.S., 'International Institutions Today: An Imperial Global State in the Making' (2004) *European Journal of International Law*: pp. 1–37.

Eales, Robert, 'Credit Risk Measurement in Corporate Banking – Theory and Practice' (2001).

Edopu, Peter, 'Infrastructure to Detect and Control Money Laundering and Terrorist Funding in Uganda', available at http://www.iss.co.za/pubs/Monographs/No108/Chap3.pdf (date accessed 7 January 2012).

Falk, Richard, 'Kosovo, World Order and the Future of International Law' (1999) 93 *American Journal of International Law*: pp. 847–53.

Fatuna, L.L., 'Russia: Organized Crime and Money Laundering' (1998) 1(4) *Journal of Money Laundering Control*.

Fleming, Jeremy, 'Stripping Away Assets' (2000) 97(46) *Law Society Gazette*: p. 21. Available at http://www.lawgazette.co.uk/news/stripping-away-assets (date accessed 7 January 2012).

Fowler, A., *Institutional Development and NGOs in Africa: Policy Perspectives for European Development Agencies*. Intrac, 1990.

Gariyo, Zie, 'The Role and Experience of the Civil Society in the Struggle Against Corruption in Uganda', paper presented at the Consultative Group Panel on Corruption, Kampala, 15 May 2001, pp. 1–12.

Gilmore, W.C., 'International Action Against Drug Trafficking: Trends in United Kingdom Law and Practice' (1990) 24 *International Lawyer*: pp. 388–90.

Goredema, Charles, 'Money Laundering in Southern Africa: Incidence, Magnitude and Prospects for its Control', Institute of Security Studies, occasional paper 92, October 2004.

Graham, G., 'Seychelles Condemned over Money Launderers' Charter', *Financial Times*, 2 February 1996.

Gray, B., 'The Supervision of Credit Risk in the Banking Sector – Current Approach and Future Directions', in B. Gray and C. Cassidy (eds), *Credit Risk in Banking*, Proceedings of a Conference

at the H.C. Coombs Centre for Financial Studies, 1–2 May 1997, Reserve Bank of Australia.

Hill, Jonathan, 'Choice of Law in Contract under the Rome Convention: The Approach of the UK Courts' (2004) 53 *International and Comparative Law Review*: pp. 325–50.

Ho, D.E., 'Compliance and International Soft Law: Why Do Countries Implement the Basle Accord?' (2002) 5 *Journal of International Economic Law*: pp. 647–88.

Hobbs, D., 'Professional and Organised Crime in Britain', in R. Maguire, R. Morgan and J. Fawcett (eds), *Private International Law*. London: Butterworths, 1999.

Hoffman, C.D, 'Encrypted Digital Cash Transfers: Why Traditional Money Laundering Control May Fail Without Uniform Cryptography Regulations' (1998) 21 *Fordham International Law Journal*: pp. 799–860.

Howard, C., 'The *Mens Rea* Tests for Money Laundering Offences' (1998) *New Law Journal*: pp. 118–19.

'IMF Background Paper on the Role of the Fund in Promotion, Development and Implementation of the Standards and Codes (SM/01/11, January 12, 2000)', available at www.imf.org (date accessed 10 August 2005).

Jarvie, Natasha, 'Control of Cyber Crime – Is an End to Our Time on the Internet a Price Worth Paying?' (2003) 9(3) *Computer and Telecommunications Law Review*: pp. 76–81.

Joyce, Elizabeth, 'Transnational Criminal Enterprises: The European Perspective', in T. Farer (ed.), *Transnational Crimes in the Americas*. London: Routledge, 1999, pp. 99–102.

Kaufman, George, 'Bank Contagion: A Review of the Theory and Evidence' (1994) 8 *Journal of Financial Services Research*: pp. 123–50.

Kasekende, Louis A., 'Capital Account Liberalisation: The Ugandan Experience', paper presented at the Overseas Development Institute, 21 June 2000.

Kent., C, 'The Canadian and International War Against Money Laundering: Legal Perspectives' (1995) 35 *Criminal Law Review*.

Kern, A., 'Multinational Effort to Combat Financial Crimes and the Financial Action Task Force' (2000) 2(5) *Journal of International Financial Market*: pp. 178–95.

Kumar, M.S. and Persaud, A., 'Pure Contagion and Investors' Shifting Risk Appetite: Analytical Issues and Empirical Evidence', IMF Working Paper (01/134), 2001, available at www.imf.org/external/pubs/ft/wp/2001/wp01134.pdf (date accessed 6 January 2012).

Krueger, Anne and Yoo, Jungho, 'Crony Capitalism and Capital Account Liberalisation, in setting the stage for the Currency Financial crisis in Korea', Discussion Paper, October 2002.

Mann, Erika, 'A Parliamentary Dimension to the WTO – More than Just a Vision?' (2004 (7(3) *Journal of International Economic Law*: pp. 659–65.

McCheney, Robert and Chomsky, Noam, 'The Struggle Against Neoliberalism' (1999) 50 *Monthly Review*: pp. 40–47.

McClean, D., 'Seizing the Proceeds of Crime: The State of the Art' (1989) 38 *International Criminal Law Quarterly*: pp. 334–60.

McCorquodale, R. and Fairbrother, R., 'Globalization and Human Rights' (1999) 21(3) *Human Rights Quarterly*: pp. 735–6.

McDonald, M.F., 'The Globalization of Criminology: The New Frontier is the Frontier' (1998) 1 *Transnational Organized Crime*: pp. 1–22.

McDonnell, Rick, 'Money Laundering Methodologies: International and Regional Counter-Measures', National Crime Authority, NSW, paper presented at the Australian Institute of Research, Sydney, 1998.

McDonnell, Rick, 'Regulatory Challenges for the 21st Century', paper presented at the Australian Institute of Criminology, Sydney, 1998.

Mugarura, Norman, 'The Subdued Giant: The Predicament of the Law in Harnessing Global Markets' (2009) 2 *African Journal of International Comparative Law*: pp. 321–52.

O'Brien, P., 'Trafficking Narco-Dollars: The Evolution of a Potent Weapon in the Drug War' (1990) 21 *Inter-American Law Review.*

Palmer, A, 'Global Crusade Can Never Be Won', *Sunday Telegraph,* 31 August 1997.

Perts C. Van Duyne, 'Money Laundering: Estimates in the Fog' (2007) 2 *Journal of Asset Protection and Financial Crime.*

Peterson, N.H., 'Towards a European Security Model for the 21st Century' (1997) *NATO Review*: p. 4. Available at http://www.nato.int/docu/review/1997/9706-02.htm (date accessed 7 January 2012).

Quiroz Rendon, David, 'The Formal Regulatory Approach to Banking Regulation', available at www.badellgrau.com/legalbanking.html (date accessed 20 August 2007).

Rider, B., and Ashe, M. (eds), A.K, 'Taking the Profits Out of Crime' (2001) *Journal of Money Laundering Control*: pp. 2–3.

Rotman, E., 'The Globalization of Criminal Violence' (2000) 10(1) *Cornell Journal of Law and Public Policy*: pp. 1–43.

Sappideen, Razeen, 'The Regulation of Credit, Market and Operational Risk Management under the Basel Accords' (2004) *Journal of Business Law*: pp. 61–70.

Sarooshi, Dan and Smith, Herbert, 'Sovereignty, Economic Autonomy, the United States and the International Trading System: Representations of Relationship' (2004) 15(651) *Economic Journal of International Law*: pp. 1–11.

Savona, E.U. and De Foe, M.A., 'International Money Laundering Trend and Prevention/Control Policies', in E.U. Savona (ed.), *Responding to Money Laundering: International Perspectives*. New York: Harwood Academic Publishers, 1997.

Schiff, Maurice, 'Regional Integration and Development of Small States', Development Research Group of the World Bank, available at www.worldbank.org (date accessed 12 June 2005).

Schneider, Benu, 'Capital Account Liberalisation: A Developing Country's Perspective', Overseas Development Institute, 21 June 2000.

Shams, Heba, 'Using Money Laundering Control to Fight Corruption: An Extraterritorial Instrument' (2001) 7 *Law and Business Review of the Americas*: pp. 85–133.

Shelley, Louise, 'Privatization and Crime: The Post Soviet Experience' (1995) 11(4) *Journal of Contemporary Criminal Justice*: pp. 244–56.

Shelley, Louise, 'Transnational Organised Crimes: A New Authoritarianism', in H. Richard Friman and Peter Andreas (eds), *The Illicit Global Economy and State Power*. Lanham, MD: Rowman & Littlefield, 1998, pp. 25–40.

Slaughter, Anne-Maria, 'Sovereignty and Power in a Networked World Order' (2004) *Stanford Journal of International Law*: pp. 286–92.

Sproule, D.W. and St-Denis, P., 'The UN Drug Trafficking Convention: An Ambitious Step' (1998) *Canadian Yearbook of International Law*: pp. 263–70.

Stewart, D.P., 'Internalising the War on Drugs: The UN Convention Against Illicit Trafficking in Narcotic Drugs and Psychotropic Substances' (1990), 18 *Denver Journal of International Law and Policy*.

Stone Sweet, A. 'Integration and Europeanisation of the Law', Queen's Paper on Europeanisation, No. 2/2002, Nuffield College, University of Oxford.

Strawson, John, 'Islamic Law and the English Text' (1995) VI(1) *Law and Critique*: pp. 21–38.

Sundhya, Pahuja, 'This is the World: Have Faith' (2004) 15 *European Journal of International Law*: pp. 1–11.

Teubner, G., 'Legal Irritants: Good Faith in British Law or How Unifying Law Ends Up in New Divergences' (1998) 61 *Modern Law Review*.

Wiener, Jarrod, 'Money Laundering: Transnational Criminals, Globalization and the Forces of Redomestication' (1997) 1 *Journal of Money Laundering Control*; pp. 54–66.

Williams, P., 'Transnational Criminal Organisations and International Security' (1994) 36 *Survival*: pp. 96–113.

Williams, P. (ed.), 'Emerging Issues: Transnational Crimes and Its Control' (1999) *in Global Report on Crimes and justice*, Graeme Newman, pp. 225–226.

Zagaris, Bruce and Macdonald, Scott, 'Money Laundering, Financial Fraud, and Technology: The Perils of an Instantaneous Economy' (1992) 26 *George Washington Journal of International Law and Economics*.

Books

Abdullah A. An-Na'im, *The Contingent Universality of Human Rights: The Case of Freedom of Expression in African and Islamic Context: Law, Morality and Politics*. Oxford: Oxford University Press, 2000.

Adelman, Sammy and Caesar Espiritu, The Debt Crisis, Underdevelopment and the Limits of the Law (1996), pp. 173–95.

AFDB, *Globalisation and Africa, Africa Development Report*. Oxford: Oxford University Press, 2003.

Alldridge, P., *Money Laundering Law*. Oxford: Hart Publishing, 2003.

Anderson, J., *Policing Across National Boundaries*. London: Pintes, 1995.

Anderson, M., *Policing the World: Interpol and the Politics of International Police Cooperation.* Oxford: Oxford University Press, 1998.

Bantekas, Ilias and Nash, Susan, *International Criminal Law.* London: Cavendish Publishing, 2003.

Bhagwati, Jagdish, *In Defence of Globalisation*. Oxford: Oxford University Press, 2004.

Birks, Peter, *Laundering and Tracing*. Oxford: Clarendon Press, 1997.

Blaxter, L., Hughes, C. and Tight, M., *How to Research.* Buckingham: Open University Press, 2001.

Bond, Patrick, *Against Global Apartheid: South Africa Meets the World Bank, IMF and International Finance*. Cape Town: University of Cape Town Press, 2001.

Bradley, A.W. and Ewing, K.D., *Constitutional and Administrative Law,* 12th edn. London: Longman, 1999.

Buzan, B., *People, States and Fear: An Agenda for International Security Studies in the Post-Cold War Era*. Brighton: Harvester Wheatsheaf, 1991.

Cassesse, Antonio, *International Criminal Law*. Oxford: Oxford University Press, 2003.

Craig, Paul and DeBurca, Graine, *EU Law: Text, Cases, Materials*, 3rd edn. Oxford: Oxford University Press, 2002.

Cranston, Ross, *Principles of Banking Law*, 2nd edn. Oxford: Oxford University Press, 2002.

De Sousa Santos, Boaventura, *Towards a New Legal Common Sense: Globalisation, Law and Emancipation*, 2nd edn. London: Butterworths, 2002.

Dine, Janet, *Companies, International Trade and Human Rights*. Cambridge: Cambridge University Press, 2004.

Dumbro, J., *Dragons of Crime*. Markham, Ontario: Octopus Publishing Group, 1992.

Ellinger, E.P., Lomnicka, E. and Hooley, R.J.A., *Modern Banking Law* (3rd) (2002).

Feyerabend Paul K., 'History of Philosophy of Science', in Oxford Companion 414 (Ted Honderich ed., 1995) at pp.806–07.

Fitzpatrick, Peter, *The Mythology of Modern Law*. London: Routledge, 1992.

Findlay, Mark, *The Globalisation of Crime*. Cambridge: Cambridge University Press, 1999.

Friman, H. Richard and Andreas, Peter, *The Illicit Global Economy and State Power*. Lanham, MD: Rowman & Littlefield, 1999.

Gilmore W.C. (ed.), *International Efforts to Combat Money Laundering*. Cambridge: Grotius Publications, 1992.

Gilmore, W.C., *Dirty Money: The Evolution of Money Laundering Counter-Measures*. Strasbourg: Council of Europe Publishing, 1999.

Graziano, A.M. and Raulin, M.L., *Research Methods: A Process of Inquiry*. New York: HarperCollins, 1989.

Hall, Andrew and Rees, Edward, *Blackstone's Guide to the Proceeds of Crime Act*. Oxford: Oxford University Press, 2002.

Higgins, Rosalyn, *International Law and How We Use it: Problems and Process*. Oxford: Oxford University Press, 1994.

Jamieson, Alison, *Global Drug Trafficking*. University of Michigan: Research Institute for the Study of Conflict and Terrorism, 1990.

Keh, Douglas I., *Drug Money in a Changing World: Economic Reform and Criminal Finance*. Oxford: Oxford University Press, 2004.

Kent Fry, 'Credit assessment in retail banking – A Portfolio Management Perspective', in P. Krugman and M. Obstfeld (eds), *International Economics: Theory and Policy*, 5th edn. 2000, pp. 659–67.

Kern, Alexander, Rahul, Dhumale and Eatwell, John, *Global Governance of Financial Systems: International Regulation of Systemic Risk*. Oxford: Oxford University Press, 2006.

LaMond, Tullis, *Unintended Consequences: Illegal Drugs and Drug Policies in Nine Countries*. Boulder, CO: Lynne Reinner Publishers, 1995.

Likosky, Michael (ed.), *Transnational Legal Processes: Globalization and Power Disparities*. London: Butterworths, 2002.

Lloyd, Leonard-Jason, *The Law on Money Laundering*. London: Frank Cass, 1997.

Lowenfeld, Andreas F., *International Economic Law*. Oxford: Oxford University Press, 2002.

Morgan, Rod, New Man Tim, *The Future of Policing*. Oxford: Oxford University Press, 1997.

Oxfam, *World Development Report: Fifty Years of the World Bank and IMF*. Milton Keynes, Open University Press, 2001.

Patten, Chris, *Globalisation and the Law*. London: Human Rights Lawyers Association, 2006.

Pavarin M., Primera Conferentia, quoted in Valsamis Mitsileges, *Money Laundering Counter-measures in the European Union: A New Paradigm of Security Governance Versus Fundamental Legal Principles*. Dordrecht: Kluwer Law International, 2003, at pp. 25–30.

Phillips, E. and Pugh, D.S., *How to Get a PhD*. Buckingham, Open University Press, 1999.

Possamai, Mario (ed.), *Money on the Run*. Toronto: Viking, 1997.

Raine, L.P. and Cilluffo, F.J. (eds), *Global Organized Crime: The Empire of Evil*. Washington DC: Center for Strategic and International Studies, 1994.

Reiner, R. (ed.), *The Oxford Handbook of Criminology*. Oxford: Oxford University Press, 1994.

Reiner, R., *The Politics of the Police*. Oxford: Oxford University Press, 2000.

Rider, Barry (ed.), *Corruption: The Enemy Within*. Dordrecht: Kluwer Law International, 1997.

Robinson, J., *The Laundrymen*. London: Pocketbooks, 1995.

Robinson, J., *How Organised Criminal Groups are Taking Up Canada*. Toronto: McClelland Stewart Inc, 1999.

Rondo, Cameron (ed.), *Banking and Economic Development: Some Lessons of History*. New York: Columbia University Press, 1979.

Rose-Ackerman, Susan, *Corruption and Government: Causes, Consequences and Reform*. Cambridge: Cambridge University Press, 1998.

Rose-Ackerman, Susan (ed.), Empirical Themes in Political Economy of Corruption, Stockholm University, Stockholm Sweden (2000).

Ruggiero, V., Scheinost, M. and Valkenburg, V. (eds), *Cross-border Crimes in a Changing Europe*. New York: Nova Publishers, 2000.

Sands, Philip, *The Lawless World*. London: Penguin, 2005.

Sen, Amartya, *Development as Freedom*. Oxford: Oxford University Press, 1999.

Sharma, R., *Due Diligence and Money Laundering*. London: EMIS Professional Publishing Ltd, 2005.

Sheptycki, J.W.E, *Issues in Transnational Policing*. London: Routledge, 2000.

Stalker, Peter, *The No-Nonsense Guide to International Migration*. London: Verso, 2001.

Steiner, Henry and Alston, Philip, *International Human Rights in Context: Law, Morality and Politics*. Oxford: Oxford University Press, 2000.

Stiglitz, Joseph, *Globalisation and its Discontents*. London: W.W. Norton & Co, 1999.

Tabb, William K., *The Amoral Elephant: Globalization and the Struggle for Social Justice in the Twenty First Century*. Berkeley, CA: Monthly Review Press, 2001.

Walker, George, A., *Principles of International Banking Law*. Dordrecht: Kluwer, 1991.

Walker, R.J.B., Security, Sovereignty, and the Challenges of World Politics Alternative vol. 15, (2004) p.4.

Walter, Ingo, *The Secret Money Market: Inside the Dark World of Tax Evasion, Financial Fraud, Insider Trading, Money Laundering, and Capital Flight*. London: HarperCollins, 1990.

Wiener, J., 'International Crime in the New Geopolitics: A Core Threat to Democracy', in W.F. McDonald (ed.), *Crime and Law Enforcement in the Global Village*. Highlands Heights, KY and Cincinnati, OH: Academy of Criminal Justice Science and Anderson Publishing Co, 2000.

Index

For Product Safety Concerns and Information please contact our EU representative GPSR@taylorandfrancis.com Taylor & Francis Verlag GmbH, Kaufingerstraße 24, 80331 München, Germany